NATIONAL
GEOGRAPHIC

2ND EDITION

ANIMAL ENCYCLOPEDIA

2,500 ANIMALS WITH PHOTOS, MAPS, AND MORE!

DR. LUCY SPELMAN

NATIONAL GEOGRAPHIC
WASHINGTON, D.C.

TARPON AND SILVERSIDES

RED-EYED TREE FROG

EASTERN FOX SQUIRREL

AFRICAN ELEPHANT

COMMON CHAMELEON

WESTERN MEADOWLARK

LEOPARD

MEERKATS

SPINNER DOLPHINS

MANDRILL

GENTOO PENGUIN

SEA OTTER

GREEN SEA TURTLE

GIANT PANDA

ARCTIC FOX

MUGGER CROCODILE

CONTENTS

BIRDS 98

MAMMALS 28

REPTILES 146

AMPHIBIANS 170

FISH 188

INVERTEBRATES 222

HOW TO USE
THIS BOOK

The *National Geographic Animal Encyclopedia* is divided into eight parts. The first part introduces you to the world of animals by exploring topics such as animal life cycles and babies, senses and communication, homes and habitats, adaptations and camouflage, endangered species, and animal conservation.

The second through seventh sections present the major animal groups: mammals, birds, reptiles, amphibians, fish, and invertebrates. Each section begins with an opener followed by a gallery spread of photographs. Since it is impossible to include every animal on Earth in one volume, these galleries are designed to portray as much animal diversity as is possible on two pages. Following the gallery is the "What Is" spread, which introduces the groups of animals within each section. The spreads that follow introduce each animal group, featuring specific species along with key facts about them, including their common and scientific names, endangered status, habitat, range, size, diet, and a short text block about each species. In addition, illustrated diagrams convey information about animal life cycles, size comparisons, and much more.

Throughout the book you will find 17 "From the Field" reports and six "From the Lens" images. The reports present accounts from National Geographic explorers, grantees, and photographers in the field. Each "From the Lens" features a stunning animal photograph. Concluding each chapter are animal records. These pages are full of animal superlatives from the tallest and biggest, to the smallest and smelliest animals.

The eighth section in this book is a listing of more than 1,000 additional animals. Like the gallery spreads, this list serves as a tool to give you a sense of the vast diversity and size of the animal kingdom. Here you will find common and scientific names and size, diet, range, and habitat information about animals in each of the six animal groups (mammals, birds, reptiles, amphibians, fish, and invertebrates).

HOW THE ANIMAL KINGDOM IS ORGANIZED

The kingdom Animalia includes one phylum, Chordata, for animals with a backbone (vertebrates) and eight phyla for those without one (invertebrates). The vertebrates belong to eight classes: one each for mammals, birds, reptiles, amphibians, and four for fish. The eight invertebrate phyla are Arthropoda (insects, arachnids, centipedes and millipedes, and horseshoe crabs), Mollusca (squid, octopus, cuttlefish, and snails), Cnidaria (corals, jellyfish, and hydras), Annelida (earthworms, leeches, and polychaetes), Platyhelminthes (flukes and tapeworms), Nematoda (roundworms), Echinoderms (sea stars, sea urchins, and sea cucumbers), and Porifera (sponges).

SIZE ABBREVIATIONS

cm: centimeters	kg: kilograms	m: meters
ft: feet	km: kilometers	mm: millimeters
g: grams	L: liters	oz: ounces
in: inches	lb: pounds	t: metric tons

ENDANGERED STATUS

Throughout this book you will notice solid-colored circles accompanying animal photographs as well as the list of animals in the back of the book. These colors represent different conservation statuses. Below is a key identifying each status, along with its definition. With the exception of "Domesticated," these statuses are based on information from the International Union for Conservation of Nature (IUCN) Red List of Threatened Species 2020.

● **ALERT** Animal species that are endangered and at very high or extremely high risk of dying out. Some may even be extinct in the wild and exist only in places such as zoos or wildlife sanctuaries.

● **IN TROUBLE** Animal species vulnerable to becoming threatened or with a high risk of becoming endangered without conservation action.

● **STABLE** Animal species that have been determined not to be vulnerable, endangered, or at risk of extinction.

● **UNDER STUDY** Scientists are still studying these animals to assess their risk of extinction.

● **NOT LISTED** Animal species that have not yet been listed in the IUCN Red List.

● **DOMESTICATED** Animal species domesticated for food, clothing, sport, and companionship. Their numbers are plentiful.

RANGE MAPS

You will find two kinds of range maps in this book. The range maps that appear on the "Records" spreads illustrate ranges for all the record-holding animals presented on those pages. The range maps that appear with the "From the Field" reports illustrate the range of the featured species.

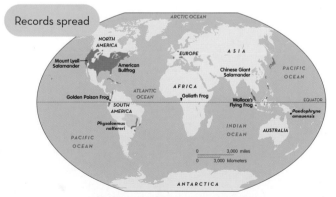

Records spread

From the Field report

Bold headings introduce the animal group for each section of the book.

Color-coded tabs appear on every page to tell you which section you are in and help you navigate the book.

Opening text introduces you to each animal section and describes the general characteristics of the animals you will read about in the section.

Diagrams depict the unique physical features and anatomy of the animals in the section.

Colorful boxes provide fun animal facts.

Classification boxes explain the way in which animals in each section are grouped.

WHAT IS A MAMMAL?

MAMMALS ARE AMONG THE MOST ADAPTABLE ANIMALS.

CLASSIFICATION OF MAMMALS

MAMMAL TRAITS

Bold headings highlight the specific species on each spread.

Color-coded tabs appear on every page to tell you which section you are in and help you navigate the book.

Opening text introduces you to the species on the page and provides an overview of the species on the page or spread.

Illustrated diagrams portray information such as animal life cycles and special features.

Habitat icons represent the type of environment each animal lives in. Descriptions are detailed on page 16.

Fact boxes provide common and scientific names and key facts for each featured species.

PENGUINS

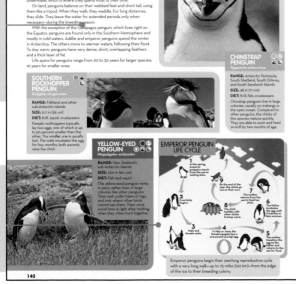

9

INTRODUCTION TO THE ANIMAL KINGDOM

The animal kingdom is an amazing, diverse group of living organisms. It includes microscopic mites, gigantic whales, migrating butterflies, marching penguins, 100-year-old tortoises, regenerating worms, air-breathing fish, mouth-brooding frogs, and bamboo-eating bears.

To keep track of biodiversity, scientists use a classification system. Organisms with similar features, or traits, are grouped together. The largest group is a kingdom. The smallest is a species. In between are phylum, class, order, family, and genus. The phrase "kids prefer cheese over fried green spinach" is one way to remember how it all works. Examples of traits used to classify animals are body structure, life cycle, and social behavior.

So what does a fly have in common with a chimpanzee? How is a human like a gecko? Like all members of the kingdom Animalia—1.3 million species and counting—they share the following traits. They are multicellular, they must find their own food, they develop into adult forms, and they are capable of movement.

Genetic studies are also used to classify animals. Related species share a common ancestor and more of the same genes. They usually look alike, but not always. The genome is full of surprises.

NAMING OF SPECIES

Remembering the different subcategories can be difficult. To make things easier, scientists use only the last two—genus and species—when referring to a specific animal. For example, a common house cat's genus is *Felis* and its species is *catus*. So scientists refer to it as *Felis catus*. This is the cat's binomial nomenclature, or scientific name.

Why can't scientists just use a common name when referring to an animal? That can get complicated. Some animals have many common names. For example, a "panther" in one region may be called a "cougar" in another; this can cause people to believe that the same cat is two different animals. Because the scientific name is always the same, it eliminates confusion.

When coming up with a genus and species name for an animal, scientists have a few rules they must follow. The name must be Greek or Latin. Or it can be a "Latinized" version of a word such as a place or a person's name. Some scientists have a sense of humor when naming organisms. In 1993, arachnologist Norman I. Platnick named a spider *Calponia harrisonfordi* in honor of Harrison Ford, the actor who portrayed Han Solo in the *Star Wars* movies.

COLD-BLOODED VS. WARM-BLOODED

All organisms within the animal kingdom are either cold-blooded or warm-blooded. Warm-blooded animals, such as mammals and birds, have a body temperature that remains constant even when the temperature of their environment varies. In mammals, body temperature is controlled by the hypothalamus in the brain. If the body becomes too warm, the hypothalamus signals the sweat glands to cool it by releasing sweat. If body temperature begins to drop, the hypothalamus signals that the body should shiver to warm itself.

In birds, special air sacs that extend from the lungs help the body perform heating and cooling functions. In addition, birds have feathers to help trap heat, and mammals have hair.

In cold-blooded animals, which include reptiles, amphibians, fish, insects, and arthropods, body temperature rises and falls with the temperature of their environment. To keep body temperature constant, these animals have developed a variety of behaviors. For example, a crocodile may bask in the sun to keep itself warm, and move to a shady area to cool off.

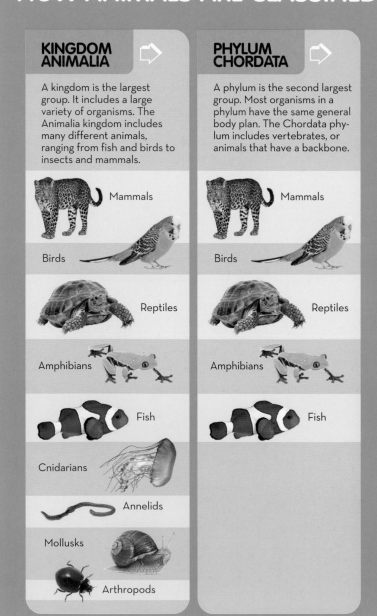

HOW ANIMALS ARE CLASSIFIED

KINGDOM ANIMALIA

A kingdom is the largest group. It includes a large variety of organisms. The Animalia kingdom includes many different animals, ranging from fish and birds to insects and mammals.

Mammals
Birds
Reptiles
Amphibians
Fish
Cnidarians
Annelids
Mollusks
Arthropods

PHYLUM CHORDATA

A phylum is the second largest group. Most organisms in a phylum have the same general body plan. The Chordata phylum includes vertebrates, or animals that have a backbone.

Mammals
Birds
Reptiles
Amphibians
Fish

VERTEBRATE OR INVERTEBRATE?

All organisms in the animal kingdom are either vertebrates or invertebrates. But which is which?

YELLOW TANG FISH

MACAWS

RED-EYED TREE FROG

ARCTIC FOXES

SEA TURTLE

Vertebrates are animals with a backbone. They are grouped into a single phylum (Chordata) with eight classes: amphibians, reptiles, birds, mammals, and four classes of fish.

RED AND SILVER DEWDROP SPIDER

BROWN GARDEN SNAIL

EARTHWORMS

Invertebrates are animals that do not have a backbone. Many invertebrates have an exoskeleton, a hard skeleton on the outside of the body, to protect the delicate organs inside. Invertebrates include earthworms (annelids), insects and spiders (arthropods), jellyfish (cnidarians), and snails (mollusks).

CLASS MAMMALIA ⇨

A class shares more traits than those in a phylum. Animals in the class Mammalia are warm blooded mammals that have a backbone, fur, or hair, and can nurse their young with milk.

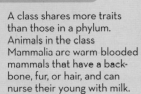
red panda

platypus

kangaroo

white-tailed deer

beaver

bat

tree shrew

leopard

human

ORDER PRIMATE ⇨

An order consists of organisms that share even more common traits than those of a class. Primate is a group of mammals that includes humans, apes, monkeys, and lemurs.

ring-tailed lemur

potto

black howler monkey

olive baboon

tarsier

white-handed gibbon

chimpanzee

FAMILY HOMINIDAE ⇨

A family is a smaller grouping of organisms. The Hominidae family includes the great apes as well as humans.

human

chimpanzee

bonobo

western lowland gorilla

eastern mountain gorilla

Sumatran orangutan

Bornean orangutan

GENUS PAN ⇨

A genus is a group of different organisms that are closely related but cannot produce offspring together. The genus *Pan* includes the chimpanzee and the bonobo.

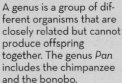
chimpanzee

bonobo

SPECIES PAN TROGLODYTES

A species is the smallest and most closely related group of organisms. Members of a species can produce offspring with one another. *Pan troglodytes* is the chimpanzee species.

chimpanzee

"SUCCESSFUL" SPECIES

Throughout the book you will see some species described as "successful." What does that mean? It means that a species has done well adapting to its environment and has been able to endure and reproduce over many generations.

LIFE CYCLE AND BABIES

Every animal starts out life as an egg produced by a female. Most eggs that develop into adult animals have been fertilized with sperm produced by a male. There are exceptions, though. Worker honeybees, for example, lay eggs that are never fertilized; they develop into male bees called drones.

The fertilized eggs of vertebrate animals develop into embryos. In mammals—except for the platypus—these grow inside the female's body, developing organs and limbs over time until she gives birth to live young. This is also the case for some fish and reptiles. But for most, and for all birds and amphibians, their young develop inside eggs laid by the female.

After an animal is born, it must learn to survive in the wild. Some learn by imitating their parents, whereas others must fend for themselves. The animal grows until it reaches maturity. At this point, it is ready to mate—producing an offspring of its own and enabling another life cycle to begin.

LIVE BIRTH
SHORT-BEAKED COMMON DOLPHIN ○ ◉
Delphinus delphis

Like most mammals, short-beaked common dolphins give birth to live young. The female gestates, or carries her calf, for 10 to 12 months. At the end of that period, the calf is born underwater. The young dolphin feeds only on its mother's milk for the first six months. After that it starts to eat solid food, such as fish and mollusks.

EGG
GENTOO PENGUIN ○ ◉ ◉
Pygoscelis papua

Gentoo penguins lay eggs to reproduce. The female bird deposits two eggs inside a nest—usually a small depression in the ground lined with pebbles or grass. Then the female and her mate take turns keeping the clutch warm. One penguin spends eight to 12 days incubating the eggs while the other goes in search of food. This continues until the eggs hatch (up to 37 days).

GROWING UP
EASTERN MOUNTAIN GORILLA ●○⊛
Gorilla beringei beringei

Eastern mountain gorillas weigh only four pounds (2 kg) at birth and spend about four years sharing a nest with their mother. A lot happens during that time. When the babies are two months old, they begin to crawl. At six months, they learn to walk, but often hitch a ride on their mother's back to travel. The next three years are spent play-fighting and imitating older members of their troop.

METAMORPHOSIS
EASTERN TIGER SWALLOWTAIL ●○⊕
Papilio glaucus

During its life cycle, the eastern tiger swallowtail butterfly undergoes a complete change, called a metamorphosis, in four stages. A butterfly begins life as an egg. After four days, a caterpillar, or larva, hatches. For two weeks, it feasts on its eggshell and milkweed plants. Then it becomes a pupa by forming a protective shell called a chrysalis. Two weeks later, a butterfly emerges.

CARING FOR YOUNG
MALLARD (DUCK) ○⊘⊕⊘
Anas platyrhynchos

A mallard mother is very protective of her young. Shortly after her ducklings have hatched, she leads them to a water source, keeping a watchful eye along the way. If a predator, such as a red fox, is lurking nearby, the mother bird will pretend to be injured to distract the fox from her brood.

Did you know? A group of ducklings is called a brood.

SENSES AND COMMUNICATION

All animals have five senses: sight, hearing, touch, taste, and smell. They use them to find food, shelter, and each other, as well as to navigate, communicate, avoid predators, and attract a mate.

Depending on their lifestyle and evolutionary history, some animals have more developed senses than others. Eagles, for instance, have excellent vision, and, like other birds, humans, and some rainforest primates, they can see in color. Dogs and their relatives have an incredible sense of smell. Naked mole rats and other burrowing animals live mostly by feel, using their extra-sensitive whiskers and hairs to find their way in the dark. For aquatic animals like fish, dolphins, and whales, hearing is by far the most important sense. For one thing, sounds travel farther underwater than through air. For another, there is very little light in the deep ocean. Taste is used by all animals to test their food for chemicals, such as toxins that may be harmful.

Some species have a sixth—or even a seventh—sense. For example, sharks find their prey by picking up electrical signals, and snakes can detect heat.

The senses are part of the nervous system. Animals collect sensory information using different types of specialized cells, called sensory receptors. Examples are photoreceptors (light), mechanoreceptors (pressure), thermoreceptors (heat), and chemoreceptors (chemicals)—better known as taste buds in humans!

SOUND
BELUGA WHALE
Delphinapterus leucas

Beluga whales use clicks, whistles, and chirps to communicate with members of their pod. They also use sound—in the form of echolocation—to find food. While hunting, the whale emits sounds that travel underwater until they encounter an object. The sounds then bounce back to the whale, revealing the location of its target.

SIGHT
SHARP-SHINNED HAWK
Accipiter striatus

The sharp-shinned hawk can see twice as far as a human. Its eyes are packed with sensory cells called rods and cones that allow it to see with great clarity. In addition, like many birds it can see more colors than humans can. This ability allows these hawks to easily pick out prey that may be camouflaged.

TASTE
SUMATRAN ORANGUTAN
Pongo abelii

Like all mammals, orangutans have taste buds on their tongues. Most animals rely on these receptors to determine what they can—and cannot—eat. Typically, bitter, unripe fruits can be toxic, so most animals stay away from them. But orangutans eat them. They also eat soil rich in minerals that apparently help neutralize the toxins.

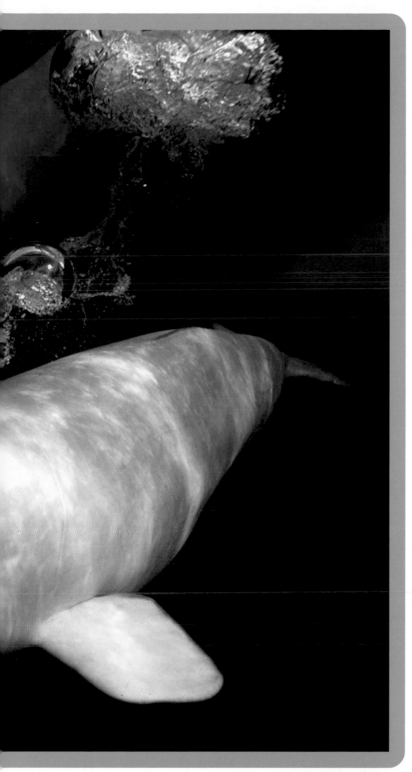

ELEPHANT
COMMUNICATION

Elephants use a variety of sounds to communicate. They trumpet at the sight of a predator to warn the herd. They rumble to greet each other. They also make long-distance contact calls. These travel by seismic, or ground, vibrations. They are so low in frequency that humans cannot hear them. But the elephants can, as long as they are listening. To listen for a contact call, elephants rest their trunks on the ground and hold one leg up. This position helps the sound waves travel through the elephant's feet, up its body, and into its ears. Elephants are not the only animals that use seismic communication. Others include spiders, scorpions, kangaroo rats, and golden moles.

SMELL
DOG
Canis familiaris

All dogs have keen sniffing abilities, but the bloodhound's sense of smell is among the strongest. It has about 230 million olfactory receptors, or scent cells, inside its nose. That's 40 times as many as humans! The large number of receptors increases the dog's ability to pick up odors. In addition, bloodhounds can remember scents for several days.

TOUCH
CHANNEL CATFISH
Ictalurus punctatus

Catfish are named for the whisker-like organs that extend from each side of their mouths. These organs—called barbels—help the fish feel for prey in the murky water at the bottom of a lake. Some species—like the channel catfish—have up to four pairs of barbels.

HOMES AND HABITATS

All animals and plants need a place to live. Most choose— or are born into— particular habitats. Habitats are places in nature that provide food, protection from predators and unfavorable weather, and a home in which to raise young.

Habitats are characterized most often by climate and location. They can range from warm, moist areas near the Equator— such as the Amazon rainforest— to cold polar areas such as the Arctic.

The animals and plants that live in a particular habitat have adaptations that allow them to survive there. For example, spider monkeys—which live in the trees of some tropical forests—have flexible tails that allow them to grasp and balance along branches. And a cactus that grows in the desert has spines that help collect and retain moisture.

Some animals build homes in their habitat. Beavers use wood and mud to construct lodges; some toads dig burrows. Other animals don't have to do such work. They find their homes in natural places such as caves and trees.

To the right, you'll find sets of icons that represent different habitats around the world, as well as descriptions for each one. These icons appear throughout the book. Refer to this page whenever you see a habitat icon as you read.

HABITATS

	Habitat	Description
	SHRUBLAND/BUSH	Bushy areas where the main plants found are branched woody plants, or shrubs. Other plants include grasses, herbs, and plants with underground root systems.
	GRASSLAND	Open areas covered with wild grasses and few trees. Found everywhere except Antarctica. Grasslands can be wet, flooded, or frozen during certain times of the year.
	SAVANNA	Grassy areas with numerous trees widely spaced that allow plenty of light to reach the ground, or open canopy. Found in warm and hot climates. Most have seasonal rainfall.
	DESERT/DRY/ DRY AND ROCKY	A large area of land that receives less than 10 inches (25 cm) of precipitation each year. Some deserts, like the Sahara, are hot all year, while others, like the Gobi, are cool.
	TROPICAL FOREST/ SUBTROPICAL/RAINFOREST	Forests near Earth's Equator that receive at least 160 inches (406 cm) of rainfall each year; tropical dry and moist forests; cloud/montane forests.
	TEMPERATE FOREST/ WOODLAND	Forests that experience four seasons, and are characterized by tall trees with broad leaves.
	CONIFEROUS FOREST/ WOODLAND	Forests with pine-producing trees that experience long, cold winters and short, moist summers.
	MOUNTAINS/HIGHLANDS/ SLOPES/TEMPERATE AND TROPICAL	Masses of rock pushed upward. Climate in these rocky regions becomes cooler as the elevation increases.
	POLAR REGIONS/ARCTIC/ TUNDRA AND ANTARCTIC	Vast, treeless regions where temperatures can dip below 32°F (0°C) for 10 months a year. These areas have permafrost, a layer of soil that is frozen all year.
	FRESHWATER/FLOWING/ RIVERS/STREAMS	Bodies of water flowing continuously in one direction. These areas may vary in oxygen content, level of dissolved nutrients, and clarity.
	FRESHWATER/STILL/ WETLANDS/BOGS/ SWAMPS/PONDS/LAKES	Bodies of standing water that are home to many aquatic plants and have very low salt concentration.
	OCEANS AND OPEN SEA	Bodies of salt water that cover 75 percent of Earth's surface. The presence of sunlight in this habitat is great near the surface, but decreases with depth.
	COASTAL/INSHORE AREAS (INCLUDES MANGROVE SWAMPS)	Areas along the shoreline that are characterized by salt water, and may be subject to strong winds and waves; inshore areas such as inlets, bays.
	CORAL REEFS/SEAGRASS	Structures found underwater composed of calcified material made by living coral animals combined with minerals and organic matter; reef grasses, macroalgae, and kelp marine habitats.
	CAVES AND CAVERNS	Open spaces in the ground or in hillsides with rocky walls. These structures can occur naturally or be human-made.
	URBAN AREAS/CITIES/ INDOOR PARKS/GARDENS	Areas in which the food supply and environmental conditions are largely controlled or influenced by humans.
	FARMLAND/RURAL AREAS/ ABANDONED STRUCTURES	Land where agricultural products such as food and livestock are raised. These places have less human development and are more open than urban areas.

HOMES

HIVE
A container in which a colony of honeybees lives and produces honey. Hives are often built by people to collect the bees' honey.

INSECT GALL
A swelling of a plant tissue caused by some insects, parasites, and mites. Gall-making animals may use the gall as shelter and a food source.

NEST
A structure made by some birds, insects, or small mammals to lay eggs and live in. Nests are often made of sticks, leaves, fur, and other found objects.

LODGE
A dome of sticks and mud built in a body of water. A lodge has underwater entrances that lead to a plant-lined living area above water level.

BURROW
A hole or tunnel dug in the ground by an animal that lives or hides in it.

HOLE
A cavity or hollow place in a solid object such as a tree. Some animals, such as woodpeckers, peck holes in trees and then roost inside them.

DEN
A burrow used for hibernation and where females raise young.

SHELL
A hard bone covering that protects some animals' bodies. Some animals—such as turtles—grow their own shell, while others—like the hermit crab—find one and move into it.

WEB
A net of silky threads spun by some spiders to trap prey. Webs can vary in shape, ranging from spiral to tube-shaped.

TERMITE MOUND
A tall mound built by termites using saliva and soil. A termite mound contains hundreds of air tunnels to help cool the structure when the weather is hot.

CAVE
A large natural hole in a hillside or cliff, or underground. Caves provide a cool, dark shelter for animals that have little or no vision—such as eyeless shrimp and some bats.

HOLLOW
A cavity or space within an object that is often the result of natural forces. Animals such as raccoons and some owls may use tree hollows for shelter.

TREE TRUNK
Many birds, insects, and other animals seek protection from predators and weather inside tree trunks. They may peck holes inside tree trunks, or move into existing tree hollows.

TREES
Trees provide a safe place for animals that want to avoid predators on the ground. Trees are often homes to animals whose bodies are adapted for climbing and balancing on branches.

AQUATIC PLANTS
Some plants—such as duckweed and water lilies—thrive in aquatic environments. These plants can provide shade and are a protective shelter for some frogs and fish.

MIGRATIONS

Many animals move from one area to another on a regular basis, a behavior known as migration. Animals migrate in search of food, water, shelter, or a mate, usually in response to changing seasons. When and where they go depend on the species. The albatross, for example, flies around the world—every year. Elephants walk from one watering hole to the next. Wood frogs hop from dry land to shallow ponds and back again. What keeps them on track? Genetics play a role, as do environmental cues such as certain smells, changes in air or water temperature, water currents, the position of the sun and stars, and the Earth's geomagnetic field. In some cases, we do not yet understand how migrating animals find their way. But one thing is clear: They are programmed to move!

WOOD FROG
Lithobates sylvatica

Wood frogs range in size from two to three inches (5 to 8 cm). They live in swamps, ravines, and wooded areas, where they feed on ground-dwelling creatures. These include insects, spiders, and earthworms. When it's time to breed, the frogs migrate about a half mile (1 km) to seasonal wetlands, or vernal pools.

ARCTIC OCEAN

NORTH AMERICA

The wood frog range is shown here in dark blue.

ATLANTIC OCEAN

PACIFIC OCEAN

Migration routes shown are some of the longer examples for the particular species.

SOUTH AMERICA

0	2,000 miles
0	2,000 kilometers

AFRICAN SAVANNA ELEPHANT
Loxodonta africana

Elephants migrate in search of water, following the same routes every year. As each elephant travels, it consumes up to 660 pounds (300 kg) of roots, grasses, fruit, and bark daily. The large meal is necessary to sustain its large frame, which measures nine to 12 feet (3 to 3.7 m) tall at the shoulder.

ANTARCTICA

ARCTIC
TERN
Sterna paradisaea

Arctic terns are only 13 to 15 inches (33 to 39 cm) long. But don't let their small size fool you. These seabirds are capable of great migrations. Each year, the birds fly an average of 44,000 miles (70,900 km) round-trip between their summer breeding grounds in the Arctic to summer in Antarctica. Along the way, they may stop to feed on small fish and crustaceans.

CHRISTMAS ISLAND
RED CRAB
Gecarcoidea natalis

The red crab, which measures three to five inches (8 to 13 cm), is found only on Australia's Christmas Island. Most of the year, it lives on the rainforest floor, feeding on leaves, fruits, seedlings, and flowers. But during the rainy season, it migrates up to one mile (1.6 km) to the sea to breed. Millions of crabs take part in this migration, crossing roads and stopping traffic along the way.

EUROPE

ASIA

PACIFIC OCEAN

The African elephant range is shown here in gold.

AFRICA

EQUATOR

INDIAN OCEAN

The red crab range is shown here in the teal circle.

AUSTRALIA

LEATHERBACK SEA
TURTLE
Dermochelys coriacea

The leatherback is the world's largest turtle. Most measure six to 7.2 feet (1.8 to 2.2 m) long. During breeding season, these giant reptiles migrate to the same region where they hatched to lay their eggs. After the eggs hatch, the young turtles head to the sea, perhaps guided by geomagnetic forces, the frequency of the waves, or both. Adults feed mainly on a diet of jellyfish and salps, a type of tunicate.

BLUE
SHARK
Prionace glauca

These sharks migrate to find cooler water. They prefer water temperatures in the range of 45 to 61°F (7 to 16°C). Blue sharks grow six to 13 feet (2 to 4 m) and eat a diet of bony fish and squid.

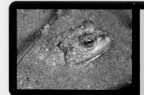

ADAPTATIONS FOR SURVIVAL

Life in the wild has many challenges. Animals must find enough food to survive, endure the climate of their environment, and protect themselves from predators. Fortunately, animals have adaptations—body parts or behaviors—that help them meet these challenges.

TOUGH SKIN, SCALES, SHELLS
A tough exterior can protect an animal from bites and cuts. The three-banded armadillo has a body shield of bony plates that protects it when under attack.

CLAWS
Sharp claws can be used as weapons. The brown bear has sharp claws on each paw, which it uses to climb, forage for food, and slash enemies when provoked.

TEETH
Carnivores, like the jaguar, have sharp teeth to tear into meat. The teeth also are used as a weapon if the animal is attacked.

HOOVES
Some animals, like goats, have hooves at the tips of their toes. Thanks to these tough hooves, goats can navigate difficult and rocky terrain.

TAILS
When a predator grabs a leopard gecko's tail, it breaks off! This tail shedding ability surprises the predator and allows the lizard to escape.

HORNS AND ANTLERS
Horns are made of keratin, like fingernails. Antlers are made of bone covered in skin that is shed just before the breeding season. Horns and antlers are both useful for headbutting.

ADAPTATIONS FOR PROTECTION

To avoid being eaten, many animals have body parts that they use as weapons, such as claws and horns. Others find ways to confuse or hide from their predators.

SPITTING
The fulmar is a type of seabird that can spit oil from its stomach onto its enemies. The oil can damage its attackers' feathers or fur.

CAMOUFLAGE
Camouflage is an animal's ability to disguise its appearance, often by using its coloring or body shape to blend in with its surroundings.

STINGING
Sharp organs called stingers can be used to pierce the skin of attackers and deliver venom. Bee stingers release venom for several minutes after the stinger has entered its target.

ODOR
A foul odor can ward off some predators. Skunks let loose a terrible-smelling spray that can linger for weeks.

TUSKS
Tusks are long, pointy teeth that grow from an animal's head. Elephants use their tusks for digging, marking trees, and even fighting.

TONGUES
Snakes flick their tongues to smell their surroundings. This helps them know when danger is nearby.

POISON
The strawberry poison dart frog has glands in its skin that are packed with poison. The poison isn't made inside the frog's body. It comes from formicine ants that the frog eats.

WEBBED FEET
Many water animals, such as ducks and some frogs, have a thin membrane, or web, between their toes. This allows them to paddle through water and walk on muddy surfaces.

WHISKERS
Whiskers can help an animal navigate at night. A tiger's whiskers have sensory nerves at the base. This helps the tiger detect movement. (It also helps the tiger determine where to bite its prey.)

BEAKS
All birds use their beaks to feed. A toucan uses its long, colorful beak to reach fruits on high branches. The beak is also serrated like a knife, to tear apart the bird's meal.

ADAPTATIONS FOR LIFE IN UNIQUE HABITATS
Over time, animals adapt to the environments in which they live. These adaptations, which include traits like fur and wings, allow them not only to survive, but also to reproduce, even in extreme temperatures, on remote islands, and underwater.

GILLS
All fish need oxygen to breathe underwater. Organs called gills absorb oxygen from the water and then send it to the fish's bloodstream.

WINGS
Wings allow many birds to cover large distances while searching for food. Birds may use their wings to fly through the air or glide from tree to tree.

SCALES
Reptiles have scales that cover their skin. A crocodile's tough scales protect it against rocky surroundings, whereas desert-dwelling lizards and snakes have scales to help keep in moisture. A snake's scales also help reduce friction as it moves.

FEATHERS
A bird's feathers vary depending on the habitat. Some desert birds, such as the sand grouse, have barbs on their feathers that help retain water. Meanwhile, seabirds, like the pelican, have water-repellent feathers.

FUR
Arctic animals, like the polar bear, have fur to help keep warm. A polar bear's fur consists of an undercoat, which traps body heat against the skin, as well as a thick coat of water-repellent guard hairs on top.

MORE ON CAMOUFLAGE

COLORS Many animals have coats, feathers, or skin that naturally match their environment. A prairie dog's reddish brown coat matches its earthy surroundings.

PATTERNS Patterns can also help an animal match its environment. A peacock flounder can change its pattern to match the pebbly ocean floor.

BLENDING If animals can't rely on their skin color and patterns to match their environment, they may use objects to blend in. A dresser crab places pieces of coral and sponge on its body to conceal itself from predators.

MIMICRY Some animals can mimic, or copy, another organism's appearance or behavior. The walking stick is an insect that mimics a stick.

SPOTS False eyespots can make an animal look like a larger and scarier animal. The two large spots behind a hawk moth caterpillar's head make it look like a snake.

STRIPES Stripes can create an optical illusion. When zebras stand in a herd, it's hard to tell where one zebra ends and another begins. This makes the herd look like one giant animal.

SKIN Special skin cells that contain pigment allow some animals—like the octopus—to change the color of their skin to match the environment.

FUR Some animals have fur that changes color seasonally to match their surroundings. The arctic fox's coat changes from white in the cold, snowy winter to brown or gray in the spring and summer to match the rock-covered terrain.

FEATHERS Some birds, such as the willow ptarmigan, molt their white winter feathers to make way for brown feathers in the spring and summer.

ENDANGERED ANIMALS

Many animal species are at risk of becoming extinct, or dying out. Although natural causes can be a factor, humans are largely responsible. Activities such as logging, farming, and construction have destroyed many animal habitats, and illegal hunting and climate change have only added to the problem. A group called the International Union for Conservation of Nature (IUCN) surveys different animal populations to determine if they are at risk. According to the IUCN, the animal species shown here are endangered and at very high or extremely high risk of dying out.

NORTH
AMERICA

ATLANTIC
OCEAN

PACIFIC
OCEAN

SOUTH
AMERICA

GRAY
PARROT
Psittacus erithacus

Gray parrots, also called African grays, are known for their fantastic ability to mimic human speech and other sounds. They're outgoing and social, and tests show that they can solve logic problems about as well as a five-year-old child. That's why they're popular pets all around the world. But between the illegal pet trade and loss of the forests they live in, these birds are quickly disappearing.

0   2,000 miles

0   2,000 kilometers

BORNEAN
ORANGUTAN
Pongo pygmaeus

Bornean orangutans were once widespread throughout Southeast Asia. Today, these tree dwellers are found only in small patches of rainforest on the island of Borneo. It is estimated that farming and logging have claimed more than 80 percent of their habitat. Illegal hunting and the illegal pet trade are problems, too. Fewer than 100,000 Bornean orangutans live in the wild today. Their risk of extinction is very high.

ANTARCTICA

GRAND CAYMAN
BLUE IGUANA
Cyclura lewisi

In 2002, Grand Cayman blue iguanas became the most endangered iguana on Earth, with fewer than 25 adults remaining in the wild. Humans brought new predators such as cats, rats, and dogs to the island. They also destroyed the iguana's habitat as they built farms, homes, and roads. The population is now increasing, but the iguanas can only survive in small protected areas.

WHALE
SHARK
Rhincodon typus

Commercial fishing of whale sharks is banned in many places. But it's still the biggest problem for the world's biggest fish. In some parts of the world, there is a high demand for whale shark meat, fins, and oil. Whale sharks can also get caught in gear used to catch other types of fish. People swimming with or taking tours to watch whale sharks are also threats because they interrupt the shark's feeding.

RANGES OF SELECTED ENDANGERED ANIMALS

- Bornean Orangutan
- Chinese Giant Salamander
- Grand Cayman Blue Iguana
- Gray Parrot
- San Francisco Forktail
- Whale Shark

EUROPE

ASIA

AFRICA

PACIFIC OCEAN

EQUATOR

INDIAN OCEAN

AUSTRALIA

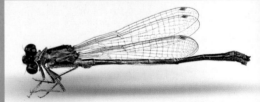

SAN FRANCISCO
FORKTAIL
Ischnura gemina

Loss of habitat is the biggest threat to the San Francisco forktail's survival. Some small ponds where it lives have dried up naturally. Humans have destroyed many more by draining wetlands for housing and industry and rerouting creeks to control flooding. This damselfly sometimes mates with a closely related species, resulting in offspring with traits of both species. That pushes this damselfly species even closer to the edge of extinction.

CHINESE
GIANT SALAMANDER
Andrias davidianus

The Chinese giant salamander is an ancient species. But in the 1970s, this six-foot (1.8-m)-long amphibian was suddenly in danger. Markets for its meat and body parts—used to make traditional medicines—both grew. People built thousands of farms to raise captive giant salamanders, but illegal hunting of wild salamanders continued. Dams and pollution also destroyed natural habitats. Today, these salamanders are a rare find in the wild.

CONSERVATION

According to the IUCN, more than 31,000 animal and plant species are at risk of becoming extinct, many due to the actions of humans. Contributing factors include illegal trade and hunting, overfishing, habitat destruction, invasive species, emerging diseases, and climate change.

Although extinction is a normal process, the historical rate based on the fossil record was 10 to 100 species per year—for all species everywhere. The current rate is at least 1,000 times higher.

In response, scientists are working together with research and conservation organizations, communities, and governments to gather the information needed to protect animals at risk. Their methods include monitoring population size, protecting ecosystems, and captive breeding.

On this map are animal species whose future depends on whether we take steps to conserve them, or not.

MEKONG GIANT
CATFISH
Pangasianodon gigas

Overfishing, development, and dams have driven the Mekong giant catfish to the edge of extinction. It is now illegal to catch them. Some captive giant catfish have been bred on farms with a similar species. But the wild population in the Mekong River is disappearing. Researchers and local fishers are working together to save them. They report any illegal fishing and also work with governments and developers to protect the fish's natural habitat.

ARCTIC OCEAN

NORTH AMERICA

ATLANTIC OCEAN

0   2,000 miles

0   2,000 kilometers

PACIFIC OCEAN

SOUTH AMERICA

AFRICAN
ELEPHANT
Loxodonta africana

Habitat loss and centuries of poaching have taken a heavy toll on African elephants. In 1800, there were up to 26 million African elephants. An estimated 400,000 remain today. To protect them, governments have passed anti-poaching laws and banned the ivory trade. National parks give the elephants a safer place to live, and wildlife corridors help them travel safely from one park to another. Local people are working with conservationists as wildlife scouts, helping to monitor and protect the elephants.

ANTARCTICA

KEMP'S RIDLEY
SEA TURTLE
Lepidochelys kempii

In the past, people over-harvesting eggs was a major problem for the Kemp's ridley sea turtle. Today, laws protect the beaches where this species goes to nest. Now the turtle's biggest threat is in the ocean. Kemp's ridleys often get caught in fishing gear, especially shrimp nets. To prevent this, many fishing boats now use special gear that allows the turtles to escape. Some areas where the turtles live are permanently closed to shrimp trawling.

LEMUR LEAF
FROG
Agalychnis lemur

In the past 15 years, the lemur leaf frog's numbers have plummeted by up to 80 percent—largely due to chytridiomycosis, a deadly fungal disease. To reintroduce the frogs to their native forests in Costa Rica, researchers have created artificial breeding sites on a small, privately owned reserve. They add tadpoles to the ponds each year and are also breeding the frogs in captivity so the species will live on even if the wild frogs disappear.

EUROPE

ASIA

AFRICA

PACIFIC OCEAN

EQUATOR

RANGES OF SELECTED ENDANGERED ANIMALS

- African Elephant
- Kemp's Ridley Sea Turtle
- Lemur Leaf Frog
- Mekong Giant Catfish
- Monarch Butterfly
- Whooping Crane

AUSTRALIA

INDIAN OCEAN

MONARCH
BUTTERFLY
Danaus plexippus

In the 1990s, hundreds of millions of monarch butterflies flew each fall from Canada and the northern U.S.A. to central Mexico. Today, just a fraction of that number makes the trip. Loss of habitat, increased use of pesticides, and climate change are to blame. To track the monarch's migrating patterns, people are sending scientists photos of butterflies they see. People are also planting flower gardens and milkweed, where monarchs lay their eggs, to attract the butterflies. And they are restoring grassland habitats along the butterfly's migratory route.

WHOOPING
CRANE
Grus americana

In 1941, whooping cranes had nearly vanished. People had overhunted them and destroyed their wetlands habitats. Then the U.S. and Canadian governments, conservationists, and volunteers banded together to save them. They protected around 20 cranes that were left and bred more in captivity. They restored the wetlands and even trained young cranes to follow an ultralight aircraft to teach them how to migrate. Today, there are about 440 whooping cranes in the wild and 160 in captivity, and their population is growing.

NEWLY DISCOVERED CREATURES

How many species live on Earth? Estimates run as high as one trillion, but the truth is no one knows for sure. What we do know is that new species are being discovered every day. Insects are the most common type of new species found. It's rare to find a new mammal.

Many of these discoveries happen because scientists are going to remote places that haven't been well studied before. Others occur in the lab when they examine genetic codes. Scientists even find new species when they study fossils of organisms that lived millions of years ago.

On these pages are animals that have recently been discovered. Because they are so new, some don't even have a common name yet. Use the map to learn where they were found and read the descriptions to learn a little bit about them.

APHRODITE
ANTHIAS
Tosanoides aphrodite

In 2017, researchers discovered Aphrodite anthias, a new type of coral reef fish. It lives around a group of small islands in the middle of the Atlantic Ocean. The fish's bright pink and yellow neon colors were so spectacular that scientists named it after the ancient Greek goddess of love and beauty. Although similar fish live in the Pacific Ocean, this is the only fish of its genus ever found in the Atlantic.

NORTH AMERICA

ATLANTIC OCEAN

PACIFIC OCEAN

SOUTH AMERICA

ANTARCTICA

VOGELKOP SUPERB
BIRD OF PARADISE
Lophorina niedda

Male superb birds of paradise put on quite a show when they court females. Typically, they hop around and fan their feathers into a black oval with a blue smiley face. But one observed in 2016 instead slid smoothly from side to side. Its black feathers formed a crescent and its blue feathers frowned. Genetic testing confirmed that this was a new bird of paradise species. Named the Vogelkop superb bird of paradise, it is endemic to, or found only on, the Vogelkop Peninsula of New Guinea.

SORTING HAT
SPIDER
Eriovixia gryffindori

A team of scientists discovered a new spider in southern India in 2015. The spider was less than 0.3 inch (7 mm) long. Its spotted, grayish brown body blended in with the dried-up leaves around it. But the scientists noticed something else. It was shaped just like the Sorting Hat in the Harry Potter books! Huge fans of the series, they named the spider in the hat's honor.

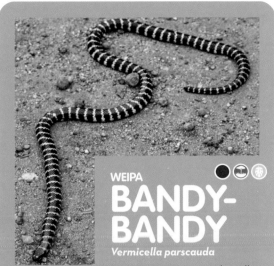

WEIPA
BANDY-BANDY
Vermicella parscauda

In 2018, scientists accidentally discovered a new species of bandy-bandy snake in Queensland, Australia. *Vermicella parscauda*, part of the cobra family, is a small, nocturnal, venomous snake. Bandy-bandies are burrowing snakes, so researchers were surprised to find this one on a concrete block by the sea. The snake had slithered over from a pile of bauxite rubble. The mining of bauxite, a soft rock used to make aluminum, is a major industry in the area. Scientists worry that mining could destroy the snake's habitat, putting its future at risk.

0 ——— 2,000 miles
0 ——— 2,000 kilometers

EUROPE

ASIA

PACIFIC OCEAN

AFRICA

EQUATOR

RANGES OF SELECTED NEWLY DISCOVERED ANIMALS

- Aphrodite Anthias
- "Mini" Frog
- Olinguito
- Sorting Hat Spider
- Vogelkop Superb Bird of Paradise
- Weipa Bandy-Bandy

AUSTRALIA

OLINGUITO
Bassaricyon neblina

In 2013, scientists introduced the world to the olinguito. It was the most recent mammal and the first carnivore discovered in the Americas in 35 years. But these raccoon relatives hadn't exactly been hiding. For more than 100 years, people had seen them in the wild, museum collections, and zoos. But they mistook them for olingos, a close relative. Olinguitos weigh two pounds (0.9 kg) and have large eyes and woolly orange-brown fur. They live in the cloud forests of Colombia and Ecuador.

"MINI" FROG
Mini mum

Scientists discovered a new species of tiny frog in southeast Madagascar in 2019. They accurately named it *Mini mum*! Males grow only up to .38 inch (9.7 mm) long. Females are slightly larger, measuring up to .44 inch (11.3 mm) in length. Both are small enough to sit on top of a staple! These little amphibians live in only one tiny part of a rainforest. There aren't very many of them, and the surrounding habitat is quickly disappearing. Scientists are trying to get them classified as a critically endangered species.

All mammals have hair at some point in their lives. (Even dolphins are born with a few hairs on their snout!) Their hair—or fur—is an adaptation that helps them survive where they live. Polar bears *(Ursus maritimus),* for example, have a thick white coat of fur that insulates them from the cold, repels water, and provides camouflage in their Arctic habitat.

MAMMALS

MEERKAT

RED PANDA

LIONS

HORSE

RED-NECKED WALLABY

SOUTHERN ELEPHANT SEAL

SIBERIAN TIGER

VIRGINIA OPOSSUM

AFRICAN ELEPHANTS

CHIMPANZEES

DOG

CHEETAH

BACTRIAN CAMEL

BOTTLENOSE DOLPHIN

GRAY WOLF

KOALA

WHAT IS A MAMMAL?

MAMMALS ARE AMONG THE MOST ADAPTABLE ANIMALS.

They are found on every continent and in every ocean, and they range in size from tiny bumblebee bats to enormous blue whales. One reason for their success is the way they move. Mammals as a group use every possible form of locomotion. Terrestrial species walk, run, jump, climb, hop, swing, dig, and burrow. Aquatic ones swim, shuffle, and dive. A few even fly.

Diet and behavior vary, too. Many carnivores, for example, are top predators that live generally solitary lives. These include jaguars, tigers, and polar bears. By contrast, lions, otters, wolves, and dolphins live in family groups. Even more social are some of the herbivores, especially hoofed animals like deer and zebra. By living in large groups, they gain both protection against becoming another animal's meal and more opportunities to breed. Among omnivores, primates are known for their high intelligence, and rodents for their high numbers.

Mammal bones, especially skulls, are used for identification, and to work out the evolutionary history of each species. The jaws of a house cat are more like those of a lion than those of a wolf, for example. The teeth of horses and zebras look alike. The ear bones of mammals were once the jaws of prehistoric reptiles. And so on.

All mammals share four traits, which can be seen in the diagram below: hair, mammary glands, a hinged jaw, and three tiny middle ear bones. Most have specialized teeth and moveable external ears.

CLASSIFICATION OF MAMMALS

1 Mammals are organized into 27 orders, but this classification scheme is not set in stone. It changes as new species and fossils are discovered and DNA studies shed new light on the relatedness of species.

2 Mammals are divided into three big groups based on how the embryo develops.

3 Monotremes such as the platypus are the egg-laying mammals.

4 Marsupials such as kangaroos have a short gestation period and give birth to young that crawl immediately into a pouch.

5 Placental mammals have a long gestation made possible by a placenta and give birth to live young.

6 More than 20 percent of all mammals are members of the order Chiroptera (bats).

7 Forty percent of all mammals are members of the order Rodentia (rodents).

8 Eight percent of all mammals are members of the order Eulipotyphla (moles, shrews, and hedgehogs).

9 Some of the more familiar mammals are in the order Carnivora such as cats, dogs, and bears.

MAMMAL TRAITS

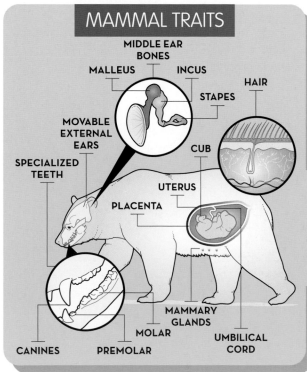

MIDDLE EAR BONES
MALLEUS
INCUS
STAPES
HAIR
MOVABLE EXTERNAL EARS
CUB
SPECIALIZED TEETH
UTERUS
PLACENTA
CANINES
MOLAR
PREMOLAR
MAMMARY GLANDS
UMBILICAL CORD

All mammals have hair—in the form of fur and whiskers—and mammary glands for nursing their young.

Did **you** **know?** No two humpback whales have the same pattern of color on their tails.

When this gentle giant, a humpback whale, surfaces to breathe, the water it sprays from its blowhole can soar as high as 30 feet (9 m) into the air.

MONOTREMES
AND MARSUPIALS

The egg-laying mammals, or monotremes, are strange-looking creatures retaining many ancient specialized characteristics. Though they were once common, there are only two species groups remaining: the platypus and the echidnas. The marsupials, or mammals with pouches, are a more familiar group, including species such as kangaroos and koalas.

Similar to other (placental) mammals, monotremes and marsupials produce milk and nurse their young, have hair, and hear as a result of the vibration of three middle-ear bones. But they are really quite different in a number of other ways! They share several unique anatomical features, for example. One is the cloaca, a common opening for their reproductive, intestinal, and urinary tracts, a structure also found in birds and reptiles.

Their reproductive strategies also differ. Monotremes lay eggs and produce milk for their young but lack nipples. Marsupials give birth to live young known as joeys and have multiple nipples located within their pouches. Some joeys remain in the pouch for as long as one year, or until the next baby is born.

Another difference is where they are found. Monotremes live only in Australia, Tasmania, and New Guinea and are represented by only five species. Most of the 379 species of marsupials also are found in Australia and New Guinea. They were once much more widespread, however. Fossils of extinct marsupials show they once lived alongside placental mammals in the Americas, for example. Today, only one survives in North America, the Virginia opossum; 125 inhabit Central and South America.

Life spans for monotremes and marsupials range up to 50 years.

COMMON BRUSH-TAILED POSSUM
Trichosurus vulpecula

RANGE: Australia, Tasmania, New Zealand

SIZE: 3.3 to 9.9 lb (1.5 to 4.5 kg)

DIET: Leaves, flowers, shrubs

In most parts of the world, small animals that live in trees, have long tails, and eat leaves are monkeys—placental mammals. In Australia, they are marsupials. The solitary and nocturnal brush-tailed possum is one example.

LIFE IN A POUCH

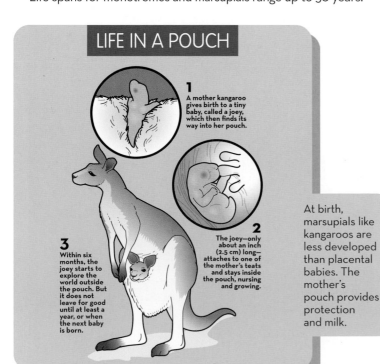

1 A mother kangaroo gives birth to a tiny baby, called a joey, which then finds its way into her pouch.

2 The joey—only about an inch (2.5 cm) long—attaches to one of the mother's teats and stays inside the pouch, nursing and growing.

3 Within six months, the joey starts to explore the world outside the pouch. But it does not leave for good until at least a year, or when the next baby is born.

At birth, marsupials like kangaroos are less developed than placental babies. The mother's pouch provides protection and milk.

VIRGINIA OPOSSUM
Didelphis virginiana

RANGE: Central America and Mexico to Ontario, Canada

SIZE: 0.7 to 14 lb (0.3 to 6.4 kg)

DIET: Insects and carrion

Though its lifespan is short (1.5 years), the opossum is a highly successful marsupial. Diet is one reason. This species eats anything, including garbage. It is also excellent at playing dead when threatened by a hungry hawk or coyote.

KOALA
Phascolarctos cinereus

RANGE: Eastern Australia

SIZE: 11.2 to 26 lb (5.1 to 11.8 kg)

DIET: Leaves and shoots of eucalyptus trees

After eating a pound of eucalyptus leaves each night, koalas spend their days resting and digesting. Sometimes, they climb down to the ground to change trees or eat soil, which helps with digestion. They rarely drink.

Did you know? Echidnas use their backward-pointing rear feet to remove soil.

SHORT-BEAKED ECHIDNA
Tachyglossus aculeatus

RANGE: Australia, New Guinea, Tasmania

SIZE: 4.4 to 15.4 lb (2 to 7 kg)

DIET: Termites, ants, other small invertebrates

Echidnas are diggers. Like the platypus, they use their sensitive snouts to find food using electroreception. These egg-laying monotremes are the only mammals with this sixth sense.

DUCK-BILLED PLATYPUS
Ornithorhynchus anatinus

RANGE: Eastern Australia, Tasmania

SIZE: 1.8 to 5.6 lb (0.8 to 2.5 kg)

DIET: Aquatic insects, larvae, fish

This unusual animal spends most of its time in water. The platypus has a supersensitive nose shaped like a bill, which it uses to hunt for aquatic insects, crayfish, shrimp, tadpoles, and worms. It finds its food by feel and by detecting electrical signals.

TASMANIAN DEVIL
Sarcophilus harrisii

RANGE: Tasmania

SIZE: 8.8 to 26 lb (4 to 11.8 kg)

DIET: Dead animals and small mammals

One look at the teeth of a Tasmanian devil and it is clear that this marsupial is a carnivore. It will eat anything ranging in size from a possum to a wallaby. Its large head and neck give it a very powerful bite.

WESTERN GRAY KANGAROO
Macropus fuliginosus

RANGE: Southern Australia

SIZE: 60 to 120 lb (27 to 54 kg)

DIET: Grasses, forbs, leaves, tree bark, shrubs

The kangaroo's long, furry muzzle hides its massive molar teeth, suited for chewing plants. This herbivore is a grazing animal, like deer and antelope (species not found in Australia). Unlike those animals, however, kangaroos do not regurgitate and rechew their food.

Lisa Dabek

TREE KANGAROO

Matschie's tree kangaroos *(Dendrolagus matschiei)* are among the rarest animals on Earth. They lead secret lives in Papua New Guinea's ancient cloud forests, spending most of their time hidden in a maze of moss-covered tree branches nearly 100 feet (30 m) above ground. I had studied tree kangaroos in captivity for nearly a decade and wanted to investigate them in the wild. Many people warned that I might never find one—that it was impossible to track them—but I wanted to learn their secrets to help save them from extinction.

At the time, area villagers tracked tree kangaroos with hunting dogs, so I flew to Papua New Guinea and for three weeks met with local landowners and the best local tree kangaroo hunter. I expressed my desire to study wild tree kangaroos, and they led me through the forest to look for one. On the very last day of the trip, one of the hunting dogs barked wildly. His eyes fixed on a red-and-brown tree kangaroo 40 feet (12 m) above our heads! It gazed down at us and tears welled in my eyes—I had finally seen a wild Matschie's tree kangaroo. Since then, local landowners and hunters have guided our team into the forest year after year to study them. Seven *years* passed before we saw another tree 'roo, but a couple of years later we *caught* one and attached a special collar that allows us to monitor its movements. And thanks to the hunters who help us track the tree kangaroos, we recently captured the first images of their secret lives in the canopy—including a female caring for a tiny joey in her pouch!

PACIFIC
OCEAN

**RANGE OF THE
DENDROLAGUS MATSCHIEI
(MATSCHIE'S TREE KANGAROO)**

0   200 miles
0   200 kilometers

ASIA

OCEANIA

New Guinea

Arafura Sea

CORAL
SEA

AUSTRALIA

OBSERVATION TIPS

1 Wear comfortable hiking boots on your trip of a lifetime to Papua New Guinea. You'll be trekking over steep hills and rugged peaks to look for tree 'roos.

2 Tree kangaroos blend into moss-covered branches—use binoculars to spot their dangling tails.

3 To track Matschie's tree kangaroos, look for nibbled leaves, scratched trees, and even poop!

4 Heads up! Matschie's tree kangaroos can safely leap 60 feet (18 m) or more from a tree branch to the ground.

Lisa Dabek is founder and director of the Tree Kangaroo Conservation Program at Woodland Park Zoo in Seattle, Washington, U.S.A. She began studying Matschie's tree kangaroos in 1987 and continues to work with local landowners in Papua New Guinea to study the animals and conserve their natural habitat.

Matschie's tree kangaroos give birth to a single baby, called a joey. The naked, lima bean–size newborn crawls up its mother's belly into her pouch to nurse on milk and continue to develop. After about 10 months, the joey permanently leaves its mother's pouch—though it still pushes its head inside to drink milk for another four months! The joey follows its mother closely, learning to navigate the maze of tree branches and how to find food before setting off to live on its own.

37

RODENTS

odents are extraordinarily successful animals that are native to every continent except Antarctica. About 40 percent of all mammals—more than 2,500 species—are rodents! They are found everywhere except Antarctica and a few islands.

Rodents also have very interesting front teeth: Their incisors are self-sharpening. The front surface of these long, curved teeth is hard, made of enamel. The back surface is soft, made of dentine. When a rodent chews, the harder tooth surfaces sharpen the softer ones, like a chisel. As a result, the animals in this group are capable of gnawing through and eating just about anything—from wood to wire.

Rodents are divided into mouselike (this page), squirrel-like (page 41), and cavy-like (page 40), based upon the way their jaws work. The mouselike rodents include mice, rats, and voles, as well as gerbils, hamsters, jerboas, lemmings, and muskrats. The animals in this group have two well-developed jaw muscles that allow them to chew and gnaw in all directions.

Life spans for mouselike rodents are usually one to three years.

BROWN RAT
Rattus norvegicus

RANGE: Worldwide, except polar regions

SIZE: 5 to 18 oz (140 to 500 g)

DIET: Anything they can find

Before ships carried rats as stowaways around the world, this species was native to northern China. Brown rats have a keen sense of smell and are highly social. They live in packs and are known for their intelligent behavior.

BARBARY STRIPED GRASS MOUSE
Lemniscomys barbarus

RANGE: North Africa

SIZE: 0.8 to 1.4 oz (24 to 40 g)

DIET: Grass stems, leaves, roots, fruit, crops, seeds

Some rodents breed year-round, but striped mice reproduce only during the rainy season, when food and water are readily available. Females give birth to two to 10 pups every 28 days for four months in a row!

HARVEST MOUSE
Micromys minutus

RANGE: Europe and Asia

SIZE: .14 to .23 oz (4 to 7.5 g)

DIET: Seeds and small insects

This tiny mouse is a climber. It uses its prehensile tail and strong, flexible toes to hold on to the narrowest of plant stems while feeding on seeds, berries, and insects. Harvest mice also build their nests high above the ground.

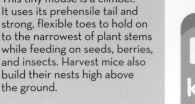

Did you know? The harvest mouse feeds for 30 minutes every three hours.

FAT-TAILED GERBIL
Pachyuromys duprasi

RANGE: North Africa

SIZE: 0.8 to 1.75 oz (20 to 50 g)

DIET: Insects, leaves, seeds

Gerbils are native to the Sahara, where they spend the hot days in burrows. At night, when temperatures are cooler, they search for insects. Some live in colonies, whereas others live as solitary animals.

GOLDEN HAMSTER
Mesocricetus auratus

RANGE: Syria and Turkey

SIZE: 3.5 to 4.4 oz (100 to 125 g)

DIET: Nuts, seeds, insects such as ants

Golden hamsters are territorial and show aggression toward their own species by chattering their teeth. These rodents are a food source for many animals, including foxes, snakes, and birds of prey such as eagles.

YELLOW-NECKED FIELD MOUSE
Apodemus flavicollis

RANGE: Europe and western Asia

SIZE: 1.2 to 2.3 oz (34 to 65.2 g)

DIET: Grass, herbs, seeds, grains, bark, tubers

This species digs burrows, where it stores food and where females give birth to their young. In the process, field mice can damage the roots of fruit trees, garden plants, and crops.

HOUSE MOUSE
Mus musculus

RANGE: Worldwide, except polar regions

SIZE: 0.4 to 1.1 oz (12 to 30 g)

DIET: Anything they can find

Rodents—especially house mice and rats—have a bad reputation. They damage tons of crops and stored goods each year. They also carry diseases. Yet they are important in the food web, both as seed dispersers and as prey.

MUSKRAT
Ondatra zibethicus

RANGE: North America, Europe, north and east Asia

SIZE: 1.25 to 4.5 lb (0.6 to 2 kg)

DIET: Aquatic and land vegetation

Muskrats are named for the musky odor they secrete to mark their territory. They dig into the banks of swamps and marshy areas. Like beavers, they have a flat tail that functions as a rudder.

RODENTS

Squirrel-like rodents (opposite page) range from all types of squirrels (tree, ground, and flying) to prairie dogs, marmots, beavers, chipmunks, and kangaroo rats. When these animals take a bite out of something, their jaws move forward. Like all rodents, they can gnaw through anything. The result, in the case of the beaver, can be disruptive. Beaver dams often cause widespread flooding, especially in urban areas.

Hibernation is another interesting feature of this group. Ground squirrels and marmots hibernate for several months during the winter, when food supplies are short. They become inactive, living off their fat stores. To conserve energy, their body temperature drops to equal that of the environment. Their heart and respiratory rates drop, too. But they are not asleep. All hibernating animals sporadically become active and warm up, usually every 10 to 15 days. Some squirrels and beavers can live more than 20 years.

The cavy-like rodents (this page) have chewing muscles that attach to both the lower and upper jaws, giving them a very strong bite. (The cavy family is a group of South American rodents that includes guinea pigs.) The animals in this group have large heads relative to their bodies, and vary greatly in size. The smallest is the mouse-size naked mole rat. The largest is the pig-size capybara, the world's largest rodent. The one with the most defenses on display is the porcupine, known for its painful quills. Many cavy-like rodents, such as the guinea pig and chinchilla, have been domesticated for food and clothing, and as pets. Life spans in this group also vary. Naked mole rats and porcupines can live as long as 20 years.

BRAZILIAN PORCUPINE
Coendou prehensilis

RANGE: Trinidad and the forests of northern South America

SIZE: 2 to 11 lb (0.9 to 5 kg)

DIET: Leaves, stems, fruit, blossoms, roots, trees, bark

Worldwide, there are 29 species of porcupines. Those found in the Americas, like the Brazilian porcupine, are good climbers. Those found in Asia, Europe, and Africa spend most of their time on the ground. All release their quills when threatened.

CAPYBARA
Hydrochoerus hydrochaeris

RANGE: Tropical areas of South America

SIZE: 77 to 145 lb (34.9 to 65.8 kg)

DIET: Grasses and aquatic plants

Despite their large size, or maybe because of it, capybaras are one of the green anaconda's favorite foods. For protection, these semiaquatic herbivores live in groups of 10 to 20. Young stay with their mothers for up to a year.

NAKED MOLE RAT
Heterocephalus glaber

RANGE: Kenya, Somalia, Ethiopia

SIZE: 1.2 oz (35 g)

DIET: Roots, bulbs, tubers, other underground plant parts

Naked mole rats live in dark, warm burrows. They find their food by smell and their way by feel, using their sensitive whiskers. They live in large colonies with a single breeding female, or queen, and dozens of workers.

NAKED MOLE RAT BURROW

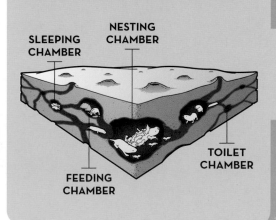

NESTING CHAMBER

SLEEPING CHAMBER

FEEDING CHAMBER

TOILET CHAMBER

Naked mole rats live in underground burrows with separate feeding, sleeping, nesting, and toilet chambers.

WOODCHUCK
Marmota monax

RANGE: Canada and eastern and central United States

SIZE: 4.4 to 13.1 lb (2 to 5 kg)

DIET: Roots, bulbs, tubers, seeds

The woodchuck is the most common species of marmot found in North America. In some places, it is also known as the groundhog or whistle pig. Woodchucks hibernate, and they breed shortly after waking in the spring.

ORD'S KANGAROO RAT
Dipodomys ordii

RANGE: Western North America

SIZE: 2 to 3.4 oz (56.7 to 96.4 g)

DIET: Seeds; some grasshoppers and moths

Kangaroo rats are solitary, nocturnal animals that hop and build burrows in sandy soil. To protect their homes and avoid the heat of the day, they kick sand over the entrance, covering the hole from the inside.

SILKY POCKET MOUSE
Perognathus flavus

RANGE: Western and southwestern United States, northern Mexico

SIZE: 0.2 to 0.3 oz (5.7 to 8.5 g)

DIET: Seeds, some green vegetation, some insects

There are several species of pocket mice. This one prefers sandy soils, though it also is found in rocky habitats. The silky pocket mouse is named for its unusually soft fur.

BLACK-TAILED PRAIRIE DOG
Cynomys ludovicianus

RANGE: Western United States

SIZE: 1.5 to 3.7 lb (0.7 to 1.7 kg)

DIET: Grasses and other vegetation

These highly social rodents live in large colonies known as prairie dog towns. They not only share their burrows and food, but they also warn each other at the first sight of predators such as a hungry hawk or black-footed ferret.

AMERICAN BEAVER
Castor canadensis

RANGE: North America, except deserts and tundra

SIZE: 29 to 70 lb (13 to 32 kg)

DIET: Tree bark, especially willow, maple, poplar, beech, birch, alder, aspen

Beavers are mostly aquatic rodents, with huge incisors for cutting through wood—their primary food. Young are born fully furred with their eyes open and can swim within 24 hours. They spend up to two years with their parents.

EASTERN GRAY SQUIRREL
Sciurus carolinensis

RANGE: Eastern to midwestern United States

SIZE: 0.7 to 1.6 lb (0.3 to 0.7 kg)

DIET: Nuts, buds, flowers of trees

There are more than 100 species of tree squirrels, and each plays a role in plant dispersal. As winter approaches, the eastern gray squirrel buries more food than it will recover. The buried seeds and nuts germinate the following spring.

BATS

Like birds, bats have wings and can fly. The difference is that instead of flying by flapping feathered arms, bats hold out their elbows and flap their webbed, outstretched hands. The bat wing is a special double layer of skin that stretches from one finger to another and attaches to the side of the bat's body, like a fan.

Because they fly, bats are one of the most successful groups of animals on Earth. Twenty percent of all mammals are bats—about 1,386 species. They are also beneficial. Bats eat massive amounts of insects. They also help pollinate a variety of plants. There are two main groups of bats: microbats and megabats.

Bats are among the longest-living mammals, with average life spans of 10 to 25 years and a longevity record of 33 years. This is unusual, since small animals rarely live as long as large ones. Some experts think this is because bats have such an efficient metabolism that there is less wear and tear on their tissues over time. This type of age-related damage is known as oxidation. Hibernation also limits this damage because it essentially serves as a rest period.

COMMON VAMPIRE BAT
Desmodus rotundus

RANGE: From Mexico to Argentina and Chile

SIZE: 0.5 to 1.7 oz (15 to 50 g)

DIET: Blood of other vertebrates

Many people fear bats because of their behavior: They are nocturnal, secretive animals that rest by hanging upside down by their feet. Another reason? Some bat species drink blood! Vampire bats are the only mammals that feed entirely on blood. (They favor sleeping cattle and horses.)

CALIFORNIA LEAF-NOSED BAT
Macrotus californicus

RANGE: United States, Mexico

SIZE: 0.4 to 0.7 oz (12 to 20 g)

DIET: Moths; also beetles, flies, other small insects

The ridges on the inside of this bat's ears and the flap of skin over its nose help focus sounds. They also help the bat detect very soft sounds, like insect wings flapping. All of these features are important in echolocation.

MEXICAN FREE-TAILED BAT
Tadarida brasiliensis

RANGE: Most of North, Central, and South America

SIZE: .25 to 0.4 oz (7 to 12 g)

DIET: Moths, beetles, dragonflies, flies, true bugs, wasps, bees, ants

Millions of free-tailed bats migrate from Mexico to Texas each year to breed. They are following migrating moths and will fly as high as 10,000 feet (3,000 m) to catch them. The moths are a problem because they feed on crops like corn. The bats limit the damage by eating 1,000 tons (907 t) a night!

GEOFFROY'S ROUSETTE
Rousettus amplexicaudatus

RANGE: Southeast Asia, from Myanmar to Papua New Guinea

SIZE: 2.8 to 6 oz (80 to 170 g)

DIET: Fruit

This species is unusual among fruit bats because it uses echolocation as well as sight to find its food. The Geoffroy's rousette fruit bat is also known for its roosting behavior: Thousands live together in caves.

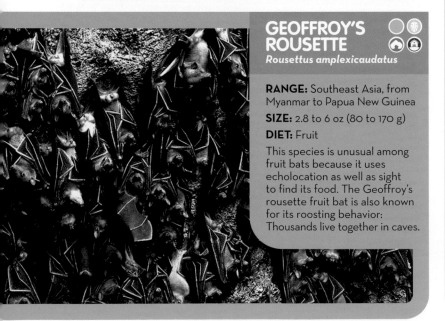

GREAT FRUIT-EATING BAT
Artibeus lituratus

RANGE: Central and South America

SIZE: 2.3 oz (65 g)

DIET: Fruit

The great fruit bat has especially sharp canines used to cut into its food: mostly unripe figs, which have very tough skin. It also uses the claw at the end of its first digit—the equivalent of a thumb—to hold on to the fig.

CHESTNUT SHORT-TAILED BAT
Carollia castanea

RANGE: Honduras to northern South America

SIZE: 0.5 oz (14 g)

DIET: Fruit of the piper plant

This species is one of many in the group known as leaf-nosed bats. Although it is capable of using echolocation, the chestnut short-tailed bat eats fruit, rather than insects, and plays an important role in seed dispersal in tropical forests.

WAHLBERG'S EPAULETTED FRUIT BAT
Epomophorus wahlbergi

RANGE: Sub-Saharan Africa

SIZE: 1.9 to 4.4 oz (54 to 125 g)

DIET: Fruit, especially guava, figs

Guava is one of the favorite foods of Wahlberg's epauletted fruit bat. This species is common in southern Africa, where it feeds on both wild and farmed fruits. It finds its food by detecting the smell of ripening fruit.

INDIAN FLYING FOX
Pteropus giganteus

RANGE: Tropical parts of Central Asia

SIZE: 1.3 to 3.5 lb (0.6 to 1.6 kg)

DIET: Fruit, including guava, mango, and fig

The Indian flying fox is a fruit bat that roosts in trees during the day. Like most bats, they are very social: Hundreds may be found in a single tree. If they get too hot in the sun, they fan themselves with their wings.

STRAW-COLORED FRUIT BAT
Eidolon helvum

RANGE: Sub-Saharan Africa and southwest Arabian Peninsula

SIZE: 8.1 to 12.3 oz (230 to 349 g)

DIET: Variety of fruit

The straw-colored fruit bat has long, narrow wings that it uses to fly long distances—roosts may be as far as 120 miles (193 km) apart. This species flies straighter and at higher altitudes than other fruit bats. When it feeds, it swallows the juice of fruit and spits out the fiber.

BAT ECHOLOCATION

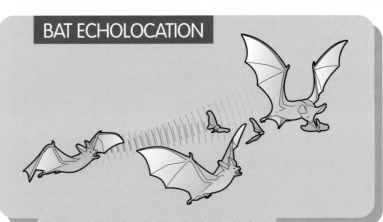

Bats hunt by making high-pitched sounds, then listening for the echoes of the sounds as they bounce off potential prey, such as moths.

RABBITS
AND RELATIVES

SNOWSHOE HARE
Lepus americanus

RANGE: Northern United States and Canada

SIZE: 3.2 to 3.4 lb (1.4 to 1.6 kg)

DIET: Green plants, grasses, twigs, shoots, buds

Snowshoe hares have reddish brown to gray fur in summer and white fur in winter. This change in coat color—known as seasonal molt—gives them better camouflage.

There are two ways to avoid becoming another animal's meal: fight or flight. Rabbits and their relatives—hares and pikas—take the second approach. These animals are capable of running or hopping with great speed and agility, turning on a dime, and finding places to hide. Two other features give them an edge: acute hearing and excellent vision.

The animals in this group have another form of defense: They reproduce quickly and in very high numbers. Eastern cottontail rabbits, for example, can breed every two months. In the course of one year, they can have up to six litters and produce as many as 35 babies. Females also start breeding at a young age: three months. As always in nature, though, there is a trade-off.

Many baby bunnies do not survive to adulthood, becoming food for predators, such as foxes, wolves, and hawks. As a result, the recorded life spans for some of the animals in this group range from one to three years. Species like the European hare live longer, up to 15 years.

AMERICAN PIKA
Ochotona princeps

RANGE: Mountains of western North America

SIZE: 4.3 to 6.2 oz (122 to 175 g)

DIET: Shrubs, plants, grasses

All pikas live in cold climates, but they do not hibernate. Instead, they prepare for winter by gathering greens and grasses and stashing them near their burrows. The pile soon turns into hay, which the pika uses for bedding and food.

EASTERN COTTONTAIL RABBIT
Sylvilagus floridanus

RANGE: Southern Manitoba and Quebec, Canada; northeast United States to the Great Plains, to central and northwestern South America

SIZE: 1.7 to 3.4 lb (0.8 to 1.5 kg)

DIET: Green vegetation, bark, twigs

Rabbits are born fully furred, with their eyes closed. The mother visits the nest to nurse them for only a few minutes a day. She begins to wean them by 10 days, and they are on their own by three to four weeks of age.

ARCTIC HARE
Lepus arcticus

RANGE: Greenland, Arctic mainland and islands in Canada

SIZE: 6.6 to 11 lb (3 to 5 kg)

DIET: Grasses, herbs, shrubs, roots, twigs

With their compact bodies and powerful rear legs, arctic hares are capable of running 30 miles an hour (48 km/h) to escape a predator. These are nocturnal animals that feed on the twigs and roots of willow and other shrubs.

ALPINE PIKA
Ochotona alpina

RANGE: China, Kazakhstan, Mongolia, Russia

SIZE: 2.5 to 10.6 oz (70 to 300 g)

DIET: Plants

The alpine pika, like its relatives, gathers bits of plants before winter to make a hay pile. It is not the only animal that benefits from this special stash of food, however. When the snow is deep, Siberian deer and reindeer will eat the pika's hay.

SHREWS AND SMALL INSECTIVORES

Shrews, tree shrews, elephant shrews, moles, golden moles, tenrecs, and hedgehogs are insect-eaters, though not exclusively. They prefer to eat worms and bug larvae, but also will eat plants, seeds, and small animals like lizards and fish.

The animals in this group are generally shy and nocturnal. Instead of relying on their vision, which is poor, they use their mobile snouts and excellent sense of smell to find their food. Some, like the hedgehog and moles, also have good hearing.

These characteristics also describe the first mammals, primitive species that evolved more than 200 million years ago. The smallest of today's insectivores, shrews and moles, are living examples of yesterday's early mammals. Their opportunistic diet, small size, and secretive behavior helped them survive 66 million years ago when other species, including the dinosaurs, went extinct.

Life spans range from two to six years.

GOLDEN-RUMPED SENGI
Rhynchocyon chrysopygus

RANGE: Forested areas of coastal Kenya in Africa

SIZE: 1.1 to 1.2 lb (0.5 to .54 kg)

DIET: Worms, spiders, insects

Sengi use their long, flexible noses to look under leaves for insects. This species also mates for life and is found in pairs. At night, they sleep in a ground nest made by digging out a hollow and lining it with leaves.

LESSER HEDGEHOG TENREC
Echinops telfairi

RANGE: Madagascar

SIZE: 6.4 oz (181 g)

DIET: Insects and other invertebrates

Like hedgehogs, tenrecs use their spines for defense by rolling up into a ball. But if the predator persists, they will unroll and attack. They can also vibrate their spines to make a rasping sound.

EUROPEAN HEDGEHOG
Erinaceus europaeus

RANGE: Europe and Central Asia

SIZE: 1.8 to 2.6 lb (0.8 to 1.2 kg)

DIET: Insects, berries, bird eggs, frogs

Except for the fur on its face and underbelly, this kind of hedgehog is covered in spines—about 5,000 of them. Each is 3/4 to 1 inch (2 to 2.5 cm) long with a white tip, and brown and black stripes. When threatened, the hedgehog curls into a ball and stiffens its spines.

STAR-NOSED MOLE
Condylura cristata

RANGE: Eastern North America

SIZE: 1.2 to 2.6 oz (34 to 74 g)

DIET: Aquatic crustaceans, small fish, water insects

This semiaquatic mole has a nose made up of 22 very sensitive, and always active, tentacles. It uses its nose to move dirt and catch prey, such as worms, leeches, and fly larvae, and uses its paddle-like feet to swim.

MADRAS TREE SHREW
Anathana ellioti

RANGE: India

SIZE: 4.8 oz (136 g)

DIET: Insects, fruit, leaves

At first glance, tree shrews look like squirrels, with their long bodies and bushy tails. They even use their feet to hold on to their food. Their diet is different, though. Tree shrews don't eat nuts.

ANTEATERS,
ARMADILLOS, AND SLOTHS

Anteaters, aardvarks, armadillos, and sloths share several features. All have powerful front legs with long claws used for digging or hanging on to tree branches, and reduced or absent teeth.

The two largest animals in this group, anteaters (South America) and aardvarks (Africa), are interesting because although they prey on tiny insects, neither is a small animal. The giant anteater weighs as much as 80 pounds (36 kg) or more and the aardvark almost twice as much at 140 pounds (64 kg). Both are known as "antbears" in the countries where they live.

Their nickname comes from their hunting strategy. Instead of looking for one insect at a time, anteaters and aardvarks learn the location of ant and termite nests, or mounds. Because these are social insects, each nest contains hundreds of thousands of them. Antbears move from one nest to another, digging a hole in each and eating what they can without getting stung too badly. The worker ants or termites repair the damage, and the nest is still there for the next visit.

Life spans for the animals in this group range from 10 to 25 years.

GIANT ANTEATER
Myrmecophaga tridactyla

RANGE: Central and South America, from Belize to Argentina

SIZE: 40 to 86 lb (18 to 39 kg)

DIET: Ants, termites, grubs

Inside its 1.5-foot (0.5-m)-long snout, the giant anteater has a two-foot (0.6-m)-long tongue—and no teeth! It also has glands that produce sticky saliva. To feed, it flicks its tongue 150 times a minute, grabbing its food.

LARGE HAIRY ARMADILLO
Chaetophractus villosus

RANGE: Paraguay, Bolivia, central Argentina

SIZE: About 4.4 lb (2 kg)

DIET: Insects, other invertebrates, small rodents, lizards, plants, carrion

Armadillos have armor-like skin to protect themselves when threatened. This protective layer is made up of flat bones, or scutes, covered by keratin, the same material that makes up hair and nails.

Did you know?
Only the three-banded armadillo can roll up into a hard ball.

HOFFMAN'S TWO-TOED SLOTH
Choloepus hoffmanni

RANGE: Central and South America

SIZE: 8.8 to 17.6 lb (4 to 8 kg)

DIET: Leaves, twigs, fruit

The sloth's curved toes help it hang on to tree branches without wasting energy. All species of sloths are similar: They eat leaves, buds, and twigs; move very slowly; and climb to the ground weekly to defecate. They rarely drink water.

COLLARED ANTEATER
Tamandua tetradactyla

RANGE: South America

SIZE: 9.9 lb (4.5 kg)

DIET: Ants and termites

This species has two other names: lesser anteater, or southern tamandua. It spends its time in the trees feeding on ants. Though much smaller than its giant cousin, the tamandua also has a very long tongue—up to 1.3 feet (0.4 m)!

PALE-THROATED THREE-TOED SLOTH
Bradypus tridactylus

RANGE: Northeast South America

SIZE: 4.9 to 12.1 lb (2.2 to 5.5 kg)

DIET: Twigs, buds, leaves

Because they live in the rainforest and rarely move, sloths often grow algae on their fur. The relationship is an example of commensalism, which means the algae have a place to live, and the sloth is better camouflaged. The algae may even be nutritious.

LINNAEUS'S TWO-TOED SLOTH
Choloepus didactylus

RANGE: South America

SIZE: 8.8 to 17.6 lb (4 to 8 kg)

DIET: Leaves, twigs, fruit

Because of their diet, sloths have a slow metabolism and cannot maintain a high body temperature. So, like reptiles, they move into the sun when they need to get warm. Their digestion is the slowest of any herbivorous mammal: around two weeks!

NINE-BANDED ARMADILLO
Dasypus novemcinctus

RANGE: Southern United States through northern South America

SIZE: 8 to 17 lb (3.6 to 7.7 kg)

DIET: Mainly insects and other invertebrates

Despite their name, nine-banded armadillos may have up to 11 bands of hard, flexible plates covering their outer bodies. Good swimmers, they can hold their breath up to six minutes as they walk along river bottoms. When startled, they jump straight up in the air.

HOW DO ANTEATERS EAT?

There are four species of anteaters, and they all have one thing in common: They are edentates, which means they lack teeth. How would you eat your food if you didn't have teeth? You would suck it up through a straw, of course. And that's about what they do. Giant anteaters creep up on a termite mound or anthill and rip it open with their sharp claws. They stick their tongues into the opening and create almost a vacuum with their throats, sucking up their prey. Their tongues are also sticky, which speeds up the process. An anteater may spend as little as one minute feasting on an anthill, flicking its tongue up to 160 times.

Smaller anteaters like the silky anteater and tamandua prefer to search trees for bugs to eat. Either way, that's some fancy feasting!

FROM THE FIELD:

Vinicius Alberici

GIANT ANTEATER

G iant anteaters *(Myrmecophaga tridactyla)* aren't easy to spot in the wild. Black and white stripes on their backs, which warn predators to stay away, help them blend in with their grassland and forest habitats. They also have a clever way of hiding. They lie on the ground and cover their bodies with their bushy, broom-like tails. They're not small animals—a giant anteater can grow up to 6.5 feet (2 m) long and weigh about 88 pounds (40 kg)!—but you can step on one without even knowing it's there.

The first time I saw a giant anteater in the wild, I was in the world's largest wetland, the Pantanal, in Brazil. I was thrilled to see that odd animal with its long snout, walking on its knuckles, sniffing around as the sun rose in the sky. It was searching for food. Giant anteaters use their powerful forelegs and sharp front claws to dig up ants and termites. They capture them with their long, sticky tongues. The ants bite and sting, so speed is important. A giant anteater flicks its two-foot (0.6-m)-long tongue up to 160 times a minute. It can eat up to 30,000 ants in a single day!

To study giant anteaters up close, you first have to catch them. One way we do that is with a big, strong butterfly net. The first time I caught a giant anteater, it was a large and magnificent female. When it blew air hard through its snout, it sounded like a bear's growl. I touched the thick hairs of its tail and saw its muscular arms and sharp front claws. That day, I realized that these were wild and fierce animals and that, despite all threats they are facing, they will not give up easily. That made me respect them even more and gave me purpose and inspiration to continue working hard to save them.

Vinicius Alberici is a biologist and a Ph.D. candidate in applied ecology at the University of São Paulo, Brazil. He works with the Brazilian NGO ICAS (Institute for the Conservation of Wild Animals) on its Anteaters & Highways Project, which investigates the impact of roads on giant anteater populations in the Brazilian Cerrado.

NORTH AMERICA

CARIBBEAN SEA

RANGE OF THE
MYRMECOPHAGA TRIDACTYLA
(GIANT ANTEATER)

0   1,000 miles
0   1,000 kilometers

SOUTH AMERICA

PACIFIC OCEAN

ATLANTIC OCEAN

OBSERVATION TIPS

1 To see them eating, search in early morning or just before sunset, when it's cooler.

2 Keep your distance! If cornered, giant anteaters will stand up, spread out their arms, and use their claws to defend themselves.

3 Observe from upwind. Giant anteaters have a great sense of smell and can detect you from a long way away.

4 Never approach a giant anteater if you have dogs with you. They may chase the anteater.

Giant anteaters are typically solitary animals that come together only to mate. Females give birth to a single baby, called a pup, each year. For the first six months after the pup is born, the mother nurses it. When she gets up to move, the pup climbs onto her back and she carries it around. The pup has a full coat of hair and looks just like its mother. The stripes on their backs line up perfectly, providing excellent camouflage against potential predators. Pups leave their mothers by age two, when they're fully grown. They start to have pups of their own one to two years later.

49

ELEPHANTS

Imagine a time when there were dozens of species of elephant-like animals roaming across Africa, each with stout legs, oversize upper lips, and special incisors made of ivory, known as tusks. This was the case in the Pleistocene epoch two million years ago. These giant, plant-eating animals belonged to a group known as the proboscids (pro-BOS-skids), named after the Latin word for "trunk."

Today, only three species of elephants remain. They are now the largest land mammals, weighing up to 13,230 pounds (6,000 kg).

Both Asian and African elephants are highly social. Herds consist of females and their young led by the oldest female, or matriarch. Males, known as bulls, live alone or in bachelor groups, interacting with the herd only to breed. They are also highly intelligent. Elephants communicate by making sounds that range from low-frequency rumbles to high-pitched trumpet calls. When a member of the herd is injured or trapped, others will work together to help. Elephants also mourn their dead.

Elephants can live up to 70 years. Unfortunately, many populations in Africa and Asia are endangered from habitat loss and illegal hunting, or poaching, for their ivory tusks.

ASIAN ELEPHANT
Elephas maximus

RANGE: India and Southeast Asia

SIZE: 4,405 to 13,216 lb (2,000 to 6,000 kg)

DIET: Grasses, leaves, shoots, fruit

Elephants are extremely agile. They place one foot in front of the other, leaving behind a remarkably narrow trail. In the forests where they live, Asian elephants easily climb up and down muddy, slippery slopes.

AFRICAN SAVANNA ELEPHANT
Loxodonta africana africana

RANGE: Sub-Saharan Africa

SIZE: 4,405 to 13,436 lb (2,000 to 6,100 kg)

DIET: Leaves, shoots, twigs, roots, fruit

Savanna elephants are known for their incredibly large herds and for the great distances they travel in search of water. Crop damage often results, causing conflict with people. Fences made of active beehives help keep elephants away from crops.

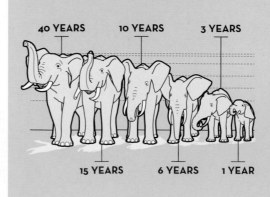

AFRICAN FOREST ELEPHANT
Loxodonta africana cyclotis

RANGE: West and central Africa

SIZE: 5,947 to 13,216 lb (2,700 to 6,000 kg)

DIET: Fruit, leaves, bark, twigs of rainforest trees

Forest elephants are smaller than savanna elephants. They have four toes on their front feet instead of five, and three on the back instead of four. They travel in small family groups of two to eight.

ELEPHANT GROWTH

40 YEARS   10 YEARS   3 YEARS

15 YEARS   6 YEARS   1 YEAR

The oldest elephants in a herd are the largest. Breeding starts in the early teens. Births occur every three to five years.

SEA COWS

ugongs and manatees are often called sea cows, but their closest living relatives are elephants. They are large, slow-moving, vegetarian marine mammals. They have big, rounded noses; nostrils with flaps they can close while underwater; and fleshy lips for grazing on seagrasses and other plants. Like other aquatic mammals, they were once a terrestrial species. They must swim up to the water's surface to take a breath of air.

Before boats and ships were common in shallow areas, dugongs and manatees were seen only rarely. Sailors who spotted them thought they were mermaids, mythical half woman–half fish sea creatures. Their order name Sirenia is based on this myth, as "siren" is another name for a mermaid.

Sea cows eat a lot—up to a quarter of their body weight in plant material each day. The gas produced by their digestive systems makes them very buoyant. To help them stay submerged, their bones, especially the ones in their flipper-like front limbs, are very dense.

Sadly, all four species of dugongs and manatees are threatened by habitat loss and injury from boat propellers. The result is that there are fewer sea cows left on Earth compared to any other single group of mammal. They can live up to 70 years.

DUGONG
Dugong dugon

RANGE: Warm coastal waters in the Indo-Pacific region

SIZE: 507 to 881 lb (230 to 400 kg)

DIET: Seaweed and seagrasses

Dugongs are marine sea cows once found along the coasts of at least 48 countries. They have a single pair of tusklike incisors and a sharply angled snout. Based on their strange anatomy, dugongs are considered relatives of hyraxes, elephants, aardvarks, and sloths.

AMERICAN MANATEE
Trichechus manatus

RANGE: Southeastern United States; Caribbean; east coast Central America; northern coast South America

SIZE: 441 to 3,304 lb (200 to 1,500 kg)

DIET: Water lettuce and water hyacinths

West Indian manatees reproduce very slowly. Females are at least seven years old before they have their first calf. Their gestation period is 12 to 14 months, and they usually have only one baby, though twins are possible.

THE AFRICAN SAVANNA ELEPHANT (*Loxodonta africana africana*) is the largest land mammal in the world. The elephant's large ears—shaped like the continent of Africa—radiate heat to help keep it cool as temperatures rise on the grassy plains and bushlands where it lives. Its long, muscular trunk—capable of grabbing small things—helps, too. The elephant uses its trunk to spray cool water or a protective coat of dust on its skin.

DOGS, WOLVES, AND RELATIVES

Smell is everything to a dog. All 34 species in the dog, or canid (KAY-nid), family use their noses to find food, track one another's whereabouts, and identify competitors as well as potential predators.

A dog's nose is also important for temperature control. Wolves, coyotes, jackals, foxes, and wild and domestic dogs lack sweat glands. They cannot shed heat by perspiration. Instead, they open their mouths and pant through their noses.

Panting is more complicated than it looks. Cooler air is inhaled and warmer air is exhaled. But the process only works if the tongue and nasal passages are wet, and the outside temperature is lower than the animal's body temperature. This is why it is dangerous—and against the law in many countries—to leave a dog in a parked car in the sun.

Though dogs are more likely to pant than most carnivores, there are several other species that use their noses to keep cool. Polar bears are one example.

Dogs, wolves, and their relatives have a life span of 12 to 15 years.

AFRICAN WILD DOG
Lycaon pictus

RANGE: Sub-Saharan Africa

SIZE: 70 to 79 lb (32 to 36 kg)

DIET: Antelopes, impalas, zebras, wildebeest

No two African wild dogs have the same markings on their coat. Also known as painted dogs, they hunt in packs and have the strongest bite relative to their body size of all living carnivores!

FENNEC FOX
Vulpes zerda

RANGE: Sahara of North Africa

SIZE: 1.7 to 3.3 lb (0.8 to 1.5 kg)

DIET: Small rodents, birds, insects, lizards

The smallest canid, this fox is highly specialized for life in the desert. Its huge ears help to get rid of heat as well as gather sound. Fennec foxes hunt by listening for rodents, reptiles, and insects moving under the sand.

COYOTE
Canis latrans

RANGE: North and Central America

SIZE: 15 to 46 lb (6.8 to 21 kg)

DIET: Rodents, rabbits, snakes, insects, carrion, fruit, berries, grasses, fish, frogs, crustaceans

Coyotes are a very successful species, especially in places where there are no wolves. This is one reason why they are now common in cities and urban areas. Another is diet: Coyotes prefer to eat rodents.

FOX FOOD WEB

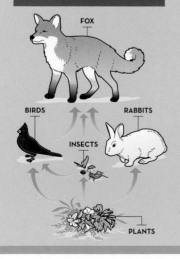

Among mammals, the top predator in a food web is often a member of the order Carnivora, such as a fox. As shown here, rabbits, birds, and insects consume plants, whereas foxes consume all of these food sources.

CARNIVORES

The order Carnivora includes 302 species of mammals divided into 16 families. The name of this group is a bit confusing, though, because not all of its members are strict meat-eaters. Many are omnivores. All share a common ancestry, however. The fossil record shows that the first mammalian carnivores appeared about 66 million years ago. They were small, shrewlike animals that ate whatever they could find, including other small animals. Over time, they evolved into two types: the doglike and the catlike carnivores. The dog group is more flexible in its choice of food and includes coyotes, foxes, raccoons, bears, civets, and mongooses. The cat group became specialized at eating meat and includes all species of cats from margays to tigers. Whatever they eat, carnivores are predators. All are capable of preying on other animals—even the bamboo-eating giant panda! One way to tell the two carnivore groups apart is to look at their tracks. Though there are exceptions, the footprints of most doglike carnivores have oval-shaped footpads and obvious toenail marks. Catlike carnivores leave behind only the impressions of their round footpads. The reason: Cats have retractable claws, whereas dogs do not.

BLACK-BACKED JACKAL
Canis mesomelas

RANGE: Southern Africa; East Africa, including Kenya, Somalia, Ethiopia

SIZE: 11 to 23 lb (5 to 10 kg)

DIET: Insects, small mammals, carrion, reptiles, birds

Black-backed jackals live in small groups, usually a male and female pair with their young. Like other members of the dog family, they will sometimes gather together in small packs to hunt down larger prey, like antelopes.

DHOLE
Cuon alpinus

RANGE: South and Southeast Asia

SIZE: 37 to 46 lb (17 to 21 kg)

DIET: Wild pigs, hares, goats, sheep, berries, insects, lizards

Though also called the Asiatic wild dog, dholes are only distantly related to wolves. They have fewer molars; a shorter, thick nose; and longer, thin legs. Dholes can jump as high as 12 feet (3.7 m) and leap more than 20 feet (6.1 m).

RED WOLF
Canis rufus

RANGE: Southeastern United States

SIZE: 35 to 90 lb (16 to 41 kg)

DIET: Small mammals; some insects, berries

The red wolf is named for the red fur on its ears and back. It also has a long, bushy tail with a black tip and white fur on its lips. Genetic studies suggest this species is more closely related to the coyote than to other wolves.

DOMESTIC DOG
Canis lupus familiaris

RANGE: Worldwide

SIZE: Less than 1 to 200 lb (less than 0.5 to 91 kg)

DIET: Mainly meats, grains, vegetables.

Since first domesticated in Asia or Western Europe at least 15,000 years ago, dogs have been used to hunt, both for food and sport. Today, they are also companions, protectors, rescuers, herders, and healers. There are dozens of specific and mixed breeds.

SKUNKS
AND STINK BADGERS

Skunks and stink badgers are nocturnal omnivores in the mephitid (meh-FIT-id) family that live in dens or burrows. Most are distinctively colored white and black. These markings act to warn predators, which include coyotes, badgers, foxes, mountain lions, civets, eagles, and owls.

The sickening smell of a skunk is difficult to ignore. Though it may seem the skunk has sprayed its oil everywhere, these animals are very accurate, aiming right between the eyes of any potential predator.

First, the skunk arches its back and stomps its feet as a warning. Unless the attacker leaves, the skunk does a handstand, of sorts, by jumping up with its rear legs off the ground. At the same time, it squeezes the muscles on either side of its anal glands—located right beneath the tail—and squirts a noxious stream of fluid over its head a distance of up to 10 feet (3 m).

Skunk life spans range from five to 10 years.

WHAT'S THAT SMELL?

What's black and white and strikes fear into the hearts of predators five times its size? A skunk. So why is something smaller than a house cat feared by so many? Its powerful scent, of course: a thick, pungent odor similar to rotten eggs that is enough to send anybody running in the other direction. But did you know that skunks themselves don't actually stink? What you're really smelling is a skunk's number one line of defense. The stinky substance comes from special glands located under their tails. The liquid is composed of compounds that contain sulfur, a naturally occurring chemical that is responsible for the icky stench.

HUMBOLDT'S HOG-NOSED SKUNK
Conepatus humboldtii

RANGE: Southern Argentina, southern Chile

SIZE: 2.4 to 10 lb (1.1 to 4.5 kg)

DIET: Mainly insects, but also small mammals, fruit

These solitary, nocturnal creatures, also called Patagonian hog-nosed skunks, have black or reddish brown fur. Two white stripes run from the top of their heads to the tip of their tails. Their long and bare noses resemble a pig's snout, which is how they got their name.

PALAWAN STINK BADGER
Mydaus marchei

RANGE: Palawan and Busuanga Islands in the Philippines

SIZE: 5.5 lb (2.5 kg)

DIET: Worms and other soil insects

The Palawan stink badger, a member of the skunk family, is skunk-like when threatened—it smells nasty. It is also a digger. Unlike skunks, it has a much more specific diet—mostly worms—and a narrow range: three islands in the Philippines.

WESTERN SPOTTED SKUNK
Spilogale gracilis

RANGE: Western United States

SIZE: 0.8 to 1.3 lb (0.4 to 0.6 kg)

DIET: Rodents, young rabbits, birds, eggs, insects, fruit

Spotted skunks are good climbers and diggers. As with other members of the skunk family, they rarely spray each other or around their dens. They don't like the smell, either.

STRIPED SKUNK

Mephitis mephitis

RANGE: North America

SIZE: 1.5 to 13.9 lb (0.7 to 6.3 kg)

DIET: Mice, eggs, insects, berries, carrion

Skunk kits are born with their eyes closed and a thin layer of fur. They stay with their mother for up to one year. Mother skunks will readily spray to protect their young.

OTTERS,
WEASELS, AND RELATIVES

O tters, weasels, and their relatives are in the mustelid (MUS-tell-id) family. This is an extremely successful group of carnivores, with 64 species distributed worldwide. Most are small, with short ears and noses, elongated bodies, long tails, and soft, dense fur. All are expert hunters.

Otters, for example, are just one type of mustelid. There are species of otters in Asia, Europe, Africa, North America, and South America. Though most live in freshwater rivers, lakes, and wetlands, a few are found in the Pacific Ocean—the sea otter, and the smaller, lesser-known marine otter.

Species of weasels, badgers, and martens are found in different parts of the world.

Otters and their relatives were once hunted extensively for their fur—many to the point of near extinction. Despite regulations designed to protect them, many species remain at risk from pollution and habitat loss.

Life spans range from 10 to 20 years.

AMERICAN BADGER
Taxidea taxus

RANGE: Great Plains region of North America

SIZE: 8.8 to 26 lb (4 to 12 kg)

DIET: Small animals

Digging is what American badgers do best. They dig for their food—small animals that live underground, including pocket gophers, moles, marmots, prairie dogs, kangaroo rats, deer mice, wood rats, hibernating skunks, ground-nesting birds, and insects.

ASIAN SMALL-CLAWED OTTER
Aonyx cinereus

RANGE: Southeast Asia

SIZE: 5 to 11 lb (2.3 to 5 kg)

DIET: Clams, mussels, crabs

This is the smallest—and least aquatic—of the otter species. Asian small-clawed otters prefer shallow water and wetlands. They hunt by feel, using their fingerlike toes to search in the mud for mollusks and crustaceans.

LEAST WEASEL
Mustela nivalis

RANGE: Europe, Asia, North America, North Africa

SIZE: 1 to 1.8 oz (30 to 50 g)

DIET: Small rodents, bird eggs, chicks, small reptiles, lizards

Among the carnivores, the least weasel is the smallest. Even so, it is capable of killing a rabbit up to 10 times its own weight by clamping down on the animal's neck and biting until it's dead. This weasel is also food for other predators, such as foxes, snakes, and owls.

WOLVERINE
Gulo gulo

RANGE: Scandinavia, Russia, Siberia, Canada, Alaska, western United States

SIZE: 19 to 66 lb (8.6 to 29.9 kg)

DIET: Reindeer, roe deer, wild sheep, elk or red deer, marals, moose; also berries

The scientific name for the wolverine comes from the word "glutton." This large mustelid is capable of killing and eating anything it can find in the snow. Wolverines have snowshoe-like footpads that help them run down reindeer and moose.

ERMINE
Mustela erminea

RANGE: Circumpolar Northern Hemisphere

SIZE: 0.9 to 4 oz (25.5 to 114 g)

DIET: Rodents, rabbits, birds, eggs, fish, insects

The ermine, or stoat, has a narrow head and long body typical of its relatives. It, too, is an excellent hunter. The ermine listens for insects and sniffs out rodents. In winter, its coat turns white, giving it the advantage of camouflage.

BEARS

The fossil record for the ursid (ER-sid), or bear, family is one of the most complete for all carnivores. It shows that the eight species alive today are the descendants of a 30-million-year-old bearlike animal that resembled a cross between a dog and a raccoon.

Much has changed since then! All modern bears are larger, stocky animals with nonretractable claws, shaggy fur, an excellent sense of smell, and short tails. They are solitary, except for mothers with cubs, and generally diurnal. During the time of year when food is scarce, most bears have an effective survival solution: sleep.

All bears are considered omnivores—and all love the taste of honey—yet each species has a preferred diet. Polar bears are carnivores, for example, preferring to eat seals. American black bears prefer berries and insect larvae whenever they are available. Giant pandas prefer bamboo, and sloth bears prefer ants and termites.

Bears are generally long-living, with life spans of up to 25 years in the wild and 50 in captivity.

BROWN BEAR
Ursus arctos

RANGE: North America, Siberia, Europe

SIZE: 176 to 1,322 lb (80 to 600 kg)

DIET: Fruit, nuts, roots, seaweed, grasses, moss, bulbs, insects, fish, small vertebrates, carrion, mice, ground squirrels, marmots

Some brown bears eat more salmon than others. Those found along the coast of Alaska eat the most—and are the largest. Those found in the Rocky Mountains, also known as grizzly bears, are smaller, but not by much!

SLOTH BEAR
Melursus ursinus

RANGE: India, Sri Lanka, Bangladesh, Nepal, Bhutan

SIZE: 121 to 308 lb (55 to 140 kg)

DIET: Insects; also leaves, honey, flowers, fruit

The name given to these bears is misleading. They are very fast runners—and eaters. A sloth bear can tear a hole in a termite mound, push its nose inside, and inhale a full meal in just a few seconds.

A sloth bear is the only bear that carries its babies on its back.

Did you know?

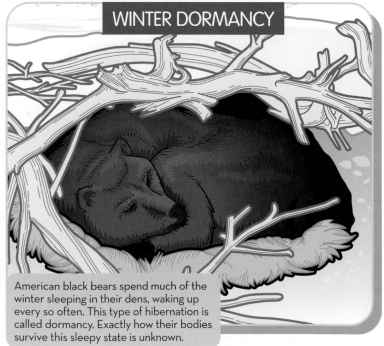

WINTER DORMANCY

American black bears spend much of the winter sleeping in their dens, waking up every so often. This type of hibernation is called dormancy. Exactly how their bodies survive this sleepy state is unknown.

58

ASIATIC BLACK BEAR
Ursus thibetanus

RANGE: Asia

SIZE: 143 to 330 lb (65 to 150 kg)

DIET: Mainly plant matter; also fruit, nuts, insect larvae, ants; may also prey on cattle, sheep, goats

These bears are known for their opportunistic eating habits. Mostly they are vegetarians, but they will also eat small animals and carrion—typically left over from a tiger's kill. Their main predator is the Siberian tiger.

POLAR BEAR
Ursus maritimus

RANGE: North of the Arctic Circle to the North Pole

SIZE: 330 to 1,762 lb (150 to 800 kg)

DIET: Seals, walruses, seabirds and their eggs, small mammals, fish

Female polar bears breed in the spring and give birth in the fall, but only if they have not lost too much weight over the summer. This species normally builds up its fat stores during winter by hunting ringed seals from the pack ice. Global warming threatens their life cycle.

GIANT PANDA
Ailuropoda melanoleuca

RANGE: Sichuan, China

SIZE: 176 to 275 lb (80 to 125 kg)

DIET: Bamboo

Giant pandas almost always eat only bamboo. To survive on such a high-fiber, low-calorie diet, pandas spend all day eating. They have massive chewing muscles—and an appealing round face—as a result.

SUN BEAR
Helarctos malayanus

RANGE: Nepal, China, Myanmar, Malay Peninsula

SIZE: 59.5 to 143 lb (27 to 65 kg)

DIET: Bees, termites, earthworms; also fruit

This is the smallest member of the ursid family. Sun bears have long tongues to pull termites and bees out of their nests and honey from hives. They also will scavenge garbage and raid crops like bananas.

SEALS, SEA LIONS, AND FURRED SEALS

There are three families of carnivores that spend most of their time in salt water. These are the eared seals, or otarids; the true seals, or phocids; and walruses. Together, these animals are often called pinnipeds (PIN-uh-pedz), which means "fin-footed" in Latin. All hunt a variety of marine prey, including fish, mollusks, and, in some cases, each other. They are also highly social during the breeding and calving seasons, when they gather in large, often noisy herds on beaches and rocky areas.

Seals, sea lions, and walruses have streamlined bodies for swimming, and large eyes so they can see their prey underwater. Their lungs are reinforced with cartilage to withstand the pressure changes when they dive. To save energy, their heart rate also goes down during a dive.

The eared seals have doglike earflaps. These are the sea lions and their close relatives, the furred seals. In water, they swim with their front flippers. On land, they pull their rear flippers up and under their bodies and use them like feet. True seals, by comparison, do not have earflaps and cannot use their rear flippers for walking. They move like inchworms on dry land. True seals are also excellent divers and can hold their breath for up to two hours.

Life spans for seals, sea lions, furred seals, and walruses range from 15 to 30 years.

BROWN FUR SEAL
Arctocephalus pusillus

RANGE: Off coasts of Africa and Australia

SIZE: 79 to 793 lb (36 to 360 kg)

DIET: Mostly fish; also crustaceans, squid, octopus

Male pinnipeds often weigh hundreds of pounds more than females of the same species. The brown fur seal is one example. The female (shown here) weighs 79 to 220 pounds (36 to 110 kg). The male weighs 440 to 793 pounds (200 to 360 kg).

GALÁPAGOS SEA LION
Zalophus wollebaeki

RANGE: Galápagos Islands

SIZE: 110 to 551 lb (50 to 250 kg)

DIET: Fish, octopus, crustaceans, squid

When not in the water hunting, sea lions "haul out" on dry land. Female sea lions often sunbathe together on the beach. The lead male patrols the beach to fight off competitors. When he can, he rests in the shade under a tree or rock cliff.

SOUTHERN ELEPHANT SEAL
Mirounga leonina

RANGE: Antarctica, Australia, Argentina, New Zealand, South Africa, South Sandwich and South Georgia Islands

SIZE: 1,322 to 3,304 lb (600 to 1,500 kg)

DIET: Sharks, fish, squid, shrimp, crabs

Male southern elephant seals are larger than any other carnivore. Females are much smaller. Both have short front flippers for steering and webbed back flippers for propelling forward.

Did you know? Mother and baby fur seals recognize each other by their calls.

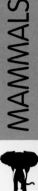

NORTHERN ELEPHANT SEAL ⬤◖◖ ◖
Mirounga angustirostris

RANGE: Off coast of North America, from Gulf of Alaska to Baja California, Mexico

SIZE: 1,322 to 5,066 lb (600 to 2,300 kg)

DIET: Squid, octopus, fish, small sharks, skates

Male elephant seals have a large nose called a proboscis. By filling it with air, they can make loud calls that establish breeding rights. These seals can dive as deep as a mile (1,500 m) and stay down for more than an hour.

LEOPARD SEAL ◖◖ ▲
Hydrurga leptonyx

RANGE: Antarctic coast and islands, coasts of South Africa and southern Australia, Tasmania, New Zealand, Cook Islands, South America

SIZE: 661 to 1,101 lb (300 to 500 kg)

DIET: Krill; other seals, especially fur and crabeater; penguins; also squid, fish

Leopard seals are top predators in the Antarctic. About a third of their diet is krill, which they filter using special molars. Other seals make up another third. The rest is penguins, fish, and squid.

BEARDED SEAL ◖◖ ▲ ◖
Erignathus barbatus

RANGE: Arctic Ocean

SIZE: 441 to 947 lb (200 to 430 kg)

DIET: Crustaceans and mollusks

Bearded seals prefer shallow Arctic waters with plenty of fish—and floating ice. This species has no need for dry land. Instead, it climbs onto a piece of ice and drifts with it, migrating north in winter and south in summer.

WALRUSES

The walrus is more like a seal than a sea lion except that it can bend its back flippers forward. It is found only in Arctic waters, where it uses its whiskers and snout to find food.

The modified canine teeth of the walrus are used in fighting with other males. Though this species can hold its breath, the longest it can stay underwater is 10 minutes. Walruses tend to stay near the shoreline, as they are a favorite food of the killer whale.

Did you know? Walruses use their large ivory tusks to haul their huge bodies out of the water onto the ice and to make breathing holes in the ice. Males also use their tusks to fight.

WALRUS ◖◖ ▲ ◖◖
Odobenus rosmarus

RANGE: The Arctic

SIZE: 880 to 3,740 lb (399 to 1,696 kg)

DIET: Bottom-living invertebrates, such as mollusks, mussels, crustaceans; some fish, seals

Walruses are the most social marine carnivores. Thousands often haul out together, though males and females only mix during the breeding season. To attract females, males do more than display their tusks: They sing, click, cluck, bellow, and whistle.

RACCOONS,
RED PANDAS, AND RELATIVES

Raccoons, kinkajous, coatis, cacomistles, and olingos are members of the raccoon family. All are omnivores and most have banded tails, facial markings, or a bandit-like mask. Most are also smaller animals. The exception is the North American raccoon, which can weigh up to 23 pounds (11 kg). This species is also known for its dexterous front paws, which it uses like hands, and excellent sense of touch.

The raccoon family is most closely related to the seal family—both are descendants of the doglike carnivore group. The same is true for the red panda. Scientists studying the genes of this endangered animal found evidence suggesting that there are actually two separate species of red panda: the Himalayan red panda (*Ailurus fulgens*) and the Chinese red panda (*Ailurus styani*). Red pandas are omnivores, though they prefer bamboo leaves and shoots.

Most raccoons and their relatives have short lives in the wild—from five to 10 years.

NORTHERN RACCOON
Procyon lotor

RANGE: North America and Central America

SIZE: 4 to 23 lb (1.8 to 10.4 kg)

DIET: Frogs, fish, small land animals, birds, turtle eggs, fruit, corn, nuts, seeds

Raccoons use their front feet like hands. They pick up their food to eat, washing it first whenever possible. They feel for insects in tree trunks, eggs in nests, and crayfish in mud. They can even pry the lid off a garbage can.

RED PANDA
Ailurus fulgens

RANGE: Himalaya in Asia

SIZE: 8 to 14 lb (3.6 to 6.4 kg)

DIET: Grasses, roots, fruit, acorns, berries, blossoms, bamboo leaves, small leaves of other plants, bird eggs

Bamboo is a major part of the red panda's diet. Like the giant panda, this relative of the raccoon has an extra wrist bone, which it uses to grasp the bamboo stalk while it fills its mouth with leaves.

Kinkajous can turn their feet backward to run in any direction.

Did you know?

SOUTH AMERICAN COATI
Nasua nasua

RANGE: Colombia, Venezuela, Uruguay, northern Argentina

SIZE: 6.6 to 13.2 lb (3 to 6 kg)

DIET: Fruit, scorpions, centipedes, eggs, beetle larvae, termites, lizards, spiders, ants, small mammals, rodents, carrion

Coatis (kuh-WAH-teez) hunt with their long noses held close to the ground. They prefer insects to other food. Males are solitary, but females, their young, and juvenile males travel together in groups of up to 20.

KINKAJOU
Potos flavus

RANGE: Mexico to Brazil

SIZE: 4.4 to 10 lb (2 to 4.6 kg)

DIET: Fruit, insects, nectar, flowers

Kinkajous are sometimes mistaken for monkeys, even though they are active only at night. They are small, furry animals with prehensile tails, and they pluck fruit from trees with their tiny hands. They even live in small groups and groom one another.

HYENAS AND AARDWOLVES

There are four species in the hyena family—three types of hyena and the aardwolf. Though these animals at first appear doglike, they are more closely related to cats, civets, and mongooses.

The front legs of a hyena are so long compared to the back ones that the animal looks like it is walking uphill. Hyenas also have very round faces because of their massive chewing muscles. Combined with big ears, they look almost friendly. On the contrary, these are aggressive animals, capable of killing live prey or scavenging dead carcasses. Male and female hyenas are indistinguishable.

The aardwolf is a small version of a striped hyena, except it eats only termites. It cannot tear open a termite mound on its own, however. Instead, it either wanders around looking for termites, or it follows and scavenges after the aardvark, a totally unrelated species that can dig into termite mounds.

Life spans for these animals are up to 25 years.

AARDWOLF
Proteles cristata

RANGE: South and East Africa

SIZE: 17 to 31 lb (7.7 to 14.1 kg)

DIET: Termites

Aardwolves eat only a particular type of termite—a species that nests in dried grass. As a result, both predator and prey are found only in certain areas. One aardwolf requires about 1.5 square miles (3.9 sq km) of territory.

SPOTTED HYENA
Crocuta crocuta

RANGE: Sub-Saharan Africa

SIZE: 99.1 to 176 lb (45 to 80 kg)

DIET: A variety of hoofed mammals, including wildebeest, zebras, gazelles, impalas; also porcupines, jackals, ostrich eggs, bat-eared foxes, termites

Spotted hyena cubs are born covered in black fur and with their eyes open. Newborns of the same sex are capable of fighting with one another—until one dies. Yet the cubs stay with their mother for up to three years.

STRIPED HYENA
Hyaena hyaena

RANGE: North and eastern Africa, Middle East, Asia

SIZE: 55 to 99 lb (25 to 45 kg)

DIET: Carrion and human refuse; also fruit, insects, small animals such as hares, rodents, reptiles, birds

The striped hyena is tough enough to steal a fresh kill from a lion or cheetah. But it will not even try to defend its meal from a spotted hyena. Wherever they are found together, striped hyenas act submissively toward their larger relative.

Did you know? Aardwolves can consume up to 300,000 termites in one night.

RED PANDA

Red pandas (*Ailurus fulgens*) are shy, quiet, and very hard to find. Their reddish brown coat helps them camouflage well with the reddish brown moss that covers fir and oak trees in their Himalayan forest home. They live in trees and mostly stay on the high branches. They mark their territory each day by rubbing scent-producing glands at the base of their tail on branches.

The most difficult part of studying them is venturing into their habitat. The mountainous terrain is rugged, and you have to make your way through dense bamboo thickets. Searching for red pandas requires many days of rigorous hiking and climbing trees, which is very tiring.

I had seen red pandas in zoos, but the first time I saw one in the wild was a truly special experience. I was with a group on a weeklong trek through one of the red panda's most important habitats in northeastern India. It was mid-January, and it was freezing in the mountains. At about 9:30 in the morning, we saw footprints on a snowy tree branch. We were excited because they couldn't have been made by anything but a red panda.

It was hard to see through the mist and snow, and it was the wrong time of day. (Red pandas are most active at dawn and dusk.) But we followed the footsteps, and suddenly we spotted something moving from one tree branch to another just ahead of us. It looked like a big domestic cat, but its long, thick, bushy tail—which was about as long as its body—is what caught my attention. The red panda was looking right at us. For about 20 minutes, we didn't move or make a sound as we watched it sitting in the tree. Then we slowly moved in closer and took pictures. Finally, it started moving and vanished into the thick foliage.

RANGE OF THE
AILURUS FULGENS
(RED PANDA)

0   800 miles
0   800 kilometers

ASIA

Himalaya

BAY OF
BENGAL

INDIAN
OCEAN

SOUTH
CHINA
SEA

ASIA

OBSERVATION TIPS

1 Wear waterproof hiking boots. The terrain is rugged, steep, and densely forested.

2 Follow their footprints in muddy or snowy patches. Or search for red panda poop on tree branches.

3 Look up. Red pandas prefer high, mossy branches in oak, maple, and rhododendron trees surrounded with bamboo patches.

4 Red pandas have a sweet tooth! You might spot them near kiwi, berry, or other wild fruit plants.

Moumita Chakraborty is studying for a Ph.D. in wildlife science from Saurashtra University, in affiliation with the Wildlife Institute of India. She is investigating the status of red pandas and their habitat in the Sikkim Himalaya in India. By sharing her results with people living in the area, she hopes to help create a long-term conservation plan that will save this endangered species.

Red pandas are solitary animals, but the mature male and female come together from January to April to mate. Come summer, the mother gives birth to cubs in a den that she has built mostly inside the tree hollows. In the wild, single births or twins are most common; in captivity, there can be up to four cubs in one litter. Newborns are covered with a thick gray fur that eventually turns red. They call to their mother with a high-pitched whistle when they need her. At three months, cubs begin to explore outside the den. At about 18 months, they are ready to live on their own.

CIVETS, FOSSAS,
AND RELATIVES

C ivets, fossas, and their relatives in the viverrid (vie-VER-rid) family resemble cats more than dogs. Most of these species have small heads and long tails, and are just as comfortable high up in the trees as on the ground. Their dietary preferences differ from those of cats, though. They eat insects and some fruit, in addition to rodents, birds, and eggs.

Civets in particular are believed to look—and act—like the earliest carnivores. They are nocturnal, secretive, and solitary omnivores. Based on the fossil record, the civet has changed very little in more than 20 million years!

Life spans are not well known; they are likely to range up to 25 years.

AFRICAN CIVET
Civettictis civetta

RANGE: Southern and central Africa

SIZE: 26.4 to 33 lb (12 to 15 kg)

DIET: Rodents, insects, eggs, carrion, birds; also millipedes and some fruit

Civets have a distinctive masked face, striped fur around their necks, and spotted fur down their backs. Like many carnivores, they communicate by scent marking. The oil in their glands, diluted many times, has been used to make perfume.

BINTURONG
Arctictis binturong

RANGE: India, China, Cambodia, Vietnam, Myanmar, Thailand, Southeast Asia

SIZE: 19.8 to 44 lb (9 to 20 kg)

DIET: Fruit and other plant matter, insects, eggs, birds

The binturong, or Asian bearcat, is one of only two carnivores (the other is the kinkajou) with a prehensile tail, which it uses to hang upside down in the trees. Though it eats a variety of foods, this animal prefers figs.

COMMON GENET
Genetta genetta

RANGE: Africa, Europe

SIZE: 2.2 to 6.6 lb (1 to 3 kg)

DIET: Small mammals, birds, reptiles, insects

The genet is so agile it can squeeze through a hole the size of its head. Its tail is also incredibly long—up to one and a half times its body length. Though mostly catlike, it has a long nose like a dog.

Did you know?

Sharp claws help fossas to climb down trees headfirst.

FOSSA
Cryptoprocta ferox

RANGE: Madagascar

SIZE: 15.4 to 26.4 lb (7 to 12 kg)

DIET: Mostly lemurs; also rodents, other small animals

Fossas and their preferred food, lemurs, are endemic to the island of Madagascar, meaning they are found only there. With its long tail and semi-retractable claws, this carnivore hunts by day and night, on the ground and in the trees.

MONGOOSES

Most species in the herpestid (HER-pes-tid) family are found in Africa. All are excellent hunters, but meat is not their only food. Many also eat insects, seeds, plants, and fruits. Mongooses are considered a more primitive form of carnivore, like the members of the civet family. The difference is they are more active during the day.

Most mongooses live in small groups. The meerkat, or slender-tailed mongoose, is unusual because of its highly social behavior.

Meerkats live in packs with up to 30 individuals and three family groups. Members of the pack serve a variety of important roles. One is the role of lookout, or sentinel. These meerkats sound an alarm call at the first sight or smell of a predator like an eagle or jackal. Packs also raise their young cooperatively. Older meerkats share food with young ones, and nonbreeding members act as aunts and uncles, helping to take care of young so nursing mothers can take the time to feed.

Most mongooses have life spans of 10 years in the wild.

BANDED MONGOOSE
Mungos mungo

RANGE: Africa, south of the Sahara

SIZE: 2.2 to 3.3 lb (1 to 1.5 kg)

DIET: Insects, fruit, snakes, lizards, eggs, frogs

All mongooses have short legs and ears, slender bodies, and long claws for digging up insects and invertebrates. Banded mongooses are known to eat toxic animals, including frogs. They first roll them around in the dirt to remove the poisons.

RING-TAILED VONTSIRA
Galidia elegans

RANGE: Madagascar

SIZE: 1.5 to 2 lb (0.7 to 0.9 kg)

DIET: Small animals, eggs, fruit

This mongoose is the most common carnivore on the island of Madagascar. It is also known for its exceptional climbing ability. Ring-tailed mongooses have large footpads for gripping and a bushy tail for balance.

EGYPTIAN MONGOOSE
Herpestes ichneumon

RANGE: Spain, Portugal, Israel, most of Africa

SIZE: 3.7 to 8.8 lb (1.7 to 4 kg)

DIET: Invertebrates, fish, small vertebrates, fruit, eggs

Eggs are a favorite food of the Egyptian mongoose. To eat one, the mongoose picks it up with its front feet and throws it against a hard surface, either straight down on the ground, or back between its hind legs, as if hiking a football.

DWARF MONGOOSE
Helogale parvula

RANGE: Ethiopia, Angola, southeastern region of Africa

SIZE: 0.6 lb (0.3 kg)

DIET: Mainly insects; also small vertebrates, eggs, fruit

Dwarf mongooses live in small groups in which only one pair breeds, and females are dominant over males. The breeding female is number one in the social hierarchy, her mate number two, and their youngest female offspring number three.

MEERKAT
Suricata suricatta

RANGE: Southern Africa

SIZE: 1.5 to 1.8 lb (0.7 to 0.8 kg)

DIET: Mainly insects; also small vertebrates, eggs, plants

Female meerkats are capable of giving birth to as many as 12 cubs a year, or three cubs every four months. When the young leave the burrow at three weeks of age, the adults in the group surround them for protection.

LARGE CATS

The "large cats" are the lion, tiger, leopard, jaguar, and snow leopard. Based on their skull and voice box anatomy, they are grouped together in the same genus, *Panthera*, and are known as the "roaring" or "great" cats. (Clouded leopards are the exception—they belong to the genus *Neofelis*.)

Though there are just five species of large cats, there seem to be many more! This is because there are variations, or subspecies, of each. These include Asiatic and African lions; Bengal, Sumatran, and Siberian tigers; and nine subspecies of leopards found across Asia, Europe, and Africa.

Cats are not the only animals that exist as subspecies. Geographic variation is common in the animal kingdom. Each subspecies is given a three-part name. The first two parts identify the species (*Genus species*). The third part is specific to the subspecies. For example, all leopards are *Panthera pardus* (*P.p.*). The subspecies in Kenya is called *P.p. pardus*, whereas the one in the Russian Far East, Korean Peninsula, and northeast China is *P.p. orientalis*.

AFRICAN LION
Panthera leo

RANGE: Sub-Saharan Africa

SIZE: 278 to 599 lb (126 to 272 kg)

DIET: Gazelles, antelopes, zebras, buffalo; also smaller animals, birds

Lions are by far the most social species of cat. They live in family groups, or prides. The females are related and will often nurse each other's cubs. Lions have two unique features: a tufted tail and, in the males, a mane.

JAGUAR
Panthera onca

RANGE: Warmer regions of North and South America

SIZE: 150 to 300 lb (68 to 136 kg)

DIET: Peccaries, tapirs, deer; also caimans, turtles, snakes, porcupines, capybaras, fish, large birds

Jaguars are excellent swimmers. They also depend on water to keep cool. Like leopards, they have a genetic color mutation known as melanism. The gene is dominant, which means black phase jaguars, or black panthers, are relatively common.

CLOUDED LEOPARD
Neofelis nebulosa

RANGE: South of Himalaya in Nepal, Bhutan, Myanmar, India, southern China, Taiwan

SIZE: 24.2 to 50.7 lb (11 to 23 kg)

DIET: Birds, fish, monkeys, deer, rodents

Clouded leopards are very secretive. They spend much of their time in trees, where they hunt monkeys and birds. They have the greatest size difference between sexes among cat species—males are twice the size of females.

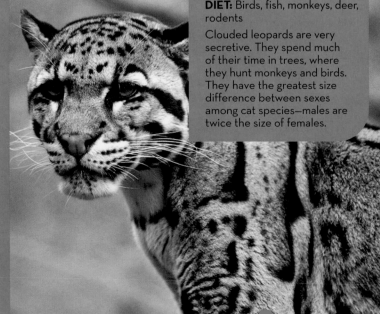

SNOW LEOPARD
Panthera uncia

RANGE: Parts of Nepal, Mongolia, Afghanistan, Pakistan, China

SIZE: 55 to 165 lb (25 to 75 kg)

DIET: Wild boar, wild sheep, mice, deer, hares, marmots, other small mammals; birds; sometimes domestic livestock

Snow leopards live in cold, mountainous areas, where they hunt blue sheep, ibex, rodents, and birds. To keep warm, they curl up underneath their long, furry tail. Unlike the other large cats, snow leopards have gray-green instead of yellow-gold eyes.

SIBERIAN TIGER
Panthera tigris altaica

RANGE: East Asia, in Russia, China, North Korea

SIZE: 200 to 710 lb (90.7 to 322 kg)

DIET: Hoofed animals

This tiger subspecies is the largest cat. Siberian tigers also have the longest canine teeth—up to four inches (10 cm)—and can eat up to 40 pounds (18 kg) of meat at one meal.

FELIDS

The 46 species in the cat, or felid (FEE-lid), family are remarkably similar. All have excellent vision, hearing, and sense of smell. They are ambush hunters with sharp retractable claws, powerful jaws, and teeth specialized for grabbing and tearing meat.

Cats are strong, agile predators. They either hide and wait for their prey, or walk silently behind on padded feet, pouncing when the time is right. They are also obligate carnivores. The definition is not simply that they eat only meat. Cats must also eat skin and bones to get the nutrition they need.

Except for lions, cats are nocturnal, secretive, and solitary. They hunt at night and interact with each other only to defend territory or breed. Even so, cats communicate in plenty of other ways—through scent and scratch marks.

Not every species of cat is the same, of course. They differ in size and fur color. Whether or not they can roar depends on their anatomy. All can purr, but only lions, tigers, leopards, and jaguars can roar.

Cat life spans range from 15 to 25 years.

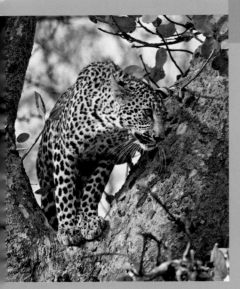

LEOPARD
Panthera pardus

RANGE: Africa, Europe, Asia

SIZE: 37.4 to 143 lb (17 to 65 kg)

DIET: Small antelopes, gazelles, deer, pigs, primates, domestic livestock; also birds, reptiles, rodents, arthropods, carrion

Asiatic and African leopards are similar, apart from their fur. In the rainforests of Asia, these cats are more likely to be melanistic, or black—a color mutation caused by a recessive gene that allows better camouflage. In the right light, their rosettes, or spots, are still visible.

BENGAL TIGER
Panthera tigris tigris

RANGE: Myanmar, Bangladesh, India, Nepal, Bhutan

SIZE: 200 to 570 lb (90.7 to 259 kg)

DIET: Hoofed animals

Bengal tigers socialize through scent markings and scratch marks. One male's territory may overlap that of one to seven females. These cats use their body weight to knock their prey to the ground before going for the neck.

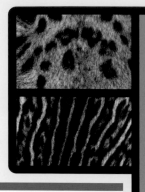

SMALL AND MEDIUM CATS

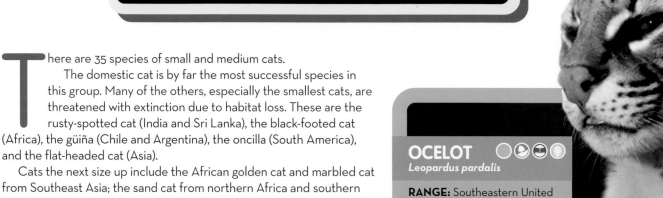

There are 35 species of small and medium cats.
The domestic cat is by far the most successful species in this group. Many of the others, especially the smallest cats, are threatened with extinction due to habitat loss. These are the rusty-spotted cat (India and Sri Lanka), the black-footed cat (Africa), the güiña (Chile and Argentina), the oncilla (South America), and the flat-headed cat (Asia).

Cats the next size up include the African golden cat and marbled cat from Southeast Asia; the sand cat from northern Africa and southern Asia; and, from South America, the Andean cat, Geoffrey's cat, and sand margay.

The medium-size cats range in size from wild cats found in parts of Europe, Africa, and Asia to cheetahs (Africa) and mountain lions (North and South America). The diversity in this group includes five species found in the Americas (ocelots, jaguarundis, caracals, bobcats, and the Canada lynx), three in Asia (fishing cats, Asiatic golden cats, and marbled cats), two in Africa (African golden cats and servals), and two in Europe (the Spanish and Eurasian lynx). The largest of the medium cats are the cheetah and the mountain lion.

OCELOT
Leopardus pardalis

RANGE: Southeastern United States to south-central South America

SIZE: 18 to 35 lb (8.2 to 15.9 kg)

DIET: Mostly small rodents, reptiles, medium-size mammals, birds, crustaceans, fish

These medium-size cats have two black stripes on their cheeks, a white spot on the backs of their ears, and a ringed tail. As with other striped and spotted cats, individual ocelots can be identified by their unique markings.

FISHING CAT
Prionailurus viverrinus

RANGE: India, Sri Lanka, Nepal, Bangladesh, Vietnam, Thailand, Java, Sumatra

SIZE: 13 to 26 lb (5.9 to 11.8 kg)

DIET: Mostly fish and shellfish

When hungry, these cats go fishing. If the water is shallow, they wade in. In deeper water, they swim or dive in after their prey. Fishing cats also hunt from the water's edge, using their sharp claws like fishhooks.

CANADA LYNX
Lynx canadensis

RANGE: Canada, Alaska, northwestern United States

SIZE: 9.5 to 38 lb (4.3 to 17.2 kg)

DIET: Mainly snowshoe hares; also rodents, birds, fish

In areas where Canada lynx prefer snowshoe hares to any other prey the hare population gradually declines, followed by the lynx population. With fewer lynx around, the hare population increases again. This cycle repeats every nine to 10 years.

SERVAL
Leptailurus serval

RANGE: Mainly southern Africa

SIZE: 20 to 40 lb (9.1 to 18.1 kg)

DIET: Rats, mice, shrews, birds, insects, frogs, lizards

Servals listen for their next meal using their huge ears. As soon as this long-legged cat picks up the sound of a rodent rustling in the grass, it moves closer. Then it pounces—from up to 12 feet (3.7 m) away.

MARGAY
Leopardus wiedii

RANGE: Northern Mexico to Uruguay and northern Argentina

SIZE: 5.5 to 9 lb (2.5 to 4.1 kg)

DIET: Mammals, birds and their eggs, reptiles, amphibians, arthropods, fruit

Margays are close relatives of the ocelot. They look alike—though the margay is smaller—and they hunt the same prey and live in the same areas. What distinguishes them is their behavior. Margays are arboreal and diurnal. Ocelots are terrestrial and nocturnal.

CHEETAH
Acinonyx jubatus

RANGE: Africa and northern Iran

SIZE: 34 to 160 lb (15.4 to 72.6 kg)

DIET: Hares, jackals, small antelopes, gazelles

The cheetah runs faster than any other animal for a variety of reasons. Its nose is one of them. Compared to other cats, cheetahs have wider nostrils and larger nasal passages. Both allow it to take in more oxygen with each running breath.

BOBCAT
Lynx rufus

RANGE: North America

SIZE: 8 to 33 lb (3.6 to 15 kg)

DIET: Mainly small mammals, such as rabbits and rodents; also small ungulates, large ground birds, reptiles

Throughout its range, the fur color and markings of the bobcat vary. For example, bobcats living in northern forests have darker coats than those living in southern deserts. Each distinct form is considered a subspecies.

HERE, KITTY, KITTY!

Although the origin of many animal species is a bit fuzzy, most scientists agree that today's domestic cat descended from a Middle Eastern wildcat, *Felis silvestris*, which means "cat of the woods." Dogs were domesticated well before cats because humans were a society of hunters, and gray wolves (the ancestor of domestic dogs) were tamed to be their hunting companions. It wasn't until people began to settle down and live together in communities, farm the fields, and construct mills to store crops that cats became necessary. Wild cats began to wander into town, attracted by the mice and small prey lured by silos and mills chock-full of grain. Humans liked this natural pest control and welcomed them. As time went on, people chose cats with more docile personalities to live on their farms, and as generations had kittens and grandkittens, the "wild" was eventually bred out completely.

MAMMALS

71

Beverly and
Dereck Joubert

LEOPARD

eopards *(Panthera pardus)* are silent and secretive animals—the ghosts of the forest. Their yellowish fur and black spots camouflage their bodies as they slink through the shadows and slither through the grass, eluding predators and surprising their prey. And they almost always avoid humans. That's why the highlight of our lives began the day we met a little leopard cub in the Okavango Delta, in Botswana. She was just eight days old when we spotted her, and we decided to spend the next four years watching her grow up.

Three months after we saw her, a horrible storm broke out while the cub's mother was off hunting. The sky turned black, rain pounded the ground, and lightning crackled all around us. Dereck and I huddled together in our jeep, but on the ground, the cub shivered with fear. It was her first storm. Suddenly, a bolt of lightning struck a nearby tree. There was a deafening crash, leaves showered us, and a pungent smell filled the air. We thought the cub would run away—but she came charging out of the thicket, straight toward us, and sat down next to Dereck's feet! After that, we called her Legadema, which means "light from the sky," or "lightning."

NORTH AMERICA

ARCTIC OCEAN

ATLANTIC OCEAN

EUROPE

ASIA

AFRICA

PACIFIC OCEAN

INDIAN OCEAN

The Jouberts' base camps

RANGE OF THE *PANTHERA PARDUS* (LEOPARD)

AUSTRALIA

0   2,000 miles

0   2,000 kilometers

OBSERVATION TIPS

1 Leopards are sneaky. You usually have to follow their paw prints to find them!

2 To see leopards behaving naturally, you have to watch for a long time—even at night, which is usually when they hunt.

3 Watch nature unfold from a respectable distance, and never interfere.

4 Stay alert! There are many other wild—and dangerous—animals in the area.

Beverly and Dereck Joubert have spent more than 25 years studying, filming, and photographing animals all over Africa, dedicating their lives to understanding and conserving Earth's magnificent places and creatures. This multi-award-winning team lives in the wild surrounded by the animals they love.

Leopard cubs have a lot to learn about living in the wild. They're easy targets for hungry predators, so they stay with their mothers for about two years while they figure out where the best hiding spots are, which trees are easiest to climb, and how to hunt. If a predator does approach, the cub can be carried to safety. But life in the forest isn't always serious—there's plenty of time to play, too!

COWS, SHEEP, AND GOATS

Cows, sheep, and goats are some of the best known hoofed animals. These species—and their relatives—are known as ruminants. All have an even number of toes and a series of four digestive chambers, the largest of which is known as the rumen.

Ruminants are experts at digesting plants that are very high in fiber, or cellulose. To start the process, they chew their food twice. A cow that is chewing its cud, for example, is breaking up its meal into tiny bits and mixing it with saliva. This process is called rumination.

Next, the food moves into the rumen, which is filled with partially digested plant material and millions of microbial organisms like protozoa and bacteria. These microbes eat the plant fiber and release energy—fat, glucose, and methane gas. This type of digestion is called fermentation.

From the rumen, the plant material passes into a much smaller chamber called the reticulum, where it is filtered. Larger pieces stay in the rumen and are "unswallowed" and rechewed. Smaller pieces pass into the third chamber, the omasum, where water and other nutrients are absorbed. Only then does the food pass into the true stomach, or fourth chamber, called the abomasum. From there, digestion proceeds much the way it does in nonruminant mammals.

Many species of cows, sheep, and goats have been domesticated and bred on farms worldwide for their meat, milk, wool, and leather. Others are kept as pets. Their life spans range up to 30 years.

TAKIN
Budorcas taxicolor

RANGE: Eastern Himalaya in Asia

SIZE: 330 to 881 lb (150 to 400 kg)

DIET: Leaves, grasses, herbs

Takin look as though they are part cow, part goat, and part antelope. They live high in the mountains during the summer, and in very large herds. During winter, they break into smaller groups and move down to the forested valleys.

AMERICAN BISON
Bison bison

RANGE: Protected areas of the western U.S. and Canada (before near extinction: range was North America, from Alaska to northern Mexico)

SIZE: 700 to 1,982 lb (318 to 900 kg)

DIET: Mostly grasses; also other vegetation such as sagebrush

There were once 60 million American bison. Their presence— they grazed in large herds—helped to maintain the prairie ecosystem. They were hunted to near extinction, however, by 1890; today, they are found only in protected areas.

HOOFED MAMMALS

The hoofed mammals are the most successful group of herbivores. There are more than 350 species found all over the world.

One reason for their success is their ability to digest cellulose, the fiber found in grass. Another is their ability to escape predators. Not only do they have excellent vision and an acute sense of smell, but they are also strong and fast runners. Most hoofed mammals also have either antlers or horns. These are used for defense as well as for breeding displays.

Depending on the species, hoofed mammals stand on one, two, three, or four elongated toe bones. In other words, they bear weight on their tiptoes! They have equally long tendons running down the backs of their legs that connect to the hoof. These give the animals a spring in their step and the power to run and kick.

The hoofed animals that stand on an even number of toes are divided into three groups: ruminants (cows, sheep, goats, deer, antelopes, giraffes), hippos and pigs, and camels and llamas.

The odd-toed hoofed mammals are divided into two groups: horses and relatives, and rhinos and tapirs.

BIGHORN SHEEP
Ovis canadensis

RANGE: Rocky Mountains of North America from southern Canada to Colorado, U.S.A.; deserts from Nevada, U.S.A., to Mexico

SIZE: 117 to 280 lb (53 to 127 kg)

DIET: Grasses, herbs, sedges, forbs

Bighorn sheep live only in drier deserts or mountainous areas. Their small hooves are adapted to fit the narrow ledges between rocks, but they are too blunt to claw through snow to find food.

DOMESTIC MOUFLON SHEEP
Ovis aries

RANGE: Worldwide

SIZE: 44 to 440 lb (20 to 200 kg)

DIET: Mainly grasses; also a wide variety of hays and oats

Mouflon sheep were first domesticated about 10,000 years ago in the Middle East and Central Asia. Since then, they have been bred for their meat, hide, milk, and wool. With more than 200 breeds, domestic sheep now outnumber all other species of sheep.

NUBIAN IBEX
Capra nubiana

RANGE: Northern Africa and Middle East

SIZE: 55 to 154 lb (25 to 70 kg)

DIET: Herbs, shrubs, tree foliage, buds, fruit, grasses

Nubian ibex have a special strategy for protecting their young from predators. They lead them into a nursery of sorts—a walled-in area, like a canyon. The mothers leave the nursery to graze, returning often to nurse their young.

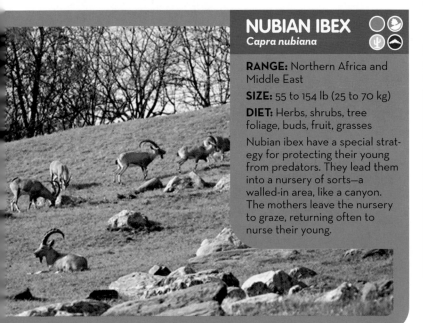

MOUNTAIN GOAT
Oreamnos americanus

RANGE: Northern Rocky Mountains in North America

SIZE: 125 to 180 lb (57 to 82 kg)

DIET: Grasses, woody plants, mosses, lichens, herbs

Mountain goats have oval hooves with rubberlike soles that help them grip rocks. Each year, they migrate—vertically. At the end of winter, they shed their thick coats and climb up to 16,000 feet (4,877 m). By summer, they are back down at 3,200 feet (975 m).

DOMESTIC COW
Bos taurus

RANGE: Worldwide

SIZE: 324 to 3,002 lb (147 to 1,363 kg)

DIET: Grasses and stems

Cows were domesticated 10,000 years ago in India, the Middle East, and North Africa. Today there are more than 800 breeds. Cows are used for plowing and moving heavy loads, and as sources of meat, milk, cheese, glue, soap, leather, and fertilizer.

YAK
Bos mutus

RANGE: Asia's Tibetan Plateau

SIZE: 660 to 2,200 lb (300 to 1,000 kg)

DIET: Low-lying grasses and grasslike plants

Wild yaks live at very high elevations, up to 17,700 feet (5,395 m). Domesticated yaks are smaller, but equally well adapted to the altitude. For thousands of years, yaks have been used as pack animals as well as sources of meat, milk, cheese, clothing, blankets, and tents.

CAMELS AND RELATIVES

Instead of hooves, camels and their relatives walk on two padded toes. All are grazers. They have a three-chambered stomach that includes a fermentation compartment for digesting plant fiber.

The animals in this group are extremely hardy. They are found in some of the harshest, driest habitats in the world—in Africa and Asia as well as the Americas. The Bactrian camel is native to the deserts of Central Asia; the dromedary to North Africa and South Asia. The vicuña and guanaco are native to the high-altitude grasslands of the Andes, mountains in western South America.

All four camel species have been domesticated—kept and bred—for transportation as well as for their milk, meat, and hair. There are more than 14 million domestic dromedaries in Africa and Asia, and another million running free in Australia, the descendants of animals brought there for transport. Wild dromedaries are extinct. There are far fewer domestic Bactrian camels: about 1.4 million, with only about 1,000 left in the wild. Domesticated guanacos are llamas. Domesticated vicuñas are alpacas.

Camel life spans range from 25 to 50 years.

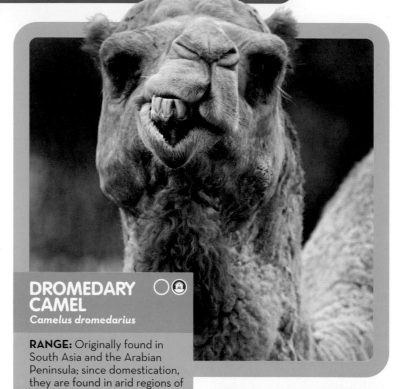

DROMEDARY CAMEL
Camelus dromedarius

RANGE: Originally found in South Asia and the Arabian Peninsula; since domestication, they are found in arid regions of the Middle East, India, Africa

SIZE: 660 to 1,518 lb (300 to 689 kg)

DIET: Leaves, plants, grasses

Dromedary camels (one hump) have been extinct in the wild since the time of their domestication 2,000 years ago. They are excellent pack animals in hot, dry regions. To conserve water, they do not sweat until their body temperature reaches 106°F (41°C).

GUANACO
Lama guanicoe

RANGE: Northern Peru to southern Chile

SIZE: 253 to 308 lb (115 to 140 kg)

DIET: Grasses and other plants

The guanaco (gwa-NAH-koh) rarely drinks water. Instead, it relies on the moisture in its plant diet, including the dew on cactus leaves. When threatened, the guanaco, like its relative the llama, makes a bleating sound. It also spits.

BACTRIAN CAMEL
Camelus bactrianus

RANGE: Asia north of Himalaya

SIZE: 990 to 1,100 lb (449 to 499 kg)

DIET: Leaves, roots, tubers, wood, bark, stems, seeds, grains, nuts, fruit

About 1,000 wild Bactrian camels (two humps) remain in the Gobi, a desert in China and Mongolia, where they thrive despite extreme heat and cold. After a drought, these camels can drink up to a quarter of their body weight at one time.

VICUÑA
Vicugna vicugna

RANGE: Andes in South America

SIZE: 77 to 143 lb (35 to 65 kg)

DIET: Grasses

Unlike other members of the camel family, the vicuña (vih-KOON-yuh) cannot go without water. It is also much smaller, has rodent-like incisors for grazing, and lives only at high elevations—up to 18,800 feet (5,750 m).

HORSES AND RELATIVES

H orses and their 14 relatives are members of the equid (EE-quid) family. The animals in this group differ from even-toed, hoofed mammals in several ways. For one thing, they bear weight on a single digit. They are odd-toed.

They also digest their food differently, fermenting it in a dilated portion of their large intestine rather than in a rumen. This process, known as hindgut fermentation, is not nearly as efficient as rumination. As a result, horses and zebras eat constantly. Other herbivores like rabbits use the same strategy—and face the same challenge. The need to graze puts the animals at risk of greater predation, which is one reason these animals are able to run so fast.

Equids are among the most graceful animals on Earth. The faster they gallop, the more amazing they are to watch. The horse, domesticated 6,000 years ago, is also one of the most important animals in human history, having been used for work, transportation, war, and pleasure.

Life spans range from 10 to 30 years for horses and their relatives.

HORSE
Equus caballus

RANGE: Original species: steppe zone of Europe and Asia; domesticated 6,000 years ago and now worldwide

SIZE: 500 to 1,982 lb (227 to 900 kg)

DIET: Grasses, but often have domestic diets that include grains and hays

Domestic horses are likely descendants of the now extinct wild horse (*Equus ferus ferus*) that once lived in Europe and Asia, although multiple geographic and genetic origins of the horse are likely. The animals called wild horses, such as mustangs and brumbies, are escaped domestic horses.

AFRICAN WILD ASS
Equus africanus

RANGE: Northern Africa, Arabian Peninsula; domesticated subspecies is the donkey, which is found worldwide

SIZE: 400 to 550 lb (181 to 249 kg)

DIET: Grasses and herbs

The donkey is the same species as the African, or Somali, wild ass. Like all equids, they have long jaws lined with molars for chewing grass, large eyes with binocular vision, and large, sensitive ears.

KIANG
Equus kiang

RANGE: Tibet, parts of China, Nepal, India

SIZE: 550 to 970 lb (249 to 440 kg)

DIET: Grasses and plants

The kiang is the largest species of wild ass. They are found at high elevations of up to 23,000 feet (7,010 m) and live in close-knit family groups led by an older female. Single males, called stallions, follow the herd and fight for breeding rights.

BURCHELL'S ZEBRA
Equus quagga burchellii

RANGE: Africa

SIZE: 385 to 847 lb (175 to 384 kg)

DIET: Primarily grasses; also herbs, leaves, twigs

There are three species of zebras: mountain, Grevy's, and plains. The most widespread is the plains zebra, which exists as several subspecies, including Burchell's, shown here. Plains zebras live in groups called harems that include one stallion and up to six females with foals.

RHINOS AND TAPIRS

Rhinos and tapirs (TAY-peerz) are another type of odd-toed, hoofed mammal. Unlike horses, however, they walk on three digits and a footpad.

The other interesting thing about rhino and tapir feet is that they differ depending on where the animal lives. Species that live on firm grassland, like the black and white rhinos of Africa, have relatively short toes and a flat, firm footpad. Species that live in the tropics and swampy areas, like the greater one-horned rhino and Brazilian tapir, have longer toes and a soft footpad for better traction in mud.

Hair is another feature that varies among the species in this grouping. African rhinos have hairy ear tips and eyelashes. Asian rhinos have tufts of hair on their ears and tails. The Sumatran rhino has hair all over its body, an adaptation for life in the buggy tropics.

Like most rhinos, tapirs have very little hair. Only the mountain species has a thick coat. The others have bristly manes, right in the location where a jaguar would take its first bite.

Life spans range up to 30 years for tapirs, and up to 50 for rhinos.

BRAZILIAN TAPIR
Tapirus terrestris

RANGE: South America

SIZE: 330 to 551 lb (150 to 250 kg)

DIET: Fruit, leaves, other plant material

Like all tapirs, the Brazilian, or lowland, tapir is mostly nocturnal, lives in dense forest near water, and has a mobile nose called a proboscis, which it uses to grasp its food. It is more vocal than its relatives, however, and makes a loud, piercing whistle when disturbed.

BLACK RHINOCEROS
Diceros bicornis

RANGE: Once found throughout sub-Saharan Africa; now only in Cameroon, Kenya, South Africa

SIZE: 1,760 to 3,080 lb (800 to 1,400 kg)

DIET: Leaves, buds, shoots of bushes and small trees

Compared to the white rhino, also found in Africa, the black rhino is smaller and usually has darker skin. Both have two horns. The way to identify the black rhino for certain is to look at its lips. Since black rhinos are browsers, they have a pointed, mobile upper lip for grabbing leaves, twigs, and other plants.

WHITE RHINOCEROS
Ceratotherium simum

RANGE: Once found in central, eastern, and southern Africa; now only in game reserves and parks

SIZE: 2,200 to 7,930 lb (1,000 to 3,600 kg)

DIET: Grasses

White rhinos are grazers. Also called the square-lipped rhino, they have a flat upper lip for cropping grasses. Though some white rhino populations are well protected, all rhinos, both in Asia and Africa, are threatened with extinction because of poaching for their horns.

MALAYAN TAPIR
Tapirus indicus

RANGE: Swamps in Malaysia and Sumatra

SIZE: 500 to 800 lb (227 to 363 kg)

DIET: Aquatic vegetation, grasses, leaves, buds, fruit

The Malayan tapir looks different from its three South American relatives. The light gray fur around its body helps to provide camouflage in the shadows of the rainforest. Also, it eats aquatic plants in addition to land vegetation.

JAVAN RHINOCEROS
Rhinoceros sondaicus

RANGE: Once widespread in Indonesia, India, China; now fewer than 50 animals in two parks in Southeast Asia

SIZE: 3,300 to 4,400 lb (1,500 to 2,000 kg)

DIET: Leaves, young shoots, twigs, fruit

This species is also known as the lesser one-horned rhino. It looks very similar to its larger Asian relative and was once the most common rhino in Asia. Sadly, the Javan rhino has been killed for its horn and is one of the rarest animals on Earth.

GREATER ONE-HORNED RHINO
Rhinoceros unicornis

RANGE: Northern India and southern Nepal

SIZE: 3,300 to 4,400 lb (1,500 to 2,000 kg)

DIET: Grasses, weeds, twigs, fruit, leaves, branches, aquatic plants, farm crops

Also known as the Indian rhinoceros, this massive mammal is a browser. Like the black rhino, it has a pointed upper lip that it uses to eat tall grasses. Its skin has thick folds and bumps on the surface that make it look like armor.

SUMATRAN RHINOCEROS
Dicerorhinus sumatrensis

RANGE: Asia, from foothills of Himalaya in India and Bhutan to Thailand, Malaysia, Indonesia

SIZE: 1,760 to 4,400 lb (800 to 2,000 kg)

DIET: Plants, fruit, twigs

The Sumatran rhino is smaller than its relatives and has more hair—especially the calves. The only Asian rhino with two horns, it lives in forested areas near water or in swamps. It, too, is critically endangered because of poaching.

BAIRD'S TAPIR
Tapirus bairdii

RANGE: Mexico, Central America, Colombia

SIZE: 330 to 661 lb (150 to 300 kg)

DIET: Leaves, fruit, twigs, flowers, grasses

Baird's tapirs are the largest of the tapir species found in South America. To stay cool, they rest in the shade or in shallow pools of water. Despite their size, they are very fast—on land and in water.

ANTELOPES AND PRONGHORNS

Most of the 91 species of traditional antelopes are found in the grasslands of Africa. A few—such as the saiga and Tibetan antelopes—live in Asia. The pronghorn is a closely related species found only in North America.

All are browsers, grazers, or both. This explains their diversity. There may be several species of antelopes in one area, but each specializes in a different part of the available plants. Gerenuks, for example, browse on tree leaves by standing on their hind legs. Thomson's gazelles graze on short, fine grasses. Wildebeest nip off the tips of larger, tough grasses.

Like all ruminants, antelopes have horns that are bony structures made of keratin that grow continuously. Some are straight; others are curved. A few species, like kudus and elands, have elaborate, spiraled horns.

Antelopes live in social groups that vary in size from a few individuals to hundreds. Every dry season in East Africa, several species of antelopes join together in huge herds, along with zebras, buffalo, and elephants, in search of water.

Life spans for antelopes and pronghorns range from 15 to 20 years.

PRONGHORN
Antilocapra americana

RANGE: Western North America

SIZE: 80 to 150 lb (36.3 to 68 kg)

DIET: Sage, forbs, grasses, cacti

Pronghorns are in a family all their own. Like African antelopes, they are flighty and fast. Like deer, they shed their prongs once a year. Unlike both, they cannot jump. As a result, pronghorns are afraid of fences.

THOMSON'S GAZELLE
Eudorcas thomsonii

RANGE: Kenya and Tanzania

SIZE: 33 to 77 lb (15 to 34.9 kg)

DIET: Short grasses, foliage, twigs, seeds, leaves

Thomson's gazelles are mostly grazers. During the rainy season, when the grass is very tall, they are often found in mixed herds of zebras and wildebeest. They wait their turn to graze until the larger herbivores make the first cut.

GERENUK
Litocranius walleri

RANGE: Somalia, eastern Ethiopia, Kenya, Tanzania

SIZE: 63 to 127 lb (29 to 58 kg)

DIET: Leaves, shoots, fruit, flowers, buds

Among the gazelle species, gerenuks (JER-a-nooks) have unusually long legs and necks. Their name means "giraffe-necked" in Somali. Gerenuks feed on whatever they can reach that other antelopes cannot.

BLUE WILDEBEEST
Connochaetes taurinus

RANGE: Eastern and southern Africa

SIZE: 260 to 600 lb (118 to 272 kg)

DIET: Grasses; rarely, leaves

Wildebeest live in small herds led by a territorial bull. Unlike many of their smaller relatives, they cannot survive without water. Wildebeest migrate up to 75 miles (120 km) from one home range to the other, depending on the time of year.

DEER
AND ELK

Deer and elk live mostly in wooded or forested areas and are found in Europe and the Americas, as well as Asia and Africa. Most of the male animals in this group have antlers—they grow a new set each year—instead of horns.

Antlers start out as living tissue covered in soft, furred skin, known as velvet. When they reach their final length and shape, they lose their blood supply, and the velvet falls off, leaving a dry, bone-like structure. Now the male is ready for rut, a type of breeding display also known as horning and adorning. After the breeding season, the antlers fall off, usually within a day or two of each other. The three-dimensional shape of the antlers is unique to each male and is the same each year, like a fingerprint.

Instead of antlers for displays and defense, some smaller deer use their teeth. Muntjacs, for example, have four razor-sharp canines.

Life spans for deer, elk, and their relatives range from 10 to 15 years.

CARIBOU
Rangifer tarandus

RANGE: Circumpolar Northern Hemisphere

SIZE: 120 to 700 lb (54.4 to 318 kg)

DIET: Grass, plants, lichens

Caribou, or reindeer, are unusual among deer because both males and females have antlers. Their calves also mature incredibly fast. New-borns nurse within minutes of birth, follow their mother within an hour, and can run full speed after one day.

ELK
Cervus canadensis

RANGE: Formerly northern Europe, Asia, Africa, North America; now western North America

SIZE: 145 to 1,100 lb (65.8 to 499 kg)

DIET: Grasses, sedges, forbs; also clover, dandelions, violets

Elk, or wapiti, are one of the most vocal species in the deer family. During the mating season, males roar, or bellow, loudly and repeatedly to attract females and advertise their territory. This behavior is called bugling.

WHITE-TAILED DEER
Odocoileus virginianus

RANGE: North, Central, and South America, as far south as Bolivia

SIZE: 125 to 300 lb (56.7 to 136 kg)

DIET: Grasses, weeds, shrubs, twigs, fungi, nuts, lichens

Like many other herbivores, a female white-tailed deer protects her young by leaving it alone. The doe hides, or "tucks," her newborn on the forest floor or in tall grass. With its neck stretched out and white spots for camouflage, the fawn blends right in.

MOOSE
Alces alces

RANGE: Circumpolar Northern Hemisphere

SIZE: 595 to 1,698 lb (270 to 771 kg)

DIET: Stems, twigs, leaves, shoots

During winter, moose are found in forests where there is snow cover. Their large bodies retain heat, and they have no problem staying warm. During summer, they often are found standing in lakes or swamps to keep cool.

GIRAFFES AND OKAPIS

Giraffes and okapis are found only in Africa, and both have fur that allows them to camouflage themselves from predators.

Giraffes blend right in among the bush and acacia trees. An entire herd can disappear into a thicket! Their blotchy brown spots blend in perfectly with the shadows created by the thorny branches. Okapis are difficult to see in the forest, where the sunlight creates shadows. Against the alternating light and dark of the forest, their striped legs and dark bodies are almost invisible. They also walk and run differently from most other hoofed animals. They pace, meaning they move the front and rear legs on the same side at the same time. This is their only gait, yet they are surprisingly agile.

Both are also very quiet. Giraffes and okapis communicate using sounds most animals—including humans—cannot hear. A giraffe, for example, will arch its neck to force air through its long windpipes. This action creates very low-frequency sounds, known as infrasound.

Life spans are up to 25 years.

NUBIAN GIRAFFE
Giraffa camelopardalis

RANGE: Africa

SIZE: 2,600 to 4,250 lb (1,180 to 1,930 kg)

DIET: Leaves, flowers, seed pods, fruit; also soil

Previously, giraffes were divided into subspecies based on their coat patterns and where they lived. Genetic analysis suggests that giraffe groups are more distinct from one another, placing them into distinct species that don't interbred in the wild. However, genetic data are undergoing constant reanalysis, so this division may change in the near future!

SOUTHERN GIRAFFE
(Giraffa giraffa)

RANGE: Africa

SIZE: 2,600 to 4,250 lb (1,180 to 1,930 kg)

DIET: Leaves, flowers, seed pods, fruit; also soil

All giraffes share several unique traits. One is a series of valves in the arteries and veins of their necks. These help to maintain a constant blood pressure in the giraffe's head, whether it is held high or lowered to eat or drink.

MASAI GIRAFFE
Giraffa tippelskirchi

RANGE: Africa

SIZE: 2,600 to 4,250 lb (1,180 to 1,930 kg)

DIET: Leaves, flowers, seed pods, fruit; also soil

Masai giraffes are the tallest of the species, reaching 20 feet (6 m). Their coats have dark brown patches with jagged edges surrounded by white. For comparison, southern giraffes have larger brown patches with fewer notches, and reticulated giraffes have large, light brown patches separated by thin white lines.

OKAPI
Okapia johnstoni

RANGE: Northeastern Democratic Republic of the Congo

SIZE: 440 to 660 lb (200 to 299 kg)

DIET: Leaves, buds, shoots

Okapis and giraffes are similar in many ways. Both have bluish black tongues—long enough to reach their ears—that they use for plucking leaves. Both also have a type of horn unique among mammals: It is made of bone covered by furred skin.

HIPPOS AND PIGS

Hippos and pigs and their relatives are grouped with one another, ruminants, and camels mostly because of their hooves. All stand on an even number of toes. The difference is that hippos, pigs, peccaries, and warthogs stand on four toes, rather than two.

They are different in many other ways, too. Hippos, for example, are semiaquatic. They graze on land, only at night, and spend their days resting in the water, and digesting. Their closest relatives may be whales. Instead of a rumen, they have a compartmentalized stomach.

Pigs, warthogs, and peccaries, on the other hand, are omnivores. They also have special snouts: The very end is made up of cartilage and bone so they can use it like a bulldozer.

The most visible features shared by hippos and pigs are their tusk-like canines. These modified teeth are used for fighting as well as digging. If provoked, they can inflict severe wounds.

For example, hippos kill more people in Africa each year than any single disease, except malaria. Unfortunately, they are often surprised at night by people visiting the river to fetch water, bathe, or wash their clothes.

Life spans range from 15 to 20 years for pigs and relatives, and 55 to 60 years for hippos.

HIPPOPOTAMUS
Hippopotamus amphibius

RANGE: Sub-Saharan Africa

SIZE: 1,400 to 8,000 lb (635 to 3,629 kg)

DIET: Short grasses and other plants; fallen fruit

With their eyes, ears, and nostrils just above the surface, hippos let their body sink under the water. This behavior is related to eating—hippos need to rest to digest all of the food they eat.

COLLARED PECCARY
Pecari tajacu

RANGE: Southern United States, Central America, South America

SIZE: 33 to 60 lb (15 to 25 kg)

DIET: Roots, fungi, bulbs, nuts, fruit, eggs, carrion, small reptiles, fish

Collared peccaries are found in two very different habitats: rainforests and deserts. In both places, they eat a variety of plant roots and bulbs. In the desert, there is one plant they need: the prickly pear. Without it, they would die of thirst.

COMMON WARTHOG
Phacochoerus africanus

RANGE: Africa

SIZE: 110 to 330 lb (50 to 150 kg)

DIET: Short grasses, roots, berries, bark of young trees; sometimes carrion

The "wart" in "warthog" refers to bumps made of cartilage-like tissue on the animal's face. There are warts above and below the eyes, as well as along the lower jaw. These warts also have long white bristles, which give the warthog a beard.

WILD BOAR
Sus scrofa

RANGE: Europe, Asia, North Africa

SIZE: 110 to 770 lb (50 to 349 kg)

DIET: Tubers, bulbs, grains, nuts, fruit, fungi, other plant material; manure, insect larvae, eggs, small vertebrates, invertebrates

The wild boar is the ancestor of the domestic pig. There are now more than 100 breeds of domestic pig—each a different mix of coat color, size, tail length, and shape of the ears and snout. All are the same species, *Sus domesticus*, and all like the same thing: wallowing in mud.

GIRAFFE

Since giraffes (*Giraffa camelopardalis*) are widely distributed and easy to spot in the wild, people assume that their population numbers are going up. But really, they are going down. Giraffes, as a single species, have declined by about 35 percent over the past 30 years. This decline has mostly been a result of habitat loss and fragmentation, climate change, and illegal killings.

In 2016, I participated in the first ever translocation of giraffes across the Nile River in Uganda's Murchison Falls National Park. Oil drilling was about to begin in the northern section of the park, which is home to more than half of the world's Nubian giraffe population. In partnership with the Uganda Wildlife Authority, we moved several giraffes to a new refuge in the southern part of the park. It was larger, didn't have any giraffes at the time, and had the same habitat.

Capturing the giraffes was quite an intense undertaking. A trained vet darted each giraffe from a vehicle. When we examined the giraffes, they were fully awake. We blindfolded them when they were down so that they would stay calm as measurements were being done. After we measured and examined each giraffe, we led them to a cart that carried them to a *boma,* or enclosure, next to a ranger post near an entry gate. We removed the blindfolds just before the giraffes were led into the boma.

Usually giraffes don't come to this part of the park because of all the people and vehicles. We were surprised when other giraffes came up to the boma to check out what was going on. It reminded us that we still know very little about how giraffes communicate. Participating in this operation was an emotional roller coaster because anything could have gone wrong at any time. Luckily, everything went smoothly. It was rewarding seeing the giraffes run toward their new homes, knowing that we made a difference.

SAFETY FIRST

It isn't safe for people—even trained researchers—to approach a wild animal. If the animal feels threatened, it will either fight back or attempt to flee. To keep the animal and the people studying it safe, a trained veterinarian may dart the animal to sedate it. The medicine makes the animal calm just long enough for researchers to safely examine it.

Arthur Muneza is a wildlife ecologist and the East Africa Coordinator for the Giraffe Conservation Foundation. He decided to study giraffes because they are understudied and there is still a lot to learn. Their numbers are declining, especially in East Africa. Through his work, he hopes to secure the future of the Masai, Nubian, and reticulated giraffes, which are East Africa's regional species.

EUROPE

ASIA

AFRICA

INDIAN OCEAN

ATLANTIC OCEAN

RANGE OF THE
GIRAFFA CAMELOPARDALIS (GIRAFFE)

0   1,000 miles
0   1,000 kilometers

OBSERVATION TIPS

1 Giraffes are huge, so they're easy to spot in the wild. Just don't get too close or make too much noise.

2 Giraffes are usually calm and very rarely chase after vehicles.

3 Look for giraffe droppings or footprints on the ground.

4 Examine the color and pattern on a giraffe's body and legs. Each subspecies has different markings.

Giraffes, the world's tallest animals, live in groups called towers. After a 14-month pregnancy, females give birth standing up—which means the newborn's first experience is falling five feet (1.5 m) to the ground! The baby, called a calf, is about six feet (1.8 m) tall and can stand up on its own in half an hour. About 10 hours after it's born, it can run. Mothers nurse their calves for about a year. Females join together to form nursery groups—some mothers watch over the calves while others get food.

DOLPHINS, PORPOISES, AND OTHER TOOTHED WHALES

Dolphins, porpoises, and whales are marine mammals belonging to the order Cetacea. They are highly social and intelligent animals with relatively large brains and fishlike bodies. Though they live in water, all breathe air. Their nostrils are located on the top of their heads, just inside the blowhole. When a cetacean exhales, it blows both water and air out the hole, creating a spray. Based on the fossil record, their common ancestor was a land mammal related to the hippo.

The animals in this group are divided into two suborders, the toothed and baleen whales.

There are 80 species of toothed whales. They include dolphins, porpoises, orcas, sperm whales, and beaked whales. All have teeth, which they use to grab their prey, and a single blowhole. Most have a special sensory organ known as the "melon" located between their eyes. The melon is used to gather and focus sound waves.

Sounds travel farther in water than in air, and toothed whales rely on their hearing more than any other sense. They communicate using clicks, whistles, moans, calls, and songs. Many also echolocate, meaning they use sound to find each other, forage for food, and navigate.

Life spans for dolphins, porpoises, and other toothed whales range from 40 to 90 years.

COMMON BOTTLENOSE DOLPHIN
Tursiops truncatus

RANGE: Indian, Atlantic, and Pacific Oceans; Mediterranean Sea

SIZE: 573 to 1,101 lb (260 to 500 kg)

DIET: Fish, invertebrates, squid

In shallow water, bottlenose dolphins take several breaths per minute, compared to one breath every two minutes between dives in deeper water. Females breed once every three to six years beginning at the age of 20, and can reproduce past the age of 40.

HARBOR PORPOISE
Phocoena phocoena

RANGE: All oceans in Northern Hemisphere

SIZE: 99 to 132 lb (45 to 60 kg)

DIET: Fish, squid, crustaceans

Compared to dolphins, porpoises are smaller and have a more rounded nose. They also reproduce faster and have shorter life spans. Female harbor porpoises, for example, give birth to one calf a year, starting at age five. They live eight to 10 years.

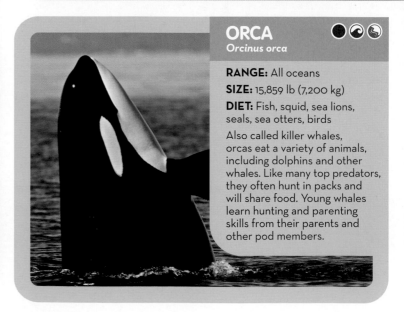

ORCA
Orcinus orca

RANGE: All oceans

SIZE: 15,859 lb (7,200 kg)

DIET: Fish, squid, sea lions, seals, sea otters, birds

Also called killer whales, orcas eat a variety of animals, including dolphins and other whales. Like many top predators, they often hunt in packs and will share food. Young whales learn hunting and parenting skills from their parents and other pod members.

BALEEN WHALES

The baleen whales include the blue whale, right whale, bowhead whale, fin whale, and gray whale. All have a two-part, V-shaped blowhole. They are filter feeders. Like toothed whales, they use sound to communicate.

Instead of a row of teeth like other mammals, these whales have a brushlike structure known as a baleen plate. The baleen is a bristly material that hangs down from a plate attached to the inner surface of the whale's upper jaw. Like hair and nails, baleen is made of keratin. It grows slowly over time as the ends wear out. To feed, the whale fills its lower jaw with water, closes its mouth, and pushes its tongue up against the baleen. This traps the whale's food—zooplankton like krill, copepods, and small fish—against the baleen. All it has to do next is squirt out the excess water and swallow. Filter feeding is incredibly efficient. Baleen whales can eat up to four tons (3.6 t) of food a day.

Baleen whales prefer warmer waters and migrate to avoid cool water during winter. The record for the longest migration is for the humpback whale: 5,176 miles (8,330 km). The life spans range from 60 to 70 years, possibly as long as 100 or more for some individuals.

NORTH ATLANTIC RIGHT WHALE
Eubalaena glacialis

RANGE: North Atlantic Ocean

SIZE: 121,145 to 209,251 lb (55,000 to 95,000 kg)

DIET: Zooplankton—mainly krill and copepods

These whales were hunted to near extinction for their meat and oil. Though protected, their future remains uncertain. They live in shallow coastal waters, where they often are struck by ships, caught in fishing nets, and harmed by pollution—including underwater noise.

BOWHEAD WHALE
Balaena mysticetus

RANGE: Coastal polar waters of the Northern Hemisphere

SIZE: 165,347 to 220,462 lb (75,000 to 100,000 kg)

DIET: Zooplankton—krill and other crustaceans

The bowhead whale is named for the U shape of its lower jaw. Its head is huge compared to its body, and its baleen plates are the largest of any whale species. For insulation, it has a two-foot (0.6-m)-thick layer of blubber!

SEI WHALE
Balaenoptera borealis

RANGE: All oceans and seas, except polar and tropical waters

SIZE: 44,092 to 55,116 lb (20,000 to 25,000 kg)

DIET: Zooplankton—krill, other crustaceans, small fish

Sei whales are big—and fast. Most are 50 feet (15 m) long and can swim up to 31 miles an hour (50 km/h). They are not divers, however; they feed only at the surface, swimming on their sides with their mouths open through a swarm of zooplankton.

BLUE WHALE
Balaenoptera musculus

RANGE: All oceans

SIZE: Up to 418,502 lb (190,000 kg)

DIET: Zooplankton—mainly krill, and some copepods

Blue whales are the largest whales. They also eat more krill in a day than any other species: up to 40 million! They communicate using low-pitched calls, or songs. The male's song can travel thousands of miles in the deep ocean.

LEMURS AND RELATIVES

Lemurs are found only on the island of Madagascar and the Comoros Islands. Biologists are still working out how to organize this group—there may be more than 100 species. Because they more closely resemble ancestral forms, lemurs are considered primitive primates.

Lemurs are known for their incredible diversity. This group includes the smallest primate on Earth, the 0.9-oz (25-g) pygmy mouse lemur. Some, like the dwarf lemur, are small, shy, nocturnal, and arboreal. Others, like the ring-tailed lemur, are diurnal and more often seen on the ground. There are lemurs with thick fur (woolly lemurs) as well as colorful fur (red, black, brown, and white-and-black ruffed lemurs). Many have distinct vocalizations. The indri, for example, makes a sad, siren-like call.

Another unusual feature among the social lemurs is female dominance. Females decide the hierarchy within a group. The males are responsible only for territorial defense.

Life spans for ring-tailed lemurs and sifakas are 25 to 30 years. Smaller lemurs live shorter lives (10 to 15 years) because of predation.

COQUEREL'S SIFAKA
Propithecus coquereli

RANGE: Northern Madagascar

SIZE: 8 to 9.4 lb (3.6 to 4.2 kg)

DIET: Leaves, seeds, flowers, fruit, bark

Sifakas are herbivores that prefer fresh leaves over anything else. As with other social lemurs, females are dominant over males. When the troop finds a choice patch of leaves, the females eat first.

RED RUFFED LEMUR
Varecia rubra

RANGE: Northeastern Madagascar

SIZE: 7.5 to 7.7 lb (3.4 to 3.5 kg)

DIET: Mainly fruit, nectar, pollen; also leaves and seeds

Red ruffed lemurs are very vocal primates. They bark to stay together while feeding, and squawk to warn each other of danger. Their calls are essential to survival—Madagascar is also home to the fossa, a marsupial that feeds exclusively on lemurs.

VERREAUX'S SIFAKA
Propithecus verreauxi

RANGE: Western and southwestern Madagascar

SIZE: 6.6 to 15.4 lb (3 to 7 kg)

DIET: Mainly leaves, seeds, flowers, fruit, bark

Sifakas (se-FA-kas) are known as leaping, or dancing, lemurs because of the way they move. In the trees, they leap from one branch to another without injury. On the ground, they hop sideways on two legs, holding their short arms up in the air.

GREATER DWARF LEMUR
Cheirogaleus major

RANGE: Eastern and northern Madagascar

SIZE: 0.4 to 1.3 lb (.18 to 0.6 kg)

DIET: Fruit, flowers, nectar; also insects

These small lemurs are nocturnal. During the drier months, when food is scarce, they become inactive to save energy, living off fat stored in their tails. This behavior is called torpor.

RING-TAILED LEMUR
Lemur catta

RANGE: Southern and southwestern Madagascar

SIZE: 5 to 7.7 lb (2.3 to 3.5 kg)

DIET: Fruit, leaves, bark, grass

Lemurs communicate using vocalizations, body language, and scent. Ring-tailed lemurs set up "stink battles." They rub secretions from their scent glands into their tails and wave them at the opposition.

POTTOS,
LORISES, AND GALAGOS

Like the lemurs, the species in this grouping are considered primitive primates. Galagos and pottos are found in Africa. Lorises are found in Asia. All are small, arboreal primates with large, round eyes and dense fur. Galagos are known for their ability to leap—up to 39 feet (12 m)—from one branch to another. Lorises and pottos move deliberately from one branch to another and are excellent climbers. They can walk along the underside of a branch just as well as along the top.

Life spans for pottos, lorises, and galagos are up to 20 years.

WEST AFRICAN ○ ⊛
POTTO
Perodicticus potto

RANGE: Equatorial Africa
SIZE: 1.3 to 3.5 lb (0.6 to 1.6 kg)
DIET: Mostly fruit; also insects, snails, plant gums

Though they eat mostly fruit, pottos also hunt for insects. They use their excellent sense of smell to find them and their humanlike fingers to catch them. They tend to eat spiny or bad-smelling species like ants, beetles, caterpillars, millipedes, and spiders.

GREATER ● ⊛ 🐾
SLOW LORIS
Nycticebus coucang

RANGE: Sumatra, Malaysia, Thailand, Singapore
SIZE: 2.2 to 4.4 lb (1 to 2 kg)
DIET: Fruit, insects, birds, leaves

This loris moves slowly along branches and prefers to eat fruit. Like other lorises, it has skin glands on its forearms that produce an oily substance used to mark territory. This secretion is also toxic.

RED SLENDER ○ ⊛
LORIS
Loris tardigradus

RANGE: Sri Lanka
SIZE: 4.5 to 8 oz (128 to 227 g)
DIET: Insects and small animals, especially lizards and geckos

The slender loris and its relatives communicate with each other through a variety of whistles, hums, growls, and screams. They also use body language, facial expressions, huddling, grooming, and urine and scent marking.

SENEGAL ○ ⊛
GALAGO
Galago senegalensis

RANGE: Sub-Saharan Africa
SIZE: 3.3 to 10.6 oz (95 to 300 g)
DIET: Insects, birds, eggs, fruit, seeds, flowers, plant sap, tree gum

Galagos (guh-LAY-gohz) are known as bush babies because their alarm calls sound like human babies crying. These small primates hunt for grasshoppers, beetles, and other insects by listening with their large ears, which they can wrinkle and bend.

PRIMATES

Primates descend from species that once lived strictly in trees. Today, most live in or near forests, but many spend time on the ground, too.

A number of features shared by primates reflect their arboreal, or tree-living, history. All have binocular-style vision, with eyes that face forward and are protected by a bony rim, or orbit. They have opposable thumbs (except for colobus monkeys) and big toes, as well as very mobile upper arms—the result of a combination of a ball-and-socket shoulder joint with bones in the arms (radius and ulna) and legs (femur and tibia) that allow for rotation, and a clavicle, or collarbone. All primates have either a tail or the bones to support one. In humans, these bones are fused together and known as the coccyx, or tailbone; it is easily bruised! All primates communicate using gestures, body language, and vocalizations.

Primates are divided into two main groups: one that includes monkeys, apes, and tarsiers (sometimes called higher primates), and a second that includes lemurs, galagos, lorises, and pottos (sometimes called lower or prosimian primates). In both groups, many species are at risk of extinction due to loss of their habitat.

MONKEYS

OLD WORLD MONKEYS

The easiest way to identify a monkey as Old World (Africa, Asia, Europe) or New World (Americas) is to look at the shape of its nose and the length of its tail.

Old World monkeys have a downward-turned nose with large nostrils and short, or absent, tails. The males also have very long and sharp upper canines, which they use to display. In addition, the primates in this group have hard pads where they sit down, and males are often two to three times the size of females.

Most species in this group, which include baboons, mandrills, and macaques, are omnivores and have large cheek pouches that they use to store food. A few, like the colobus monkey and langur, eat mostly leaves.

All Old World monkeys are highly social and live either in large multi-male troops, or in harems with many females and a single breeding male. Life spans range up to 40 years.

RHESUS MONKEY
Macaca mulatta

RANGE: South, Central, and Southeast Asia

SIZE: 8.8 to 26.4 lb (4 to 12 kg)

DIET: Roots, herbs, fruit, insects, crops, small animals

This species has the widest geographic range (Asia) of any primate apart from humans. They are also highly social. Rhesus monkeys live in large groups of up to 200 and communicate with each other through body language, facial expressions, and calls.

OLIVE BABOON
Papio anubis

RANGE: Equatorial Africa

SIZE: 30 to 55 lb (13 to 25 kg)

DIET: Grasses, pods, seeds, fruit, roots, leaves, buds, bark, flowers, insects, meat

Olive baboons live in troops of related females and unrelated males. This is because female babies never leave, but males do. Before they reach adult size, young male baboons will join a different troop, working their way up the dominance ladder to gain breeding rights.

ANGOLAN COLOBUS
Colobus angolensis

RANGE: Central and East Africa

SIZE: 13 to 26 lb (6 to 12 kg)

DIET: Mainly leaves; also stems, bark, flowers, buds, shoots, fruit

Of all the African monkeys, the colobus is the most specialized for life in the trees. They eat mostly leaves, and lots of them—several pounds a day. Like cows, they have a complex stomach that allows them to digest plant fiber.

MANDRILL
Mandrillus sphinx

RANGE: Parts of central West Africa

SIZE: Up to 119 lb (54 kg)

DIET: Fruit, nuts, leaves, insects; small invertebrates and vertebrates

Compared to the female, the colors on the face of the male mandrill are much brighter. They also have a larger yellow beard. Their hard pads, where they sit down, are purple. Females are attracted to the more brightly colored males.

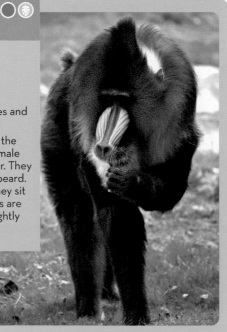

NEW WORLD MONKEYS

New World monkeys have flat, upturned noses and long tails. All are strictly arboreal. They include marmosets and tamarins, capuchin and squirrel monkeys, owl monkeys, titi and saki monkeys, and the species best known for their prehensile tails—howler monkeys and spider monkeys.

There is no single social organization common to this group. Squirrel monkeys are often found in very large groups of 100 or more, often traveling with several dozen capuchins and a small family group of saki monkeys. Marmosets and tamarins live in small family groups in which the younger members help raise the offspring. Spider monkeys have a social system similar to chimpanzees in which groups of males and females mix, split, and mix again. Howler monkeys live in family groups and move slowly among the treetops. Their distinctive calls are used to advertise their location to avoid conflict with other families.

Life spans for New World monkeys range from 15 to 25 years.

GOLDEN LION TAMARIN
Leontopithecus rosalia

RANGE: Brazil

SIZE: .75 to 1.5 lb (0.3 to 0.7 kg)

DIET: Fruit, plant sap, insects, lizards, small birds, bird eggs

Like all tamarins and marmosets, this species is tiny, active, and athletic. Golden lion tamarins move easily through dense rainforest, running along small branches and jumping among tangled vines. To meet their energy needs, they eat a high-calorie diet.

COTTON-TOP TAMARIN
Saguinus oedipus

RANGE: Northwest Colombia

SIZE: 9 to 13 oz (260 to 380 g)

DIET: Insects, fruit, sap; small reptiles and amphibians

Family life for this species is similar to that of other tamarins: The male raises the young with help from older offspring. What makes the cotton-top different is that twice a year the female gives birth to nonidentical twins. The babies ride around on the back of their father and older siblings.

SQUIRREL MONKEY
Saimiri sciureus

RANGE: South America

SIZE: 1.5 to 2 lb (0.7 to 0.9 kg)

DIET: Fruit; also leaves, seeds; some insects

The white fur around the eyes of the squirrel monkey makes it look as though it is wearing a mask. These monkeys prefer to move along the narrowest of branches—no wider than an inch (2.5 cm)—using their long tails for balance.

BLACK-AND-GOLD HOWLER
Alouatta caraya

RANGE: Central South America

SIZE: 8.8 to 22 lb (4 to 10 kg)

DIET: Leaves; some fruit, buds, flowers

Howlers live in family groups of five to 20 monkeys. They move slowly through the treetops, eating leaves as they go, using their prehensile tails like a fifth arm to hold on to branches. They come down only during the dry season to drink water.

RED-HANDED HOWLER
Alouatta belzebul

RANGE: Amazonian Brazil

SIZE: 10 to 17 lb (4.5 to 7.7 kg)

DIET: Leaves; sometimes tree bark or woody twigs; also fruit during rainy seasons

Howlers are the largest and loudest of the New World monkeys. They roar, bark, and grunt to keep track of one another and howl in unison—often before dawn. Their early morning chorus can be heard a mile (1.6 km) away.

APES AND TARSIERS

Apes are large primates with an upright or semi-upright stance capable of bipedalism—walking on two legs. All have flat nails on their fingers and toes. The lesser apes, siamangs and gibbons, have perfected the action of swinging through trees and have exceptionally long arms.

The great apes, which include gorillas, chimpanzees, orangutans, and bonobos, have flattened forearms and large brain cases. They are also our closest relatives. (For more, see "We Are Family" on the opposite page.)

Tarsiers are a very primitive species related to apes and monkeys. Today, they are found only in Asia, but their fossils—as much as 40 million years old—are found in North America, Europe, and North Africa.

Primate brains differ from those of other mammals in terms of how they process information. This is especially true among the great apes. More nerve cells, for example, are devoted to processing sight compared to smell. The front part of the brain—the cerebral cortex—is also larger in highly social primate species. Intelligence, thinking, planning, and communicating are among the many functions of the cerebrum.

Life spans for apes are from 35 to 60 years.

NORTHERN WHITE-CHEEKED GIBBON
Nomascus leucogenys

RANGE: Southeast Asia

SIZE: 10 to 13.2 lb (4.5 to 6 kg)

DIET: Pulp of fruit; also leaves, flowers, insects

The adult females of this species are cream-colored, and the males are black. As babies, they all look like females. Then, at two years of age, their fur changes, and they all begin to look like males. Their final coat color does not appear until they approach breeding age at six or seven years old.

CHIMPANZEE
Pan troglodytes

RANGE: Central Africa

SIZE: 50 to 175 lb (23 to 79 kg)

DIET: Plant material, including fruit, nuts, leaves, bark, shoots; also eggs and insects

Among the great apes, chimpanzees and bonobos have the most in common with humans. For example, both primates use tools. Chimps are more aggressive than bonobos, planning hunts or organizing attacks against their rivals.

SUMATRAN ORANGUTAN
Pongo abelii

RANGE: Sumatra

SIZE: 60 to 200 lb (27 to 91 kg)

DIET: Figs, leaves, flowers, bark, insects

Adult orangutans are solitary, except for females with their offspring. Juveniles stay with their mothers until they are nine or 10 years old. They spend some of this time learning how to survive, and the rest of it playing.

WHITE-HANDED GIBBON
Hylobates lar

RANGE: Southeast Asia

SIZE: 9.7 to 16.7 lb (4.4 to 7.6 kg)

DIET: Ripe leaves, buds, and fruit

Also known as lar gibbons, they live in small family groups made up of a male and female pair and their young. Like all gibbons, this species defends its territory by using loud calls. Males and females usually call out together.

PHILIPPINE TARSIER
Carlito syrichta

RANGE: Rainforests of the Philippines

SIZE: 3 to 6 oz (85 to 170 g)

DIET: Insects, spiders, lizards, small vertebrates

Tarsiers are nocturnal insectivores with huge eyes and excellent vision, as well as acute hearing. They also are specialized leapers. They use their long tails for balance and their long fingers and toes to grab on to branches.

BONOBO
Pan paniscus

RANGE: Democratic Republic of the Congo, Congo Basin

SIZE: 59 to 134 lb (27 to 61 kg)

DIET: Mostly fruit; also nuts, stems, shoots, leaves, roots, tubers, flowers

Compared to the chimpanzee, bonobos have darker skin and longer hair. They are more likely to walk on two legs, and they are much less aggressive toward each other. Instead of fighting, bonobos groom and mate with each other.

WE ARE FAMILY

The great apes, with their expressive eyes, playful attitudes, and intelligent behavior, seem like not-too-distant cousins of humans. As it turns out, that's exactly what they are. We belong to the same family, called Hominidae. Scientific research shows that humans and great apes are descended from a common ancestor, one that lived about 14 million years ago. And that we share 98 percent of our DNA. It's no wonder that great apes can learn, express emotion, and even reason like humans. So, does all this mean that in some prehistoric time your ancestor was a chimpanzee? Not exactly. Within the hominid family, humans, chimps, and bonobos are the most closely related. But the connection is still pretty distant. Our common ancestor was a chimp-like ape that lived six to eight million years ago.

BORNEAN ORANGUTAN
Pongo pygmaeus

RANGE: Borneo

SIZE: 60 to 200 lb (27 to 91 kg)

DIET: Mainly fruit; also leaves, seeds, young birds, eggs

Orangutans rarely leave the trees. Their legs are weak and short compared to their long, strong arms. They swing from one limb to the next, or use their huge hands to pull themselves along the length of the branches.

EASTERN MOUNTAIN GORILLA
Gorilla beringei beringei

RANGE: Virunga volcanoes, Rwanda; Uganda, Democratic Republic of the Congo, central Africa

SIZE: 130 to 400 lb (59 to 181 kg)

DIET: Roots, leaves, stems, vines, shrubs, bamboo

Compared to western lowland gorillas, eastern mountain gorillas have stockier bodies and shorter arms for climbing, longer fur for keeping warm, and larger jaws for crushing bamboo and other plants. Their behavior is different, too. Mountain gorilla groups often include several breeding males.

SIAMANG
Symphalangus syndactylus

RANGE: Sumatra and mountains of the Malay Peninsula

SIZE: 20 to 30 lb (9 to 14 kg)

DIET: Fruit, especially figs; also flowers, leaves, shoots, some insects, bird eggs

Siamangs mate for life and live in pairs. Both males and females have large throat sacs used to amplify their calls. They sing a duet to mark their territory, a song that starts with a series of hoots and ends in a whooping noise.

MOUNTAIN GORILLA

The mountain gorillas (*Gorilla beringei beringei*) that I study live in Bwindi Impenetrable National Park, in southwestern Uganda. When I first arrived there in 1994 to conduct one month's research on gorilla parasites and bacteria, I developed a nasty cold and was not allowed to track the gorillas until I got better. This made me realize how important it was to not pass on human diseases to the critically endangered mountain gorillas.

In 1996, three years after gorilla tourism had begun at Bwindi, I was hired as the first full-time veterinarian for Uganda Wildlife Authority. I led a team to investigate the first scabies skin disease outbreak in mountain gorillas. Most of the infected gorillas recovered, but only after being treated with an antiparasitic medicine.

We traced the fatal disease back to the human communities around the park. People had put out scarecrows to keep gorillas and other wildlife away from their gardens. They dressed the scarecrows in their dirtiest clothing, which had scabies mites on it. When the gorillas touched the clothing, the mites spread to them.

Since then, we have worked hard to help people coexist with gorillas and other wildlife. Gorillas are falling sick less often, and people are more positive about the gorillas and conserving their habitat. For example, when an aging silverback gorilla, Ruhondeza, decided to settle on community land because he was too old to keep up with the rest of his family, we worked with the local people. We helped them understand the gorilla so they would tolerate it when he took a few bananas and coffee berries from them. When he died, they all came to pay their last respects.

Gorillas are so similar to us. We share 98.4 percent of the same genetic material. We learn a lot from them that we can apply to our lives. By studying them, we gain a greater understanding of them and their needs and are better able to protect them.

RANGE OF THE
GORILLA BERINGEI BERINGEI
(MOUNTAIN GORILLA)

0   300 miles
0   300 kilometers

Lake Turkana

Lake Albert

Lake Edward

Lake Victoria

Lake Kivu

Lake Tanganyika

AFRICA

INDIAN OCEAN

Lake Mweru

Lake Nyasa

OBSERVATION TIPS

1 Make sure you're healthy. Humans can easily pass illnesses on to gorillas.

2 Stay at least 23 feet (7 m) away so you can observe their natural behaviors.

3 Don't talk loudly or use a flash on your camera. Both disrupt the gorillas.

4 Go with a local guide and pay attention. The guide will help you get the best views while also keeping you and the gorillas safe.

Gladys Kalema-Zikusoka is a wildlife veterinarian and conservationist. Her award-winning organization, Conservation Through Public Health (CTPH), helps people, gorillas, and other wildlife coexist by improving animal health, human health, and community livelihoods. The program has become a model for communities located near other protected areas in Africa.

Mountain gorillas live in family groups, called troops, that are led by one dominant male silverback. A troop can have up to 30 members, consisting of younger males, females, and babies. Females usually have one baby every four years. Newborns are very weak and only weigh about four pounds (1.8 kg). They depend on their mothers for everything—they nurse on her milk and she carries them everywhere. After about three years, the babies start to eat plants and fruit with the adults. Like human children, they love to play. They climb, tumble, swing from branches, and play chase. At night, they snuggle in a nest with their mothers.

95

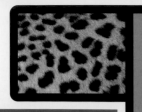

RECORDS

What mammal can paralyze a victim with its deadly venom? Which has a wingspan shorter than an unsharpened pencil? Want to find out? Then check out these mystifying record holders of the mammal world!

MOST RECORDS

Blue Whale

Balaenoptera musculus

If the animal kingdom held Olympic Games, the blue whale would swim away with the gold medal for the most gold medals. At 80 feet (24 m) long and weighing up to 418,502 pounds (190,000 kg), this massive mammal is not only the largest and heaviest animal on the planet, it boasts a few other titles, too:

Whoa, Baby! A newborn blue whale calf is the largest baby in the world: 26 feet (7.9 m) long and 4,000 to 6,000 pounds in weight (1,814 to 2,722 kg).

Loudest Blue whales communicate in deep hums and bellows that can reach 188 decibels—40 decibels louder than a jet engine.

Biggest Appetite Blue whales eat up to 11,000 pounds (4,990 kg) of krill each day, roughly the weight of an African elephant.

BIGGEST LAND ANIMAL

African Savanna Elephant

Loxodonta africana africana

Blue whales may own the seas, but on land, elephants rule. Standing up to 13 feet (4 m) tall at the shoulder and weighing as much as 13,500 pounds (6,100 kg), the African savanna elephant is the largest land animal in the world. Fortunately for other animals, these powerful pachyderms are vegetarians, eating up to 300 pounds (136 kg) of tree bark, fruit, leaves, and grasses each day.

SMALLEST MAMMAL

Bumblebee Bat

Craseonycteris thonglongyai

These itty-bitty bats—about the size of a bumblebee—have a wingspan 6.7 inches (1.7 cm) wide and weigh .07 ounce (2 g). They are the tiniest known mammals on Earth. At dawn and dusk, they emerge from limestone caves for about 20 to 30 minutes to hunt for small insects, which they catch while flying.

FASTEST RUNNER

Cheetah

Acinonyx jubatus

Now, here's a contest about which there's no debate. When it comes to fastest runner, the cheetah has this competition locked up. Able to go from 0 to 60 miles an hour (96 km/h) in just three seconds, these powerful cats are built for quick acceleration and short-distance sprinting. With physical features like a flexible spine, long legs, and a sturdy tail for balance, cheetahs win this race hands (or paws) down.

SLOWEST

Sloth

Bradypus variegatus
(three-toed sloth)

Just like a cheetah's built for speed, two- and three-toed sloths are built for, well, no speed. These mammals move a mere six to eight feet (1.8 to 2.4 m) a minute. Because sloths would be easy prey for any predator on the rainforest floor, they spend their entire lives hanging in trees, rarely ever moving to the ground.

LONGEST TONGUE

Giant Anteater

Myrmecophaga tridactyla

Boasting the longest and perhaps most useful tongue in the animal kingdom, the giant anteater's tongue can extend two feet (0.6 m) beyond its mouth. Good thing, too. Measuring more than six feet (1.8 m) in length, these medium-size mammals slurp up about 30,000 ants per day to get their fill.

MOST POISONOUS MAMMAL

Platypus

Ornithorhynchus anatinus

When it comes to venom, there is no shortage of deadly toxins in the animal kingdom. One animal takes the cake among mammals, however. The male platypus, despite its innocent appearance, actually has a venom-producing gland in its rear leg, connected to a sharp, pointy spur on the inside of its ankle. Victims as large as dingos (feral dogs) will be dead in minutes if this paralyzing predator strikes.

TALLEST

It may not be the largest animal on Earth, but standing a staggering 19 feet (5.8 m) tall, the giraffe is certainly the tallest. With a neck alone measuring more than seven feet (2.1 m), these skyscrapers of the savanna use their height to great advantage—they can reach the leaves at the tops of trees that shorter herbivores can't.

Giraffe

Giraffa camelopardalis

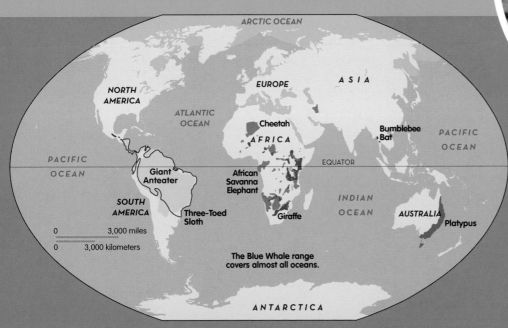

The Blue Whale range covers almost all oceans.

RANGES OF RECORD-SETTING MAMMALS

- Blue Whale
- African Savanna Elephant
- Bumblebee Bat
- Cheetah
- Three-Toed Sloth
- Giant Anteater
- Platypus
- Giraffe

Want to know where these record-holding mammals live around the world? Take a look at this range map to find out.

97

Feathers are a defining characteristic of all birds. They can vary in size and shape, and they help with many functions, such as warmth, flight, and courtship. The hyacinth macaw, the largest parrot in the world, is recognizable by its bright blue plumage as it soars through its South American home.

BIRDS

KING PENGUINS

WILLOW PTARMIGAN

COMMON KINGFISHER

SCARLET MACAW

SOUTHERN
WHITE-FACED OWL

MALLARD DUCKLING

RHODE ISLAND RED CHICKEN

YELLOW BITTERN

RED-FOOTED BOOBY

BALD EAGLE

PILEATED
WOODPECKER

SANDHILL CRANE

AMERICAN ROBINS

BARNACLE GEESE

KEEL-BILLED TOUCAN

101

WHAT IS A BIRD?

BIRDS ARE VERTEBRATE ANIMALS ADAPTED FOR FLIGHT.

Many can also run, jump, swim, and dive. Some, like penguins, have lost the ability to fly but retained their wings. Birds are found worldwide and in all habitats. The largest is the nine-foot (2.7-m)-tall ostrich. The smallest is the two-inch (5-cm)-long bee hummingbird. Everything about the anatomy of a bird reflects its ability to fly. The wings, for example, are shaped to create lift. The leading edge is thicker than the back edge, and they are covered in feathers that narrow to a point. Airplane wings are modeled after bird wings.

The bones and muscles of the wing are also highly specialized. The main bone, the humerus, which is similar to the upper arm of a mammal, is hollow instead of solid. It also connects to the bird's air sac system, which, in turn, connects to its lungs. The powerful flight muscles of the shoulder attach to the keel, a special ridge of bone that runs down the center of the wide sternum, or breastbone. The tail feathers are used for steering.

Birds have a unique digestive system that allows them to eat when they can and digest later. They use their beaks to grab and swallow food. Even the way a bird reproduces is related to flight. Instead of carrying the extra weight of developing young inside their bodies, they lay eggs and incubate them in a nest.

The fossil record shows that birds evolved alongside the dinosaurs during the Jurassic period 160 million years ago. The best known fossil bird is *Archaeopteryx*, which was about the size of a crow.

CLASSIFICATION OF **BIRDS**

There are about 10,700 bird species organized into 41 orders. The largest is the order Passeriformes, known as the perching birds. Of the 36 orders, the most familiar groupings are:

1 DUCK, GEESE, AND SWANS **(Anseriformes)**

2 CHICKENS AND RELATIVES **(Galliformes)**

3 PENGUINS **(Sphenisciformes)**

4 EAGLES, FALCONS, HAWKS, AND OWLS **(Falconiformes, Accipitriformes, and Strigiformes)**

5 PARROTS **(Psittaciformes)**

6 PERCHING BIRDS **(Passeriformes)**

BIRD TRAITS

Anatomical features found in birds but not in other vertebrates include feathers, air-filled bones, a keel, a crop (most species), and a gizzard.

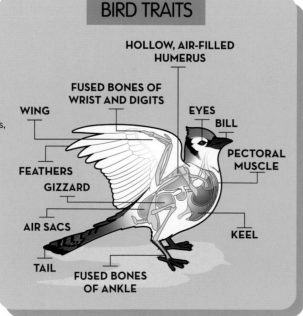

HOLLOW, AIR-FILLED HUMERUS

FUSED BONES OF WRIST AND DIGITS

WING

EYES

BILL

PECTORAL MUSCLE

FEATHERS

GIZZARD

AIR SACS

KEEL

TAIL

FUSED BONES OF ANKLE

Did you know? Birds are the only animals that have feathers.

Female robins weave nests made out of twigs, grass, feathers, and mud. Inside, soft grasses cushion delicate eggs. Males and females work together to raise their young.

EAGLES, FALCONS, HAWKS, AND OWLS

Eagles, falcons, hawks, and owls are top predators that hunt from the air. All are strong fliers with excellent vision, a hooked beak, powerful feet, and sharp nails known as talons. Because of their hunting style, they are known both as birds of prey and as raptors, from the Latin word *rapere*, which means "to take by force."

Eagles can spot their prey from a mile (1.6 km) or more away. Owls, which also have excellent hearing and soft, quiet feathers, hunt at night. Buzzards and kestrels hover over their prey. Hawks are ambush hunters, like cats. Falcons dive or swoop through the air.

Many birds of prey have dietary preferences, too. Ospreys eat only live fish, honey buzzards eat wasps, peregrine falcons eat other birds, and secretary birds eat snakes. Vultures and condors prefer dead animals, known as carrion.

There is also quite a range in the size of birds in this group. The smallest, the falconet, is about the size of a sparrow. The largest is the condor, which has a 10-foot (3.2-m) wingspan. Life spans vary from 20 years for smaller species to 60 years for larger ones.

AMERICAN BALD EAGLE
Haliaeetus leucocephalus

RANGE: North America, including northern Mexico

SIZE: 27.6 to 37.2 in (70 to 95 cm)

DIET: Fish, reptiles, amphibians, mammals, carrion

Bald eagles are large, powerful, aggressive birds known for stealing food—even garbage—from others. They are named for their bright white feathers. In animals, "bald" means "an area marked with white."

SAKER FALCON
Falco cherrug

RANGE: Eastern Europe, Central Asia, parts of Africa

SIZE: 17.7 to 21.7 in (45 to 55 cm)

DIET: Mostly small mammals and birds

The saker falcon is known for hunting its prey while flying close to the ground. It will pursue prey as small as a lizard and as large as a gazelle. Like other falcons, sakers have curved talons that they use to grasp their prey.

ANDEAN CONDOR
Vultur gryphus

RANGE: Western South America throughout the Andes

SIZE: 39.4 to 50.4 in (100 to 120 cm)

DIET: Carrion

Unlike most other birds of prey, Andean condor males are larger than females and have a colorful face. They have fleshy red tissue at the base of their beak similar to a male rooster—the top piece is a comb, the bottom is a wattle.

LAPPET-FACED VULTURE
Torgos tracheliotos

RANGE: Africa

SIZE: 31 to 45 in (78 to 115 cm)

DIET: Mostly carrion; also small reptiles, fish, birds, mammals

The lappet-faced vulture, like other condors and vultures, is bald for a reason: to keep clean. These birds splatter blood on their faces as they tear into their meals. Vultures have a strong digestive system that allows them to eat bacteria-covered prey without getting sick.

RED-TAILED HAWK
Buteo jamaicensis

RANGE: North and Central America

SIZE: 17.7 to 25.5 in (45 to 65 cm)

DIET: Rodents, reptiles, birds

Red-tailed hawks hunt from a carefully chosen perch, usually a tree branch, fence post, or telephone pole located along the edge of an open field. They dive with their legs stretched behind them and their wings open.

SNOWY OWL
Bubo scandiacus

RANGE: Northern North America

SIZE: 20.5 to 28 in (52 to 71 cm)

DIET: Small mammals, birds, fish

Snowy owls are the heaviest owls found in North America not just because of their size, but also because of their heavy, thick, insulating feathers. These owls live mostly in the Arctic tundra. Only some individuals fly south in winter.

GALÁPAGOS HAWK
Buteo galapagoensis

RANGE: Galápagos Islands

SIZE: 21.5 in (55 cm)

DIET: Lizards, rats, doves, centipedes, both land and marine iguanas, boobies, grasshoppers, carrion

Galápagos hawks hunt together in groups of two or three either for live prey or for a carcass. The dominant hawk gets to eat first. These days, their diet includes several introduced species, such as chickens and rats.

BURROWING OWL
Athene cunicularia

RANGE: North and South America

SIZE: 8.5 to 11 in (21.6 to 27.9 cm)

DIET: Insects, frogs, small mammals

These owls often will nest in holes in the ground dug by other animals, including prairie dogs and skunks. In addition to small mammals, the burrowing owl eats a wide variety of insects, including scorpions and dung beetles.

Did you know?

The California condor is the largest flying bird in North America.

GREAT HORNED OWL
Bubo virginianus

RANGE: North and South America

SIZE: 18 to 25 in (45.7 to 63.5 cm)

DIET: Mammals and birds

This owl is named for the feather tufts above its ears that look like horns. Its hooting call sounds like *whoo, whoo-hoo, whoo, whoo.* When a male hoots to establish his breeding territory, a female will often respond.

CALIFORNIA CONDOR
Gymnogyps californianus

RANGE: Western United States

SIZE: 45.6 to 51.6 in (110 to 130 cm)

DIET: Carrion

The California condor can soar for miles without flapping its wings. It is nearly extinct because it scavenges on animals shot by hunters with lead bullets and on garbage. Plastic, lead, and other metals are toxic to these birds.

Washington Wachira

CROWNED EAGLE

Birds of prey are very charismatic and full of character. To me, they are as exciting as the predator species of the mammal world—tigers, lions, leopards, and jaguars. There is never a dull moment watching them.

For many years, I have studied crowned eagles (*Stephanoaetus coronatus*), which are found only in sub-Saharan Africa. Although these majestic birds have a wingspan stretching more than five feet (1.5 m) wide, they aren't the biggest eagles in Africa. But they are the most powerful. A crowned eagle can use its long talons to capture everything from antelopes and monkeys to large birds and reptiles. It can on occasion kill prey weighing more than 45 pounds (20 kg).

Studying eagles is a lifestyle that leads to many tough days in the field, sitting and walking in the hot equatorial sun. Some days I spend long hours searching for eagles in the forest without success. Over time, I have learned many bird calls, and I often use them to detect where eagles are if they are calling.

Photography, which started as a hobby for me when I was in high school, has also become an important part of my work. I photograph chicks from the day they hatch to the day they leave the nest. This has helped me get to know the eagles as individuals. When I see an eagle again, I am able to tell which nest and territory it belongs to, how old it is, and even whether it's male or female.

Nairobi, where most of my work is focused, is a big success story for crowned eagles. With more than three million people, the city is transforming rapidly. This could be a problem for crowned eagles, which require a large area for their territory. But through my project, I have been able to increase community awareness of crowned eagles and their habitats. The scientific knowledge that I provide has helped guide decisions on where to build roads, railroads, and industries. Most important, my study has helped increase people's love toward the crowned eagle, and certainly, we humans always tend to protect and care for that which we know and love.

WACHIRA WITH A VERREAUX'S EAGLE-OWL

RANGE OF THE
*STEPHANOAETUS
CORONATUS*
(CROWNED EAGLE)

EUROPE

ASIA

AFRICA

INDIAN
OCEAN

ATLANTIC
OCEAN

0   1,000 miles
0   1,000 kilometers

OBSERVATION TIPS

1 The best time to observe crowned eagles is when they are breeding. Look for nests in tall trees along rivers.

2 Watch the nests at dusk and dawn. That's when most eagles are in their nests.

3 Be patient. Crowned eagles don't spend their days being super active.

4 Pay attention to details. Small details can lead to very interesting discoveries that help you understand crowned eagles.

Washington Wachira is a naturalist, award-winning photographer, and one of East Africa's top birders. He's studying the urban ecology of the crowned eagle. His work has attracted local and international conservationists, and he regularly spends time in the forest showing visitors these beautiful eagles and other birds of prey.

Crowned eagles mate for life. Pairs build a huge nest—up to eight feet (2.4 m) wide and 10 feet (3 m) deep—high up in a tall tree. In East Africa, females lay one or two eggs every two years. Females in South African populations may lay eggs each year. If both eggs hatch, the stronger chick kills the weaker one. Most times, the father brings food and the mother protects the surviving hatchling in the nest. After about two months, the down-covered chick's flight feathers start to appear and it hops and flaps its wings to strengthen its flight muscles. The fledgling takes its first flight at about four months, but it still needs its parent for up to a year while it learns to hunt for itself.

DUCKS,
GEESE, AND SWANS

Ducks, geese, and swans have streamlined bodies and webbed feet for swimming, thick feathers for warmth, and short, powerful wings for flying. They live in both freshwater and saltwater habitats. Many migrate long distances between their summer breeding grounds and where they spend the winter.

Many are vegetarians. They have wide, flat beaks for feeding on aquatic plants or grazing on grass. The diving ducks are the exception. Mergansers, for example, have narrow beaks with teethlike edges to grasp slippery fish.

Preening is especially important for birds that live in the water. This behavior involves using the beak to spread an oily substance, secreted by a gland located above the base of the tail, throughout the feathers. The oil creates a waterproof surface, like a raincoat.

Taking too much time to preen can be risky, though. Ducks and their eggs, in particular, are the favorite food of foxes, snakes, owls, crows, and humans. Escape is an option, except for the time of year when these birds lose their flight feathers, known as the annual molt. Growing up very quickly helps, too. Chicks hatch with downy feathers and can walk or swim with their parents within hours. Though they can live up to 30 years, the average life span is shorter because of predation.

SWAN GOOSE
Anser cygnoides

RANGE: Russia, Mongolia, China

SIZE: 32.4 to 37.2 in (80 to 90 cm)

DIET: Plants and snails and other pond life

Some domesticated geese are descendants of the Chinese, or swan, goose, the males of which have a knob at the base of their upper bill. This species is easily identified by its black bill and orange legs and feet.

CANADA GOOSE
Branta canadensis

RANGE: North America

SIZE: 30 to 43.2 in (76 to 110 cm)

DIET: Grasses, insects, snails, aquatic plants, seeds, berries

Some populations of Canada geese fly south during winter to find food, whereas others have no need to migrate. Parks and golf courses, for example, provide plenty of grass. Geese also feed on crop grains like wheat and barley.

INSIDE A BIRD'S NEST

WOOD DUCK NEST

MADE OF FEATHERS

WEAVER SPARROW NEST

MADE OF GRASSES

Bird nests differ from one species to the next, and each nest has its own style of architecture—including location, materials, and shape. For example, wood ducks nest in hollow tree cavities lined with feathers. Pairs of yellow weavers collect grasses and twigs and weave them together to create an apartment complex of hanging basketlike nests.

AMERICAN WOOD DUCK
Aix sponsa

RANGE: Much of North America, but most common in southern states

SIZE: 18.5 to 21.3 in (47 to 54 cm)

DIET: Seeds, insects, arthropods; sometimes nuts and grain

Wood ducks are named because of where they like to nest: in tree holes in wooded swamps. Their short wings help them fly among the trees with ease. These ducks are omnivores, meaning they eat both plant and animal foods.

HOODED MERGANSER
Lophodytes cucullatus

RANGE: North America

SIZE: 15.8 to 19.2 in (40 to 49 cm)

DIET: Aquatic insects and fish

Like wood ducks, hooded mergansers nest in wooded swamps and ponds. Their feeding habits are different, though: They are fish-eaters that dive for their food. During winter, they fly south only as far as needed to find ice-free ponds, lakes, and rivers.

SNOW GOOSE
Anser caerulescens

RANGE: North America

SIZE: 27.6 in (70 cm)

DIET: Aquatic vegetation and wild rice

Some snow geese migrate from the Gulf of Mexico in winter to the Arctic tundra in spring, and back again in the fall. Hundreds of thousands stop to rest along the way. From a distance, their huge flocks look like snow.

AUSTRALIAN SHELDUCK
Tadorna tadornoides

RANGE: Eastern Australia, Tasmania

SIZE: Up to 27.6 in (70 cm)

DIET: Green grass, insects, algae, mollusks

Ducks and geese make a wide range of sounds, in addition to the familiar *quack, quack* and *honk, honk*. The sounds are unique to each species. The Australian shelduck, for example, is known for being very noisy when it flies.

BLACK-NECKED SWAN
Cygnus melancoryphus

RANGE: South coastal and inland lakes of South America

SIZE: 39.6 to 48 in (100 to 120 cm)

DIET: Aquatic vegetation

Both male and female black-necked swans have a distinctive upper bill. Where the beak meets the skin under the eyes, there is a bright red, two-lobed knob known either as a comb or caruncle (CAR-uncle). This species also has pink legs.

SMEW
Mergellus albellus

RANGE: Northern taiga of Europe and Asia

SIZE: 20 to 25.2 in (51 to 64 cm)

DIET: Aquatic insects and fish

With their compact bodies and hooked upper bills, smew (a type of merganser) are expert divers and fishers. Like many ducks, the male and female have very different coloration. Males are white with distinctive black lines. Females are gray with a brown head crest.

HARLEQUIN DUCK
Histrionicus histrionicus

RANGE: Coastal parts of northeastern and northwestern North America, Greenland, Iceland, Russia

SIZE: 14 to 20 in (35.6 to 50.8 cm)

DIET: Aquatic insects and fish; crabs and mollusks

These ducks find their food by dabbling, swimming, and diving. They also have dense feathers that make them very buoyant. This versatile duck spends the winter on rocky coasts by the ocean, and the breeding season near freshwater.

GULLS, PUFFINS,
AND SANDPIPERS

All of the birds in this group feed in, or near, water. Some, like terns and puffins, live in marine environments. Others, like the pheasant-tailed jacana, are freshwater species. All eat other animals, with one exception: the seedsnipe.

Each species has a different hunting strategy, however. Gulls, for example, are opportunistic feeders. They eat everything from human garbage to fish, eggs, clams, small birds, and mammals. To feed, they use their strong beak to grab their prey and their hooked upper beak to tear it apart. Jacanas, by comparison, walk on floating plants—like the leaves of water lilies—and use their short, narrow beak to probe for insects and seeds. The American avocet, a long-legged bird, wades in shallow water and sweeps its long beak back and forth through the water, picking up tiny bits of food.

Life spans range from five years for smaller species to 30 years for puffins, and up to 50 years for herring gulls.

RING-BILLED GULL
Larus delawarensis

RANGE: North America

SIZE: 16.9 to 21.3 in (43 to 54 cm)

DIET: Fish, insects, small mammals, grain

Like all gulls, the ring-billed gull is a strong, acrobatic flier. This species is very common in urban and agricultural areas across North America because of its opportunistic diet. It also nests inland, near freshwater.

ATLANTIC PUFFIN
Fratercula arctica

RANGE: North Atlantic

SIZE: 11.5 to 13.5 in (29.2 to 34.3 cm)

DIET: Fish, mollusks, crustaceans

Atlantic puffins use their short, wide wings for swimming underwater to catch fish, as well as for flying. They cannot take off without a running start. During the breeding season, the puffin's bill turns bright yellow, blue, and orange.

RUDDY TURNSTONE
Arenaria interpres

RANGE: Breeds in Arctic, migrates worldwide

SIZE: 6.3 in (16 cm)

DIET: Insects and marine invertebrates

This sandpiper relative is named for the way it feeds. It has a short, flat, wide bill that it uses to poke under rocks and sticks. Then it flips them over, looking for insects to eat.

BIRD-BRAINED

Birds have amazing adaptations that help them with their everyday chores. Some species, like the macaw, have strong beaks with which to crack open nuts. Others, like the toucan, have long beaks that allow them to pluck fruit from the end of a branch. But for some birds, adaptation just isn't enough; they make their own tools to help them survive. For example, crows on the island of New Caledonia have been seen using their beaks as scissors to create hooks out of twigs. They then stick the hooks down into a tree trunk to fish out whatever they cannot reach with their beaks. Even gulls, generally considered a nuisance to beachgoers, have been observed using tools. And the lesser black-backed gull is known to throw bread into the water to lure fish to the surface!

BLACK SKIMMER
Rynchops niger

RANGE: Atlantic coast and southern Pacific coast of North America, the Caribbean, and most of South America

SIZE: 15.7 to 19.7 in (40 to 50 cm)

DIET: Mostly small fish

Skimmers fish by flying with their long, wide lower bills just under the water's surface. They are also a very social species and warn each other of predators. Their warning call sounds like a barking dog.

INCA TERN
Larosterna inca

RANGE: Chile and Peru

SIZE: 16 in (41 cm)

DIET: Small fish

Inca terns catch small fish using their spear-like beaks, either from the air in a plunge dive, or from the surface of the water while swimming. Like many seabirds, they live in large colonies. Their call sounds like a cat's meow.

COMMON MURRE
Uria aalge

RANGE: Coastlines and islands in the Northern Hemisphere

SIZE: 15 to 16.9 in (38 to 43 cm)

DIET: Fish and other marine vertebrates

This seabird is penguin-like. It dives to fish, has a white underside for camouflage in the water, stands up to walk, and nests in colonies. The male and female in a pair alternate duties incubating a single egg.

Did you know? Atlantic puffins nest at the same place each year.

PHEASANT-TAILED JACANA
Hydrophasianus chirurgus

RANGE: India, Southeast Asia, Indonesia

SIZE: 5.5 to 9.8 in (14 to 25 cm); tail: 9.8 to 13.8 in (25 to 35 cm)

DIET: Insects, invertebrates, some vegetation

Jacanas live among floating leaves, such as water lilies. Using their huge feet, they walk, run, and hop from one leaf to another. Male jacanas build nests and raise the young, while females defend them.

SEMIPALMATED SANDPIPER
Calidris pusilla

RANGE: Central and eastern North America, northern South America

SIZE: 5.9 in (15 cm)

DIET: Insects

The term "palmated" means "webbed." This sandpiper has partially webbed toes, an adaptation for life near water. This small bird breeds in the open tundra during summer and migrates in large numbers to the coast of northern South America in winter.

SNOWY PLOVER
Charadrius nivosus

RANGE: West and Gulf Coasts of United States to South America

SIZE: 5.9 to 6.7 in (15 to 17 cm)

DIET: Insects and other invertebrates

Snowy plovers breed only on sandy beaches and brackish inland lakes, places where there are a lot of people and housing developments. This tiny bird makes a small, shallow, difficult-to-see nest in the sand.

ALBATROSSES,
PELICANS, AND RELATIVES

Fish—both freshwater and marine—are central to the diets of many birds, especially those that rarely stray far from open waters. These include ocean birds that spend very little time on land, like albatrosses, petrels, shearwaters, boobies, tropicbirds, and some species of pelicans.

What and how these birds hunt is evident in the shape and size of their bodies, beaks, and feet. Pelicans are large birds with four webbed toes and a throat pouch. They scoop up their meals. Albatrosses are gull-like birds with very long wings. They fish on the fly, grabbing squid from just beneath the surface of the water with their hooked beaks. The giant petrel has a huge beak, which it uses to feed on seal, penguin, and whale carcasses. Gannets straighten their bodies like an arrow and plunge-dive into the water; if they catch a fish, they swallow it instantly. They fish primarily for schooling fish like mackerel and herring, often following dolphins and bluefish feeding in the same area. Frigatebirds either skim the water for fish or steal from others.

The larger seabirds have long life spans, up to 30 years for pelicans and 50 or more for the wandering albatross.

BULLER'S ALBATROSS
Thalassarche bulleri

RANGE: Islands off New Zealand, and wanders widely

SIZE: 31.2 in (80 cm)

DIET: Fish, squid, tunicates, crustaceans

This albatross, like others, has tube-shaped nostrils located on either side of its hooked bill and an excellent sense of smell. Like most seabirds, it also has glands that remove excess salt from its body.

BROWN PELICAN
Pelecanus occidentalis

RANGE: Atlantic and Pacific coasts of the Americas, from central U.S. to Venezuela, including the Gulf Coast, parts of the Caribbean

SIZE: 39.4 to 53.9 in (100 to 137 cm)

DIET: Mainly fish

Pelicans are large birds, but they weigh relatively little. The reason: pockets of air under the skin and in their bones. All that air makes it easier for them to fly, float, and surface after a dive.

NORTHERN GANNET
Morus bassanus

RANGE: Atlantic coast of North America and northern Europe, including Quebec, Newfoundland, and Scotland

SIZE: 31.2 to 43.2 in (80 to 110 cm)

DIET: Mainly fish; some squid

Gannets nest along cliffs and ledges in large, dense colonies. The female lays just one egg, though if it is lost or damaged, she will lay another. Similar to penguins, the parents alternate incubating, protecting, and feeding the young.

SNOW PETREL
Pagodroma nivea

RANGE: Antarctica

SIZE: 14 to 16 in (36 to 41 cm)

DIET: Mainly krill; also fish, mollusks, carrion

Snow petrels, about the size of a pigeon, breed only in Antarctica and live as far south as the South Pole. Their soft white feathers help them withstand the extreme cold. These birds squirt a smelly oil to keep intruders from their nests.

MAGNIFICENT FRIGATEBIRD
Fregata magnificens

RANGE: Tropical coasts of the Americas, Cape Verde Islands, Galápagos Islands

SIZE: 34.8 to 44.4 in (90 to 113 cm)

DIET: Fish, squid, crabs

Frigatebirds spend most of their lives in flight, gliding on their long, wide wings. During the breeding season, the male inflates his bright red throat pouch, called a gular (GOO-lar) sac, and makes a drumming sound to attract females.

BLUE-FOOTED BOOBY
Sula nebouxii

RANGE: Pacific coast of the Americas from California, U.S.A., to Galápagos Islands

SIZE: 31.2 in (80 cm)

DIET: Fish

The male blue-footed booby does a dance with his colorful, oversize—and otherwise clumsy—feet to attract a female. Once bonded, the pair use their feet for another purpose: to incubate their eggs and protect their chicks.

AMERICAN WHITE PELICAN
Pelecanus erythrorhynchos

RANGE: North America; winters along Atlantic and Pacific coasts, including Gulf Coast; breeds inland on lakes in northern Great Plains and western mountains

SIZE: 48 to 66 in (120 to 160 cm)

DIET: Fish

The pelican's lower bill is unique among birds. Instead of firm beak tissue, a soft, expandable throat pouch connects the two lower jawbones. This pouch, or gular (GOO-lar) sac, is used like a basket to scoop up fish.

BIRDS

WHITE-BREASTED CORMORANT
Phalacrocorax carbo lucidus

RANGE: Sub-Saharan Africa

SIZE: 33.1 to 35.4 in (84 to 90 cm)

DIET: Fish and eels

Instead of oiling their feathers to repel water, cormorants allow them to get wet. This allows them to dive more easily. The trade-off: After a meal, the cormorant cannot fly again until it holds its wings out to dry.

NORTHERN FULMAR
Fulmarus glacialis

RANGE: Northern oceans

SIZE: 15.4 to 19.7 in (39 to 50 cm)

DIET: Fish, squid, zooplankton

Northern fulmars live mostly in the open ocean, though they nest on rocky cliffs close to the shore. They are one of the longest-living species of birds, with recorded life spans in the wild of more than 50 years.

ANHINGA
Anhinga anhinga

RANGE: Southern U.S., Central America, and much of South America

SIZE: 33.6 in (90 cm)

DIET: Fish

Anhingas are called snakebirds because they swim with their long neck and head just above water. They use their daggerlike bill to spear fish underwater.

HERONS, FLAMINGOS, AND RELATIVES

Herons and their relatives—storks, egrets, ibises, and spoonbills—and the five species of flamingos are found in wetlands, waterways, and ponds.

These birds often are referred to as wading birds because of their hunting strategy. Most stand or walk in shallow water to feed. They have long legs and long necks so their beaks can reach the water.

Beak styles vary with diet. Herons, for example, are spear fishers. They have long, sharp beaks, which they use to pierce fish and frogs. Shoebills catch similar prey, but they do so by scooping it out of the mud. Cattle egrets have short, sharp beaks for catching insects and other invertebrates disturbed by larger animals, like cows. Flamingos use an entirely different approach. They are filter feeders. To make this work, though, they have to hold their head upside down with their beak underwater. Life spans for the birds in this group range up to 25 years.

GREAT BLUE HERON
Ardea herodias

RANGE: North and Central America, Caribbean, northern South America

SIZE: 39.4 to 51.2 in (100 to 130 cm)

DIET: Fish, frogs, invertebrates

For better aerodynamics in flight, the great blue heron curls its long neck into an S shape. These grayish blue birds have rust-colored feathers on their thighs, green legs, and a black band above their eyes.

ROSEATE SPOONBILL
Platalea ajaja

RANGE: Southern North America, Central America, Caribbean, northern South America

SIZE: 27.6 to 35.4 in (70 to 90 cm)

DIET: Mainly fish

Instead of a pointed tip, the end of the roseate (ROW-zee-yate) spoonbill's beak is round and flat. The bird uses this spoonlike structure to catch minnows, other aquatic organisms, and plants by sweeping it from side to side in shallow water.

GREATER FLAMINGO
Phoenicopterus roseus

RANGE: Coastal South America, Caribbean, Galápagos Islands, southern Florida

SIZE: 31.5 to 59.1 in (80 to 150 cm)

DIET: Bacteria, worms, crustaceans, insects, small fish

Turning its head upside down, a flamingo filters water through its beak for bits of food like brine shrimp and blue-green algae. These tiny plants and animals contain the chemicals that give the greater flamingo its brilliant pink-red color.

WHITE IBIS
Eudocimus albus

RANGE: Southern North America, Central America, Caribbean, northern South America

SIZE: 19.7 to 27.6 in (50 to 70 cm)

DIET: Crustaceans and insects

White ibises are social birds. They fly, roost, nest, and feed together. They find crayfish, crabs, and insects by probing the water with their long beaks. Ibises usually wash the mud off their food before swallowing it whole.

SCARLET IBIS
Eudocimus ruber

RANGE: Caribbean, northern South America

SIZE: 19.7 to 23.6 in (50 to 60 cm)

DIET: Crayfish, crabs, insects, frogs, mollusks, small snakes, fish

Scarlet ibises share their habitat with other wading birds, including spoonbills. The benefit to such a mix of species is safety in numbers. Flocks of birds are better able to detect and confuse potential predators.

MADAGASCAR CRESTED IBIS
Lophotibis cristata

RANGE: Madagascar

SIZE: 19.7 in (50 cm)

DIET: Invertebrates, frogs, reptiles

Not all ibises live in wetlands. The Madagascar crested ibis is a forest bird that hunts for invertebrates, frogs, and reptiles on the forest floor. Breeding pairs build a large, platform-like nest high up in the tree canopy.

CHILEAN FLAMINGO
Phoenicopterus chilensis

RANGE: Parts of South America

SIZE: 31.5 to 59.1 in (80 to 150 cm)

DIET: Algae, aquatic plants and seeds

Flamingos are known for their copycat-style breeding displays. One male starts by making a specific motion, like opening his wings, or side-stepping. A second male copies him, then another, and so on—like a wave.

CATTLE EGRET
Bubulcus ibis

RANGE: Native to Africa and Asia; spread in 19th century to South America; now in North and Central America

SIZE: 18.1 to 22 in (46 to 56 cm)

DIET: Insects, spiders, frogs

Cattle egrets are found in wet as well as dry grassland habitats. They are common in agricultural areas, where they often perch on the backs of cattle or follow tractors. Both stir up insects from the grass, which the egret catches.

Saddlebill storks are known to build large, flat nests 66 to 98 feet (20 to 30 m) high in trees.

Did you know?

SADDLEBILL STORK
Ephippiorhynchus senegalensis

RANGE: Sub-Saharan Africa

SIZE: 59.1 in (150 cm)

DIET: Fish, frogs, crabs

Saddlebill storks are tall wetland birds. Their wingspan is eight to almost nine feet (2.4 to 2.7 m). Males and females look alike—both have a long, colorful, sharp bill for spearing their prey.

SHOEBILL
Balaeniceps rex

RANGE: East-central Africa

SIZE: 39.4 to 55.1 in (100 to 140 cm)

DIET: Fish, especially lungfish; water snakes, other reptiles

The shoebill stork has a strange way of catching food. It lunges forward into the water, grabs the fish or reptile along with some vegetation in its bill, gets up, shakes the grasses out of its mouth, and decapitates its prey.

PAINTED STORK
Mycteria leucocephala

RANGE: Parts of Asia, including India, Sri Lanka, southern China

SIZE: 36.7 to 40.2 in (93 to 102 cm)

DIET: Fish, insects, crustaceans, reptiles

With their bill held open under the water, painted storks hunt for fish and other aquatic animals by feel. They walk slowly, stirring up the mud with their feet. When a fish moves, they snap it up.

LOONS AND GREBES

Some waterbirds are so streamlined for life in the water that they can barely stand up on dry land. This is the case with the diving birds—the loons and grebes.

Loons, for example, are heavy birds with short legs set way back on their bodies close to the tail. The result is they have trouble balancing on two feet. Most ducks, by comparison, run and walk easily. In the water, loons have the advantage. They can dive as deep as 250 feet (75 m) while hunting for fish or escaping predators.

In addition to their body shape, grebes are known for their in-the-water courtship rituals. A pair of male and female western grebes, for example, will begin with the "rush" dance. They flap their wings and run across the surface of the water, side by side. If all goes well, they continue with the "weed" dance, in which the pair dive and retrieve clumps of weeds for each other.

Life spans for loons and grebes range from 20 to 30 years.

RED-THROATED LOON
Gavia stellata

RANGE: Northern Hemisphere

SIZE: 20.9 to 27.2 in (53 to 69 cm)

DIET: Marine and freshwater fish

Loons are fish-eaters that find their food by diving. They have good underwater vision and sharp beaks for catching their prey. They have no trouble taking off from the water, but only the red-throated loon can take off from land.

GREAT CRESTED GREBE
Podiceps cristatus

RANGE: Europe, Asia, Africa, Australia

SIZE: 18.1 to 20 in (46 to 51 cm)

DIET: Fish, crustaceans, insects, small frogs

Great crested grebes nest along the edges of lakes and carry their newly hatched chicks—which are striped—on their backs. The parents show their chicks how to fish by leaving them on the surface of the water while they dive.

COMMON LOON
Gavia immer

RANGE: North America

SIZE: 27.5 to 35.4 in (70 to 90 cm)

DIET: Fish and other aquatic animals

Common loons are easily disturbed by people. They only nest on secluded ponds and lakes, where male and female pairs make flutelike calls, including one known as a wail.

AUSTRALASIAN GREBE
Tachybaptus novaehollandiae

RANGE: Australia, New Zealand, and nearby Pacific islands

SIZE: 9.8 to 10.6 in (25 to 27 cm)

DIET: Small fish and insects

Like many waterbirds, Australasian grebes are brightly colored during the breeding season. Males and females have a chestnut neck stripe and white face patch. These birds carry their striped chicks on their backs.

Did you know? Unlike other birds, loons have solid bones that enable them to dive deep to catch food.

CRANES, BUSTARDS, AND RELATIVES

Cranes are tall, long-legged, long-necked wetland birds. They live in pairs during the breeding season and in small family groups during the rest of the year—often in large flocks. Cranes are known for their courtship dances and songs. These include alternating calls between the male and female known as duets. Breeding pairs of sandhill cranes, for example, sound like trumpets playing.

Bustards are a related species of long-legged ground bird found in Africa, Europe, Asia, and Australia. These birds also dance and make loud calls during the breeding season. The male kori bustard, for example, spreads its wide tail feathers in a fan, inflates its neck, and makes a loud booming sound.

The many relatives of cranes and bustards include a variety of omnivorous birds with long legs and noisy courtship dances. Examples are trumpeters, sunbitterns, seriemas, rails, coots, and crakes.

Life spans for this group range up to 25 years.

SANDHILL CRANE
Antigone canadensis

RANGE: North America to the Russian Far East; also northern Mexico and Cuba

SIZE: 47.2 in (120 cm)

DIET: Grains, seeds, insects

During its winter migration, the sandhill crane flies south from Canada and the northern United States to New Mexico and Florida, U.S.A. Along the way, these birds stop to rest in huge numbers—up to 40,000—along the Platte River in Nebraska, U.S.A..

GRAY CROWNED CRANE
Balearica regulorum

RANGE: Sub-Saharan Africa

SIZE: 39.4 to 43.3 in (100 to 110 cm)

DIET: Insects and other invertebrates; small reptiles and mammals; grass seeds

When the gray crowned crane makes its breeding call, it fills the bright red gular sac under its throat with air and makes a loud honking sound. The male and female look similar, but the male is larger.

GRAY-WINGED TRUMPETER
Psophia crepitans

RANGE: Amazon River Basin and northeastern South America

SIZE: 16.9 to 20.9 in (43 to 53 cm)

DIET: Vegetation, including fruit; also insects, snakes

The thick black feathers on the trumpeter's head and neck look like velvet. These birds are named for their trumpetlike alarm calls. They also make a drumming sound while feeding, usually in groups, along the forest floor.

KORI BUSTARD
Ardeotis kori

RANGE: Sub-Saharan Africa

SIZE: 41.3 to 50.4 in (105 to 128 cm)

DIET: Lizards and other small reptiles, insects, mammals, birds, vegetation, carrion

Kori bustards walk slowly through the grass, taking huge steps, looking mostly for lizards. They take dust baths to stay clean. Bustards weigh up to 42 pounds (19 kg), making them one of the heaviest flying birds.

Otgontuya Batsuuri

SIBERIAN CRANE

The Siberian crane *(Leucogeranus leucogeranus)* is one of the rarest bird species in Mongolia. It is a snow-white bird with black tips on its flying feathers. It has a flaming red mask, golden yellow eyes, and long, elegant red legs. These birds live near freshwater lakes and wetlands where they can find plenty of amphibians, insects, and plant roots to eat. In relatively dry Mongolia, a small population of the birds can be found mostly near the wetlands and lakes in the northeastern part of the country during summer.

Little has been studied about the Siberian cranes that make their home here because there are so few of them. But these critically endangered birds are highly dependent on water and wetlands, and current climate and environmental changes are a big threat to their survival. So it's important that we study them and conserve their habitat.

In late June, some of the birds lose their flying feathers and regrow new ones. This takes about two to three weeks, and it's the best time for us to try to capture them. It takes a team of four to five well-trained researchers working together to succeed. A spotter finds the birds and gives directions to runners, who circle the birds and guide them out of the water to a catcher on land. As soon as a bird is captured, we put a hoodie on its head and wrap it in a cloth like a baby to keep it safe. Then we examine and measure the bird, attach a GPS transmitter to its leg, and release it. We keep an eye on the bird to make sure it is OK.

This may sound easy, but it's not. Siberian cranes are really fast runners! Plus, they live in wetlands. Sometimes, they run into shallow water to get away from us, but we've chased them through water that was waist-deep, too. The hardest part about chasing them is the mud. Sometimes it sucks our shoes off our feet. When that happens, we often lose our balance and fall in the water. And we have to continue chasing the birds in our bare feet!

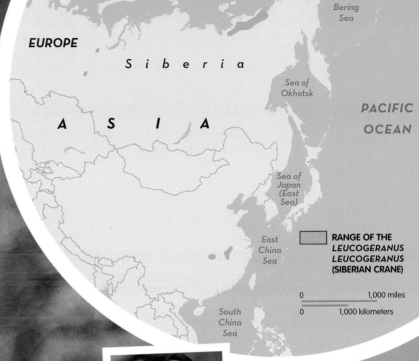

ARCTIC OCEAN

EUROPE

Siberia

ASIA

Bering Sea

Sea of Okhotsk

PACIFIC OCEAN

Sea of Japan (East Sea)

East China Sea

South China Sea

RANGE OF THE
LEUCOGERANUS
LEUCOGERANUS
(SIBERIAN CRANE)

0   1,000 miles
0   1,000 kilometers

Otgontuya Batsuuri is a National Geographic Photo Ark EDGE Fellow focusing on the critically endangered Siberian crane. Since graduating with a B.Sc. in biology from the National University of Mongolia, Batsuuri has worked as a science teacher at a local private school.

OBSERVATION TIPS

1 Never forget to bring your rain boots!

2 Bring a telescope or binoculars to view them from a distance. Also bring a sun hat and mosquito repellent.

3 Be careful! When Siberian cranes are injured or feel threatened, they sometimes attack people's eyes.

4 Leave no trace. It is important to protect the bird's habitat.

Siberian cranes mate and form a strong bond with one partner. During courtship, the partners sing, dance, and call to each other. The female lays two eggs in spring or summer in a nest located in a marsh, bog, or wetland. After about 29 days, the eggs hatch. The babies have cinnamon-colored plumage and blue eyes, which turn yellow after about six months. Usually, only one chick survives. Both parents incubate eggs and protect and feed their young, but the males spend more time feeding chicks than females do. After about 75 days, the chick develops wing feathers and takes its first flight.

CHICKENS,
TURKEYS, AND RELATIVES

There are nearly 300 relatives of chickens and turkeys. These include partridges, pheasants, quail, chachalacas (cha-cha-LOCK-as), and curassows. All are potential prey for a host of predators, including humans.

In addition to being the favorite food of many, the birds in this group share two additional features.

First, the males have conspicuous colors, and their breeding displays often include crowing or clucking. Red jungle fowl, the wild ancestor of the domestic chicken, is one example. The common peafowl, or peacock, is another.

Second, these are ground-dwelling birds. They have short legs for digging up roots and short beaks for pecking seeds and insects. When startled or threatened, they head for the cover of bushes or the safety of a high tree limb. They lack stamina, however, and many are poor fliers.

Life spans are generally short (two to seven years) because of the high risk of being eaten.

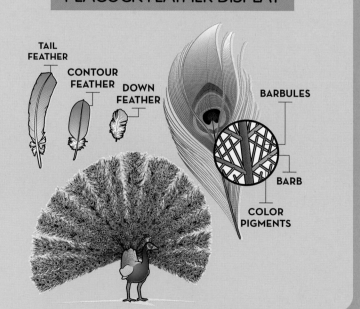

RED JUNGLE FOWL
Gallus gallus

RANGE: Asia

SIZE: 15.7 to 27.6 in (40 to 70 cm)

DIET: Vegetation, grain, worms

Red jungle fowl are tropical pheasants first domesticated in Asia thousands of years ago. They were bred with gray jungle fowl to produce domestic chickens. Compared to females, the males are much larger, with red combs and colorful wattles (folds of skin that hang from the neck).

RUFFED GROUSE
Bonasa umbellus

RANGE: Northern North America

SIZE: 15.7 to 19.7 in (40 to 50 cm)

DIET: Insects, leaves, twigs, acorns

The ruffed grouse is named for the way the male puffs out his neck feathers and fans his tail while defending his territory or trying to attract a mate. He also beats his wings against his sides to create a drumming sound.

A peacock's feather display does not actually involve its tail feathers.

Did you know?

CRESTED GUINEA FOWL
Guttera pucherani

RANGE: Sub-Saharan Africa

SIZE: 19.7 in (50 cm)

DIET: Insects, seeds, roots

The crested guinea fowl is named for the soft, curly black feathers on its head. The male also has colorful bare skin around his eyes and neck. During the breeding season, he repeatedly brings food to the female.

PEACOCK FEATHER DISPLAY

TAIL FEATHER

CONTOUR FEATHER

DOWN FEATHER

BARBULES

BARB

COLOR PIGMENTS

As in all birds, the brightly colored feathers of the male peacock result from a combination of color pigments and the way the barbules reflect light.

WILD TURKEY
Meleagris gallopavo

RANGE: North America

SIZE: 35.8 to 39 in (91 to 99 cm)

DIET: Acorns, seeds, insects, fruit

In addition to a colorful comb and wattle, male wild turkeys have a snood—fleshy skin that hangs from the top of their bill. The domestic turkey is the same species, except it has been bred for meat and often becomes too heavy to fly.

OCELLATED TURKEY
Meleagris ocellata

RANGE: Yucatán Peninsula, Belize, Guatemala

SIZE: 35 in (89 cm)

DIET: Seeds, berries, insects

Compared to wild turkeys, this species is more colorful. Ocellated turkeys have copper and violet blue spots on their tail. This pattern is called ocellated, for "ocelli," which means "spots."

RING-NECKED PHEASANT
Phasianus colchicus

RANGE: Europe and Asia

SIZE: 16.7 to 21.1 in (42.5 to 53.6 cm)

DIET: Vegetation, seeds, insects, other small invertebrates

Ring-neck, or common, pheasants are ground birds that roost in trees. But they can also fly. When surprised, they launch themselves vertically into the air, a behavior known as flushing.

GAMBEL'S QUAIL
Callipepla gambelii

RANGE: Southwest U.S.A.

SIZE: 9.8 in (25 cm)

DIET: Seeds, fruit, insects

Gambel's quails live in groups called coveys. The weather in the desert from one year to the next affects their populations. Quail can raise more young during wetter years because there is more vegetation to eat.

CRESTED PARTRIDGE
Rollulus rouloul

RANGE: Myanmar, Thailand, Malaysia, Sumatra, Borneo

SIZE: 26 in (66 cm)

DIET: Fruit, seeds, invertebrates

Like many of their relatives, crested wood partridges use their feet to find their food. They scratch and dig among the leaves looking for insects, seeds, and fruit. They often follow wild pigs, eating their half-eaten leftovers.

121

PIGEONS AND DOVES

The common pigeon found in cities all over the world is called the rock pigeon (Columba livia). It is the most abundant of the more than 300 other species of pigeons and doves. Often, but not always, the smaller species are named doves and the larger ones pigeons. City pigeons, for example, are descendants of the wild rock pigeon, native to parts of Europe, Asia, and North Africa.

Pigeons and doves are strong fliers capable of traveling long distances. Most live in tropical forests and feed on a variety of seeds or fruits. Like all plant-eating birds, they are also prey for a number of other species. When threatened, they take off, flapping their wings loudly to surprise the potential predator.

Unfortunately, many doves and pigeons are endangered. Some have been hunted to near extinction, either for food or because they are considered pests that damage crops. Others are very susceptible to habitat destruction. The dodo bird and passenger pigeon, for example, are already extinct.

In the wild, doves and pigeons have relatively short life spans: three to five years.

WHITE-WINGED DOVE
Zenaida asiatica

RANGE: North America to Panama

SIZE: 9.1 to 13.4 in (23 to 34 cm)

DIET: Seeds

Millions of white-winged doves are hunted each year. Yet they still are extremely common. The reason: There is plenty of food for them in urban areas and on farms—they eat seeds off the ground. Telephone wires also make good perches.

VICTORIA CROWNED PIGEON
Goura victoria

RANGE: New Guinea and surrounding islands

SIZE: 29.1 in (74 cm)

DIET: Fruit and seeds

The Victoria crowned pigeon is the largest in the pigeon family. Sadly, it is in trouble due to a combination of hunting and logging. This brightly colored forest bird is easily spotted when disturbed, making it an easy target.

SUPERB FRUIT-DOVE
Ptilinopus superbus

RANGE: Australia, New Guinea, Solomon Islands, Philippines, Indonesia

SIZE: 8.7 to 9.4 in (22 to 24 cm)

DIET: Berries and fruit, especially drupes and palm fruit

Only the male superb fruit-dove is brightly colored, with a purple cap, orange neck, and gray breast. The female is mostly green, with a small blue spot on her head. Figs are another favorite food of this rainforest species.

NAMAQUA DOVE
Oena capensis

RANGE: Sub-Saharan Africa, Madagascar, Arabian Peninsula, Turkey

SIZE: 8.7 in (22 cm)

DIET: Small seeds; grasses, sedges, weeds

The namaqua (nam-AH-kwa) dove is one of the smallest in the pigeon family. About the size of a budgerigar, it feeds on the ground, picking up tiny seeds. This species is known also as the cape or masked dove.

NICOBAR PIGEON
Caloenas nicobarica

RANGE: India's Nicobar Islands, Myanmar, Thailand, peninsular Malaysia, Cambodia, Vietnam, Indonesia

SIZE: 15.7 in (40 cm)

DIET: Seeds, fruit, buds

Nicobar pigeons live in large flocks that often roost at night in areas with less food and fewer predators, returning during the day to feed in the lowland rainforest. They may be the closest living relative to the extinct dodo bird.

KINGFISHERS,
HORNBILLS, AND RELATIVES

Though they are found all over the world, kingfishers, hornbills, bee-eaters, and hoopoes are related to each other.

One of the features they share is their shape. All have large heads and beaks relative to their body size, and brightly colored feathers. A second shared feature is the way they kill their food. After catching an insect or fish, they use a branch or the ground to stun or kill it.

For example, when a kingfisher spots a fish, it plunges into the water, grabs it, and flies up to a nearby perch. Once there, it slaps the fish against a branch to stun it before swallowing it. Bee-eaters have a similar behavior. After catching their prey, they fly to a perch and smash the bee to expel the venom in its stinger before eating it. The much larger great Indian hornbill, which eats small mammals, birds, amphibians, and reptiles in addition to fruit, also uses a branch to kill its prey.

Life spans in this group range from up to 18 years for smaller species and 40 years for the larger hornbills.

WREATHED HORNBILL
Aceros undulatus

RANGE: Northeastern India, Bhutan, Southeast Asia

SIZE: 30 to 32 in (76 to 81 cm)

DIET: Mostly fruit; insects, small reptiles, amphibians during nesting

All hornbills have large, curved bills. Many, like the wreathed hornbill, have an added helmetlike structure on top known as a casque (CASK). To support the weight of the bill, these birds have two fused neck vertebrae (VER-te-BRAY).

LILAC-BREASTED ROLLER
Coracias caudatus

RANGE: Sub-Saharan Africa

SIZE: 14.2 in (36 cm)

DIET: Insects and amphibians

This species is named for the color of its feathers and its courtship display. To attract a mate, the male swoops downward, rocking—or rolling—his body from side to side and calling to the female.

GRAY-HEADED KINGFISHER
Halcyon leucocephala

RANGE: Sub-Saharan Africa and the Arabian Peninsula

SIZE: 7.9 in (20 cm)

DIET: Insects and small reptiles

Most of the 90 species of kingfishers live in forested areas near rivers and lakes, where they eat mostly fish. But some, like this one, live in dry woodlands, making their diet quite different from that of other kingfishers.

COMMON HOOPOE
Upupa epops

RANGE: Africa, Europe, Asia

SIZE: 10.6 in (27 cm)

DIET: Insects

The hoopoe (HOO-poh) nests in tree cavities but feeds on the ground, using its long bill to probe for food. It eats mostly crickets, locusts, beetles, and ants, killing them first by beating them on a hard surface.

CARMINE BEE-EATER
Merops nubicus

RANGE: Equatorial and subequatorial Africa

SIZE: 13.8 in (35 cm)

DIET: Bees, grasshoppers, locusts

Bee-eaters perch out in the open, where they have a better chance of catching a meal. The carmine bee-eater sometimes uses a moving perch: It hunts for bees and grasshoppers from the back of a much larger bird, the kori bustard.

CUCKOOS AND RELATIVES

Cuckoos are secretive birds capable of moving through the forest or brush without making a sound. When they do make noise, it is a distinctive call. Most sound something like *woo-hoo hoo hoooo.*

Their relatives, while not as widely distributed, are also more likely to be seen than heard. These include the roadrunner, ani (aah-NEE), turaco (tu-RAH-koh), and hoatzin (hoh-WAT-zin).

Among the features that distinguish cuckoos and their relatives from the perching birds (see pages 132–139) are their feet. Like woodpeckers and parrots, they have two forward-facing and two rear-facing toes.

Another is a behavior known as brood parasitism. Instead of building their own nest, many cuckoos lay their eggs in the nest of another bird whose eggs look similar. The victim is typically a smaller-size perching bird. When the cuckoo chick hatches, the female who built the nest—not the cuckoo—feeds it. Because the young cuckoo is larger, it gets most of the food and grows faster.

Life spans for cuckoos and their relatives are up to nine years.

ROSS'S TURACO
Musophaga rossae

RANGE: Central and southern Africa

SIZE: 15 to 18 in (37.5 to 45 cm)

DIET: Fruit, flowers, buds, termites, snails

Turaco feathers contain blue and red pigments not found in other birds. Yet even with its bright coloring, this bird is more likely to be heard than seen. Its call sounds as if it is saying *go away.*

GREATER ROADRUNNER
Geococcyx californianus

RANGE: Mojave, Sonoran, Chihuahuan, and Great Basin Deserts in the southwestern United States and Mexico

SIZE: 20.5 to 21.3 in (52 to 54 cm)

DIET: Insects, scorpions, birds, lizards, snakes, rodents, fruit

Roadrunners are a type of ground cuckoo capable of running up to 20 miles an hour (32 km/h) after their prey. As omnivores, they eat anything they can find in the desert—even venomous scorpions and snakes.

HOATZIN
Opisthocomus hoazin

RANGE: South America in the Amazon and Orinoco River Basins

SIZE: 24 to 26 in (61 to 66 cm)

DIET: Leaves, flowers, fruit

Also called a stinkbird, the hoatzin has a unique digestive system. It eats mostly leaves and has a very large crop that acts like a fermentation vat. The result is a bird that smells like manure and can barely fly.

GREAT BLUE TURACO
Corythaeola cristata

RANGE: Central and West Africa

SIZE: 28 to 30 in (70 to 76 cm)

DIET: Fruit, flowers, buds, insects

Like all turacos, the great blue is a weak flier. Instead, it runs and jumps among tree branches, using its tail for balance. Turacos can also rotate one of their two back toes for a better grip.

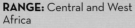

GUIRA CUCKOO
Guira guira

RANGE: Southern South America east of the Andes

SIZE: 13 in (34 cm)

DIET: Insects, frogs, eggs, small birds, rodents

The guira (goo-EAR-ra) cuckoo is a social species. Small flocks feed together in one area, hopping among the tree branches, or from a branch to the ground. These cuckoos also build community nests.

NIGHTJARS, POTOOS, AND RELATIVES

Nightjars and their relatives are very difficult to observe. All are nocturnal and active only in short bursts while hunting. Most fly with their wide mouths held open to trap insects.

During the day, the birds in this group are incredibly well camouflaged. Most roost either on the ground or in trees, where they sit as if frozen. The potoo, a speckled gray-brown color, often perches on the top of broken tree trunks. From a distance, it looks like a branch or piece of the trunk. The European nightjar has speckled brown feathering. It often rests among dried leaves or on a horizontal branch, where it, too, blends right in.

Several species make distinctive calls. One example is a species of nightjar called the whip-poor-will. It is most active on moonlit nights. The male's call sounds like he is saying his name over and over—very loudly.

Another way to find a night bird is to shine a flashlight and look for two bright dots against a dark background. Like many other nocturnal animals, its eyes reflect the light.

Life spans are up to 15 years.

TAWNY FROGMOUTH
Podargus strigoides

RANGE: Australia, Tasmania

SIZE: 9 to 21 in (22.9 to 53.3 cm)

DIET: Insects, invertebrates; sometimes mice

Like owls, frogmouths have large eyes and good night vision. Both make noise by clapping their beaks. But the frogmouth hunts differently. It perches and waits for prey to pass by, then grabs it in its beak.

GREAT POTOO
Nyctibius grandis

RANGE: Tropical Central and South America

SIZE: 13 to 16 in (33 to 41 cm)

DIET: Large flying insects

The female potoo (poe-TWO) lays her egg in a depression on top of a broken tree trunk. She and the male blend right in while they take turns incubating the egg and, later, caring for the chick.

FELINE OWLET-NIGHTJAR
Aegotheles insignis

RANGE: Southeast Asia

SIZE: 10 to 11 in (26 to 28 cm)

DIET: Insects

Nightjars and their eggs are prey for owls, hawks, adders, and foxes. When camouflage fails, these birds create a distraction by pretending to be dead, opening their mouths wide and hissing, or flapping their outstretched wings.

LESSER NIGHTHAWK
Chordeiles acutipennis

RANGE: Northern South America, mostly in the Amazon Basin

SIZE: 8 to 9.2 in (20 to 23 cm)

DIET: Insects

Nighthawks feed on a number of insects that are potentially harmful to humans, including mosquitoes. As a result, they play an important role in the ecosystem. Yet these birds, which nest on the ground in open areas, are rarely seen.

HUMMINGBIRDS
AND SWIFTS

Hummingbirds are tiny, fast, acrobatic birds with a very high metabolic rate. Not only can they fly forward at speeds of up to 34 miles an hour (54 km/h), but they can also hover in one place and even fly backward. No other bird can do this.

To maintain this level of activity, they need a constant supply of highly digestible and readily available calories. For this reason, hummingbirds are never far from flowering plants. They are nectarivores, meaning they eat nectar. All have long, narrow beaks adapted to reach deep into a flower. Among the 350 or so species, many are adapted to feed only on certain plants. Their beaks are shaped to fit precisely inside a particular flower.

Though they eat insects, swifts are grouped with hummingbirds because of their wing structure. Both have very stiff elbows and flexible wrists and digits. Swifts also have the ability to use their toes to grasp smooth surfaces like rock walls.

Life spans for hummingbirds and swifts range up to seven years.

COSTA'S HUMMINGBIRD
Calypte costae

RANGE: United States, Mexico

SIZE: 3 in (7.6 cm)

DIET: Nectar

Costa's hummingbirds live in dry deserts, though they move to cooler areas during the heat of summer. They feed on the nectar of a variety of flowering desert plants, including desert honeysuckle, saguaro cactus, agave, and chuparosa.

CALLIOPE HUMMINGBIRD
Selasphorus calliope

RANGE: Canada, United States, Mexico

SIZE: 3.5 in (9 cm)

DIET: Nectar

The calliope hummingbird is the smallest bird in North America, and the smallest migrating bird in the world. It weighs only 0.1 oz (2 to 3 g) yet it can fly as far as 5,600 miles (9,000 km) to spend the winter in southern Mexico.

WHITE-THROATED SWIFT
Aeronautes saxatalis

RANGE: North and Central America

SIZE: 6.5 in (16.5 cm)

DIET: Insects

Swifts are among the fastest flying animals. All, including the white-throated swift, spend their days in the air, hunting flying insects. At dusk, they gather to spend the night in cavities along cliffs and in large rocks. Hundreds enter the roost at once.

GREAT DUSKY SWIFT
Cypseloides senex

RANGE: Argentina, Brazil, Paraguay

SIZE: 5.5 in (14 cm)

DIET: Insects

Swifts rarely perch, except to roost at night, and even then, their feet never touch the ground. They are known for their remarkable ability to catch insects in the air. In flight, their wings look like boomerangs.

PARROTS

All parrots have relatively large, round heads with curved beaks, colorful feathers, dexterous feet, and noisy social behavior. Most eat a variety of seeds, fruits, and flowers. A few, like the lories and lorikeets, have a specialized tongue used for drinking nectar.

Parrots are found in tropical forests and wooded areas of the Americas, Africa, Asia, and Australia. A few, like the kea and thick-billed parrot, live in cooler climates and can even tolerate snow.

All are experts at eating slippery or difficult-to-reach foods. They often use one foot to perch and the other to bring food to their beaks. Like woodpeckers and toucans, they have a toe arrangement known as zygodactyl (zi-go-DACK-til). Their first and last toes face backward and the middle two face forward.

Their beaks are also much stronger than they look. Even parakeets can crack open a nutshell. Macaws in particular have powerful beaks adapted for eating the fruit, seeds, and nuts of palm trees. When they need to climb, parrots use their beaks like a third limb.

Most parrots form pair bonds for life, but they live in large flocks. Life spans range from 10 years for smaller ones up to 60 years for larger ones.

PINK COCKATOO
Lophochroa leadbeateri

RANGE: Australia

SIZE: 15.7 in (40 cm)

DIET: Seeds, nuts, grains, fruit, tubers

Also known as Major Mitchell's cockatoo, the male and female of this species look similar. Females are smaller and have more yellow on their crest. They build nests of sticks and stones in hollow trees—and return to the same nests each year.

CUBAN AMAZON
Amazona leucocephala

RANGE: Cuba, Bahamas, Cayman Islands

SIZE: 13 in (33 cm)

DIET: Fruit, leaves, seeds

There are many species of Amazon parrots. All are mostly green with colorful feathers on their head, wings, and tail. They are very social and noisy, especially while feeding and flying. Cuban parrots have white foreheads and pale red chins.

AFRICAN GRAY PARROT
Psittacus erithacus

RANGE: West and Central Africa

SIZE: 13 in (33 cm)

DIET: Palm nuts, seeds, fruit, leaves

African gray parrots have been studied for their ability to speak and understand human language, solve problems, and mimic sounds. Unfortunately, many have been taken out of the wild to be kept as pets, and their populations are now in trouble.

RED-AND-GREEN MACAW
Ara chloropterus

RANGE: North-central South America

SIZE: 39.4 in (100 cm)

DIET: Fruit, seeds, nuts

Red-and-green macaws, like most parrots, visit cliffs, where they eat bits of clay and other minerals that help with digestion. Macaws eat a variety of foods that contain toxins, such as cashews and palm.

127

MANY BIRDS GET THEIR COLOR from pigments found naturally in their feathers or borrowed from the foods they eat. Others, like the blue feathers on the back of the common kingfisher (*Alcedo atthis*), refract light. Long barbs at the base of each feather split light into brilliant shades of sapphire and emerald. As a result, this flashy little hunter looks like a shimmering streak of turquoise as it dives head-first into the water to capture prey.

129

WOODPECKERS,
TOUCANS, AND RELATIVES

Woodpeckers, toucans, and barbets are forest birds that nest in holes in tree trunks. All are excellent tree climbers, and their feet are adapted for this purpose. Like parrots, these birds are zygodactyls: The first and fourth toes face backward, and the middle two face forward. Other forest birds with similar feet—and the ability to move with great speed along tree trunks and branches—are the jacamars, honeyguides, and puffbirds. Many of these birds also feed on nectar and nest in termite mounds or on the ground.

Trogons are different. They are also a forest bird that nests in tree holes, but they barely use their feet. The arrangement of their toes is known as heterodactyl (het-er-oh-DACK-til). Their first two toes face backward, and the second two forward, which means they can balance but not grasp. They use their wings to catch and grab their food.

Life spans are up to 12 years for woodpeckers and 20 for toucans.

TOCO TOUCAN
Ramphastos toco

RANGE: South America

SIZE: 24 in (61 cm)

DIET: Fruit

Toco toucans use their oversize, colorful bills to pluck fruit from tree branches. Breeding pairs also toss food to each other as part of a breeding display. This bird is always on the move, looking for the next tree full of fruit.

PILEATED WOODPECKER
Dryocopus pileatus

RANGE: United States and Canada

SIZE: 15.7 to 19.3 in (40 to 49 cm)

DIET: Mostly carpenter ants and beetle larvae; other insects, fruit, nuts

The pileated (PIL-ee-ated) woodpecker is a noisy bird. Both males and females call loudly to each other and drum on tree trunks. They also can be heard hammering at dead wood to find their food.

Did you know?

It takes about three years for male quetzals to grow their long tail feathers.

RESPLENDENT QUETZAL
Pharomachrus mocinno

RANGE: Central America

SIZE: 13.8 in (35 cm)

DIET: Fruit, insects, frogs, reptiles

Even with its three-foot (1-m)-long tail, the resplendent quetzal (ket-SAHL), feeds like other trogons. It hops off its perch, grabs its food—a piece of fruit or an insect—while still in flight, and then swoops back to its perch to eat.

BEARDED BARBET
Lybius dubius

RANGE: Tropical West Africa

SIZE: 10 in (26 cm)

DIET: Fruit, especially figs; insects

Barbets are fruit-eating specialists. They have ridges along the cutting edge of their upper bill that help to tear open fruit, especially figs. Like all fruit-eating forest birds, they play an important role in dispersing seeds.

RATITES

Ostriches, emus, cassowaries, rheas, and kiwis are flightless birds known as ratites (ra-TITES), which means raft-like. Their group name refers to their skeletal structure, unique among birds. They lack a keel, the ridge of bone along the breastbone where the flight muscles attach in other birds. The result is that they have very weak wings and cannot fly.

Ratite feathers are also different. They lack the tiny hooks, or barbules, that interlock the feathers of other birds. They also have more of what are known as "after feathers"—the light, wispy strands at the base of the feather shaft. As a result, their feathering is over-all lighter and fluffier than that of other birds. Ostrich feathers, in particular, are used to decorate hats, fans, and pens. They are also used to make feather dusters.

The larger species—ostriches, emus, and cassowaries—have been traded as well as owned and bred for their meat, leather, oil, and feathers.

Life spans for ratites range from 20 to 30 years.

SOUTHERN CASSOWARY
Casuarius casuarius

RANGE: New Guinea and northeastern Australia

SIZE: 40.2 to 66.9 in (102 to 170 cm)

DIET: Fruit, insects, vertebrates

The bony crest, or casque (CASK) on the top of the cassowary's head is used to push through dense vegetation. But this bird has a more powerful weapon: its legs, each with three toes and long, sharp claws.

EMU
Dromaius novaehollandiae

RANGE: Australia

SIZE: 69.6 in (170 cm)

DIET: Seeds, fruit, flowers, leaves, insects

Emus, the second largest land bird after the ostrich, are known for following the rains in search of their food. They move toward dark rain clouds and the sound of thunder.

Did you know? Ostriches' eyes are the largest of any land animal.

GREATER RHEA
Rhea americana

RANGE: Southeastern South America

SIZE: 58.8 in (150 cm)

DIET: Plants, seeds, fruit

Compared to other flightless birds, the rhea (REE-yah) has long wings. If chased by a predator, rheas try to dodge the threat by running in a zigzag pattern, using one wing at a time like a rudder.

OSTRICH
Struthio camelus

RANGE: Africa

SIZE: 108 in (270 cm)

DIET: Plants

Ostriches live in habitats where the temperatures often vary greatly, by as much as 72 degrees Fahrenheit (40 degrees C). When necessary, they cover the featherless areas on their upper legs to conserve heat and expose them to cool off.

BROWN KIWI
Apteryx australis

RANGE: New Zealand

SIZE: 17.7 to 21.3 in (45 to 54 cm)

DIET: Invertebrates, especially worms, insects, crawfish; also amphibians, eels, fruit

Kiwis are shy birds with strong legs, poor eyesight, good hearing, and an excellent sense of smell. They are the only birds with nostrils at the end of their bill, which they use to poke around in the soil for food.

131

ANTBIRDS
AND RELATIVES

Antbirds and their relatives are perching birds found in the forests of Central and South America. Most live in the understory—either among tree branches or on the ground. The birds in this group are small with strong legs. Many have a hooked bill for grabbing insects. Some, like the ant-thrush, eat mostly ants. Others, like the antshrike and woodcreeper, find their food by following swarms of army ants. These ant-followers eat grasshoppers, the larvae of butterflies and moths, and a variety of other insects.

Mixed flocks are common among antbirds. As the ant swarm goes by, different species position themselves in different locations to grab a meal. Most are much easier to hear than see. Their calls are a simple series of repeated chirps.

Life spans range from two to five years.

BLACK-STRIPED WOODCREEPER
Xiphorhynchus lachrymosus

RANGE: Central America and South America

SIZE: 9.1 in (23 cm)

DIET: Primarily insects

Woodcreepers are ant-followers that feed on insects found in tree trunks. They hunt by hopping short distances or creeping along a tree limb. They also eat spiders, centipedes, millipedes, and even lizards.

MANICORE WARBLING-ANTBIRD
Hypocnemis rondoni

RANGE: South America (Brazil)

SIZE: 4.5 in (11.3 cm)

DIET: insects

The Manicore warbling-antbird lives in gaps where sunlight peeks through the thick understory of the Amazon rainforest. Like all warbling antbirds, it sings. Its song usually has four quick, screechy but clear notes that get higher pitched, one after another.

CINEREOUS ANTSHRIKE
Thamnomanes caesius

RANGE: South America

SIZE: 18 in (45 cm)

DIET: Insects

Antshrikes are one of the dominant species in a mixed flock of antbirds, meaning they lead the effort to follow army ants. They hunt insects either from a perch, called gleaning, or from the air, called sallying.

PERCHING BIRDS

Half of all birds are in the order Passeriformes. The almost 6,000 species in this large group are known as "perching birds." All have feet adapted for gripping. Most (about 5,000 species) are "songbirds."

Perching birds have a toe arrangement known as anisodactyl (an-ee-so-DACK-til). They have three toes that face forward and one that faces backward. When wrapped around a perch, these birds have an excellent grip. Their feet also have muscles and tendons that lock their toes in place. As a result, perching birds can hold on with minimal effort to feed, and even sleep.

Perching birds are found all over the world in every type of habitat. Their diets are also varied. Many eat insects. Others eat seeds, grains, nectar, and berries.

About half of the smallest perching bird is the .15-ounce (4.2-g) short-tailed pygmy tyrant. The largest is the 57-ounce (1,625-g) raven.

CHESTNUT CROWNED GNATEATER
Conopophaga castaneiceps

RANGE: Central and South America

SIZE: 4.4 in (11.2 cm)

DIET: Insects and larvae

The gnateater is another insect-eater that follows ant swarms. It perches on low branches and jumps down to the ground to grab its prey, which also includes spiders, caterpillars, grasshoppers, and beetles.

SHORT-TAILED ANTTHRUSH
Chamaeza campanisona

RANGE: South America

SIZE: 8 in (20 cm)

DIET: Insects, especially ants

The short-tailed antthrush has very strong legs for hopping after its prey and a very short tail that allows it to move quickly over the ground. It rarely flies long distances.

FLYCATCHERS
AND RELATIVES

There are about 400 species of tyrant flycatchers. These are perching birds found primarily in the Americas. They are grouped together because, like antbirds and their relatives, their calls are simple and nonmusical.

The antbirds and New World flycatchers have a simple syrinx (SEAR-inx), the bird equivalent of human vocal cords. The result is that their calls sound like a stream of single notes, rather than a song.

Despite their name, flycatchers eat more than flies. Most of the species found in North America catch their food while in flight. This behavior is called sallying, or hawking. The bird flies out from a perch, grabs an insect out of the air, and returns to the same or a different perch to eat it. Many Central and South American species catch their meals from a standstill, picking the insect off the ground or a leaf. This behavior is called gleaning.

Life spans range from two to five years.

SCISSOR-TAILED FLYCATCHER
Tyrannus forficatus

RANGE: Central North America and Central America

SIZE: 14.5 in (37 cm)

DIET: Insects

Also known as the Texas bird of paradise, the scissor-tailed flycatcher is distinctive for its long tail feathers and pink coloring. It is known to use artificial materials such as paper, cloth, string, and fuzz from carpets in building its nests.

GREAT KISKADEE
Pitangus sulphuratus

RANGE: Southwestern United States, Central America, South America

SIZE: 8.3 to 10.2 in (21 to 26 cm)

DIET: Fish, frogs, reptiles, insects

The great kiskadee is named for its call, which sounds like *KISK-α-DEE, KISK-α-DEE.* These are among the largest of the tyrant flycatchers, and they have the most varied diet.

EASTERN KINGBIRD
Tyrannus tyrannus

RANGE: North, Central, and South America

SIZE: 7.7 to 9.1 in (19.5 to 23 cm)

DIET: Insects and fruit

The eastern kingbird is a very territorial insect-eater during the breeding season. It will defend its nests even from much larger birds like crows and hawks. In winter, it changes its behavior, becoming a social fruit-eater.

VERMILION FLYCATCHER
Pyrocephalus rubinus

RANGE: Southwestern U.S., Central America, central South America, Galápagos Islands

SIZE: 5.1 to 5.5 in (13 to 14 cm)

DIET: Insects

The male vermilion (which means "red") flycatcher is more brightly colored than the female. Both feed from a low perch, usually a tree out in the open, sallying out to catch flies, grasshoppers, and beetles in midair.

BLUE-WINGED PITTA
Pitta moluccensis

RANGE: Australia and Southeast Asia

SIZE: 8.1 in (20.6 cm)

DIET: Worms, insects, snails

Pittas live on the forest floor, where they eat by probing with their beak in the leaf litter. Their brightly colored feathers are mostly under their wings and tail, to help hide them from predators.

133

CROWS
AND RELATIVES

Crows and their relatives—magpies, shrikes, and jays—are large birds known for their social, intelligent behavior. Some species raise their young together and are found in extended family groups that include a breeding pair and juveniles. Most crows, for example, stay with their parents and help raise new chicks until they are at least five years old. These young birds can be observed playing a variety of games, including "king-of-the-mountain," and learning how to balance sticks or use them as tools to find food.

Birds of paradise, found in New Guinea and parts of Australia, have crow-like bodies with very colorful feathers. Most are found in tropical forests, where they eat fruits and insects.

Vireos are medium-size, mostly dull-green birds found in the Americas. Most sing from the treetops, where they also feed on caterpillars and other insects and fruits. Their calls are flutelike and simple.

Life spans are longest for ravens, members of the crow family: up to 15 years.

AMERICAN CROW
Corvus brachyrhynchos

RANGE: North America

SIZE: 15.7 to 20.9 in (40 to 53 cm)

DIET: Grains, seeds, nuts, berries, insects, aquatic animals

The American crow has a distinctive call that sounds like *caaw-caaw, caaw-caaw*. These birds are common because they eat anything, including garbage. Crows sometimes use tools such as sticks or rocks to obtain their food.

COMMON RAVEN
Corvus corax

RANGE: North America, Europe, north Africa, and Asia

SIZE: 22 to 27.2 in (56 to 69 cm)

DIET: Carrion; small animals, including reptiles and baby birds; eggs, insects, fish, plants, human food, garbage

Ravens are usually seen alone or in pairs looking for food. In the air, they are acrobats. In mid-flight, ravens will often drop a stick, and then dive to catch it. They are also excellent mimics.

RED BIRD OF PARADISE
Paradisaea rubra

RANGE: Indonesia

SIZE: 13 in (33 cm)

DIET: Fruit and berries

All birds of paradise have amazingly colorful and elaborate feathers, which they use in breeding displays. The male red bird of paradise does not develop his long red feathers until he is five or six years old.

BLUE JAY
Cyanocitta cristata

RANGE: North America

SIZE: 9.8 to 11.8 in (25 to 30 cm)

DIET: Insects, nuts, seeds, grain

The blue jay is another social, vocal bird. It communicates using a combination of calls as well as face, crest, and body movements. A jay with its crest up is aggressive. Acorns from oak trees are their preferred food.

FORK-TAILED DRONGO
Dicrurus adsimilis

RANGE: Sub-Saharan Africa

SIZE: 9.8 in (25 cm)

DIET: Insects

The fork-tailed drongo is known for its ability to mimic other bird species. It is also an aggressive bird that will attack hawks and other large birds if its young are threatened.

MAGPIE SHRIKE
Urolestes melanoleucus

RANGE: Sub-Saharan Africa

SIZE: 19.7 in (50 cm)

DIET: Insects, small birds, reptiles, mammals

The magpie shrike has an intelligent way of capturing its prey: It impales them on thorns or sharp tree branches. It has a hooked beak and can catch insects as well as lizards. By killing its prey first, the magpie shrike avoids stingers and toxins.

WARBLING VIREO
Vireo gilvus

RANGE: North America; migrates to Mexico and Central America

SIZE: 4.7 in (12 cm)

DIET: Insects; also berries

The singing behavior of the warbling vireo is typical of many songbirds. The male arrives in the breeding range first and establishes his territory by singing. Then the females arrive, and he attracts them with his continued singing.

COMMON GREEN MAGPIE
Cissa chinensis

RANGE: Asia

SIZE: 14.4 to 15.2 in (37 to 39 cm)

DIET: Invertebrates, small reptiles, mammals, young birds

The green color of the common magpie is a combination of the yellow pigments the feathers contain and the way they are structured to reflect light that looks blue. The yellow and blue combine to make green.

SUPERB LYREBIRD
Menura novaehollandiae

RANGE: Australia

SIZE: 39.4 in (100 cm)

DIET: Insects

The male superb lyrebird has the most complicated song of any species. It is a combination of his own unique song plus mimicked sounds that may include other birds, koalas, dingos—even chain saws and barking dogs.

EURASIAN JACKDAW
Corvus monedula

RANGE: Europe, North and Central Asia, northwestern Africa

SIZE: 13 to 15 in (34 to 39 cm)

DIET: Plants, invertebrates, garbage

All members of the crow family like to pick up shiny objects. Carl Linnaeus, the scientist who created the animal classification system, named the Eurasian jackdaw for this behavior. Their scientific name comes from the Latin word *moneta*, meaning "money."

With long, strong legs and sturdy feet, the superb lyrebird is a swift runner.

Did you know?

BIRDS

135

CARDINALS
AND OTHER SONGBIRDS

Songbirds have highly developed vocal organs that allow them to produce musical notes and string them together into songs. Most of the perching birds are songbirds. Cardinals, robins, wrens, thrushes, and blackbirds are among the most well-known songbirds. By comparison, other perching birds, like antbirds, do not sing. Their calls may sound musical, but they have simpler vocal organs and don't sing true songs. Songbirds are also called passerines (pas-ser-EENS).

Male songbirds sing to establish their territory and to attract females. Each species has a distinctive courtship song. Learning bird songs is one of the best ways to identify birds. The male cardinal, for example, makes a song that sounds like a two-part whistle that ends in a trill. Both the male and female cardinal make a song that sounds like a flute playing *cheer-cheer-cheer*, followed by *birdie-birdie-birdie*.

Life spans for most songbirds range from five to eight years. Larger birds like mockingbirds can live up to 15 years.

BLACK-CAPPED CHICKADEE
Parus atricapillus

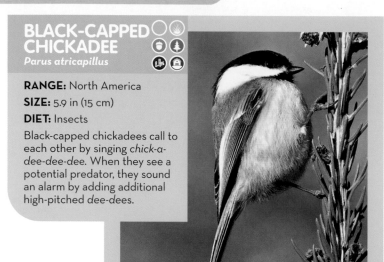

RANGE: North America

SIZE: 5.9 in (15 cm)

DIET: Insects

Black-capped chickadees call to each other by singing *chick-a-dee-dee-dee*. When they see a potential predator, they sound an alarm by adding additional high-pitched *dee-dees*.

GOLDEN-BELLIED GROSBEAK
Pheucticus chrysogaster

RANGE: Colombia, Ecuador, Peru

SIZE: 9.1 in (23 cm)

DIET: Seeds

The golden-bellied grosbeak is a songbird in the cardinal family and is named for the bright coloration of the male and for the size of its beak—"grosbeak" means "large beak" in French. There are also grosbeaks in the finch family.

CURVE-BILLED THRASHER
Toxostoma curvirostre

RANGE: Southwestern North America

SIZE: 9.1 in (23 cm)

DIET: Insects, seeds, berries

These birds have a long, curved, dark bill, which they use to dig holes in the soil and probe around looking for insects. This behavior is called thrashing. Curve-billed thrashers build their nests in cholla cactus and other spiny shrubs.

BALI MYNAH
Leucopsar rothschildi

RANGE: Bali in Indonesia

SIZE: 9.8 in (25 cm)

DIET: Fruit, seeds, worms, insects

The Bali mynah is an all-white starling, except for black tips on its wings and tail and a bare blue area around its eyes. It lives only on the island of Bali, where it is almost extinct—the result of illegal capture for the pet trade.

INDIGO BUNTING
Passerina cyanea

RANGE: Canada, United States, Central America, Caribbean, Colombia

SIZE: 8.3 to 9.1 in (21 to 23 cm)

DIET: Insects, seeds, berries, buds

Indigo buntings have a fast, whistling song that sounds like *sweet-sweet-chew*. They often sing from the tops of trees or telephone poles. These are migratory birds that fly at night, using the stars to find their way.

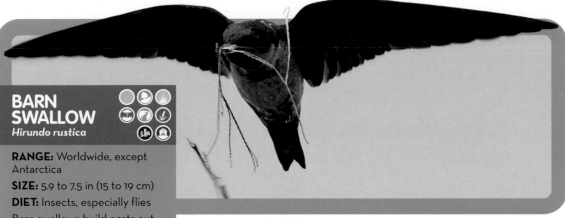

BARN SWALLOW
Hirundo rustica

RANGE: Worldwide, except Antarctica

SIZE: 5.9 to 7.5 in (15 to 19 cm)

DIET: Insects, especially flies

Barn swallows build nests out of mud almost exclusively in human-made structures. They start by collecting mud in their bills and then build it up to make a cup-shaped nest. Finally, they line it with grass and feathers.

SUPERB STARLING
Lamprotornis superbus

RANGE: East Africa

SIZE: 7.5 in (19 cm)

DIET: Insects and fruit

Superb starlings are very common in East Africa, where they can be found in shrub lands and savanna. They live in large social groups, in which the males and females share the responsibilities of building nests, incubating eggs, and feeding their young.

CACTUS WREN
Campylorhynchus brunneicapillus

RANGE: Southwestern North America

SIZE: 7.1 to 8.7 in (18 to 22 cm)

DIET: Insects and spiders

Cactus wrens feed on the ground, mostly on insects and spiders, but they also eat lizards and frogs and can survive without drinking water. They nest in cactus or thorn trees and will actively attack predators like squirrels.

CEDAR WAXWING
Bombycilla cedrorum

RANGE: North America

SIZE: 5.5 to 6.7 in (14 to 17 cm)

DIET: Fruit and insects

This bird is named for its red-tipped wings and for its favorite food: the berries of the red cedar tree, a type of juniper. In winter, cedar waxwings live in large flocks, visiting berry bushes and birdbaths.

NORTHERN CARDINAL
Cardinalis cardinalis

RANGE: North and Central America

SIZE: 8.3 to 9.1 in (21 to 23 cm)

DIET: Seeds, fruit, insects

Many male birds develop brightly colored feathers for the breeding season, and then lose them. Not the male northern cardinal. He is bright red all year—and he sings for much of that time. The female sings, too, mostly in spring.

BIRD SONGS

Have you ever wondered how birds are able to sing their beautiful songs? Birds have a special structure in their throats called a syrinx, which functions similarly to human vocal cords. The syrinx is made of cartilage (the same as your ear) and is located at the base of the trachea, which connects the back of the throat to the lungs. Birds vary the pitch and volume of their voices by relaxing the muscles of the syrinx. This changes the airflow and creates vibrations that come out as sound. Birds with the best control of these movements are called songbirds. Some birds create their own sounds, but others, like mockingbirds, mimic other birds' songs. The nightingale knows more than 300 songs!

NORTHERN MOCKINGBIRD
Mimus polyglottos

RANGE: North America

SIZE: 8.2 to 10 in (20.8 to 25.5 cm)

DIET: Insects, seeds, berries

Male mockingbirds can be heard singing day and night. In cities, their calls sound like all the neighborhood bird songs combined. They are also very active defenders of their territory and will dive-bomb or fly tight circles around any intruder.

ROBINS
AND OTHER SONGBIRDS

ongbirds take advantage of their ability to perch on a treetop, a high branch, or even a tuft of grass to better project—or broadcast—their calls. Most are heard before they are seen. Some may be easier to spot than others. The American robin, for example, is rarely hard to find. In urban areas, these birds often are seen perching on, and singing from, fence posts, telephone wires, and lawn furniture.

Like most other birds, songbirds also make contact calls to each other, and to their chicks, as well as alarm calls. Compared to other birds, even these calls sound like music. Some species also sing a dawn song that differs from their daytime song. Others sing all year, even outside the breeding season.

With about 5,000 species of songbirds, and many that sound—and even look—alike, the key is to learn the song of the breeding male.

RED-WINGED BLACKBIRD
Agelaius phoeniceus

RANGE: Canada, United States, Mexico

SIZE: 8.3 to 9.8 in (21 to 25 cm)

DIET: Insects and fruit

Red-winged blackbirds are easy to identify. The males sit on a high perch, flash their red and yellow wing feathers, and sing *oak-a-lee*. The brown female is harder to find. One male may have up to 15 mates.

EASTERN BLUEBIRD
Sialia sialis

RANGE: Eastern North America, Central America

SIZE: 8.3 in (21 cm)

DIET: Insects, fruit

Male bluebirds have bright, royal blue feathers on their head and wings, contrasting with rust-colored breast feathers. They often are seen perching on low branches, telephone wires, and nest boxes set out just for them.

When they are ready to eat, bluebirds swiftly swoop to the ground and pounce to catch their prey.

Did you know?

ANTILLEAN EUPHONIA
Euphonia musica

RANGE: Caribbean islands, especially Hispaniola and islands in the Lesser Antilles

SIZE: 4.7 in (12 cm)

DIET: Fruit of mistletoe; also a few other fruits and seeds

Euphonias are small, colorful fruit-eaters related to finches. By feeding on mistletoe, the antillean helps disperse its seeds. Its call sounds like a tiny bell tinkling.

BOAT-TAILED GRACKLE
Quiscalus major

RANGE: Canada, United States, Mexico

SIZE: 10 to 17 in (26 to 43 cm)

DIET: Insects, eggs, frogs, seeds, berries, grain, small birds, small fish

The male and female boat-tailed grackle look like separate species. The male has shiny black-purple feathers on his body and greenish black ones on his wings and tail. The female is half his size, with a dark brown body and light brown belly.

OLIVE THRUSH
Turdus olivaceus

RANGE: East Africa

SIZE: 9.4 in (24 cm)

DIET: Insects, fruit, snails

Olive thrushes are common in East Africa and are readily seen foraging on the ground for food. Their songs are a pleasing mixture of flutelike phrases, whistles, and trills.

WESTERN TANAGER
Piranga ludoviciana

RANGE: Western North America

SIZE: 7.5 in (19 cm)

DIET: Insects and fruit

Western tanagers are forest birds that feed on a variety of insects, either by gleaning or hawking. They nest in spruce, pine, fir, and aspen trees and migrate during winter to Mexico and Costa Rica.

AMERICAN ROBIN
Turdus migratorius

RANGE: Canada, United States, Mexico

SIZE: 6.3 to 8.3 in (16 to 21 cm)

DIET: Insects, berries, earthworms

American robins sing at the first hint of spring. Their morning song starts before sunrise and is a series of cheery whistles and chirps. Robins are common in suburban areas, where they hunt for earthworms on grassy lawns.

GOULDIAN FINCH
Erythrura gouldiae

RANGE: Australia

SIZE: 5.9 in (15 cm)

DIET: Grass seeds, especially sorghum

The colorful Gouldian finch lives in a specific type of habitat in Australia: open tropical, grassy woodlands with eucalyptus trees. It is endangered due to habitat loss.

WHITE-HEADED BUFFALO WEAVER
Dinemellia dinemelli

RANGE: East Africa

SIZE: 7.5 in (19 cm)

DIET: Insects, especially beetles and butterflies; also fruit and seeds

This weaver often follows African buffalo, grabbing beetles and butterflies as they are stirred up out of the grass. Like its relatives, the white-headed buffalo weaver builds a tubelike nest that hangs from a tree branch above the ground.

OLIVE-BACKED SUNBIRD
Cinnyris jugularis

RANGE: Southern Asia to Australia

SIZE: Up to 5 in (12 cm)

DIET: Nectar and insects

Sunbirds are specialized nectar-feeders. Their lifestyles are very similar to that of hummingbirds found in the Americas, and honeyeaters found in Australia. Though they can hover to feed, they usually perch.

RED CROSSBILL
Loxia curvirostra

RANGE: North America and Central America

SIZE: 5.5 to 8.3 in (14 to 21 cm)

DIET: Pinecone seeds

The red crossbill is a type of finch with a very limited diet: pinecone seeds. Instead of meeting perfectly, its upper and lower bills cross. When it bites down on the scale of a pinecone, it uses its tongue to pull out the seed.

PENGUINS

Penguins are another group of flightless birds. They have a keel and large shoulder muscles, but instead of flapping their wings to fly, they use them like flippers to swim. Unlike most birds, their wing bones are dense and flattened, and their wrist and elbow joints are stiff. This gives penguins incredible power underwater, which is where they spend most of their time.

On land, penguins balance on their webbed feet and short tail, using them like a tripod. When they walk, they waddle. For long distances, they slide. They leave the water for extended periods only when necessary—during the breeding season.

With the exception of the Galápagos penguin, which lives right on the Equator, penguins are found only in the Southern Hemisphere and mostly in cold waters. Adélie and emperor penguins spend the winter in Antarctica. The others move to warmer waters, following their food. To stay warm, penguins have very dense, short, overlapping feathers and a thick layer of fat.

Life spans for penguins range from 20 to 30 years for larger species; 10 years for smaller ones.

CHINSTRAP PENGUIN
Pygoscelis antarcticus

RANGE: Antarctic Peninsula; South Shetland, South Orkney, and South Sandwich Islands

SIZE: 28 in (71 cm)

DIET: Krill, fish, crustaceans

Chinstrap penguins live in large colonies, usually on icebergs in the open ocean. Compared to other penguins, the chicks of this species mature quickly. They are able to swim and feed on krill by two months of age.

SOUTHERN ROCKHOPPER PENGUIN
Eudyptes chrysocome

RANGE: Falkland and other sub-Antarctic islands

SIZE: 21.7 in (55 cm)

DIET: Krill, squid, crustaceans

Female rockhoppers typically lay two eggs, one of which is up to 50 percent smaller than the other. The smaller one is usually lost. The male incubates the egg for four months; both parents raise the chick.

YELLOW-EYED PENGUIN
Megadyptes antipodes

RANGE: New Zealand's sub-Antarctic islands

SIZE: 23.6 in (60 cm)

DIET: Fish and squid

The yellow-eyed penguin nests in pairs, rather than in large colonies like other penguins. They nest under trees or logs, and only where other birds cannot see them. Their most social time is right after molting, when they often hunt together.

EMPEROR PENGUIN LIFE CYCLE

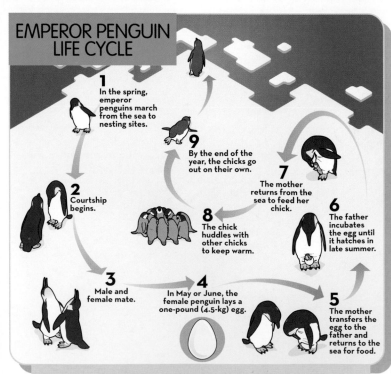

1 In the spring, emperor penguins march from the sea to nesting sites.

2 Courtship begins.

3 Male and female mate.

4 In May or June, the female penguin lays a one-pound (4.5-kg) egg.

5 The mother transfers the egg to the father and returns to the sea for food.

6 The father incubates the egg until it hatches in late summer.

7 The mother returns from the sea to feed her chick.

8 The chick huddles with other chicks to keep warm.

9 By the end of the year, the chicks go out on their own.

Emperor penguins begin their yearlong reproductive cycle with a very long walk—up to 75 miles (120 km)—from the edge of the ice to their breeding colony.

ADÉLIE PENGUIN
Pygoscelis adeliae

RANGE: Antarctic coast and islands, especially in Ross Sea

SIZE: 27.6 in (70 cm)

DIET: Krill

Penguins communicate using calls, eye contact, and body language. To attract a mate and establish territory, the male Adélie penguin performs a "salute," a behavior in which he arches his neck, stands tall, and pokes his beak in the air.

MAGELLANIC PENGUIN
Spheniscus magellanicus

RANGE: Falkland Islands, southern coasts of Chile and Argentina

SIZE: 24 to 29.9 in (61 to 76 cm)

DIET: Fish

For much of the year, Magellanic penguins live in the open ocean. During the breeding season, they migrate to the coast of South America and nearby islands, where they nest in dense colonies of up to 200,000.

EMPEROR PENGUIN
Aptenodytes forsteri

RANGE: Antarctic region

SIZE: 43 in (109 cm)

DIET: Crustaceans, fish, cephalopods

During their nine-month breeding cycle, emperor penguins endure long stretches without food and long marches back and forth to the open ocean. Each pair alternates taking care of a single egg and—if all goes well—a single chick.

GENTOO PENGUIN
Pygoscelis papua

RANGE: Antarctic Peninsula and sub-Antarctic islands, especially Falkland Islands

SIZE: 29.5 in (75 cm)

DIET: Fish, crustaceans, cephalopods

Gentoo penguin chicks look like their parents, except for the white patch above the eye and the bright orange beak—features that appear when they become adults. These penguins swim faster than any other bird underwater—up to 18.6 miles an hour (30 km/h).

LITTLE PENGUIN
Eudyptula minor

RANGE: Coasts of New Zealand and New South Wales in Australia

SIZE: 11.8 in (30 cm)

DIET: Fish, squid, crustaceans

The chicks of this species are a brighter blue than the adults. The little penguin, also called the fairy blue penguin, is the smallest of the penguins. At hatching, chicks weigh from 1.3 to 1.7 ounces (36 to 47 g).

AFRICAN PENGUIN
Spheniscus demersus

RANGE: Coastal southwest Africa

SIZE: 17.7 in (45 cm)

DIET: Fish, squid, crustaceans

African penguins spend their days in the water feeding on anchovies, pilchards, mackerels, and herring. They swim an average of 68 miles (110 km) on each trip to find food. At night, they come on shore, where they live in large colonies.

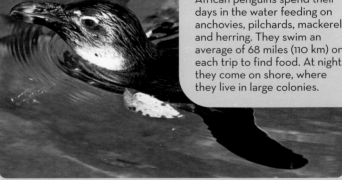

Pablo García Borboroglu

MAGELLANIC PENGUIN

When I was a small boy, my grandmother used to tell me fantastic stories of when she used to visit penguin colonies along the coast of Patagonia, Argentina, in the early 20th century. When I was 19, I visited a colony of penguins for the first time. I felt an incredible emotional connection with them and realized that protecting them would be my mission in life.

In 1991, there was a massive oil spill off the Patagonian coast and 17,000 penguins were affected in two months. With a group of friends, I organized a rehabilitation center. I later founded the Global Penguin Society (GPS), an international organization that protects penguins all around the world.

One species we study is the Magellanic penguin (*Spheniscus magellanicus),* which is my neighbor here in Patagonia. I've worked with Magellanics for 32 years.

Magellanic penguins are a species that tends to breed with the same partner every year, at the same location, and in the same nest. But in 2009, we discovered that six pairs of these penguins had created a new colony in an area of Patagonia called Pedral. One of those pairs were penguins that we called Clarita and Honorio.

When the penguins first arrived, Pedral was littered with trash, the fledgling colony was harassed by dogs, and people burned bushes where penguins nest to make barbecues on the beach. Clarita earned the title "Mother of Pedral" after she hatched the first chick born in the colony—while sharing her nest with a large plastic soda bottle. Through GPS, we worked with the local government and landowners to make Pedral a protected wildlife refuge with a thriving ecotourism operation. It is now a beautiful, secluded coastline boasting an impressive 2,600 pairs of Magellanic penguins—a population that keeps growing.

RANGE OF THE
SPHENISCUS MAGELLANICUS (MAGELLANIC PENGUIN)

NORTH AMERICA

SOUTH AMERICA

PACIFIC OCEAN

ATLANTIC OCEAN

ANTARCTICA

0   1,000 miles
0   1,000 kilometers

OBSERVATION TIPS

1 Penguins can't fly, so always let them pass first.

2 Don't interfere with penguins as they're returning from the ocean. They're probably bringing food to waiting chicks.

3 Keep your distance and don't try to touch penguins. Penguins look friendly, but they are wild animals.

4 Don't leave any garbage behind. After all, the colony is the penguins' home.

Pablo García Borboroglu, founder of the Global Penguin Society (GPS), is a marine biologist who has studied penguins for 32 years. Through GPS, he has helped 2.4 million penguins and protected more than 32 million acres (13 million ha) of penguin habitat. To inspire future conservationists, he has also taken thousands of kids to visit colonies, where they saw penguins for the first time.

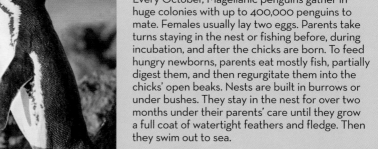

Every October, Magellanic penguins gather in huge colonies with up to 400,000 penguins to mate. Females usually lay two eggs. Parents take turns staying in the nest or fishing before, during incubation, and after the chicks are born. To feed hungry newborns, parents eat mostly fish, partially digest them, and then regurgitate them into the chicks' open beaks. Nests are built in burrows or under bushes. They stay in the nest for over two months under their parents' care until they grow a full coat of watertight feathers and fledge. Then they swim out to sea.

143

RECORDS

E ver seen an ostrich speed by or a pelican swoop into the water like a rocket out of the sky? Well, these are just some of the amazing things birds can do. Want to know more? Check out these superstar record holders of the bird world!

LONG-DISTANCE TRAVELER
Arctic Tern
Sterna paradisaea

Each year, the Arctic tern migrates an incredible 44,055 miles (70,900 km) on average—some as far as 55,330 miles (81,600 km). These birds, which weigh about 3.5 oz (100 g), fly from the Arctic to the waters off Antarctica. Because terns can live up to 30 years, that's 1.5 million miles of travel in one lifetime—roughly three trips to the moon and back.

FASTEST FLIER
Peregrine Falcon
Falco peregrinus

Soaring through the air at speeds of what many believe to be 200 miles an hour (322 km/h), the peregrine falcon is so fast that it has completely stumped scientists. There is much debate about the accuracy of this number, though experiments in several countries have ranged from an impressive 124 miles an hour (200 km/h) to a whopping 217 miles an hour (350 km/h). Whatever the real number may be, scientists aren't sure how they manage to dive that fast without blacking out entirely.

BIGGEST BIRD
Ostrich
Struthio camelus

Measuring up to nine feet (2.7 m) tall and weighing up to 350 pounds (160 kg), ostriches are the biggest birds on Earth. Much of that height is made up of their long legs, which can cover an incredible 16 feet (4.9 m) in one stride! Perhaps that's why ostriches are also the fastest bird on land, reaching speeds of up to 45 miles an hour (72 km/h). And those legs aren't just made for running. One kick from this bad bird can chase a lion away! Top that off with the fact that they travel in groups—this is one bird that's best left alone.

SUPER SWIMMER
Gentoo Penguin
Pygoscelis papua

Like most penguins, gentoos are awkward on land. But get them in the water and watch out: These penguins are diving machines! Standing about 30 inches (75 cm) tall and weighing only 12 pounds (5.4 kg), gentoo penguins easily dive in water at speeds of up to 22 miles an hour (35 km/h)—about the same speed as a bottlenose dolphin. And the impressive stats don't end there. Foraging for food and avoiding predators, gentoo penguins can dive 655 feet (220 m) deep as many as 450 times a day, staying underwater for up to seven minutes!

HIGHEST FLIER

→

Bar-Headed Goose
Anser indicus

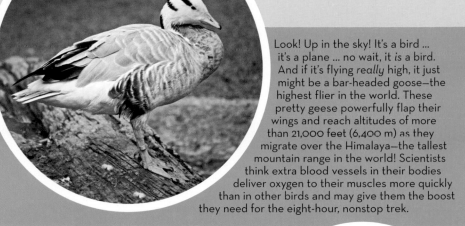

Look! Up in the sky! It's a bird ... it's a plane ... no wait, it *is* a bird. And if it's flying *really* high, it just might be a bar-headed goose—the highest flier in the world. These pretty geese powerfully flap their wings and reach altitudes of more than 21,000 feet (6,400 m) as they migrate over the Himalaya—the tallest mountain range in the world! Scientists think extra blood vessels in their bodies deliver oxygen to their muscles more quickly than in other birds and may give them the boost they need for the eight-hour, nonstop trek.

SMALLEST BIRD

→

Bee Hummingbird
Mellisuga helenae

At a maximum length of just over two inches (5 cm) and a weight of a mere .06 ounce (2 g)—about the same as a dime—the bee hummingbird is named after an insect for a reason. These itty-bitty birds are the smallest in the world, roughly a tenth of the size of the largest hummingbird and less than an inch (2.5 cm) larger than the biggest bee. What it lacks in size it makes up in ability: This humble hummingbird can flap its wings at a rate of 50 to 80 times per second.

WONDERFUL WINGS

→

Wandering Albatross
Diomedea exulans

When it comes to an amazing wingspan, there's no denying that the wandering albatross wins—wings down. This sensational seabird boasts wings that span an incredible 11 feet (3.4 m)—about the length of two adult humans lying end to end. But easy flying is key when you live your life above the ocean, as albatrosses rarely go on land. They spend their days gliding through the air—sometimes never even flapping their massive wings—or resting on the surface of the ocean, waiting for their next meal to swim by.

BIGGEST BILL

→

Australian Pelican
Pelecanus conspicillatus

There's no competition in the biggest bill category: The bill of the Australian pelican can be up to 20 inches (50 cm) long. This fierce feeder is not shy when it comes to eating—it even steals fish from other birds' mouths. But it's this pelican's bill that is most impressive. It is super sensitive, which helps the pelican find fish in murky water. There's a hook on the end for stabbing and grabbing. And the huge pouch beneath serves as a net by scooping a "bill-full" of water and fish, and holding the fish while the water drains out.

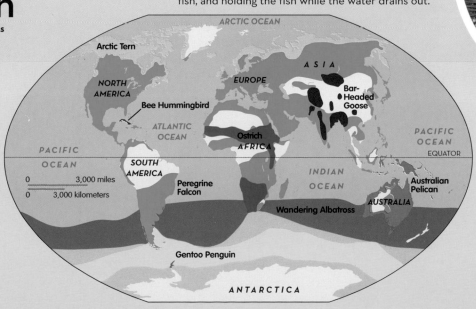

RANGES OF RECORD-SETTING BIRDS
- Arctic Tern
- Peregrine Falcon
- Ostrich
- Gentoo Penguin
- Bar-Headed Goose
- Bee Hummingbird
- Wandering Albatross
- Australian Pelican

Most reptiles, like this alligator, have scales—overlapping layers of skin—covering their bodies. A reptile's scales can protect the animal from a rocky or thorny habitat and lock in moisture to keep it from drying out.

REPTILES

GREEN SEA TURTLE

BEARDED DRAGON

DWARF CROCODILE

KING COBRA

BLUE-HEADED ANOLE

TOKAY GECKO

WESTERN DIAMONDBACK RATTLESNAKE

AMERICAN ALLIGATOR

MARINE IGUANA

BOA CONSTRICTOR

CROCODILE SKINK

YELLOW-SPOTTED AMAZON RIVER TURTLE

WEST USAMBARA TWO-HORNED CHAMELEON

COMMON AGAMA

WHAT IS A REPTILE?

REPTILES ARE AIR-BREATHING VERTEBRATES COVERED IN SPECIAL SKIN MADE UP OF SCALES, BONY PLATES, OR A COMBINATION OF BOTH.

They include crocodiles, snakes, lizards, turtles, and tortoises. All regularly shed the outer layer of their skin. Their metabolism depends on the temperature of their environment.

Birds and mammals are endotherms, meaning they create most of the heat they need and regulate their own body temperature. Reptiles, on the other hand, can't make their own heat, so they rely mostly on external heat sources to keep their internal body temperature constant. They are known as ectotherms. Without fur or feathers for insulation, reptiles cannot stay warm on a cold day, and without sweat glands or the ability to pant, they cannot cool off on a hot one. Instead, they move into the sun or into the shade as needed. During cooler parts of the year, they become inactive.

Reptile reproduction also depends on temperature. Some snakes, such as the boa constrictor and green anaconda, give birth to live young. The other species lay their eggs in a simple nest and leave. The young hatch days to months later. The soil temperature is critical during this time: It determines how many hatchlings will be male or female. Young reptiles can glide, walk, and swim within hours of birth.

The green vine snake is active during the day and sleeps at night. It moves slowly and blends easily into its surroundings, using its unique color and pattern as camouflage.

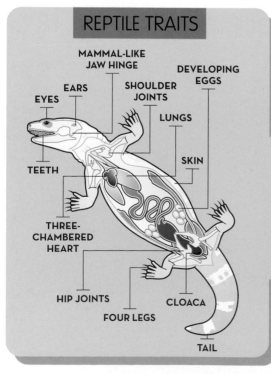

REPTILE TRAITS

- MAMMAL-LIKE JAW HINGE
- EARS
- SHOULDER JOINTS
- DEVELOPING EGGS
- EYES
- LUNGS
- TEETH
- SKIN
- THREE-CHAMBERED HEART
- HIP JOINTS
- CLOACA
- FOUR LEGS
- TAIL

All reptiles have scales, or scutes, on their skin and a mammal-like hinged jaw. Lizards also have mammal-like shoulder and hip joints.

Did you know? Reptiles first appear in the fossil record 315 million years ago.

CLASSIFICATION OF **REPTILES**

There are four reptile orders (see below). There are more than 10,000 species of reptiles, with new species being discovered on a regular basis.

1 CROCODILES, CAIMANS, AND ALLIGATORS **(Crocodilia)**

2 SNAKES, LIZARDS, AND WORM LIZARDS **(Squamata)**

3 TURTLES AND TORTOISES **(Testudines)**

4 TUATARAS **(Sphenodontia)**

CROCODILES, CAIMANS, AND ALLIGATORS

Crocodiles, caimans, and alligators—along with birds and sea turtles—are the only living direct descendants of the dinosaurs. The 25 species that exist today also look the same as they did 65 million years ago.

All are semiaquatic, meaning they require dry land to rest and lay their eggs. They spend the rest of their time in the water. They are found only in warmer climates, and most live in freshwater. All have long snouts and tails, a flattened body, a mouth full of peg-like teeth, thick armor-like scales, and webbed feet. With nostrils and eyes on the top of their heads, they are able to stay mostly submerged.

The species in this group are meat- or carrion-eaters. They hunt ambush-style and can bite with power, but cannot chew, which means they either swallow their prey whole, or kill it by drowning it and then eat it by tearing it into smaller pieces. The Nile crocodile, for example, waits along the edge of the river for a thirsty antelope and leaps out to grab it by the neck and pull it under the water.

Crocodiles and their relatives live for a long time. Their life spans range from 40 to 100 years.

NILE CROCODILE
Crocodylus niloticus

RANGE: Africa, Madagascar

SIZE: Averages 16 feet (5 m)

DIET: Zebras, antelopes, buffalo, fish, birds

Studies show the Nile crocodile has a stronger bite than any other animal tested, including alligators. Instead of chewing their food, they tear it into chunks. As a result, the muscles that open the mouth are surprisingly weak.

AMERICAN ALLIGATOR
Alligator mississippiensis

RANGE: Southeastern United States

SIZE: 9.2 to 16 ft (2.8 to 5 m)

DIET: Both small and large prey; generally fish, turtles, snakes, small mammals

American alligators use their powerful jaws to clamp down on prey of all sizes. When hunting larger animals like deer, they float just beneath the surface until the time is right to grab the animal's head, pull it underwater, and drown it.

SPECTACLED CAIMAN
Caiman crocodilus

RANGE: Northern South America, Central America, certain parts of the Caribbean, Florida

SIZE: 4.9 to 9.8 ft (1.5 to 3 m)

DIET: Insects, snails, shrimp, crabs, fish, lizards, snakes, turtles, birds, mammals

Spectacled caimans are named for the bony ridge around their eyes, which makes them look as though they are wearing glasses. This adaptable species is found in a variety of habitat types, making it the most common among all crocodilians.

Did you know?

American alligators may take shelter in swimming pools.

DWARF CAIMAN
Paleosuchus palpebrosus

RANGE: Wetlands of Brazil, French Guiana, Suriname, Guyana, Venezuela, Colombia

SIZE: 3.9 to 4.9 ft (1.2 to 1.5 m)

DIET: Tadpoles, frogs, snails, crabs, shrimp, small fish

Adult dwarf caimans have more bony plates, called osteoderms, covering their bodies than any other crocodilian. These protect them from raccoons and foxes, which prey on caiman eggs, but not from jaguars, large boas, and green anacondas.

SALTWATER CROCODILE
Crocodylus porosus

RANGE: Northern Australia, Southeast Asia, eastern coast of India

SIZE: Up to 23 feet (7 m)

DIET: Fish, reptiles, birds, mammals, amphibians

This is the largest crocodile, and the largest living reptile. Males weigh up to 2,200 pounds (1,000 kg). Females are about half the size—but no less dangerous. Saltwater crocodiles are known to attack humans.

YACARE CAIMAN
Caiman yacare

RANGE: Central South America

SIZE: 6.6 to 8.2 ft (2 to 2.5 m)

DIET: Fish, especially piranhas; birds, capybaras

This is the second-smallest species of crocodilian. Despite its size, this caiman is a significant predator. As an adult, it can eat porcupines and large rodents called pacas.

FALSE GHARIAL
Tomistoma schlegelii

RANGE: Western Malaysia, Sumatra, Borneo

SIZE: 13 to 18 ft (4 to 5.5 m)

DIET: Fish, insects, crustaceans, small mammals

Like all crocodilians, false gharials (GAH-ree-yals) have teeth that are constantly replaced throughout their lives. This happens whether or not they lose them while hunting. Underneath each visible tooth, there is a replacement ready in the socket.

AMERICAN CROCODILE
Crocodylus acutus

RANGE: Atlantic and Pacific coasts of Central and South America, Caribbean islands, southeast Florida, U.S.A.

SIZE: 8 to 14 ft (2.4 to 4.3 m)

DIET: Mostly fish, frogs, turtles; also birds and small mammals

As soon as they hatch, American crocodiles start croaking. The mother responds by uncovering them in the nest and carrying them in her mouth to the water. She will continue to look out for them for several more weeks.

ALLIGATORS VS. CROCS

With massive jaws, sharp teeth, and powerful bodies, crocodilians are among the most dangerous animals on Earth. They include 17 species of crocodile, one gharial, six caiman, and two species of alligator, the Chinese and the American. So what's the difference between an alligator and a crocodile? The first is that alligators are freshwater animals that can tolerate brackish, or salty, water. Crocodiles are found in fresh, brackish, and saltwater habitats. The second is that alligators have short, broad, U-shaped snouts. Crocodile mouths have a sharper V-shape. But the most telltale sign is the teeth. Alligators have an upper jaw that overlaps the lower jaw, and their teeth are not clearly visible when the mouth is shut. Crocodiles, on the other hand, have interlocking chompers and an oversize tooth that fits outside the mouth when the jaw is closed.

GHARIAL

Gharials (*Gavialis gangeticus*) are bizarre-looking, critically endangered animals. Once widespread across South Asia, they now survive only in several small, fragmented populations in northern India and Nepal.

I started studying gharials in the Babai River in Nepal's Bardiya National Park in 2016, but I wondered if gharials bred there since I hadn't seen any hatchlings. So, in 2019, I headed to the river for breeding season to find out. We saw breeding groups in four places, but we didn't know if the females would lay eggs.

A few months later, we went back. If gharials had laid eggs, they would have hatched by then. Unfortunately, there was a big storm a few days before we planned to leave and the road was blocked. We had to walk in the brutal heat instead. We hiked through dense forests and tall grasses, climbed hills, and crossed the Babai River several times. After four hours, we reached our destination: a long, elevated sandbank next to deep water pools. It was the perfect spot for female gharials to build their nests.

From a distance, we saw one adult male and two adult females. My heart was pounding. Seeing females meant that there could be nests. We saw three excavated nests surrounded by scattered white material that looked like egg shells. We rushed to them, and as we were examining the egg shells, I looked toward the river. About 50 to 65 feet (15 to 20 m) away, around 100 tiny gharial hatchlings were basking on the edge of the water. I was so thrilled that I ran toward them and started taking pictures. The hatchlings hurried into the water and swam away. I have never had such an adrenaline rush in my life. It had been 37 years since anyone had recorded evidence of gharials nesting here.

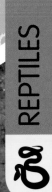

Ashish Bashyal, conservation biologist at Biodiversity Conservancy Nepal, first became fascinated with gharials when he was a child. After learning that there were fewer gharials than tigers left in the wild in Nepal, he was inspired to protect them.

RANGE OF THE
GAVIALIS
GANGETICUS
(GHARIAL)

0   800 miles
0   800 kilometers

ASIA

Himalaya

ARABIAN
SEA

BAY OF
BENGAL

SOUTH
CHINA
SEA

INDIAN
OCEAN

ASIA

OBSERVATION
TIPS

1 Wear comfortable hiking boots. You'll be trekking through dense forests, up hills, and along riverbanks.

2 Watch out for any tigers, leopards, rhinos, and elephants that you might encounter on the way.

3 Bring binoculars. Gharials are very sensitive to human presence. It's best to observe them from far away.

4 Look closely. Gharials blend in well with the sandbanks where they are usually found.

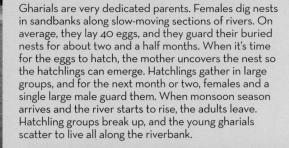

Gharials are very dedicated parents. Females dig nests in sandbanks along slow-moving sections of rivers. On average, they lay 40 eggs, and they guard their buried nests for about two and a half months. When it's time for the eggs to hatch, the mother uncovers the nest so the hatchlings can emerge. Hatchlings gather in large groups, and for the next month or two, females and a single large male guard them. When monsoon season arrives and the river starts to rise, the adults leave. Hatchling groups break up, and the young gharials scatter to live all along the riverbank.

155

TURTLES AND TORTOISES

Turtles and tortoises are the oldest reptiles. Their fossils date from 215 million years ago—long before the dinosaurs appeared—and many species have changed very little since then.

All have a domed shell that encases most of the body. The upper part is the carapace, the lower the plastron. The outer surface is made up of specialized scales known as scutes. The inner surface is attached to the ribs, as well as the spine, shoulder, and pelvis. Turtles and tortoises inhale and exhale by moving their leg muscles.

Another distinctive feature of this group is a birdlike beak that functions more like a set of jaws with teeth than a beak. Turtle and tortoise beaks have hornlike ridges lining the inner surface of the upper and lower beak. Carnivorous species have sharp ridges for slicing, whereas herbivorous ones have serrated, or toothlike, ridges for cutting through plant stems.

More than half of the species in this group are threatened with extinction, due to habitat destruction and the harvesting of the species for food, traditional Chinese medicine, and the pet trade.

Life spans are generally long. Several giant tortoises have lived more than 150 years.

EASTERN BOX TURTLE
Terrapene carolina

RANGE: Eastern North America

SIZE: 6.3 to 8.3 in (16 to 21 cm)

DIET: Snails, insects, slugs, worms, roots, flowers, berries, fungi, fish, frogs, salamanders, snakes, birds, eggs

This species is named for the "box" shape it forms when threatened. If a predator approaches, it will pull in its head, legs, and tail and close the front hinge of its bottom shell until the predator leaves.

ASIAN GIANT TORTOISE
Manouria emys

RANGE: Southern and southeastern Asia

SIZE: 19.7 to 23.6 in (50 to 60 cm)

DIET: Grasses, leaves, fruit

Like most tortoises, brown tortoises are herbivores that eat grasses, leaves, and fruit. This species lives in temperate, humid areas. On a hot day, it burrows into moist soil to keep cool, or waits until dusk to feed.

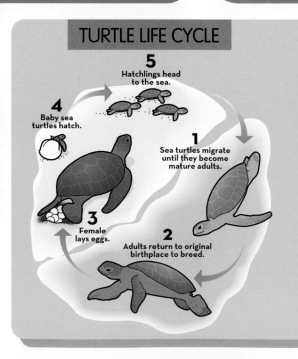

TURTLE LIFE CYCLE

5 Hatchlings head to the sea.

4 Baby sea turtles hatch.

1 Sea turtles migrate until they become mature adults.

3 Female lays eggs.

2 Adults return to original birthplace to breed.

All seven species of sea turtles follow a similar life cycle, in which young hatch on beaches and find their way to the sea to mature.

LEATHERBACK SEA TURTLE
Dermochelys coriacea

RANGE: Worldwide

SIZE: 4.3 to 6 ft (1.3 to 1.8 m)

DIET: Mainly jellyfish and salps

This species lays its eggs on the sands of tropical beaches, but it spends its life at sea in cold waters feeding on jellyfish. Sadly, leatherback turtles mistake plastic debris in the ocean for food. This is one reason they are in danger.

LOGGERHEAD SEA TURTLE
Caretta caretta

RANGE: Worldwide

SIZE: 2.3 to 3.4 ft (0.7 to 1 m)

DIET: Algae; horseshoe crabs, mollusks, sea snails, other invertebrates; fish and fish eggs

Loggerhead sea turtles are named for their large head and strong jaws adapted for crushing hard-shelled invertebrates. Young turtles eat algae and plants, but older ones are carnivores. Their size and rough, scaly skin on their head and neck protect them from predators.

GALÁPAGOS GIANT TORTOISE
Chelonoidis spp.

RANGE: Galápagos Islands, Ecuador

SIZE: Up to 4 ft (1.2 m)

DIET: Grasses, forbs, leaves

The Galápagos is the largest living tortoise, weighing up to 880 pounds (400 kg). The shape of its shell depends on the vegetation found on the island on which it lives. Tortoises that eat tall plants have a high shell opening so they can extend their necks to reach their food source.

GIANT SNAKE-NECKED TURTLE
Chelodina expansa

RANGE: Eastern Australia

SIZE: 19.7 in (50 cm)

DIET: Aquatic invertebrates, crustaceans, fish

The giant snake-necked turtle is an ambush predator. It waits for its prey, head and neck hidden inside its shell. When it strikes, snakelike, it has its mouth open, which draws in the food like a vacuum.

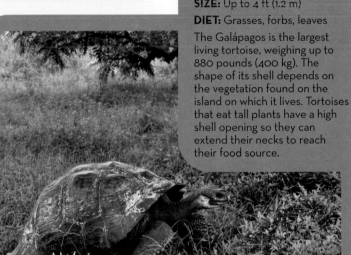

MATA MATA TURTLE
Chelus fimbriatus

RANGE: Parts of Central America, South America in Amazon and Orinoco River systems; also Trinidad

SIZE: 12 to 18 in (30 to 45 cm)

DIET: Mainly fish and aquatic invertebrates

Mata mata turtles are poor swimmers. Instead, they walk along the river bottom, using their snouts like snorkels to breathe. To find their food, they use the skin flaps on their head and neck to detect the movements of fish and invertebrates.

SNAPPING TURTLE
Chelydra serpentina

RANGE: North America

SIZE: 8 to 18 in (20 to 45 cm)

DIET: Carrion, invertebrates, small mammals, amphibians, fish, birds, aquatic vegetation

The tail of the snapping turtle looks like a saw. Its shell is also smaller than that of other species, which means its head, neck, and legs are more mobile. Snapping turtles will eat anything that fits in their beak-like jaws.

Did you know? Desert tortoises get water from the flowers and grasses they eat.

DESERT TORTOISE
Gopherus agassizii

RANGE: Southwest United States, northwest Mexico

SIZE: 10 to 14 in (25 to 36 cm)

DIET: Low-growing plants, leaves, bark, stems, fruit, shrubs, woody vines, grasses

Desert tortoises use their strong front legs and long claws to dig burrows to escape the heat or to hibernate. Some populations create a complicated burrow system big enough to share with others—usually five, with room for 25.

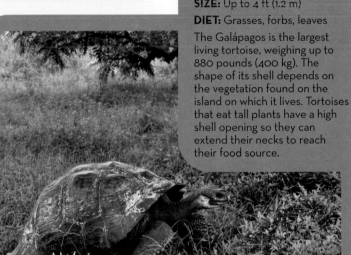

REPTILES

157

IGUANAS,
CHAMELEONS, AND RELATIVES

Lizards are the most successful group of reptiles, with about 6,900 species. They are subdivided into four groups: iguanas and relatives, geckos and relatives, skinks and relatives, and monitors and relatives.

All have tails, and most have four legs. They also have excellent vision, which they use to find food and for communication. Like birds, they can see color in both the visible (to humans) and ultraviolet (UV) spectrum.

Body language is especially important among lizards. They use a variety of postures and movements to defend their territories and attract mates. The males, in particular, show off their crests, horns, and brightly colored patches of skin by raising their heads, pointing their tails, and scurrying from one place to another.

Many of these behaviors are used for defense against predators. Some species use another tactic: With a quick jerk, they can release their tail and leave it behind as a distraction. A new tail will eventually grow back.

Iguanas and their relatives, which include chameleons, are tree-living species found in tropical forests.

Life spans for these reptiles range from five to 20 years, and up to 30 for the larger iguana species.

VEILED CHAMELEON
Chamaeleo calyptratus

RANGE: Border of Yemen and Saudi Arabia

SIZE: 10 to 24 in (25.4 to 61 cm)

DIET: Insects, some vertebrates, plants

Veiled chameleons have a very distinctive head crest, or helmet—up to two inches (5 cm) tall in a male. When threatened, it turns dark and curls into a ball. Like all lizards, chameleons shed their skin in patches.

EASTERN COLLARED LIZARD
Crotaphytus collaris

RANGE: United States, Mexico

SIZE: 8 to 14 in (20 to 35 cm)

DIET: Insects and smaller lizards; sometimes plant matter

Female collared lizards are gray with some red speckling, whereas males are bright blue. Both males and females have a black band on their necks. This species is an active predator of its food and can run as fast as 16 miles an hour (26 km/h).

ALLIGATOR LIZARD
Elgaria multicarinata

RANGE: Western United States, Mexico

SIZE: 3.1 to 7.3 in (7.8 to 18.4 cm)

DIET: Insects, spiders, centipedes, scorpions, snails, frog tadpoles, other lizards

Alligator lizards are named for the overlapping bony plates found beneath their scales and their long tails, which can be up to twice as long as their bodies. They are carnivores that eat anything they find.

CHAMELEONS AND THEIR
VISION

Chameleons are amazing lizards. They change color; have very long and sticky tongues, which they use to catch food; and have five toes, which help them grab on to tree branches. Another extraordinary trait is their 360-degree vision, which means they can see in every direction! Their eyes are cone-shaped and have an opening in the middle, where the pupil sits. They can look at different objects with each eye. Chameleons also can focus both eyes on their food before they quickly extend their long tongues and go in for the kill.

COMMON GREEN IGUANA
Iguana iguana ⚪ 🔆 🏙 🏠

RANGE: Central and South America, Caribbean islands, coastal eastern Pacific islands

SIZE: 3.3 to 6.5 ft (1 to 2 m)

DIET: Mainly plants

Like other iguanas, green iguanas also vary in color. Their skin turns darker while they bask in the sun (a change that helps them absorb heat) and lighter when it gets too hot or bright. Breeding males also turn orange or gold.

NORTH AFRICAN SPINY-TAILED LIZARD
Uromastyx acanthinura ⚪ 🌵

RANGE: Northwest Africa

SIZE: 15.7 to 16.9 in (40 to 43 cm)

DIET: Mainly plants; also ants and beetles

This lizard digs burrows up to 10 feet (3 m) deep, where it can escape from predators and extreme temperatures. Like other herbivorous desert reptiles, it does not drink but instead obtains water from grasses and desert plants.

CUBAN KNIGHT ANOLE
Anolis equestris ⚪ 🔆

RANGE: Cuba

SIZE: 13 to 19 in (33 to 48 cm)

DIET: Grubs, crickets, spiders, moths

The knight anole is twice the size of most anole lizards (more than 360 species.) All have special toes for clinging to branches and are highly territorial. Males of this species will face off with another male by standing up, turning dark green, gaping, and bobbing.

THORNY DEVIL ⚪ 🦎 🌵
Moloch horridus

RANGE: Great Sandy Desert in Australia

SIZE: 3 to 4.3 in (7.6 to 11 cm)

DIET: Ants

Thorny devils are covered in cone-shaped gold and brown scales. Their special skin gives them excellent camouflage and protection from predators. But the spines serve another role that is especially important in the Australian desert: water collection and absorption.

GALÁPAGOS PINK LAND IGUANA
Conolophus marthae ⚪ 🐾 🔆

RANGE: Isabela Island in the Galápagos

SIZE: 3 to 4 ft (1 to 1.2 m)

DIET: Mainly plants; the fruit of the prickly pear cactus

These pink land iguanas look like the Galápagos land iguana, which is yellowish brown in color and much more widespread. Genetic studies confirm the two species are closely related, but the connection is very old. Their common ancestor lived 5.7 million years ago.

PANTHER CHAMELEON ⚪ 🐾 🔆
Furcifer pardalis

RANGE: Madagascar

SIZE: 5.3 to 9 in (15.3 to 23 cm)

DIET: Insects

The panther chameleon is named for its spotted skin. Males are more brightly colored than females, and their coloring varies depending on where they live. Some are mostly red, whereas others are blue, green, or orange.

CHAMELEONS CAN QUICKLY CHANGE their colors by altering the amount of space between nanocrystals in their skin that reflect light. In a relaxed chameleon, the crystals are closer together and reflect green or brown colors. But when a chameleon is excited, the crystals move farther apart and reflect yellow, orange, and red. The panther chameleon *(Furcifer pardalis)* is famous for the kaleidoscope of colors it can display.

GECKOS, SKINKS, AND MONITORS

Geckos are known for their sticky feet, amazing camouflage, and strange-sounding calls. Most are nocturnal. At night, they chirp like birds or croak like frogs. When disturbed, they scream or hiss. These are also among the smallest lizards: The ashy gecko is just three inches (7.5 cm) long.

Skinks are the most common lizards. They are generally long and slender. Several have an unusual method of reproduction: Males are not necessary. The female produces clones of herself. This is called parthenogenesis. Some populations of skinks have no males at all!

The monitors are a diverse group that includes the largest lizard, the Komodo dragon; the only venomous lizards, the Gila monster and Mexican beaded lizard; and the legless lizards. All have a forked tongue and excellent sense of smell. Snakes are descended from this group.

Life spans range from five to 20 years for most geckos, skinks, and smaller monitors. Komodo dragons live up to 50 years.

GILA MONSTER
Heloderma suspectum

RANGE: Southwestern United States and northwestern Mexico

SIZE: 14 to 20 in (35 to 50 cm)

DIET: Small mammals; birds; lizards; eggs of quails, doves, and reptiles

Gila monsters inject venom, produced by salivary glands in their lower jaw, into their prey as they bite down. These lizards eat up to one-third of their body weight at each meal and only feed five to 10 times a year.

NILE MONITOR LIZARD
Varanus niloticus

RANGE: Sub-Saharan Africa

SIZE: Up to 8 ft (2.4 m)

DIET: Frogs, toads, rodents, reptiles, fish, birds and their eggs, beetles, crabs, earthworms, slugs, caterpillars, spiders, millipedes

The Nile monitor is a largely aquatic lizard and one of the biggest lizards in Africa. It has tough skin, which is covered by beadlike scales, and nostrils located high up on its nose—an adaptation for swimming.

CALIFORNIA LEGLESS LIZARD
Anniella pulchra

RANGE: California, U.S.A., and Mexico

SIZE: 6 to 9 in (15 to 23 cm)

DIET: Insects, insect larvae; termites, beetles, spiders, other invertebrates

This is one of many species of legless lizards. Though this reptile may look like a snake, it has several features shared by most lizards. These include eyelids, external ear openings, and a short body with a very long tail.

TOKAY GECKO
Gekko gecko

RANGE: Northeast India, southeast Indonesia

SIZE: 7 to 14 in (18 to 36 cm)

DIET: Other tokays, insects, other small vertebrates

For small animals, tokays make very loud sounds. Their mating call resembles a frog's croak, interspersed with the sound of a person calling out their name, *too-kay, too-kay.* Males are more colorful than females.

DON'T TRY THIS AT HOME

Of all the awesome reptiles in the world, climbing geckos have got to be at the top of the list for outrageous abilities. Why? These little lizards seem to defy gravity by climbing straight up walls and walking upside down across the ceiling! You might think the secret to their skill involves suction cups on each foot, but the truth is it's more like built-in Velcro than anything else. Climbing geckos have toe pads that are made up of millions of microscopic structures. The structures are so thin (only a few thousandths of a millimeter) that they fit into the spaces in between the smallest irregularities in the surface of the object they are climbing. This gives them quite an advantage over their ground-dwelling counterparts: No bug can escape to the ceiling to avoid becoming their lunch!

GOLD DUST DAY GECKO
Phelsuma laticauda

RANGE: Madagascar

SIZE: 9 to 12 in (22 to 30 cm)

DIET: Insects, spiders, crustaceans; sometimes sweet fruit or nectar

Like all geckos (there are more than 1,500 species), the gold dust day gecko can cling to any surface. They have special toe pads and muscles that allow them to bend their toes upward—so they can peel their feet off a flat surface.

RED-EYED CROCODILE SKINK
Tribolonotus gracilis

RANGE: Indonesia (New Guinea)

SIZE: Up to 10 in (25 cm)

DIET: Insects

With its rows of pointed scales on its back, this lizard looks like a little crocodile. But it doesn't act like one! When threatened by a predator, it lets out a high-pitched yelp. It also may vomit and shed its tail. If that doesn't work, it will freeze and play dead.

BLUE-TONGUED SKINK
Tiliqua scincoides

RANGE: Australia

SIZE: 18 to 20 in (45 to 50 cm)

DIET: Insects, other reptiles, snails, carrion; some plant material, fruit, berries

Like most of its relatives (there are 1,200 skink species), the blue-tongued skink has a very short neck and legs. It moves like a snake, with its belly on the ground. The blue tongue is used for defensive displays against predators.

SOFT SPINY-TAILED GECKO
Strophurus spinigerus

RANGE: Southwest Australia

SIZE: 3 to 5 in (8 to 13 cm)

DIET: Insects and other invertebrates

Instead of eyelids, geckos have clear membranes over their eyes, which they clean with their tongues. Most species, including the spiny-tailed gecko, have another unusual behavior: They can shake their tail and break it off, leaving it behind to distract a predator.

SOLOMON ISLANDS SKINK
Corucia zebrata

RANGE: Solomon Islands

SIZE: Up to 30 in (75 cm)

DIET: Mainly fruits and leaves

Unlike most other skinks, the Solomon Islands skink has a prehensile tail and long toes, adaptations for its life in the trees. This lizard is unusual in another way: It is one of the very few social reptiles.

REPTILES

163

SNAKES

Snakes are highly successful predators. Yet they lack features shared by most other vertebrate hunters. They cannot chew, they have no limbs, their hearing is limited, and their vision is poor. They cannot hunt or digest their food unless the temperature in their environment is just right.

One reason for their success is their incredible sense of smell, which they use to locate prey. When a snake flicks its forked tongue, it is sampling the air, bringing various scents into its mouth, where they are picked up by special nervous tissue called Jacobson's organ. Some species, like pit vipers, also have a sixth sense: sensors under their eyes that can pick up body heat.

Another reason is their unique anatomy. Snakes have incredibly flexible jaws, elastic skin, and expandable stomachs. Combined, these features make it possible for them to open their mouths wider than the width of their bodies, and swallow prey of all shapes and sizes. This is particularly true for constrictors like the boas and pythons.

Finally, some species have a powerful weapon: venom. The most dangerous of these are the cobras and sea kraits (elapid family), and the vipers, adders, and rattlesnakes (viper family).

Life spans range up to 40 years.

COMMON ADDER
Vipera berus

RANGE: Western Europe, Asia north to Arctic Circle and south to Mediterranean Sea

SIZE: 26 to 35 in (65 to 90 cm)

DIET: Primarily small rodents and lizards

Also known as the common viper, this shy snake has less toxic venom and is less aggressive when surprised than most vipers. Widespread in Europe and Asia, adders play an important role in controlling mice and rat populations in urban areas.

EYELASH PIT VIPER
Bothriechis schlegelii

RANGE: Mexico and Central America

SIZE: 18 to 30 in (45 to 75 cm)

DIET: Lizards, frogs, small rodents

Pit vipers, including this one, use heat detection to find their prey. The pit organ is a narrow opening in the scales between the eye and the nose. Inside the opening is a heat-sensitive membrane that transmits signals to the brain.

BOA CONSTRICTOR
Boa constrictor

RANGE: Mexico and Central and South America

SIZE: 3.2 to 13 ft (1 to 4 m)

DIET: Mostly birds and mammals

Boa constrictors hunt by ambush, often while hanging from a tree limb, and kill by constriction. They grab the animal in their mouth and coil around the rest of it, squeezing until it dies by suffocation. Boas will eat any animal that is not too big to swallow.

SNAKE DIGESTION

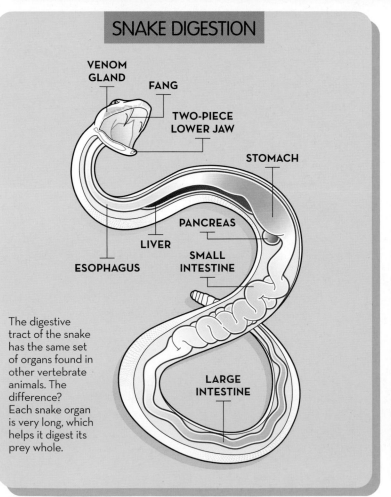

VENOM GLAND
FANG
TWO-PIECE LOWER JAW
STOMACH
PANCREAS
LIVER
SMALL INTESTINE
ESOPHAGUS
LARGE INTESTINE

The digestive tract of the snake has the same set of organs found in other vertebrate animals. The difference? Each snake organ is very long, which helps it digest its prey whole.

EASTERN BLACK-NECKED GARTER SNAKE

Thamnophis cyrtopsis ocellatus

RANGE: Southwestern United States, Mexico

SIZE: 20 in (50 cm)

DIET: Small fish, frogs, invertebrates, including earthworms

Found across North America, garter snakes are one of the few snakes that give birth to live young—from three to 80 babies in each litter. They also have mild venom, which is released only when they chew on their prey.

BALL PYTHON

Python regius

RANGE: West and Central Africa

SIZE: 3.3 to 6 ft (1 to 1.8 m)

DIET: Rodents, birds

Ball pythons prey almost entirely on rats and mice, which they kill by constriction and swallow. They are nocturnal snakes that spend most of their time in burrows. When threatened, they curl up into a ball.

SCARLET KINGSNAKE
Lampropeltis elapsoides

RANGE: Southeastern United States

SIZE: 14 to 20 in (35.5 to 50 cm)

DIET: Small lizards such as skinks; also rodents, other snakes

Kingsnakes vary in coloration, and in the southeastern U.S. can resemble the venomous coral snake. The rhyme "red on black, friend of Jack" is one way to identify these harmless scarlet kingsnakes.

TIMBER RATTLESNAKE
Crotalus horridus

RANGE: Eastern half of the United States

SIZE: 3 to 5 ft (0.9 to 1.5 m)

DIET: Mice, rats, squirrels, rabbits; sometimes birds

Rattlesnakes are venomous pit vipers found only in the Americas. They are named for their rattle, a series of button-like scales at the end of their tail. When threatened, rattlesnakes shake their tail, making a noise intended to scare potential predators.

COTTONMOUTH
Agkistrodon piscivorus

RANGE: Eastern half of the United States

SIZE: 2.2 to 6.2 ft (0.7 to 1.9 m)

DIET: Mostly fish and frogs; also mammals, snakes, birds

Also called water moccasins, cottonmouths are semiaquatic pit vipers—the only ones in the world. Most live in freshwater swamps, shallow lakes, and slow-moving streams, but they also are found in brackish and salt water.

EASTERN GREEN MAMBA
Dendroaspis angusticeps

RANGE: Coastal southern and eastern Africa

SIZE: 4.6 to 7.9 ft (1.4 to 2.4 m)

DIET: Birds, eggs, frogs, lizards, rodents, small mammals

Mambas are highly venomous snakes related to cobras. The green mamba, which is strictly arboreal, is much less aggressive when surprised or provoked, compared to its larger relative, the black mamba. Both snakes have a deadly bite.

GABOON VIPER

Venomous reptiles possess one of nature's deadliest weapons: toxic cocktails that evolved over millions of years to immobilize and kill prey and predators. But these deadly toxins also can save human lives. Scientists study their effects on the body and borrow the toxins' blueprint to develop drugs that treat diseases like heart disease and diabetes. I've traveled all over the world capturing deadly snakes and extracting their tissues—a source for the toxins' blueprint. On one trip, Baka people of the Congo Basin rainforest guided me on my search for the Gaboon viper (*Bitis gabonica*)—a snake that likely produces the most venom of any animal species.

About a week after the rainy season set in, one of the guides yelled at me to come quick. After a half-hour sprint through the forest, we stopped to stare at the ground. One of the largest vipers I have ever seen was lying barely above the leaf litter. Its head was too big to fit in the tube I had brought to shield my hands from its fangs, so I had to hold its head with my bare hands! After my assistant managed to extract a piece of tissue from the tail, we released the snake, grateful for the millions of years of potentially lifesaving information locked inside the sample.

RANGE OF THE
BITIS GABONICA
(GABOON VIPER)

0 ——— 1,000 miles
0 ——— 1,000 kilometers

EUROPE

ASIA

AFRICA

INDIAN
OCEAN

ATLANTIC
OCEAN

Zoltan Takacs began catching snakes in kindergarten. His fascination with venomous reptiles inspired him to co-invent a revolutionary technology that screens millions of toxin blueprints for potential use in making medicines.

OBSERVATION TIPS

1 Know your surroundings: Learn everything you can about the animals, environment, people, and culture *before* heading into the forest.

2 Vipers tend to be most active at the beginning of the rainy season and in the spring—and you may find them wandering into open areas at night, which is when they hunt.

3 Viper venom can easily kill a human. You must have years of experience and be prepared for an emergency when dealing with venomous snakes.

4 Watch your step. Even the largest vipers disappear into rainforest leaf litter—and beware of charging forest elephants!

Gaboon vipers are fearsome predators—they produce two teaspoons (10 mL) of venom that deliver a violent, multipoint attack on blood circulation and inject it via two-inch (5-cm) fangs! They hide motionless, camouflaged among leaf litter, to ambush their prey—including rodents and even small monkeys and antelopes! Males fight before mating—hissing and striking with closed mouths, each trying to force the other's head down—and females typically give birth to 10 to 30 live young. Born with deadly venom and fangs, the baby vipers soon disperse to live on their own.

RECORDS

E ver heard a crocodile roar like a lion? Or seen a snake smaller than a worm? If you thought you knew everything about reptiles, you had better think again. Check out these superstars of the reptile world!

LONGEST LIVING

Aldabra Giant Tortoise
Dipsochelys dussumieri

While it's difficult to know for sure the life span of certain reptiles, scientists believe that the giant tortoise lives the longest. Several species are known to live more than 150 years. But the tortoise with the longest life lived more than 200 years! His name was Adwaita, and he was originally brought from the Seychelles Islands to the Calcutta Zoo in India in 1875. When he died in 2006, a technique known as carbon dating was used to determine his age. Adwaita was 255 years old!

SMALLEST SNAKE

Barbados Threadsnake
Leptotyphlops carlae

The Barbados threadsnake was identified for the first time in 2008, and it's easy to see why it went unnoticed for so long. It averages four inches (10 cm) in length and is as thin as a spaghetti noodle. Unlike most snakes, which lay many eggs at a time, the threadsnake lays just one. The hatchling is also relatively large compared to the mother—about half her size. The reason has to do with space. The snake's body cavity must have room for all of its organs, including reproductive tract, and the egg must be large enough to house the tiniest known snake form: a baby threadsnake.

FASTEST SNAKE

Black Mamba
Dendroaspis polylepis

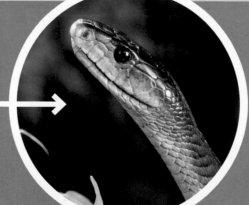

If snakes were cars, the black mamba would be a Corvette. These aggressive snakes can grow to an impressive 14 feet (4.3 m) in length and are capable of raising their heads four feet (1.2 m) in the air. When cornered, they are aggressive and explosive. As a result, black mambas are the most feared snake in Africa. But it's not only their size and temperament that make them scary, it's their speed: They are able to move in bursts of up to 12.5 miles an hour (20 km/h). Good luck outrunning this swift snake!

WEIRDEST

Texas Horned Lizard
Phrynosoma cornutum

There's no doubt about it. When it comes to self-defense, the Texas horned lizard of North America is the king. With several tricks up their sleeves, these lizards can change color to blend in with their surroundings. When threatened by a predator, they inflate themselves to look more threatening. But that's not the strange part. As a last resort, the horned lizard can actually squirt blood from its eyeballs a distance of three feet (0.9 m) to thwart attackers. Now *that's* weird.

LARGEST LIZARD

Komodo Dragon
Varanus komodoensis

Think dragons only exist in fairy tales? Think again. The Komodo dragon is real, terrifying, and not afraid to take down a water buffalo twice its size. At 10 feet (3 m) in length and weighing more than 300 pounds (136 kg), this largest of all lizards has bacteria-ridden saliva that seeps into the bite wounds of its victims, causing a slow, painful death. Komodo dragons are known to deliver their deadly bite, and then follow their victims for miles while they slowly succumb to blood poisoning. Yikes!

SMELLIEST

Common Musk Turtle
Sternotherus odoratus

If you keep one of these guys as a pet, you know why this species is also referred to as the stinkpot turtle. At a maximum of about five inches (12.7 cm) long, this turtle doesn't have much of a chance defending itself in the wild based on size alone. But it does have one feature that might keep attackers away. When threatened, it releases a foul-smelling oily substance to deter predators. Startle these turtles, and you'll certainly pay the price.

NOISIEST

American Alligator
Alligator mississippiensis

Crocodilian species are famous for lurking in muddy waters with only their eyes and snouts above the surface, barely visible to unsuspecting prey. But if you thought these reptiles were silent killers, you thought wrong. All crocodilians are able to hiss, snort, moan, and bellow, with American alligators being the loudest. Said to resemble a lion's roar, an alligator's bellow can easily be heard 500 feet (152.4 m) away. Individual alligators can even be identified by their call, much like humans can be identified by their voice.

LONGEST TONGUE

Veiled Chameleon
Chamaeleo calyptratus

Chameleons have the longest tongues, relative to body size, in the entire animal world. These lizards keep their sticky, mucus-covered tongues bunched up at the back of their mouths until needed, then shoot them out a distance of one and a half times their body length to catch an insect. It's all over in about half a second.

Want to know where these record-holding reptiles live around the world? Take a look at this range map to find out.

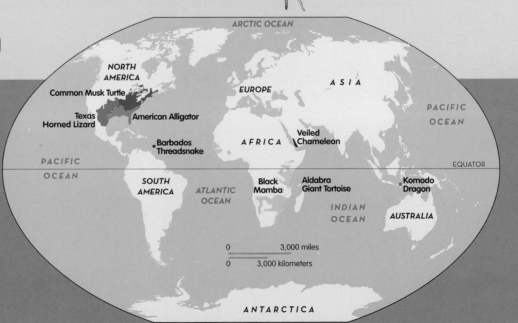

RANGES OF RECORD-SETTING REPTILES
- Aldabra Giant Tortoise
- Barbados Threadsnake
- Black Mamba
- Texas Horned Lizard
- Komodo Dragon
- Common Musk Turtle
- American Alligator
- Veiled Chameleon

ARCTIC OCEAN

NORTH AMERICA
Common Musk Turtle
Texas Horned Lizard
American Alligator
EUROPE
ASIA
PACIFIC OCEAN
AFRICA
Veiled Chameleon
Barbados Threadsnake
PACIFIC OCEAN
EQUATOR
SOUTH AMERICA
ATLANTIC OCEAN
Black Mamba
Aldabra Giant Tortoise
Komodo Dragon
INDIAN OCEAN
AUSTRALIA

0   3,000 miles
0   3,000 kilometers

ANTARCTICA

169

The name "amphibian" comes from a Greek word that means "living a double life." The term refers to the ability of some of these animals to live on land and in water. Frogs are amphibians that begin life underwater but head to land when they mature.

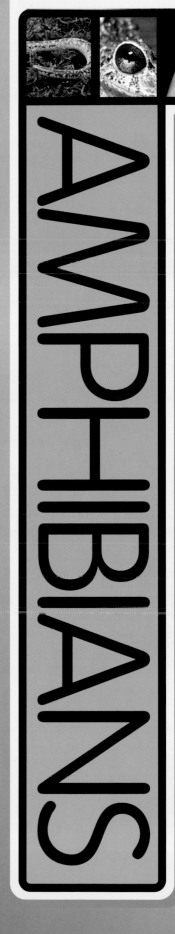

AMPHIBIANS

PACIFIC TREE FROG

AMERICAN TOAD

ROBBER FROG

PETERS' TOADLET

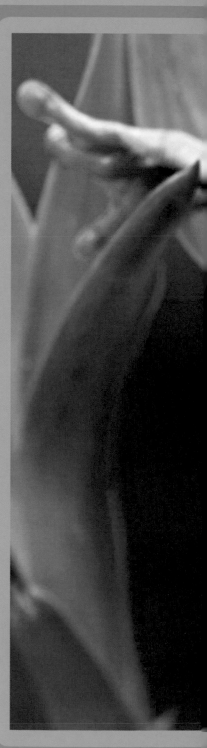

AUSTRALIAN GREEN TREE FROGS

BICOLOR CAECILIAN

AFRICAN BULLFROG

172

RED-EYED TREE FROG

HARLEQUIN FLYING FROG

RED-LEGGED FROG

GRAY TREE FROG

GLASS FROG AND EGGS

GOLFODULCEAN POISON FROG

SPOTTED SALAMANDER

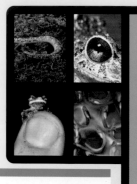

WHAT IS AN AMPHIBIAN?

AMPHIBIANS ARE VERTEBRATES THAT NEED WATER, OR A MOIST ENVIRONMENT, TO SURVIVE.

The almost 8,300 species in this group include frogs, toads, salamanders, and newts. All can absorb water and breathe through their very thin skin.

Amphibians also have special skin glands that produce useful proteins. Some transport water, oxygen, and carbon dioxide either into or out of the animal. Others fight bacteria or fungal infections. And at least one—in each species—is used for defense.

To warn potential predators, the most toxic amphibians are also the most brightly colored. Another special feature of most amphibians is their egg-larva-adult life cycle. The larvae are aquatic and free-swimming—frogs and toads at this stage are called tadpoles. At a certain size, the young develop limbs and lungs. Some also lose their tails. Eventually, they hop or climb out of the water as adults, and spend the rest of their lives on land. This process is known as metamorphosis.

Like reptiles, amphibians are ectothermic, meaning they depend on external sources to regulate their body temperature. Because of their special skin, they require very specific living conditions. Too much sun can damage their cells. Too much wind can dry their skin and dehydrate the animal. As a result, amphibians are the first to die off when their habitats are disturbed or contaminated with chemicals like weed killers. More than half of all frog species are in danger of extinction.

CLASSIFICATION OF **AMPHIBIANS**

Amphibians appear in the fossil record more than 250 million years ago. They were the first four-legged vertebrates to live on land and are considered descendants of fish and ancestors of terrestrial reptiles. They were once much larger than they are today. They exist today in three orders. Frogs and toads are by far the most numerous.

1 SALAMANDERS AND NEWTS (Caudata)

2 FROGS AND TOADS (Anura)

3 CAECILIANS (Gymnophiona)

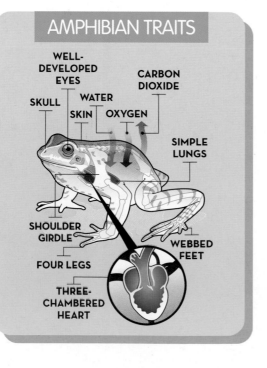

AMPHIBIAN TRAITS

Frogs, like all amphibians, have very delicate skin that allows water, oxygen, carbon dioxide, and chemicals to pass right through.

WELL-DEVELOPED EYES

CARBON DIOXIDE

SKULL

WATER

SKIN OXYGEN

SIMPLE LUNGS

SHOULDER GIRDLE

WEBBED FEET

FOUR LEGS

THREE-CHAMBERED HEART

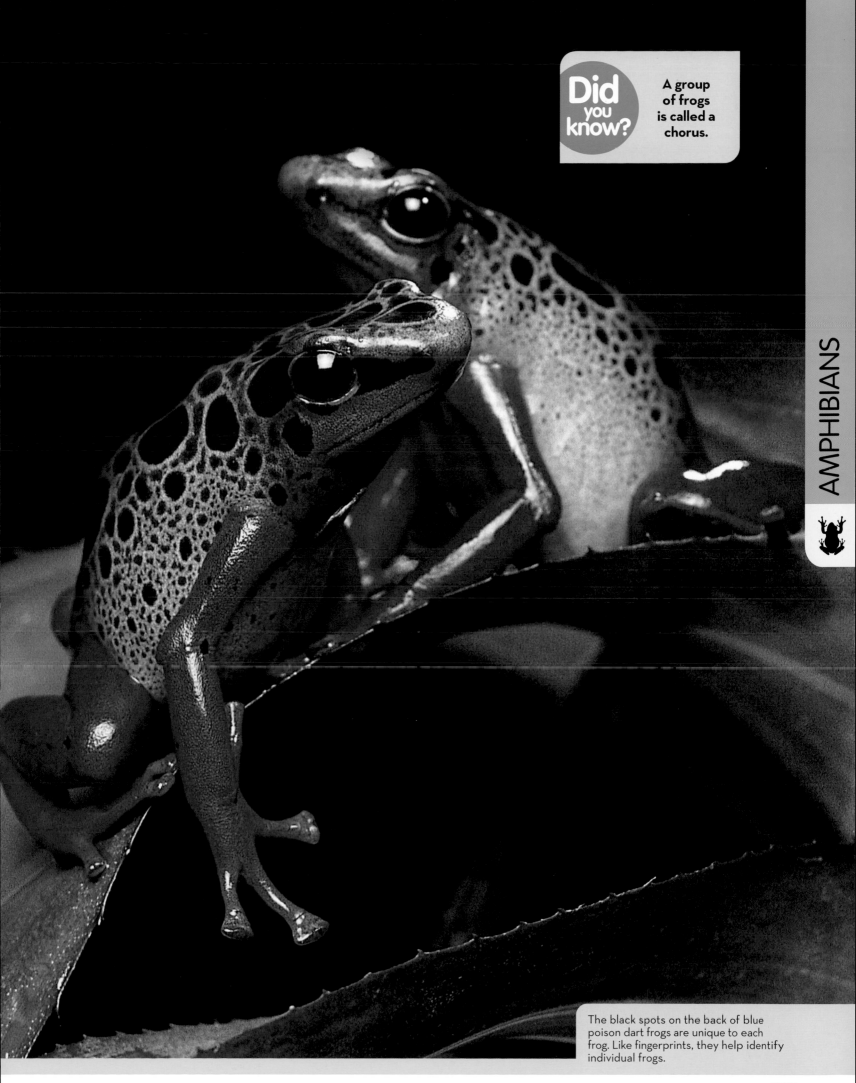

Did you know? A group of frogs is called a chorus.

The black spots on the back of blue poison dart frogs are unique to each frog. Like fingerprints, they help identify individual frogs.

175

SALAMANDERS
AND NEWTS

Salamanders have smooth, slimy skin compared to newts, which have bumpy skin. All require moist habitats such as caves, wetlands, streams, and forests. They are aquatic, terrestrial, or both, depending on their life cycle. One-third of all salamanders are found in North America, with the highest density in the Appalachian Mountains.

Most, like the tiger salamander, begin life as aquatic larvae with external gills, then change, through a process called metamorphosis, to terrestrial adults with simple lungs. Others, such as axolotl (AXE-oh-la-til), are aquatic animals throughout their life cycle. Some, such as the eastern red-spotted newt, are terrestrial while they mature, then aquatic as adults. Finally, there are lungless salamanders, which are completely terrestrial.

All are carnivorous. For defense, they produce toxins in their skin and their bright colors warn predators. Life spans range from 10 to 15 years.

AXOLOTL
Ambystoma mexicanum

RANGE: Southern Mexico

SIZE: 9.1 to 11.8 in (20 to 30 cm)

DIET: Anything that it can catch, such as mollusks, fish, arthropods

The axolotl is an aquatic salamander that does not go through a complete metamorphosis. The adults look like the larval form. They have external gills, a dorsal fin, and short legs. They also are able to regrow lost limbs.

ITALIAN NEWT
Lissotriton italicus

RANGE: Italy

SIZE: Up to 3 in (8 cm)

DIET: Plankton and other invertebrates

The rate of development of the Italian newt depends on the temperature of its environment, which is true for all amphibians. In this species, metamorphosis from larvae to juvenile takes four to six weeks in warm water, and several months in cold water.

CAVE SALAMANDER
Eurycea lucifuga

RANGE: Central eastern United States

SIZE: 4.9 to 7.1 in (12.5 to 18.1 cm)

DIET: Variety of invertebrates

There are more than a dozen species of salamanders that live in caves. The spotted-tail cave salamander is found near the entrance. It lives under rocks and in rock crevices, and has a long, prehensile tail that it uses to climb.

LESSER SIREN
Siren intermedia

RANGE: Eastern United States and northern Mexico

SIZE: 7 to 27 in (18 to 68 cm)

DIET: Aquatic invertebrates, including crustaceans, insect larvae, worms, snails

Most of the time, lesser sirens are buried in mud and debris at the bottom of slow-moving streams. If its habitat dries up temporarily, this species can survive by secreting a protective layer of mucus, like a cocoon.

ARBOREAL SALAMANDER
Aneides lugubris

RANGE: California, U.S.A.

SIZE: 4 to 7.2 in (10 to 18.4 cm)

DIET: Variety of invertebrates

This tree-climbing salamander is found in the black oak–yellow pine forests of the Sierra Nevada foothills. It has a prehensile tail and has been found as high as 60 feet (18 m) above ground! Males have visibly sharp teeth.

LONG-TOED SALAMANDER
Ambystoma macrodactylum

RANGE: Northwestern United States, Canada

SIZE: Up to 4 in (10 cm)

DIET: Worms, tadpoles, insects, small fish

The long-toed salamander can survive in all kinds of habitats, as long as there is water nearby. The adults are seen only during the breeding season. Most of the time they stay moist underground in burrows created by rodents, or under rocks and rotten logs.

HELLBENDER
Cryptobranchus alleganiensis

RANGE: United States

SIZE: 11 to 29 in (28 to 74 cm)

DIET: Crayfish, insects, fish, worms

The three species of giant salamanders—Chinese, Japanese, and American, or hellbender—are all aquatic as adults. Lacking gills, they breathe through long folds of skin. Hellbenders can weigh as much as 5.5 pounds (2.5 kg).

EMPEROR NEWT
Tylototriton shanjing

RANGE: Southern China

SIZE: 5.9 to 7.9 in (15 to 20 cm)

DIET: Small insects

The orange spots on the sides of this newt are filled with a toxic poison that is highly dangerous for potential predators like mice. They also have a relatively thick skull. These adaptations are for defense, not offense.

EASTERN RED-SPOTTED NEWT
Notophthalmus viridescens

RANGE: Eastern North America

SIZE: 2.6 to 6 in (6.5 to 15 cm)

DIET: Small invertebrates

The larval form of this species is light green. The terrestrial, immature form is bright orange-red with spots and is called an eft. The mature form is aquatic, with olive-green skin and the same orange-red spots.

WESTERN TIGER SALAMANDER
Ambystoma mavortium

RANGE: Southwestern Canada, western United States, northern Mexico

SIZE: 5.9 to 14 in (15 to 35.6 cm)

DIET: Small insects, slugs, worms; sometimes small frogs, lizards, small mice, snakes

To escape temperature extremes and dry air, tiger salamanders spend their days underground in deep burrows they dig in the soil. At night, they come out to feed, using their sticky tongues to catch prey. This tiger salamander is one of the largest in North America.

AMPHIBIANS

177

LAO WARTY NEWT

In 2002, scientists published a paper about the Lao warty newt *(Laotriton laoensis)*, a type of salamander that lives only in a small area of northern Laos. Unfortunately, wildlife traders used this information in the scientific journal to find the newts, which have distinctive bright yellow stripes on their back and an orange stomach. They began capturing them and selling them as pets. For a species that was rare to begin with, this was a problem.

The Lao warty newt was the first species of salamander ever recognized in Laos. To get more information about the newt, I began studying it in 2007. I started by showing photos of the newt to local people. The first questions I always got were "Do you want to buy it?" or "How much do you want to pay?" I had to explain that I was not visiting their village to buy the species but to learn about it.

The next step was finding the newts, which are active during the day in certain stream pools high up in the mountains. Once I found them, my team and I had to catch them. Some we were able to easily capture by hand or with a fish net. But to reach others, we had to snorkel in the cold mountain streams. Even though Laos is a tropical country, it can get very cold at high elevations. We were freezing and had to build a fire to warm up!

As a result of my study, which revealed how endangered this newt is, the Lao government banned the commercial trade of Lao warty newts. I created an educational poster about conserving them in seven languages. I went back to each village to share the posters and tell the people that they had a rare and beautiful newt in their village. In Lao, the word for "newt" is *patin*, and people still recognized me as the person who asked about the newt. Now my friends call me "Dr. Patin."

Somphouthone Phimmachak is the first Lao national to have expertise on the amphibians and reptiles of her country. In 2014, the IUCN Red List of Threatened Species listed the Lao warty newt as Endangered because of her research. Since then, she has found four additional newt species in Laos, one that is new to science and found only in that country.

ASIA

LAOS

SOUTH CHINA SEA

RANGE OF THE
LAOTRITON LAOENSIS
(LAO WARTY NEWT)

0   200 miles

0   200 kilometers

Gulf of Thailand

OBSERVATION TIPS

1 Have a local guide lead you to the right stream during the day when the newts are active.

2 Search at the right time of year. It's hard to find these newts during the rainy season.

3 Don't step on the leaf pack at the bottom of the stream. That's where these newts hide their eggs.

4 Be very quiet and still. If you startle a newt, it will swim away and hide.

Lao warty newts mate from November to February, the coldest and driest time of year. Females lay their eggs between two dead leaves or folded within one leaf at the bottom of stream pools. Many females may deposit their eggs in the same leaf pack. Newly hatched larvae, or tadpoles, live in the water. But after that they grow legs and, for a time, live only on land. Adults live mostly in the water.

FROGS AND TOADS

All toads are frogs ... but not all frogs are toads!

A toad is a type of frog that needs relatively little water. Instead of wet skin, long legs, and webbed feet, toads have dry skin, short legs, and stubby bodies. As a defense against predators, toads have a pair of paratoid glands behind their eyes that ooze poisonous fluid when they feel threatened. (See diagram on page 181.)

Otherwise, toads are very similar to other frogs. They have breathable skin, saclike lungs, and a four-stage life cycle. They also lack tails. All frogs and toads are in the order Anura, which means "tailless" in Greek.

Of the 54 frog families, one contains mostly toads, the bufonid (boo-FON-id) family. The animals in this group are known as "true toads." They include the cane toad, green toad, smooth-sided toad, Panamanian golden frog, and the limosa harlequin frog. In addition to other toad traits, they share one more: They lack teeth.

Life spans for true toads range from seven to 10 years, though some may live up to 40 years in captivity.

GREEN TOAD
Pseudepidalea viridis

RANGE: Europe, Asia, northern Africa

SIZE: 1.8 to 4.7 in (4.8 to 12 cm)

DIET: Insects, worms, butterflies, moths, caterpillars

These "green" toads vary in color, appearing also in brown, red, or black. In northern Europe, they live near open bodies of water or in places that flood seasonally. Elsewhere in their range, they inhabit arid and sandy areas.

CANE TOAD
Rhinella marina

RANGE: Texas, U.S.A.; South America to the central Amazon and parts of Peru

SIZE: 6 to 7 in (15 to 17.5 cm)

DIET: Ants, beetles, earwigs; sometimes dragonflies, grasshoppers, crustaceans, plant matter, true bugs

The cane toad was introduced to the Caribbean, Hawaii, and Australia to control sugarcane beetles. Instead, it became an invasive species, preying on native frogs. Its skin secretions are also very toxic.

SONORAN DESERT TOAD
Incilius alvarius

RANGE: Southwestern United States and northern Mexico

SIZE: 4.3 to 7.4 in (11 to 18.7 cm)

DIET: Snails, beetles, spiders, grasshoppers, lizards, mice, smaller toads

Like many toads, this species has glands containing chemicals toxic enough to kill a dog. In people, these poisons produce hallucinations. The Sonoran Desert toad is one of the largest in North America.

PANAMANIAN GOLDEN FROG
Atelopus zeteki

RANGE: Panama

SIZE: 1.4 to 2.5 in (3.5 to 7 cm)

DIET: Variety of small invertebrates

Golden frogs are symbols of good luck in Panama. They are also symbols of extinction. The numbers of this species have declined drastically in the wild as a result of pollution, habitat loss, overcollecting, and a fungal skin disease spread by global trade.

KIHANSI SPRAY TOAD
Nectophrynoides asperginis

RANGE: Tanzania

SIZE: 0.4 to 0.7 in (1 to 1.8 cm)

DIET: Insects and small invertebrates

Before this tiny toad became extinct in the wild in 2003, it lived only near the Kihansi waterfall in Tanzania. Today, it survives only in captivity. Conservation organizations are working to reintroduce them.

FROGS VS. TOADS

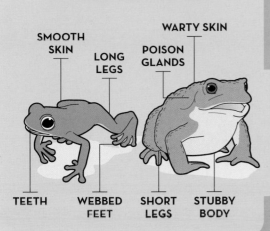

SMOOTH SKIN

LONG LEGS

WARTY SKIN

POISON GLANDS

TEETH

WEBBED FEET

SHORT LEGS

STUBBY BODY

Unlike frogs, toads have short rear legs; thick skin that is dull, dry, and covered with warts; poison glands; and no teeth.

AMERICAN TOAD
Bufo americanus

RANGE: Eastern Canada south to all U.S. Gulf Coast states except Florida

SIZE: 2 to 4 in (5 to 10.2 cm)

DIET: Insects

American toads are thriving in urban areas. As long as this species has water during the breeding season, it can survive in almost any habitat, including forests, gardens, and agricultural fields. During bouts of cold weather, they hibernate.

SMOOTH-SIDED TOAD
Bufo guttatus

RANGE: Northern South America

SIZE: 9 in (23 cm)

DIET: Insects and small mammals

The patchy light and dark brown colors of this toad help it blend in with the leaf litter on the forest floor. Smooth-sided toads are still common in South American rainforests, but they can be very hard to find.

RED-SPOTTED TOAD
Anaxyrus punctatus

RANGE: Southwestern United States and northern Mexico

SIZE: 1.5 to 2.5 in (3.8 to 6.4 cm)

DIET: Small arthropods, such as spiders and insects

Unlike so many of its relatives, populations of red-spotted toads remain stable. This toad lives in streams that run through deserts and dry areas, including grazing lands. It also likes cattle water tanks!

LIMOSA HARLEQUIN FROG
Atelopus limosus

RANGE: Panama

SIZE: 1 to 1.8 in (2.6 to 4.6 cm)

DIET: Invertebrates

In this species, the female is not only larger than the male but also has brighter coloring, with a red or orange belly. The limosa harlequin frog is another amphibian in trouble. It has largely disappeared from higher elevations in its range.

HOUSTON TOAD
Bufo houstonensis

RANGE: Southeastern Texas, U.S.A.

SIZE: 1.8 to 3.5 in (4.5 to 8.8 cm)

DIET: Ground beetles; small ants and toads

Some species of frogs and toads have small ranges, which can make them even more vulnerable to extinction. The Houston toad is one of them. It is found only in southeastern Texas and has been on the endangered species list since 1974.

AMPHIBIANS

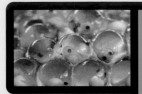

FROGS

Frogs are found everywhere except the open ocean and Antarctica. Their lifestyles differ depending on their habitats, but all require access to a moist environment, especially during the breeding season. More than half of the world's frogs are found in tropical rainforests.

Compared to toads, frogs have a shorter body, webbed feet, smoother skin, and long rear legs that allow them to swim and leap. Most also have protruding eyes and teeth on their upper jaws. Like all amphibians, frogs produce a variety of skin secretions. Poison frogs, for example, secrete chemicals known as alkaloids. The source of these toxins is the frog's insect diet, particularly ants. Other skin secretions act naturally to help the frog fight off infections from bacteria and fungi. Several of these chemicals are being studied as promising medicines for humans.

Life spans range from four to six years for smaller frogs and up to 10 for larger ones.

STRAWBERRY POISON DART FROG
Oophaga pumilio

RANGE: Nicaragua, Panama, Costa Rica

SIZE: 0.7 to 0.9 in (1.7 to 2.4 cm)

DIET: Small arthropods; mostly ants but also mites

All of the approximately 320 species in the Dendrobatidae (den-dro-BAY-tid-eye) family are called "poison dart frogs," though only some—including the strawberry poison dart frog—are so toxic that their poisonous secretions are used to coat the tips of hunting arrows.

GOLDEN POISON FROG
Phyllobates terribilis

RANGE: Pacific coast of Colombia

SIZE: 1.8 to 2 in (4.7 to 5.1 cm)

DIET: Ants; also other small invertebrates such as termites and beetles

Like the strawberry poison dart frog, skin secretions from this species are used to coat arrow tips. It is, by far, the most toxic of the poison frogs. Poison from a single frog is enough to kill 10 grown humans.

AMERICAN BULLFROG
Rana catesbeianus

RANGE: Eastern and central North America (has been introduced to South America, Europe, and Asia)

SIZE: 4.3 to 7.1 in (11 to 18 cm)

DIET: Frogs and tadpoles; snakes, insects, worms, crustaceans

Bullfrogs eat the tadpoles of other frogs and are large enough to escape predation by fish. As a result, they are rapidly increasing in number and moving west into new habitats, such as ponds stocked with fish.

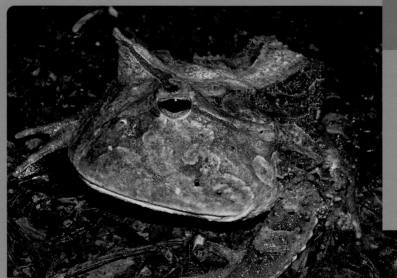

SURINAM HORNED FROG
Ceratophrys cornuta

RANGE: Amazon Basin

SIZE: 2.8 to 4.7 in (7.2 to 12 cm)

DIET: Mostly ants and beetles; other frogs, small reptiles, small mammals

The shape and coloration of this terrestrial frog give it near-perfect camouflage. Horned frogs bury themselves in the leaves on the rainforest floor and wait to ambush their unsuspecting prey.

Did you know?

A frog uses its eyeballs to push food down its throat.

COMMON COQUI
Eleutherodactylus coqui

RANGE: Puerto Rico

SIZE: 0.9 to 2.2 in (2.4 to 5.5 cm)

DIET: Mostly small arthropods

Frogs fill their vocal sacs, located under the throat, with air to make their calls louder. The frog's size determines the pitch of the call. Smaller ones, like the tiny tree frog known as the coqui (ko-KEE), make high-pitched calls.

DYEING POISON FROG
Dendrobates tinctorius

RANGE: Suriname and Brazil

SIZE: 1.2 to 1.8 in (3 to 4.7 cm)

DIET: Insects and other arthropods, especially ants, flies, mites, spiders, beetles, termites, maggots, caterpillars

Like the other species in its family, the dyeing poison frog is small and colorful and has toxic skin. It is a very territorial animal that will readily chase off or fight with intruders, of the same or different species.

RED-EYED TREE FROG
Agalychnis callidryas

RANGE: Southern Mexico, Central America

SIZE: 2.4 to 3.2 in (6 to 8 cm)

DIET: Insects, especially crickets, moths, flies, grasshoppers; sometimes smaller frogs

These brightly colored tree frogs have tiny suction cups on the bottom of their toes that allow them to cling to anything. They often rest by hanging from the underside of leaves—with their toes.

AFRICAN CLAWED FROG
Xenopus laevis

RANGE: Southern Africa

SIZE: 2 to 4.7 in (5 to 12 cm)

DIET: Insects; other vertebrates, especially anurans, fish, birds, small mammals

This aquatic frog thrives in warm, stagnant water. Instead of a tongue or teeth, it has claws on its rear feet (below) that it uses to break up its prey. Then it pumps water along with tiny bits of food into its mouth.

TOMATO FROG
Dyscophus insularis

RANGE: Madagascar

SIZE: 1.6 to 2 in (4 to 5 cm)

DIET: Invertebrates, especially crickets and waxworms; mice

When a predator grabs a tomato frog, it is in for a nasty surprise. The frog puffs up its body and secretes an irritating, thick mucus. In response, the predator—a stork, crocodile, or snake—often drops the frog.

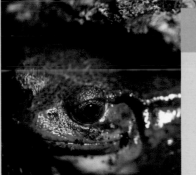

FROG LIFE CYCLE

Like all amphibians, frogs and toads require water to complete their life cycle, from egg to tadpole to adult.

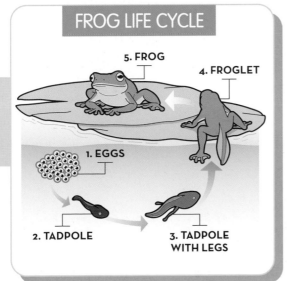

5. FROG

4. FROGLET

1. EGGS

2. TADPOLE

3. TADPOLE WITH LEGS

EMERALD GLASS FROG
Espadarana prosoblepon

RANGE: Central America and South America

SIZE: 0.8 to 1.2 in (2.1 to 3.1 cm)

DIET: Insects

Glass frogs are found in humid rainforests. They are named for the transparent skin covering the belly. This skin is so glass-like that it is possible to see the internal organs.

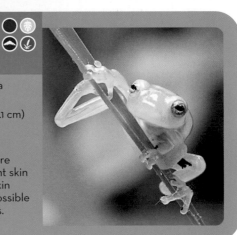

FROM THE LENS

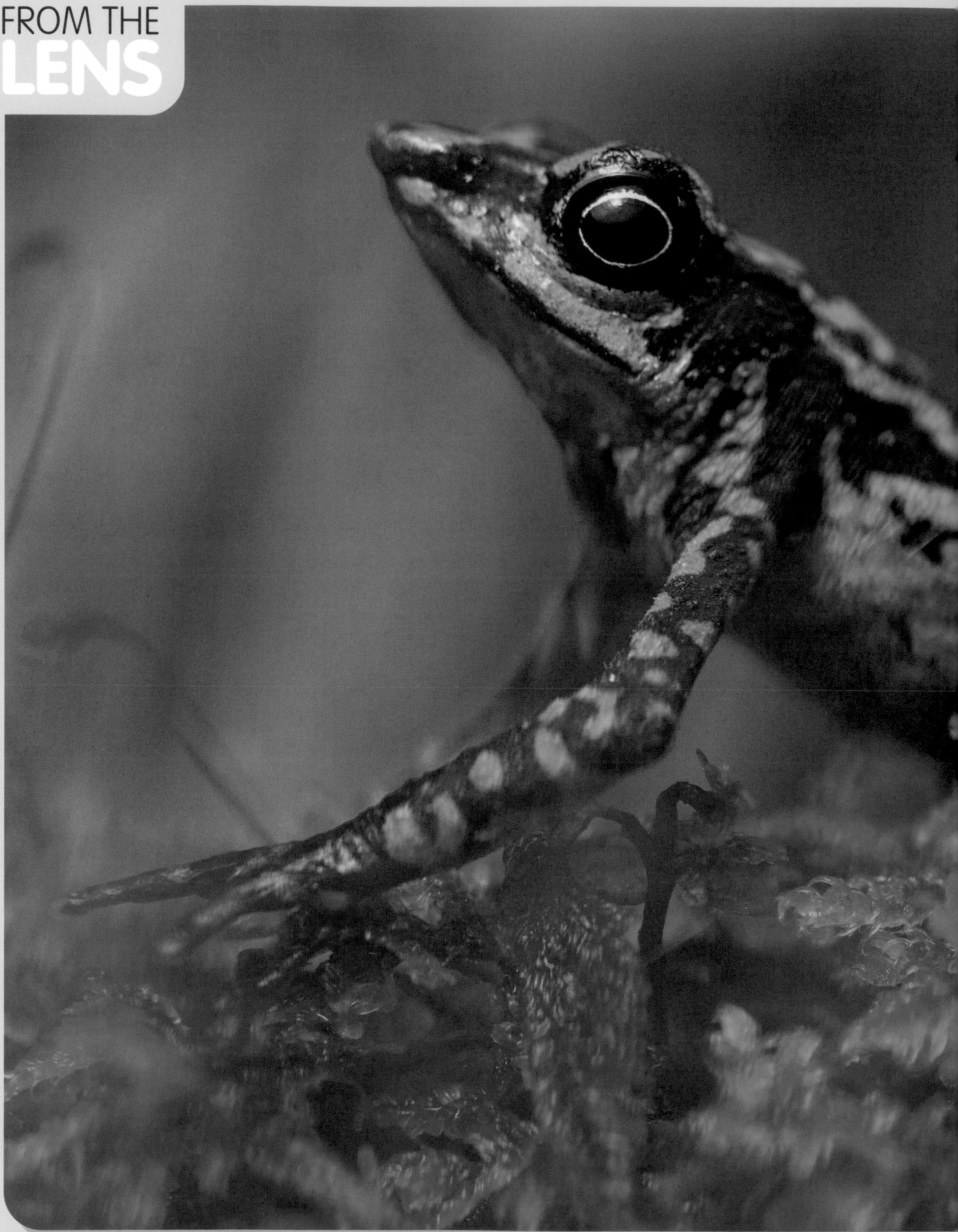

BEING CRITICALLY ENDANGERED IS
actually a step up for the webbed harlequin
(*Atelopus palmatus*). This stubbed toad species
was thought to have become extinct—like many
other amphibians, a victim of the deadly fungal
disease chytridiomycosis. Small populations were
rediscovered in the tropical rainforests of Ecuador.

185

RECORDS

E ver heard of a salamander that's as big as an adult human or a frog that can soar in the air? There are tons of incredible things amphibians can do, so hop in and check out these wet and wild record holders of the amphibian world!

LARGEST AMPHIBIAN

Chinese Giant Salamander

Andrias davidianus

Measuring up to six feet (1.8 m) in length and weighing 24 pounds (11 kg), the Chinese giant salamander can grow to be roughly the length of an adult human. This weird and wonderful amphibian has prehistoric origins, with a family lineage dating all the way back to the age of the dinosaurs. Unfortunately, today the Chinese giant salamander is considered to be one of the most endangered amphibians, as its existence is being threatened by overpopulation, pollution, and hunting.

SMALLEST AMPHIBIAN

Paedophryne amauensis

Discovered as recently as 2012, *Paedophryne amauensis* is not just the world's smallest frog; it is currently the world's smallest vertebrate. Measuring a maximum of 0.3 inch (7.7 mm), this itty-bitty amphibian is roughly the size of a housefly. It beat out the previous smallest vertebrate titleholder, a species of fish, by a mere .01 inch (0.2 mm). Talk about winning by a hair!

LOUDEST AMPHIBIAN

American Bullfrog

Lithobates catesbeianus

The American bullfrog, the largest frog in North America, has a big, bellowing call to match its substantial size. Measuring up to eight inches (20.3 cm) in length and weighing up to 1.5 pounds (0.7 kg), this loud-mouth amphibian's croak is said to resemble a cow's *moo*, which is how "bull" became part of its name. Active mostly at night, the bullfrog's deep-pitched call can be heard more than a quarter mile (0.4 km) away.

MOST TOXIC FROG

Golden Poison Frog

Phyllobates terribilis

Don't be fooled by this frog's cute and friendly appearance. That bright yellow color means "stay away." The golden poison frog stands out from its green-and-brown surroundings for a reason: Just one touch can bring on muscle paralysis and even death in a matter of minutes. Its skin contains a toxin that's so potent, one two-inch (5-cm) frog has enough toxins to kill at least 10 full-grown men.

FANCIEST FLIER →

Wallace's Flying Frog
Rhacophorus nigropalmatus

OK, so you know frogs can't really fly—but if you saw this one, you might think twice about that. The Wallace's flying frog, native to Borneo, doesn't defy the laws of gravity, but it is an accomplished glider, able to soar up to 50 feet (15.2 m) in the air from tree to tree. How does it do it? Easy. Super-webbed feet and extra skin folds help this frog catch air and glide to a halt in the trees or on the ground. Now, that is some fancy flying!

COOLEST CAMOUFLAGE →

Physalaemus nattereri

This frog doesn't have eyes in the back of its head, but it sure looks that way! The *Physalaemus nattereri* is a tiny amphibian native to South America that has one very cool feature. Two splotches on its hind end resemble the eyes of a much larger animal. If this fearless frog becomes threatened, it will raise up its rear and send predators running!

GREATEST GETAWAY →

Mount Lyell Salamander
Hydromantes platycephalus

What it lacks in size, the Mount Lyell salamander certainly makes up in style. A true rock-and-roller, this slippery salamander turns itself into a rubbery ball to get away from predators. If disturbed, it shuts its eyes, tucks in its arms and legs, and takes on a tire-like shape for a quick escape down a rocky slope.

LARGEST FROG →

Goliath Frog
Conraua goliath

It may seem like nothing compared to the six-foot (1.8-m) Chinese giant salamander, but imagine a frog the size of a house cat and try not to be impressed! The Goliath frog, native to rainforests in Africa, measures up to 12.5 inches (32 cm) in length and weighs a whopping 7.2 pounds (3.3 kg). What does it take to satisfy a frog this size? A lot of insects, fish, other amphibians, and—in some cases—bats!

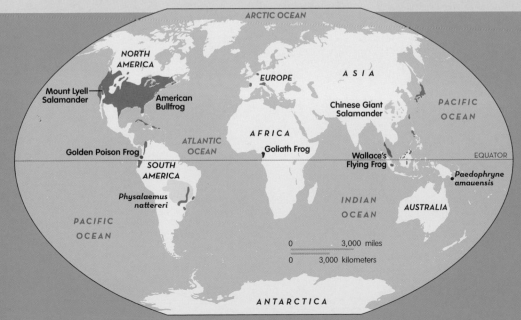

Want to know where these record-holding amphibians live around the world? Take a look at this range map to find out!

RANGES OF RECORD-SETTING AMPHIBIANS

- Chinese Giant Salamander
- *Paedophryne amauensis*
- American Bullfrog
- Golden Poison Frog
- Wallace's Flying Frog
- *Physalaemus nattereri*
- Mount Lyell Salamander
- Goliath Frog

187

All fish live in water and have a backbone, but as a group they are very diverse. Fish include four classes of animals and at least 33,000 species.

FISH

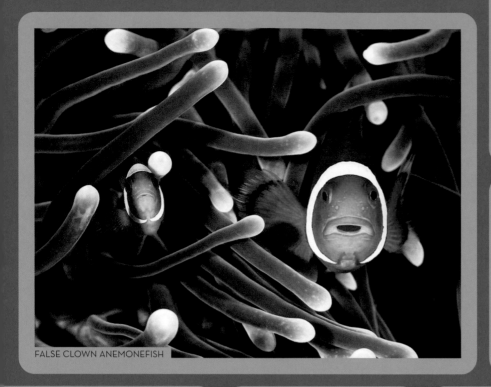
FALSE CLOWN ANEMONEFISH

CORAL GROUPER

JUMPING RAINBOW TROUT

BULLETHEAD PARROTFISH

BULL SHARK

PIRAPUTANGA

SPOTTED TRUNKFISH

NEON GOBY

DEEP SEA ROCKLING

HARLEQUIN TUSK WRASSE

ORANGE FAIRY BASSLETS
AND STONY CORAL

LONGSPINED PORCUPINEFISH
AND SEA FAN

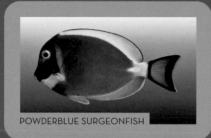

POWDERBLUE SURGEONFISH

REDCAP ORANDA GOLDFISH

SILVERSIDES

BLUE-SPOTTED STINGRAY

WHALE SHARK AND REMORA

GIANT MOTTLED EEL

191

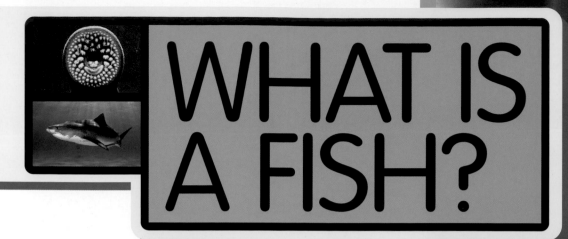

WHAT IS A FISH?

ALL FISH SHARE TWO TRAITS: THEY LIVE IN WATER AND THEY ARE VERTEBRATES.

Apart from these similarities, however, many of the species in this group differ markedly from one another. Fin fish like salmon have gills, are covered in scales, and reproduce by laying eggs. Eels, by contrast, have wormlike bodies and exceedingly slippery skin. Lungfish gulp air. Whale sharks, the largest fish, give birth to live young and eat only tiny fish, squid, and plankton. Some species, such as the weedy sea dragon, are so bizarre they seem almost unreal.

Fish have developed special senses, too. Because water transmits sounds, disperses chemicals, and conducts electricity better than air, fish rely less on their vision and more on their hearing, taste, and smell. Many can detect motion in the water using a special row of scales with sensors known as the lateral line. Others can find their prey and even navigate by detecting electrical charges.

One reason fish are so diverse is that 71 percent of the planet is covered in water. Fish are adapted to live in a variety of fresh, salt, and brackish (slightly salty) aquatic habitats, ranging from coral reefs and kelp forests to rivers, streams, and the open ocean. Another is that fish have been on Earth for a very long time—according to fossil records, more than 518 million years!

The total number of living fish species—at least 34,000—is about the same as the total of all other vertebrate species (amphibians, reptiles, birds, and mammals) combined.

FISH TRAITS

ANCIENT

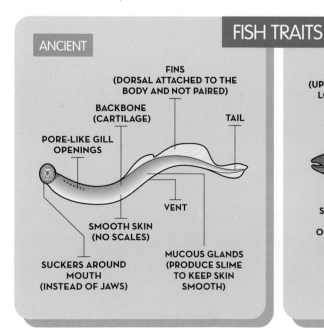

FINS (DORSAL ATTACHED TO THE BODY AND NOT PAIRED)

BACKBONE (CARTILAGE)

TAIL

PORE-LIKE GILL OPENINGS

VENT

SMOOTH SKIN (NO SCALES)

MUCOUS GLANDS (PRODUCE SLIME TO KEEP SKIN SMOOTH)

SUCKERS AROUND MOUTH (INSTEAD OF JAWS)

MODERN

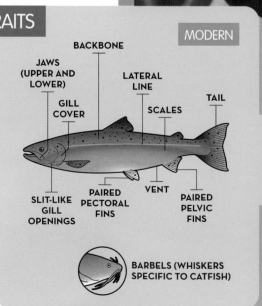

BACKBONE

JAWS (UPPER AND LOWER)

LATERAL LINE

GILL COVER

SCALES

TAIL

SLIT-LIKE GILL OPENINGS

PAIRED PECTORAL FINS

VENT

PAIRED PELVIC FINS

BARBELS (WHISKERS SPECIFIC TO CATFISH)

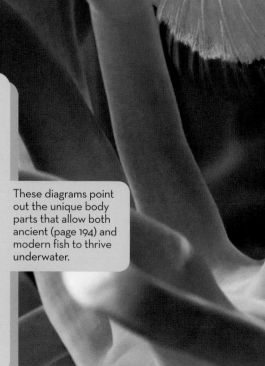

These diagrams point out the unique body parts that allow both ancient (page 194) and modern fish to thrive underwater.

CLASSIFICATION OF **FISH**

Fish can be divided into two major categories: fish without backbones (hagfish) and fish with backbones (all the others). Fish with backbones can be further subdivided into two different superclasses: fish without jaws (lampreys) and fish with jaws. Finally, fish with jaws can be divided into cartilaginous fish and bony fish (lobe-finned and ray-finned).

JAWLESS FISH

The superclass Agnatha includes Cephalaspidomorphi. These are the fish without jaws, like the sea lamprey.

JAWED FISH

The class Chondrichthyes falls under the superclass Gnathostomata and includes **cartilaginous fish,** such as chimaeras, sharks, skates, and rays.

The class Osteichthyes, or **bony fish,** also falls under the superclass Gnathostomata. The bony fish are further divided into the lobe-finned (Sarcopterygii) and ray-finned (Actinopterygii) fish.

Lobe-Finned Fish

> Today's lobe-finned fish are few in number, represented only by the lungfish and the deep-ocean-living coelacanth. Their limb-like fins share features with the fossils of the first four-legged vertebrates.

Ray-Finned Fish

> About half of all living vertebrates are ray-finned bony fish, like this sailfish. Other examples of ray-finned bony fish include the goby, from one of the largest families of fish; the emperor angelfish, one of the most colorful; and the sturgeon, one of the longest living.

FISH

A bright and colorful clownfish swims among poisonous anemone tentacles without being stung. How? A special mucus covers and protects its skin from the poison.

ANCIENT FISH

Based on studies of the fossil record, the species known as lungfish, arowana, sturgeon, and gar are some of the oldest known fish—about 200 million years old.

Two species are even older—the hagfish and the lamprey. These are the world's only remaining jawless fish. They first appear in the fossil record 500 million years ago.

Together, these species are considered "ancient" fish because they share relatively few features with modern-day fish. For example, sturgeon and gar have fins with rays like the bony fish, but their skeletons are made up mostly of cartilage. Their scales are interlocking bony plates that look like body armor. Like lungfish, gar are capable of gulping air if the oxygen levels in the water are too low.

Arowana and arapaima are bony-tongued fish. Instead of teeth in their lower jaw, they have a tonguelike structure made of bone and rimmed with teeth. Their gills also are nonfunctional. These fish must surface every few minutes to take a gulp of air.

Life spans range from 15 years for jawless fish to 100 or more for sturgeons and lobe-finned fish.

ALLIGATOR GAR
Atractosteus spatula

RANGE: United States and the Gulf of Mexico

SIZE: Up to 10 ft (3 m)

DIET: Fish, ducks, turtles, small mammals, carrion

The alligator gar is one of the largest freshwater fish in North America. Because of its size and body armor, it has few natural predators. This species was once common but is declining because of overfishing and habitat loss.

SEA LAMPREY
Petromyzon marinus

RANGE: Atlantic coasts of Europe, North America, and the western Mediterranean Sea

SIZE: Up to 4 ft (1.2 m)

DIET: Blood and skin of other fish

This parasitic fish latches on to the skin of another fish using the rim of suckers around its mouth. It then feeds on blood and flesh. It is invasive in the Great Lakes region of North America, where it preys on lake trout.

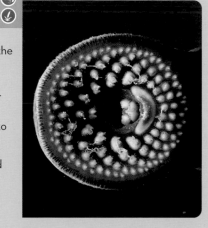

PACIFIC HAGFISH
Eptatretus stoutii

RANGE: Pacific Ocean

SIZE: 2 ft (0.6 m)

DIET: Dead or dying fish and mammals; marine invertebrates, including worms

Hagfish are also called slime eels. Like lampreys, they have a skull but no jaw. Worms are their main diet, but they will feed on—even swim into—dying or dead animals. When threatened, they excrete large amounts of slime.

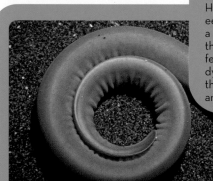

COELACANTH
Latimeria chalumnae

RANGE: Western Indian Ocean off the east African coast

SIZE: About 6.5 ft (2 m) long and nearly 220 lb (100 kg)

DIET: Cephalopods and fish

Once thought to be extinct, the coelacanth (SEE-luh-kanth) is unlike any other living fish. Its vertebrae are incompletely formed, and it has an electrosensory organ on its snout that may help it find prey. A hinged joint on its skull allows its mouth to open extra wide, and paired lobe fins move like arms and legs as it swims.

AROWANA
Osteoglossum bicirrhosum

RANGE: Amazon drainage system, South America

SIZE: Up to 3.9 ft (1.2 m)

DIET: Crustaceans, insects, smaller fish, and other animals that float on the water's surface

Arowana are ambush-style hunters. They hide beneath low-lying tree branches and will jump out of the water to grab a bird or insect. These fish are mouthbrooders, which means they hold their eggs and young in their mouth.

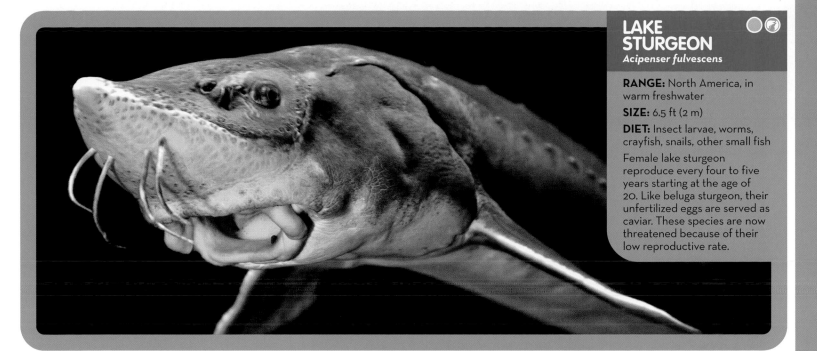

LAKE STURGEON
Acipenser fulvescens

RANGE: North America, in warm freshwater

SIZE: 6.5 ft (2 m)

DIET: Insect larvae, worms, crayfish, snails, other small fish

Female lake sturgeon reproduce every four to five years starting at the age of 20. Like beluga sturgeon, their unfertilized eggs are served as caviar. These species are now threatened because of their low reproductive rate.

LIVING FOSSIL
FISH

Most of today's fish look very different from their 250-to-200-million-year-old ancestors. But a few have changed so little that they are called "living fossils."

Lungfish (six species) are of special interest in piecing together evolutionary history. They are in a group known as the lobe-finned fish because of their large, fleshy fins. These fins are much more mobile than the fins of other fish, and they attach to the body like the limbs of terrestrial animals. Lungfish also breathe by gulping air. Their gills are too small to be useful. These features give these fish the ability to live in shallow water with low oxygen content—and even survive out of water, buried in mud. For these reasons, the lungfish are considered close relatives of the first vertebrate animals to live on land.

LONGNOSE GAR
Lepisosteus osseus

RANGE: United States and Canada

SIZE: 2 to 6 ft (0.6 to 1.8 m)

DIET: Mostly fish, small crustaceans, insects

The longnose gar hunts mostly at night. It attacks its fish prey from the side, grabbing them with rows of teeth on its long, narrow snout. Its eggs are poisonous to other animals—including humans.

ARAPAIMA
Arapaima gigas

RANGE: Brazil, Guyana, Peru

SIZE: Up to 9 ft (2.7 m)

DIET: Crustaceans and fish

The arapaima is one of the largest species of freshwater fish. An air breather, it often is found in warm, shallow water. The way to find this fish is to watch the surface of the water until it comes up for a breath, which it does every 10 minutes or so.

WEST AFRICAN LUNGFISH
Protopterus annectens

RANGE: Africa

SIZE: 3.3 ft (1 m)

DIET: Mollusks, frogs, fish, seeds, aquatic vegetation

Dwelling in swamps and backwater areas, this lungfish adapts to the dry season by cocooning itself in slime. It can remain this way for more than a year.

FISH

195

SHARKS

Sharks are a group of over 500 species. All have torpedo-shaped bodies, skeletons made of cartilage, exposed gill slits, powerful tails, teeth that are replaced throughout their lives, and pectoral fins that resemble airplane wings.

Most are predators with highly developed senses for hunting prey. Sharks have good underwater vision and acute senses of taste and smell. They can detect tiny amounts of chemicals in the water—as little as one drop of blood. They have lateral line pores for sensing sound and motion. They can pick up electrical signals as subtle as those created by the muscles of their prey.

Sharks are almost always on the move. For one thing, they are hungry. But many must swim to avoid sinking because they lack an air bladder, which helps other fish stay afloat when not moving. Others cannot pump water over their gills, so they cannot breathe unless they swim.

Life spans range from 20 to 30 years for most species. The dogfish and whale shark can live up to 100 years.

GREAT WHITE SHARK
Carcharodon carcharias

RANGE: Cold and tropical waters around the world

SIZE: 14 to 19 ft (4.3 to 5.8 m)

DIET: Bony fish, sharks, rays, seals, sea lions, dolphins, sea turtles, squid, seabirds

This shark is an ambush hunter that rams its prey. It has a long, spongy snout to absorb the impact and massive jaws supported by layers of hard tissue called tesserae (TES-ser-ray), which act like bone.

HAMMERHEAD SHARK
Sphyrna lewini

RANGE: Warm tropical and temperate waters

SIZE: 6.5 to 14 ft (2 to 4.3 m)

DIET: Lobster, shrimp, crab, fish, squid

Hammerhead sharks have an excellent prey detection system: their huge heads. The skin is covered in electrical sensors and the eyes on either side allow the shark to see above and below at once. When bottom hunting, they also use the hammer to pin down stingrays.

BASKING SHARK
Cetorhinus maximus

RANGE: North and South Pacific and Atlantic Oceans

SIZE: 16 to 32 ft (4.9 to 9.8 m)

DIET: Zooplankton

Basking sharks are filter feeders—and the second largest shark. They feed by swimming through plankton-rich water with their huge mouths open. The water flows through their gill slits, where brushlike filaments called gill rakers trap the plankton.

SPINY DOGFISH
Squalus acanthias

RANGE: Atlantic Ocean and Indo-Pacific region

SIZE: Up to 5.2 ft (1.6 m)

DIET: Fish and crustaceans

Spiny dogfish have two spines, one in front of each dorsal fin, each containing a supply of mild venom. This small, predatory shark is found worldwide and is a major source of food, shark oil, and shark cartilage.

Did you know? The smallest sharks live in the deepest parts of the ocean.

CARTILAGINOUS FISH

Sharks, rays, and skates are called cartilaginous (car-ti-LAG-i-nous) fish because their skeletons are made entirely of cartilage. This is a lightweight material that gives them an advantage in the water over bony fish. They weigh less, which means they use less energy while swimming.

These fish also have ridges on their scales, called dermal denticles, that reduce turbulence. If you rub their skin one way, it feels smooth; rub it the other way, it feels like sandpaper. They also have winglike pectoral fins that allow them to swim birdlike, gliding underwater.

Most sharks are ovoviviparous. They give birth to live young that develop in eggs inside the adult's body. Another feature of sharks, rays, and skates is their slow reproductive rate. Most do not begin to reproduce until they are several years old, and some have very long pregnancies. The dogfish shark, for example, is pregnant for 24 months, longer than the Asian elephant! This is one reason overfishing has led to the decline of so many of these species.

LEOPARD SHARK
Triakis semifasciata

RANGE: Indian and Pacific Oceans, Australian coast

SIZE: 6.5 ft (2 m)

DIET: Crab, shrimp, bony fish, fish eggs

Leopard sharks were once in trouble from overfishing. The good news is that fishing regulations worked; their numbers are stable. The bad news is that dozens of other species are declining rapidly in number for the same reason: They are used as food in shark fin soup.

WHALE SHARK
Rhincodon typus

RANGE: Tropical and warm waters worldwide

SIZE: 36 to 39 ft (11 to 12 m)

DIET: Plankton, squid, small fish

The whale shark is the largest fish in the world, yet it is a filter feeder. Like the basking shark, it has gill rakers for trapping its food. Whale sharks migrate, often timing their movement with the spawning of corals.

WHITETIP REEF SHARK
Triaenodon obesus

RANGE: Indian and Pacific Oceans

SIZE: 5.2 ft (1.6 m)

DIET: Fish, octopuses, crab, lobsters

The whitetip reef shark specializes in squeezing into crevices, cracks, and caves, looking for fish. It feeds at night, using its sense of smell to find fish hidden in the reef. Multiple sharks often hunt in the same area.

HORN SHARK
Heterodontus francisci

RANGE: Eastern Pacific Ocean

SIZE: 4 ft (1.2 m)

DIET: Fish, sea urchins, crabs

Unlike most sharks, horn sharks are oviparous. They reproduce by laying eggs in the water enclosed in a leathery case that often washes onto shore. Within a month of hatching, the young begin to feed. Horn sharks are nocturnal and solitary.

NURSE SHARK
Ginglymostoma cirratum

RANGE: Tropical and subtropical waters in western Atlantic, eastern Atlantic, and eastern Pacific Oceans

SIZE: 14 ft (4.3 m)

DIET: Lobster, shrimp, crabs, sea urchins, squid, octopuses, stingrays, bony fish

Nurse sharks are nocturnal predators. Unlike other sharks, this species can actively pump water across its gills. Like other fish, it can breathe without swimming and is often found resting on the bottom of the ocean during the day.

FROM THE FIELD:

Brian Skerry

OCEANIC SHARK
WHITETIP SHARK

The oceanic whitetip shark (*Carcharhinus longimanus*) is built like a stout but efficient airplane, with a thick fuselage-like body and long wing-like pectoral fins. It is considered to be among the "most dangerous" species to humans and has been portrayed as an animal we should fear. Although they are top predators, they are also beautiful animals that should be respected.

There are few known locations worldwide where oceanic whitetips can be predictably found. A team I was part of discovered one of these locations in the Bahamas back in 2006. I had been searching for the sharks for more than two weeks. Finally, late one afternoon, an oceanic whitetip appeared near our boat. I immediately got into the water and spent over two hours with this stunningly beautiful animal.

While we always have to be careful when interacting with wild animals, especially sharks, my experiences with the oceanic whitetip have been positive. I have learned that, despite their fearsome reputation, they can be "polite." They are usually very curious at first and will come right to me, often bouncing their noses off my camera housing. The shark usually swims away, but often it stays within my sight and will come back close to me from time to time. Often, they stay around for hours.

Few people ever get a chance to see an oceanic whitetip for themselves. Because of this, and the villainous reputation that these sharks have been given, it's easier to ignore them or be unaware of their plight. That's why I believe it's important to have photographs of animals like oceanic whitetips. I want people to see them and understand what we all have to lose by allowing these sharks to become extinct.

Brian Skerry is an award-winning photojournalist who specializes in marine wildlife and underwater environments. Over the past 40 years, he has spent more than 10,000 hours underwater and has become one of the top ocean photographers in the world.

RANGE OF THE
*CARCHARHINUS
LONGIMANUS*
(OCEANIC WHITETIP
SHARK)

NORTH AMERICA

EUROPE

ASIA

ATLANTIC OCEAN

AFRICA

PACIFIC OCEAN

SOUTH AMERICA

INDIAN OCEAN

AUSTRALIA

ANTARCTICA

0   3,000 miles
0   3,000 kilometers

OBSERVATION TIPS

1 To see these sharks in their habitat, you must be an experienced, qualified diver.

2 Work with dive operators or researchers who have great knowledge of and experience with these animals.

3 Before entering the water, have a well-formulated dive plan with safety precautions in place.

4 Enjoy the experience, but if things don't feel right or the shark seems agitated, exit the water immediately.

FISH

Oceanic whitetip sharks live in tropical and subtropical waters throughout the world. Once the most abundant large animal on Earth, their numbers have declined by an estimated 99 percent since the 1970s. Oceanic whitetips can grow up to 13 feet (4 m) long and weigh up to 370 pounds (167.4 kg). Females give birth to between one and 15 pups every other year. Older, larger females have larger litters. Oceanic whitetips are mostly solitary, but they live in parts of the ocean where food is scarce, so they will band together in large groups when a food source is present.

SKATES AND RAYS

Skates and rays have flat bodies, long tails, skeletons made of cartilage, and winglike pectoral fins. Like all fish, they breathe through their gills, but instead of taking water in through their mouths, they use a small opening behind each eye called a spiracle.

Most of the 625 species in this group are marine predators that feed along the ocean floor. Skates have small teeth for feeding on small fish in deeper water. Rays have platelike teeth for crushing snails, crabs, and other prey in shallow water.

Skates and rays are common prey for sharks and whales. For defense, skates have large, thornlike scales on their backs and sides. Rays have sharp spines about a third of the way down the length of their long tails. In stingrays, these are venomous.

Skates lay eggs in cases; rays give birth to live young. Life spans range from 15 to 50 years.

COWNOSE RAY
Rhinoptera bonasus

RANGE: Atlantic Ocean

SIZE: Disc width up to 3.6 ft (1.1 m); length 3.9 ft (1.2 m)

DIET: Invertebrates, including crustaceans and mollusks

Cownose rays often travel in schools of up to 10,000. They also hunt together by flapping their pectoral fins at the same time. The result is an underwater sandstorm that leaves their food exposed and easy to find.

GIANT MANTA RAY
Mobula birostris

RANGE: Tropical waters worldwide

SIZE: Disc width 22 to 29 ft (6 to 9 m); length 14.7 ft (4.5 m)

DIET: Plankton and fish

The giant manta is a filter feeder. Though its food is tiny, this ray is huge, weighing up to 3,100 pounds (1,400 kg.) Its large pectoral fins look like paddles. Females have just four to seven pups during their lives.

YELLOW STINGRAY
Urobatis jamaicensis

RANGE: Coastal waters of western Atlantic Ocean and the Gulf of Mexico

SIZE: Disc width up to 1.2 ft (0.4 m); length 2.2 ft (0.7 m)

DIET: Shrimp, fish, clams, worms

Yellow stingrays vary in color and pattern. The two most common are a dark green or brown ray with tiny white and yellow spots, or the reverse—a white background with tiny dark green or brown spots.

COMMON STINGRAY
Dasyatis pastinaca

RANGE: Northeastern Atlantic Ocean, and Mediterranean and Black Seas

SIZE: Disc width up to 4.6 ft (1.4 m); length up to 8.2 ft (2.5 m)

DIET: Fish, crustaceans, mollusks

Like all stingrays, the common stingray has a venom gland at the base of its spine, which is used for defense. Though this ray looks as though it has a large eye, the large oval structure is the spiracle. Their eyes are in front.

Did you know?

A species called the little skate (*Leucoraja erinacea*) is less than 20 inches (50 cm) long.

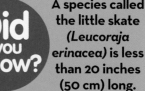

STARRY SKATE ⬤◉
Raja stellulata

RANGE: Northern Atlantic Ocean

SIZE: Length up to 2.6 ft (0.8 m)

DIET: Fish, crustaceans, worms, mollusks, cephalopods, echinoderms

Unlike rays, skates are harmless to people. Their egg cases, called "mermaid's purses," often are found washed up on the beach. The starry skate is named for its only means of protection: the 13 to 17 star-shaped thorns on its body.

BLUE-SPOTTED FANTAIL RAY ⬤◉ ◉
Taeniura lymma

RANGE: Indonesia, Japan, northern Australia, continental waters of Asia

SIZE: Disc width 1.4 ft (0.4 m); length 2.3 ft (0.7 m)

DIET: Shrimp, small bony fish, mollusks, crabs, worms

Blue-spotted fantail rays have very long tails and two venomous spines, one longer than the other. Its bright blue coloration is a warning to potential predators. This species is a favorite prey of hammerhead sharks and killer whales.

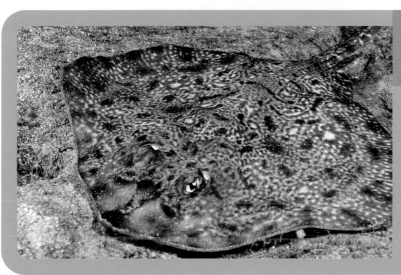

AUSTRALIAN THORNBACK SKATE ⬤◉
Dentiraja lemprieri

RANGE: Australia

SIZE: Length up to 1.8 ft (0.5 m)

DIET: Crabs, lobsters, octopuses; sometimes fish

The Australian thornback skate relies on camouflage for protection from potential predators such as large bony fish. It also surprises its prey—mostly crabs. Like all skates, it catches its prey by pouncing on and trapping it.

SPOTTED EAGLE RAY ⬤◉◉◉◉
Aetobatus narinari

RANGE: Tropical and warm temperate waters worldwide

SIZE: 8.2 ft (2.5 m), not including the tail; 16.4 ft (5 m) with tail

DIET: Small fish, shrimp, crab

Though it feeds in shallow water, the spotted eagle ray swims long distances through open water—often in large schools. Named for the graceful way it swims, it looks as though it is flying.

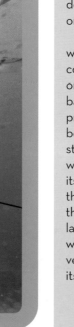

SOAKING UP SOME "RAYS"!

With an ominous name and an even more ominous-looking tail, stingrays might seem like a sea creature you'd want to steer clear of. But the truth is that they are particularly gentle animals, and certainly not out to harm you. As friendly as they are, however, stingrays are still armed with some pretty heavy defenses, which they use only if they feel threatened.

Stingrays have long, whiplike tails that can be covered with more than one knife-sharp, serrated barb. Additionally, they produce venom that can be toxic to humans. If a stingray comes in contact with a predator, it will whip its tail around and pierce the perceived threat with the sharp point, then a thin layer of skin called a sheath will break, injecting the venom into the wound of its victim.

EELS

Eels are bony fish with elongated bodies, a reduced number of fins, and, instead of scales, thick skin covered in mucus. Most are ambush predators. This group includes the electric eels and about 800 species of "true eels."

True eels, such as the moray eel, cannot swallow. Instead, they have two sets of teeth: one along the leading edge of their jaws, and one in the back of their throat. They use the front set to tear their prey into smaller pieces and the rear to pull it into their mouths.

They also have an unusual life cycle. Eggs hatch into transparent larvae called glass eels. As these mature, they darken and are called elvers. These young eels are usually found in the open ocean. They become adults after several years.

Life spans for these animals may be as long as 75 years.

SPOTTED GARDEN EEL
Heteroconger hassi

RANGE: Indian Ocean and Red Sea
SIZE: Up to 15.7 in (40 cm)
DIET: Crustaceans, small fish

Garden eels are small, social eels that live in burrows under the seafloor. At times, they are completely invisible; to feed, they poke their heads out and look like stems growing from the ground—like a garden.

SPOTTED MORAY EEL
Gymnothorax moringa

RANGE: Western and eastern Atlantic Ocean
SIZE: 6.6 ft (2 m)
DIET: Fish and crustaceans

Like all eels, spotted morays have poor vision and no lateral line pores. They find their food by smell. Divers have been injured because the eel cannot distinguish a fish from a finger. Their jaws also do not release.

STARRY MORAY EEL
Gymnothorax nudivomer

RANGE: Indo-Pacific region
SIZE: 5.9 ft (1.8 m)
DIET: Fish, crustaceans, squid

Like all true eels, the starry moray has a narrow head with wide jaws. When a moray catches prey too big to fit down its throat, it ties itself in a knot, restraining the fish or crustacean so it can tear it into smaller pieces.

ZEBRA MORAY EEL
Gymnomuraena zebra

RANGE: Indo-Pacific region, eastern central Pacific Ocean
SIZE: 4.9 ft (1.5 m)
DIET: Crabs, crustaceans, mollusks, sea urchins

Most morays eat anything that fits in their mouths. The zebra moray eel is unusual because it specializes in eating crabs. Otherwise, its behavior is similar. It waits in a hole or crevice to ambush its prey.

RAY-FINNED BONY FISH

Half of all vertebrates—animals with a backbone—are fish. Of these, most are ray-finned bony fish, or teleosts (TEE-le-osts). All have skeletons made of bone and fins made of webbed skin with bony or horny spines.

There are 27,000 species of ray-finned bony fish. They exist in all sizes, shapes, and colors, and are found all over the world. They do share some common behaviors, though.

One is migration. Though distances vary, many species in this group migrate to find food, avoid predators, or breed. Some move from salt water to freshwater, and back again. A second common behavior is shoaling, when fish move together in a group. Schooling is a specific type of shoaling, when the grouped fish are doing the same thing, such as swimming fast to avoid a predator. A third is aggression. The fish in this group tend to fight for access to food, mates, or territory.

ELECTRIC EEL
Electrophorus electricus

RANGE: Northeastern South American waters
SIZE: 8.2 ft (2.5 m)
DIET: Invertebrates, fish, small mammals

Electric eels produce two types of electricity: a weak pulsating signal for navigation, communication, and prey detection, and a strong signal—up to 650 volts—for stunning prey. Like lungfish, they are air breathers.

ANCHOVIES, HERRINGS, AND RELATIVES

Anchovies, herrings, and their relatives (shads, sardines, and menhadens) are referred to as baitfish because of their place in the food web. They feed on plankton and, in turn, are eaten by bigger fish, marine mammals and birds, and people.

These species are found in all oceans. Some also live in the brackish water of estuaries and bays. They are small- to medium-size fish, long and slender, with a single dorsal fin and a forked tail. They feed by swimming with their mouths open, collecting plankton on filaments in their gills. Most are schooling fish that swim together in large numbers in an effort to avoid or outsmart predators.

Life spans range from three years for anchovies to up to 25 years for herrings and sardines.

EUROPEAN ANCHOVY
Engraulis encrasicolus

RANGE: Eastern Atlantic Ocean and Mediterranean Sea

SIZE: 7.9 in (20 cm)

DIET: Plankton

Anchovies live in a wide range of salty waters and water temperatures. The European anchovy is a coastal species, also found in large schools like its relatives. These fish often move into lagoons, estuaries, and lakes during spawning.

ATLANTIC HERRING
Clupea harengus

RANGE: North Atlantic Ocean

SIZE: 17.7 in (45 cm)

DIET: Plankton

Atlantic herrings are found in large schools—up to several billion fish—that often stretch for miles. Their many predators include cod, bass, tuna, salmon, dogfish sharks, porpoises, whales, seals, puffins, terns, and humans.

SOUTH AMERICAN PILCHARD
Sardinops sagax

RANGE: Indian and Pacific Oceans

SIZE: 15.6 in (39.5 cm)

DIET: Plankton

There are many fish species called sardines. The South American pilchard is harvested in the greatest numbers for human use. Most of these sardines are processed into fish meal used for animal food.

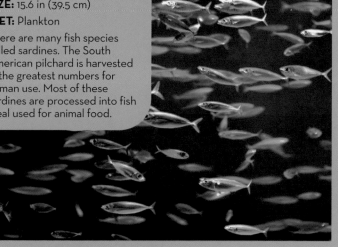

203

COD AND RELATIVES

Cod and their relatives are medium-size fish found in cooler, deeper waters. They are bottom dwellers and are sometimes referred to as groundfish. All are marine, meaning they live in saltwater environments, except for the burbot.

Their prey include baitfish like anchovies and herrings, eels, and each other. They are eaten by sharks, seals, and people.

Many species of cod and their relatives are popular foods because of their mild-tasting, flaky white meat. They are used to make cod liver oil and other nutritional supplements as well. As a result, many have become rare due to overfishing.

Groundfish like cod are caught using a method known as trawling, in which large numbers of fish—including young fish that have not had time to reproduce—are swept up in nets dragged along the ocean bottom. Some populations of Atlantic cod, for example, may never recover.

The life span for cod and cod-like fish ranges from 12 to 25 years.

HADDOCK
Melanogrammus aeglefinus

RANGE: Northeastern Atlantic Ocean

SIZE: 3.7 ft (1.2 m)

DIET: Small crustaceans, mollusks, echinoderms, worms, fish

Haddock have the same body shape and fin arrangement as cod, but with a black lateral line and a black patch behind their gill flaps. Their prey are mostly bottom-dwelling, meaning they live at or near the surface of the ocean floor.

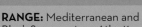

EUROPEAN HAKE
Merluccius merluccius

RANGE: Mediterranean and Black Seas, eastern Atlantic Ocean

SIZE: 4.6 ft (1.4 m)

DIET: Fish and squid

The European hake can be found living at depths of up to 3,300 feet (1,000 m). Like its relatives, it feeds on a variety of fish, but as an adult, it will also eat smaller hakes and hake eggs.

ATLANTIC COD
Gadus morhua

RANGE: North Atlantic Ocean

SIZE: 6.6 ft (2 m)

DIET: Invertebrates and fish

Atlantic, Pacific, and Greenland cod are closely related. All have rounded dorsal fins, pelvic fins that are placed very far forward, a white lateral line, and a single whisker, or barbel, on their chin used to feel for their prey.

Did you know?
Atlantic cod make a type of antifreeze to keep their blood from freezing.

BURBOT
Lota lota

RANGE: Cold freshwater in the Northern Hemisphere

SIZE: 5 ft (1.5 m)

DIET: Fish

The burbot is the only freshwater cod relative. This fish moves into deeper, cooler water during the warmer months and will burrow under mud or rocks for shelter. It also spawns during winter—under the lake ice.

COMMON LING
Molva molva

RANGE: Atlantic Ocean and Mediterranean Sea

SIZE: Up to 6.6 ft (2 m)

DIET: Lobster, fish, sea stars, squid

Like Atlantic and Pacific cod, ling have a mild taste and delicate white meat. Caught in the open ocean, they are eaten fresh, as well as dried and salted—both methods used to preserve fish. The salted eggs, or roe, of ling are a favorite food in Spain.

DEEP-SEA FISH

The largest group of deep-sea fish are the dragonfish, lightfish, and their relatives. These species are found in deep oceanic waters worldwide, from the tropics to the Antarctic. Many migrate up the water column during the day to feed on plankton and small fish.

Finding food in the depths of the ocean, where it is cold and dark and where food is scarce, is a challenge. Deep-sea fish have adapted to their unique environment in several ways.

Many are opportunistic feeders with long, sharp teeth; large mouths; and jaws that unhinge. Some have large, light-sensitive eyes. Most have reduced fins because they need only to move up or down.

Light-producing organs called photophores are their most distinctive feature. Photophores are organs that are used by fish (and invertebrates) to produce light either by chemical reaction or through symbiotic bacteria capable of bioluminescence. The fish use it to communicate, find their food, and avoid predators.

Life spans are unknown for most of these species.

FLASHLIGHT FISH
Photoblepharon steinitzi

RANGE: Red Sea and Indian Ocean

SIZE: 4.3 in (11 cm)

DIET: Zooplankton and coral

A coral reef species, flashlight fish are also capable of bioluminescence. They have a pocket beneath each eye that contains bacteria that give off a green light. These fish live in coral caves during the day and move up to the surface at night.

NORTHERN LAMPFISH
Stenobrachius leucopsarus

RANGE: Northern Pacific Ocean

SIZE: 5 in (13 cm)

DIET: Plankton and fish

The northern lampfish, one of 250 species of lanternfish, is named for its photophores, which give off light. All eat plankton, are common in the deep sea, and are an important food source for whales, dolphin, salmon, tuna, sharks, and seabirds.

SLOANE'S VIPERFISH
Chauliodus sloani

RANGE: All tropical and temperate oceans

SIZE: 13.8 in (35 cm)

DIET: Shrimp, crustaceans, other fish, squid

Viperfish are found as deep as 14,400 feet (4,400 m). Their teeth are so long they overlap the jaws. This fish catches its prey by piercing it. Like its relatives, it has a row of photophores under its belly.

ANGLER
Lophius piscatorius

RANGE: Eastern Atlantic Ocean

SIZE: 6.6 ft (2 m)

DIET: Fish and seabirds

The angler has a huge head and mouth and, instead of a dorsal fin, several long, thin spines. The first is used as a lure to catch its prey. This fish ambushes its prey by burying itself in the sand or hiding in seaweed.

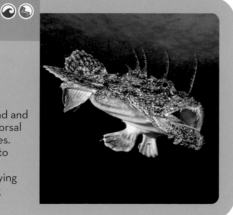

SCALY DRAGONFISH
Stomias boa

RANGE: Atlantic Ocean

SIZE: 12.7 in (32.2 cm)

DIET: Fish and crustaceans

The scaly dragonfish is also known as the boa dragonfish because of its long, slender shape. It lives at depths of 1,600 feet (500 m) or more. Like many deep-sea fish, it migrates toward the surface of the water at night to find food.

Did you know? A female angler has a dorsal spine stemming above its mouth like a fishing pole.

FISH

TROUT AND SALMON

Trout and salmon are medium-size fish with long bodies, pointed snouts, and a rounded fatty fin just in front of the tail. All spend the first part of their lives in freshwater, then return to where they hatched to breed, or spawn. After spawning, most die.

Between hatching and spawning, some species migrate to the open ocean and spend several years at sea. They return to freshwater when ready to spawn. By detecting magnetic fields beneath the ocean floor and using their sense of smell, they find their way to their home stream. Then they swim upstream, a behavior known as a run.

Life spans range from seven years for species that migrate to 30 years for nonmigrating species.

ATLANTIC SALMON
Salmo salar

RANGE: Both sides of the North Atlantic Ocean

SIZE: 4.9 ft (1.5 m)

DIET: Squid, fish, shrimp

Young Atlantic salmon have purple and red spots for camouflage. Adults at sea are silvery with a few black spots. During spawning, they turn dull brown or yellow, and the males develop hooked jaws.

BROOK TROUT
Salvelinus fontinalis

RANGE: Eastern North America

SIZE: 2.8 ft (0.9 m)

DIET: Mayflies, leeches, worms, mollusks, salamanders; anything else it can catch

Brook trout, or char, are found only in fast-running streams with clear, cold water. Most do not migrate. Those that do swim only a few miles out to sea and stay there for only a few months. They are called sea-run brook trout.

SOCKEYE SALMON
Oncorhynchus nerka

RANGE: Both sides of the northern Pacific Ocean

SIZE: 2.8 ft (0.9 m)

DIET: Plankton

Sockeye salmon are also called red and blueback salmon for the bright coloration they develop during spawning. Those that remain in freshwater for their entire lives are called kokanee salmon.

Did you know? Female salmon make a gravel nest, called a redd, where they lay their eggs.

SALMON LIFE CYCLE

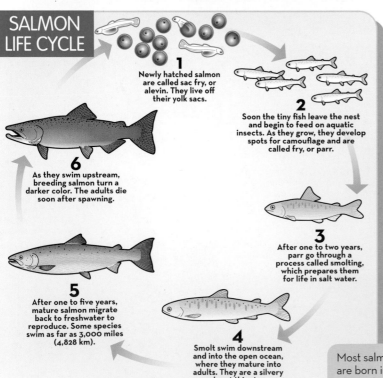

1 Newly hatched salmon are called sac fry, or alevin. They live off their yolk sacs.

2 Soon the tiny fish leave the nest and begin to feed on aquatic insects. As they grow, they develop spots for camouflage and are called fry, or parr.

3 After one to two years, parr go through a process called smolting, which prepares them for life in salt water.

4 Smolt swim downstream and into the open ocean, where they mature into adults. They are a silvery color at this stage.

5 After one to five years, mature salmon migrate back to freshwater to reproduce. Some species swim as far as 3,000 miles (4,828 km).

6 As they swim upstream, breeding salmon turn a darker color. The adults die soon after spawning.

RAINBOW TROUT
Oncorhynchus mykiss

RANGE: Pacific coast of North America

SIZE: 3.9 ft (1.2 m)

DIET: Invertebrates and small fish

Some rainbow trout migrate to the sea; others do not. Adults look different depending on where they live. Because of their silver color, ocean-living rainbow trout are called steelhead trout, even though they are the same species.

Most salmon are anadromous, meaning they are born in freshwater, migrate to the ocean, where they live for several years, and return to freshwater to reproduce.

CATFISH, PIRANHAS, AND RELATIVES

atfish, carp, piranhas, tetras, and their relatives are grouped together because of one feature: a connection between the inner ear and the swim bladder. Because of this connection, they have excellent hearing. They can make sounds for communication, too. Most species in this group share another feature: They live in freshwater.

Catfish are the exception. They are found on every continent except Antarctica, in coastal brackish water and salt water, as well as in freshwater in ponds, lakes, rivers, streams, caves, and even underground. At least one in 20 vertebrate animals is a catfish!

One reason for their success is diet: They are bottom feeders that eat just about anything—aquatic plants, other fish, decaying vegetation, fish eggs, crayfish, snails, aquatic bugs, carrion, leeches, and worms. Larger catfish also eat frogs, rodents, and ducks. A catfish has no teeth. Instead, it surrounds its prey with its pectoral fins, opens its mouth, and gulps.

Life spans for these fish range up to 40 years.

CHANNEL CATFISH
Ictalurus punctatus

RANGE: North America and parts of Europe

SIZE: 4.3 ft (1.3 m)

DIET: Fish, crustaceans, insects

Another reason for the success of catfish as a group is their skin. Instead of scales, some are armored, but many, like the channel catfish, have only a mucous covering. This allows them to breathe through their skin, like frogs.

STERBA'S CORYDORAS CATFISH
Corydoras sterbai

RANGE: Central Brazil and Bolivia

SIZE: 2.6 in (6.8 cm)

DIET: Algae

Like all catfish, corydoras use their skin sensors to taste the water and their catlike whiskers, or barbels, to feel for food. These fish are an example of an armored catfish because their skin is protected by bony plates, or scutes.

CONGO TETRA
Phenacogrammus interruptus

RANGE: Democratic Republic of the Congo

SIZE: 2.8 to 3 in (6 to 8.5 cm)

DIET: Worms, crustaceans, small insects, plant material

Tetras have six fins. The two pelvic fins under the belly are paired. The name "tetra," which means "four," refers to the single fins: the tail, dorsal, adipose, and anal fins. When the fish swims, it uses these fins like wings.

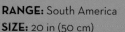

RED PIRANHA
Pygocentrus nattereri

RANGE: South America

SIZE: 20 in (50 cm)

DIET: Insects and fish

Piranhas have sharp, interlocking teeth for puncturing and tearing into their food. While feeding, these fish gather in vegetation in groups of up to 30 to wait for their prey.

GOLDFISH
Carassius auratus

RANGE: Originally Central Asia, China, and Japan

SIZE: Up to 16 in (41 cm)

DIET: Crustaceans, insects, plants

Goldfish are domesticated Prussian carp. There are now over 300 breeds of different shapes and colors. Like other carp, goldfish have teeth set way back in their mouths, attached to their gills instead of their jaws. Originally from Central Asia, China, and Japan, goldfish are now found worldwide, with adverse ecological impacts reported.

FISH

MANGROVE KILLIFISH

Mangrove killifish are amazing creatures. They can move their eyes and head like a lizard. They can live in the water like a fish. They can also live on land for weeks at a time and breathe air through their skin like a frog. To move around, they fold their two-inch (5-cm)-long, thin bodies into an S shape and—BANG!—spring forward up to 20 times their body length. And, most peculiar of all, most of these fish have characteristics of both sexes. Some of them can reproduce without a partner.

I've always liked strange fish, so when I moved to northeastern Brazil in 2015, I joined a project focusing on the neotropical mangrove killifish (*Kryptolebias hermaphroditus*). This species can actually fertilize itself. Until recently, all neotropical mangrove killifish found had both male and female traits, so we believed that was the only way they reproduced.

The second time we went into the field, it was nighttime and we were snaking among mangrove roots, searching for the killifish in dark mangrove pools. Suddenly, I saw a killifish on the water's surface. That's where these fish stay when they're in the water. They use water tension to "glue" themselves to the top of the water so they can catch small insects that fall in.

As I slowly approached the fish, it noticed me and swam deep down into the pool. But not before I saw the orange coloring on its side. It was one of the most exciting moments of my life. I had studied other types of killifish and knew that similar species had males with bright orange colors on their bodies. With patience and teamwork we waited for it to surface again. After a few tries I caught it with my own hands. We took it back to the lab, and after careful study concluded that it was a male—the first male neotropical mangrove killifish ever discovered.

CARIBBEAN SEA

RANGE OF THE
*KRYPTOLEBIAS
HERMAPHRODITUS*
(MANGROVE KILLIFISH)

0   1,000 miles

0   1,000 kilometers

SOUTH
AMERICA

PACIFIC
OCEAN

ATLANTIC
OCEAN

Helder Espírito-Santo is an expert in fish ecology. Since 2005, he has explored many Amazonian and neighboring ecosystems. His research focuses on small fish, which are often overlooked. His favorite group to study is the amphibious killifish, like the neotropical mangrove killifish, which live both on land and in the water.

OBSERVATION
TIPS

1 Be prepared for mud and mosquitoes. Mangroves are full of both.

2 Look for very shallow tide pools. Mangrove killifish live along the edge of mangrove forests, where just a bit of high tide water can reach.

3 Bring a hand net and some helpers. It's a lot easier to catch them if you work as a team.

4 Check the net carefully. Killifish aren't very colorful, but they'll jump inside the net. Sometimes they jump out of it, too!

FISH

There are two types of killifish. Annual killifish live one year. After spawning, females lay and bury eggs in shallow freshwater puddles. When the water dries up, the fish die. But their eggs remain dormant until the next rainy season, when they hatch. Mangrove killifish belong to the other group, called "amphibious killifish" because they can survive on land and in water. Mangrove killifish live in coastal mangrove forest pools. When the water dries up, they move across land for deeper pools of water. Amphibious killifish have been observed to lay their eggs on damp mud or leaves in water or near the water line.

PERCH
AND RELATIVES

P erch and their relatives form a very large group: 40 percent of all bony fish, known as Perciformes (PER-see-FOR-meez). They are also known as spiny-rayed fish because of the organization of their fins.

Fish in this group are found all over the world and in every type of aquatic habitat. Many are favorite food fish, like bass, snapper, and tilapia. Others are found on coral reefs and range in size from tiny gobies and gouramis to large groupers.

The reason for so much diversity within a single grouping of fish is that species classification is based on more than one piece of information. Physical features, like scale color and the shape of the skeleton, are important. So is behavior: where the fish lives, what it eats, how it reproduces, and whether it lives alone or in groups. Genetic information, which is found in all living things, shows similarities or differences that are useful to determine how species are related.

Life spans for these fish range from five to 30 years.

YELLOW PERCH
Perca flavescens

RANGE: North America

SIZE: 3.9 to 10 in (10 to 25.5 cm)

DIET: Fish and invertebrates

Yellow perch are in the middle of the food chain. They eat invertebrates and smaller fish and are, in turn, eaten by bigger fish, such as bass, sunfish, and lake trout. Cormorants and other waterbirds also prey on yellow perch.

DOLPHINFISH
Coryphaena hippurus

RANGE: Tropical and subtropical Atlantic, Pacific, and Indian Oceans

SIZE: 6.6 ft (2 m)

DIET: Fish, plankton, crustaceans

Though not related to dolphins, which are mammals, this fish has a dolphin-like shape, with a large head and narrow body. Dolphinfish are marine fish that eat plants. They typically grow up to 30 pounds (13.6 kg) and are known as mahi-mahi, or dorado.

SPINY-RAYED FISH

Spiny-rayed fish are ray-finned bony fish with spines in both their dorsal and anal fins and sometimes in their pectoral fins. Perch and their relatives are generally referred to as spiny-rayed fish.

The part of the fin with spines is always closer to the head. It is stiff and sharp, made up of larger bony spines covered by skin. The softer part of the fin is closer to the tail. It is flexible, made up of tiny bones covered by a web of skin.

Most spiny-rayed fish also have scales with a spiny edge. These are thin, overlapping scales that feel rough, like tiny teeth. They are called ctenoid (TEN-noyd) scales.

There are other fish with spines. The difference is in how they are arranged. Catfish, for example, have a sharp spine on their dorsal fin and both pectoral fins.

Did you know?
Dolphinfish can swim up to 40 miles an hour (64 km/h).

BLACKBANDED SUNFISH
Enneacanthus chaetodon

RANGE: North America Atlantic and Gulf Slope drainages

SIZE: 1.9 to 4.9 in (4.8 to 12 cm)

DIET: Smaller fish, insects

Though they look different, these sunfish are related to smallmouth bass. In both species, the male builds the nest, a depression in the mud, using his tail. After the female lays the eggs, he guards them.

SMALLMOUTH BASS
Micropterus dolomieu

RANGE: Temperate waters of North America

SIZE: 8.7 to 27 in (22 to 69 cm)

DIET: Crayfish, insects, smaller fish, amphibians

Smallmouth bass are top predators that eat smaller fish. Their size as adults depends on how much time they have to eat during the summer months. The largest bass are found in places with long, hot summers.

ANTARCTIC TOOTHFISH
Dissostichus mawsoni

RANGE: Southern Ocean around Antarctica

SIZE: Up to 6.5 ft (2 m) long and 176 lb (80 kg)

DIET: Fish and squid

Antarctic toothfish, which can live nearly 40 years, prey upon other fish species in Antarctica's Ross Sea. These bottom dwellers are found at depths reaching 7,200 feet (2,200 m), but they move up to feed. To survive in the salty waters that dip below the freezing point of 32°F (0°C), they produce proteins that keep their blood from freezing.

Did you know? At about four years old, female striped bass start growing faster than males.

STRIPED BASS
Morone saxatilis

RANGE: Atlantic coast of the United States

SIZE: 1.5 to 4.6 ft (0.5 to 1.4 m)

DIET: Zooplankton, insects, small crustaceans, other fish

Striped bass are popular sport fish. Also called striper, rock, or rockfish, they are caught from boats, bridges, beaches, creeks, streams, and rivers using a variety of baits. Natural populations are anadromous, meaning they are marine fish that spawn in freshwater.

PEACOCK SOLE
Pardachirus pavoninus

RANGE: Indo-Pacific region

SIZE: Up to 9.8 in (25 cm)

DIET: Crustaceans and other bottom-dwelling invertebrates

Like all flatfish, a peacock sole starts life as fish larvae with one eye on either side of its head. As it matures, one eye moves so that both are on the same side of the head—the up side. All adult soles are right-eyed.

CALIFORNIA FLOUNDER
Paralichthys californicus

RANGE: Eastern Pacific Ocean and west coast of North America

SIZE: Up to 5 ft (1.5 m)

DIET: Fish and crustaceans

California flounder, or halibut, have large mouths compared to other flatfish and very sharp teeth. They are known to bite! They are a favorite food of humans and can grow quite large. The record is five feet (1.5 m) long and 72 pounds (33 kg).

FLATHEAD GRAY MULLET

Mugil cephalus

RANGE: Worldwide tropical and subtropical waters

SIZE: 3.3 ft (1 m)

DIET: Zooplankton, algae, fish

These schooling fish gather in large numbers during the fall to swim offshore to spawn. They are known for their impressive jumps, moves made to avoid predators. Mullet are eaten by sharks, dolphins, pelicans, sea trout, and people.

FISH

A BIOLOGICAL RESERVE IN THE PACIFIC OCEAN off the southwestern coast of Costa Rica, Isla del Caño provides a safe home for a wide array of organisms, including the Mexican barred snapper (*Hoplopagrus guentherii*). During the day, this fish shelters in rocky structures and caves around the reserve's five coral reefs. At night, it emerges to hunt for crustaceans and small fish on the rocky bottom.

TUNA, MARLIN, SWORDFISH, AND RELATIVES

Tuna are among the fastest-swimming fish in the world. Streamlined for speed, they have torpedo-shaped bodies with stiff tails and tiny fins, or finlets, that decrease water turbulence. They fold their dorsal fins into grooves while they swim. They also have darker muscles than other fish, the result of high amounts of a molecule known as myoglobin, which binds oxygen.

Tuna are schooling fish that prey on smaller schooling fish, including smaller tunas and relatives like mackerel. Some swim with larger fish for protection. Yellowfin tuna, for example, school with dolphins to avoid their main predators: sharks.

Marlin, swordfish, and their relatives, which include sailfish and barracuda, are equally fast swimmers. Tuna are among their prey.

Life spans range from nine years for swordfish, 30 years for some species of marlin, and up to 50 years for bluefin tuna.

ATLANTIC BLUEFIN TUNA
Thunnus thynnus

RANGE: Atlantic Ocean

SIZE: 4.6 ft (1.4 m)

DIET: Crustaceans, fish, squid

Bluefin tuna swim at high speed for great distances. They are also one of the largest fish in the open ocean. Using heat generated by their muscles, they keep their body temperature above that of the water, a rare ability among fish.

GREAT BARRACUDA
Sphyraena barracuda

RANGE: Indo-Pacific region and eastern Atlantic Ocean

SIZE: 6.6 ft (2 m)

DIET: Fish, cephalopods, shrimp

Barracuda are predators that use bursts of speed to swim up to their fish prey and then take bites out of them with their sharp, fang-like teeth. Adults are solitary, whereas young often live together in shallow mangroves and reefs.

SWORDFISH
Xiphias gladius

RANGE: Atlantic, Indian, and Pacific Oceans

SIZE: 14.9 ft (4.5 m)

DIET: Crustaceans, fish, squid

Swordfish use their swordlike snouts to slash and injure their prey. During the day, they move to deep water. At night, they move up to the surface to feed. Swordfish typically weigh 300 to 700 pounds (140 to 320 kg).

ATLANTIC SAILFISH
Istiophorus albicans

RANGE: Atlantic Ocean

SIZE: 10.3 ft (3.1 m)

DIET: Smaller fish

To make its body more streamlined, the sailfish folds its huge, spiny-rayed fin into a ridge on its back while it swims. It then unfolds the fin to surprise and herd its fish prey. It can reach speeds of 68 miles an hour (110 km/h).

SCORPIONFISH AND SCULPINS

Found worldwide, scorpionfish and sculpins are spiny, venomous fish. Most are found in shallow water, and most are marine. All are bottom dwellers that feed on crustaceans, small fish, and invertebrates.

The fish in this group have spines with venom glands located at the base, near the skin. There are at least a dozen of these spines in the dorsal fin and more in the anal and pectoral fins. They are used only for self-defense. When pressure is applied to a spine, it releases venom. These spines are so effective that most species have few predators. Among them are sharks, rays, and moray eels.

Scorpionfish and sculpins hunt by hiding or sneaking up on their prey. They are extremely well camouflaged, with fleshy bumps and skin tags on their heads and blotchy coloration.

Life spans range from two to 10 years.

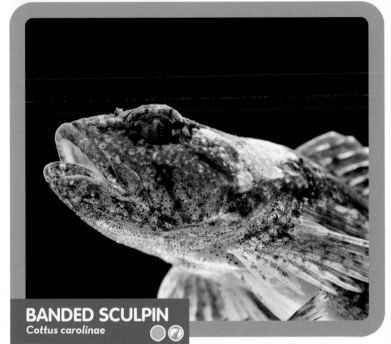

BANDED SCULPIN
Cottus carolinae

RANGE: Central United States
SIZE: 7 in (18 cm)
DIET: Invertebrates

Sculpins have flat bodies for burrowing under the sand and large pectoral fins for holding on to rocks so they can stay in one place in fast-moving water. These fish are also capable of surviving out of water for several hours.

SMALL RED SCORPIONFISH
Scorpaena notata

RANGE: Eastern Atlantic Ocean
SIZE: 9 in (24 cm)
DIET: Crustaceans and small fish

Like its relatives, the small red scorpionfish lives in shallow marine habitats, including coral reefs. It sneaks up on its prey, corners them with its pectoral fins, and then vacuums them up.

RED LIONFISH
Pterois volitans

RANGE: Indo-Pacific region
SIZE: 15 in (38 cm)
DIET: Fish and crustaceans

The red lionfish is a colorful and bold marine fish. Unfortunately, it is also an invasive species in the Caribbean and off the Florida coast. Where there were once many snapper and grouper, there are now mostly lionfish.

REEF STONEFISH
Synanceia verrucosa

RANGE: Indo-Pacific region
SIZE: 16 in (40 cm)
DIET: Crustaceans, small fish

Reef stonefish are the world's most venomous fish. They are well hidden on the seafloor and can be fatal to people if stepped on. The amount of venom injected through the dorsal spines depends on the amount of pressure applied.

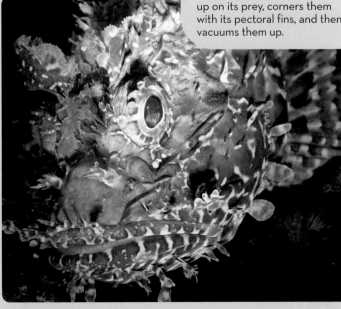

215

REEF FISH AND SEAHORSES

Coral reefs are often called rainforests of the sea. They are home to a huge amount of life, including 25 percent of all marine life, and about 4,000 species of fish. Yet there are relatively few coral reef ecosystems. They represent less than one percent of the ocean surface and are found only in tropical parts of the world, where the water, depth, current, and light conditions favor the growth of coral.

Unlike the open ocean, where silvery, streamlined bodies are common, reef fish exist in all shapes, sizes, and colors, from tiny gobies to huge groupers. Many are strangely long, narrow, flat, or round with extra, fewer, or modified fins so they can dart in and out of holes or hide under ledges. Some have spines and venom for defense; others, like the seahorses, have incredible camouflage. All are competing for the same resources: food, shelter, room to move, and a chance to breed.

The life spans vary from 60 days for some gobies to 40 or more years for the goliath grouper.

YELLOWTAIL SNAPPER
Ocyurus chrysurus

RANGE: Western Atlantic Ocean, from the U.S.A. to southeastern Brazil

SIZE: 2.8 ft (0.9 m)

DIET: Crabs, shrimp, cephalopods, worms, fish, plankton

Yellowtail snapper are reef fish that tend to stay in the same area in small groups. These smaller snapper are prey for larger snapper as well as for top predators like barracudas, groupers, and sharks.

LEAFY SEADRAGON
Phycodurus eques

RANGE: Eastern Indian Ocean to southern Australia

SIZE: 11.8 in (30 cm)

DIET: Crustaceans

This seahorse is shaped to give it near-perfect camouflage in seaweed. But the leaflike structures are not used for swimming. To move, this species uses two fins—one pectoral and one dorsal—that are so thin they are almost transparent.

FIRE CLOWNFISH
Amphiprion melanopus

RANGE: Pacific Ocean

SIZE: 4.7 in (12 cm)

DIET: Planktonic crustaceans

Fire clownfish live among the tentacles of sea anemones. Each protects the other from predators, and each provides food, either in the form of leftovers or excrement. The fish also keeps the anemone free of parasites.

LONG-SNOUTED SEAHORSE
Hippocampus guttulatus

RANGE: Eastern Atlantic Ocean: British Isles and the Netherlands to Morocco, Canary Islands, Madeira, and the Azores, including the Mediterranean and the Black Sea

SIZE: 9.8 in (25 cm)

DIET: Zooplankton, shrimp, very small fish, plants

The long-snouted seahorse has a crown on top of its head, a very long tail, and a thick nose. It can change color for better camouflage and to attract mates. It can be black, yellow, red, orange, or brown.

ATLANTIC GOLIATH GROUPER
Epinephelus itajara

RANGE: Atlantic Ocean

SIZE: 8 ft (2.4 m)

DIET: Crustaceans, spiny lobsters, turtles, fish, stingrays

Goliath groupers are large, predatory fish that weigh several hundred pounds. They are also very defensive around their home caves. They open their mouths, quiver, and contract their swim bladders to make a rumbling sound.

ORBICULAR BATFISH
Platax orbicularis

RANGE: Tropical waters of the Indo-Pacific region

SIZE: 1.6 ft (0.4 m)

DIET: Algae, invertebrates, small fish

Batfish have a distinctive shape: They are extremely thin and very round. The roundface batfish is silvery gray in color, with darker vertical bands and a black spot in front of its pectoral fin. They are often found together in schools.

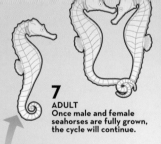

LINED SEAHORSE
Hippocampus erectus

RANGE: Western Atlantic Ocean: Nova Scotia, Canada, and northern Gulf of Mexico to Panama and Venezuela

SIZE: 6.9 in (17.5 cm)

DIET: Crustaceans and other small invertebrates

Seahorses do not have scales. Instead, their skin is attached to rings of bone. These rings give the fish its shape and, along with its spines and changeable skin coloration, help protect it from predators.

ALLIGATOR PIPEFISH
Syngnathoides biaculeatus

RANGE: Indo-Pacific region

SIZE: 11.1 in (30 cm)

DIET: Zooplankton

Like its relatives the seahorses and seadragons, the alligator pipefish has a fused jaw. It cannot open its mouth, so it feeds by using its long snout like a suction tube to inhale food.

HUMPHEAD WRASSE
Cheilinus undulatus

RANGE: Indo-Pacific region

SIZE: 7.5 ft (2.3 m)

DIET: Mollusks, fish, sea urchins, crustaceans, other invertebrates

This fish feeds on invertebrate animals found along the ocean floor that many others avoid. These include sea urchins, mollusks, and toxic species like sea hares and crown-of-thorn starfish.

SEAHORSE LIFE CYCLE

1 COURTSHIP
Male and female seahorses court each other by intertwining their tails and changing colors.

2 TRANSFER OF EGGS
The female deposits her eggs into the male's pouch at the same time he releases sperm, which fertilizes them.

3 PREGNANCY
Inside the male's pouch, the fertilized eggs develop into tiny seahorses.

4 BIRTH
The male releases the young seahorses by contracting muscles around the pouch.

5 NEWBORN SEAHORSES
Young grab hold of a floating object and each other with their tails.

6 JUVENILE
As they grow, seahorses do not change much, except for their size.

7 ADULT
Once male and female seahorses are fully grown, the cycle will continue.

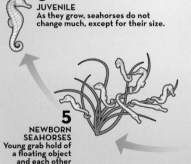

Seahorses begin their reproductive cycle with an elaborate courtship dance. Then the female deposits her eggs into the male's pouch, where they develop into young.

FROM THE FIELD:

Sylvia Earle

GRAY ANGELFISH

One of my most memorable experiences exploring coral reefs was living in an underwater habitat for two weeks with four other researchers. Our habitat was like a hotel—it had bunk beds and warm showers and a stove to cook meals—only it was on the ocean floor, and our backyard was filled with fish and other sea critters! We studied the reef day and night and became intimately acquainted with our new neighbors.

Each day, we'd wake before sunrise and slip into the sea through a hatch at the bottom of the habitat. And every morning, just as we approached the reef's edge, five gray angelfish *(Pomacanthus arcuatus)* swam over to greet us! The largest was maybe a foot (30.5 cm) across and the smallest only six inches (15 cm). They cruised the reef, grazing on seaweed and nibbling on sponges, but they were also curious and followed us around like puppies. On one occasion, I could see that I could actually tell them apart—that they had unique faces and personalities. Three were shy and hung back, while the other two swam within inches of our scuba masks. One day, a bold angelfish even nibbled a sprig of alga I held in my hand! We collected a lot of new and exciting scientific data over the two weeks, but I'll never forget those five curious angelfish that taught me that fish, like humans, are each unique and special.

NORTH AMERICA

RANGE OF THE
*POMACANTHUS
ARCUATUS*
(GRAY ANGELFISH)

0 — 1,000 miles
0 — 1,000 kilometers

Gulf of
Mexico

CARIBBEAN SEA

PACIFIC
OCEAN

ATLANTIC
OCEAN

SOUTH
AMERICA

OBSERVATION TIPS

1 Go out and get wet. Put on a face mask and snorkel around coral reefs to explore a world brimming with sea life.

2 Keep your hands to yourself. Touching coral can harm the reef, and its sharp edges can easily pierce skin.

3 Angelfish are popular reef fish and are among the first you're likely to see cruising around.

4 Reef fish—angel or otherwise—can be curious and may swim over to investigate *you!* Just be sure to respect their space.

Sylvia Earle is a world-renowned oceanographer, explorer, and author. A pioneer of underwater exploration, she researches marine algae and deep-water ecosystems, with a focus on new technology for reaching and studying the deep sea.

Adult gray angelfish typically cruise coral reefs in pairs. They nibble on sponges and algae during the day and tuck into reef crevices at night. Females swim above the reef to release their eggs, and newly hatched larvae float on plankton, where they transform into tiny angelfish. Juveniles, with their black bodies and yellow stripes, look quite different from adults. They hang out around shallow patch reefs and grassy areas and often eat parasites that latch on to the bodies of other fish.

RECORDS

D id you know there is a species of fish that can fit on your fingertip? Or that some fish can swim as fast as a car? Want to find out more? Then check out these fabulous fish record holders!

WORLD'S BIGGEST FISH →

Whale Shark
Rhincodon typus

A whale shark measures up to 65 feet (20 m) in length with an average weight of 41,200 pounds (18,700 kg). If you saw one coming toward you in the water, you would probably swim for your life. Then it would open its five-foot (1.5-m)-wide mouth, and you'd really think you're a goner. Fortunately, this giant of the sea is a gentle one, feeding only on plankton and small fish. Whale sharks suck huge amounts of water into their mouths and then strain it out through their gills, trapping the small organisms inside.

BIGGEST FRESHWATER FISH →

Mekong Giant Catfish
Pangasianodon gigas

When some people think of catfish, they think of something that fits perfectly on a dinner plate. But not the Mekong giant catfish! Measuring up to nine feet (2.7 m) long and weighing up to 650 pounds (290 kg), this river monster can grow to the size of a grizzly bear! The largest ever recorded was recently found in northern Thailand, where efforts are under way to protect giant fish in the Mekong River because many are considered critically endangered. It is rumored there are bigger fish out there, but this is the largest confirmed discovery.

SMALLEST FISH →

Paedocypris progenetica

This barely there fish is so tiny that it went undiscovered until the last decade or so. Measuring a mere 0.3 inch (8 mm) long, *Paedocypris progenetica* is a little fish with some funky features. First is a see-through body with no skeleton in the head, leaving the brain unprotected. Next is that it lives in very acidic water, and boasts fins that can grasp on to things. Little is known about this strange fish, which until 2012 was thought to be the smallest vertebrate in the world. Now that honor goes to a tiny frog named *Paedophryne amauensis* (see page 186).

FASTEST FISH →

Atlantic Sailfish
Istiophorus albicans

Racing through the water at speeds topping 68 miles an hour (110 km/h), an Atlantic sailfish sighting might be a case of "now you see it, now you don't." This sleek speedster has a compressed body perfect for darting through the water, and a long bill and jaws that help with its fancy way of fishing. Sailfish generally follow a school of fish slowly, until they are ready to attack. Then they charge full speed ahead into the school, darting left and right to stun their prey.

220

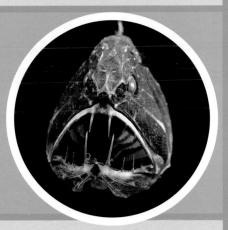

MOST POISONOUS FISH

Reef Stonefish
Synanceia verrucosa

If you're ever in the water off the coast of Australia, beware the sinister stonefish. This fiendish fish is aptly named for its resemblance to a rock, which is what makes it particularly dangerous. Its 13 venomous spines can cause pain, paralysis, and even death. Particularly vulnerable are bottom-feeding sharks and rays, and humans who accidentally step on it. Be sure to wear thick-soled shoes and walk very carefully.

FIERCEST FANGS

Fangtooth
Anoplogaster cornuta

Lurking in depths of up to 16,000 feet (4,900 m) deep there are some strange sights to behold: fish that glow, fish that dangle anglers above their heads to attract prey, and, of course, the fangtooth. The fangtooth is not a large fish, only about six inches (15 cm) in length, but what it lacks in size it makes up for in teeth. The largest two fangs in this fish's mouth are located on the lower jaw. They are so long that there are actually two sockets on either side of the fangtooth's brain so its teeth have somewhere to go when its mouth is shut. Fortunately, this freaky fish feasts only on shrimp and other fish, so you can sleep easy tonight.

HEAVIEST BONY FISH

Ocean Sunfish
Mola mola

When it comes to size, the ocean sunfish may have nothing on a whale shark, but compared to its bony fish friends it is most definitely large and in charge. That's because it maxes out at a whopping 5,000 pounds (2,300 kg)! And while it might not be the fastest fish in the sea, it certainly does get around. Sunfish are known to stay near the surface of the water to soak up some rays, but recent research shows they are quite good divers and can migrate long distances. And because they are downright puny as guppies, they also boast the biggest growth rate throughout their lifetimes—increasing in size about 60 million times!

MOST SHOCKING

Electric Eel
Electrophorus electricus

With more than five times the electric voltage of your average household electrical outlet, the electric eel is not to be messed with. These river dwellers are air breathers, meaning they must surface often for oxygen. Get too close to this feisty fish and—zap!—two of the eel's organs produce an electric pulsating current. The shock is not meant to be deadly, though—just to scare predators away.

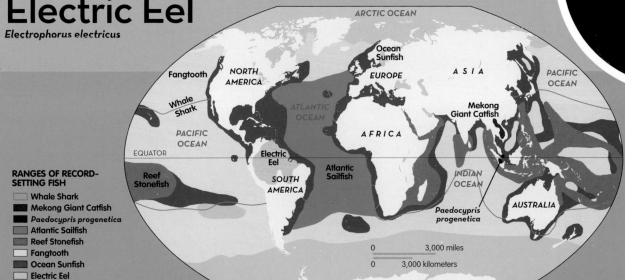

RANGES OF RECORD-SETTING FISH

- Whale Shark
- Mekong Giant Catfish
- *Paedocypris progenetica*
- Atlantic Sailfish
- Reef Stonefish
- Fangtooth
- Ocean Sunfish
- Electric Eel

ARCTIC OCEAN

Fangtooth • NORTH AMERICA • Ocean Sunfish • EUROPE • ASIA • PACIFIC OCEAN

Whale Shark • ATLANTIC OCEAN • Mekong Giant Catfish

PACIFIC OCEAN • AFRICA

EQUATOR • Electric Eel • Atlantic Sailfish • INDIAN OCEAN

Reef Stonefish • SOUTH AMERICA • Paedocypris progenetica • AUSTRALIA

0 — 3,000 miles
0 — 3,000 kilometers

ANTARCTICA

Want to know where these record-holding fish live around the world? Take a look at this range map to find out.

Ninety-seven percent of the world's animals lack a backbone. Known as invertebrates, they are the most numerous and diverse group of animals on Earth. Some go through metamorphosis, a process in which their bodies undergo extreme changes throughout their life cycles. This caterpillar, for instance, will soon spin a cocoon around its body. When it emerges, it will be a beautiful cecropia moth (*Hyalophora cecropia*), the largest moth in North America.

INVERTEBRATES

JUMPING SPIDER

GHOST CRAB

EARTHWORMS

MONARCH BUTTERFLIES

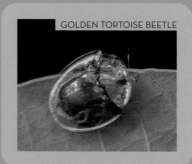

GOLDEN TORTOISE BEETLE

LAND SNAIL

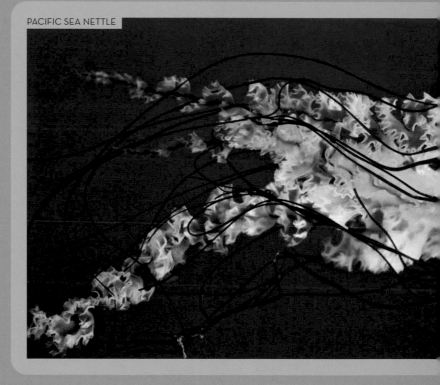

PACIFIC SEA NETTLE

SPICEBUSH SWALLOWTAIL CATERPILLAR

COMMON GREEN BOTTLE FLY

HONEYBEE

AZURE SNOUT WEEVILS

CAIRNS BIRDWING BUTTERFLY

SEA STAR

ARMY ANTS

BANANA SLUG

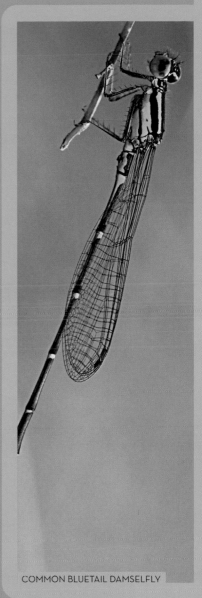
COMMON BLUETAIL DAMSELFLY

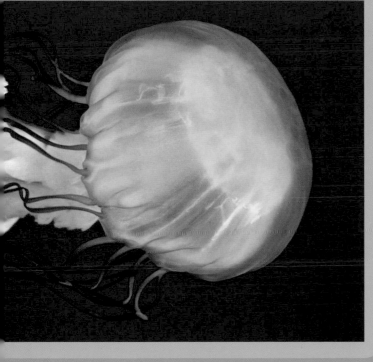

FLOWER'S MARINE FLATWORM

RED SEA URCHIN

ZEBRA LONGWING BUTTERFLY

WHAT IS AN INVERTEBRATE?

INVERTEBRATES ARE ANIMALS WITHOUT A BACKBONE OR BONY SKELETON.

They range in size from microscopic mites and almost invisible flies to giant squid with soccer-ball-size eyes.

This is by far the largest group in the animal kingdom: All but 3 percent of animals are invertebrates. So far, 1.3 million species have been described, most of which are insects, and there are millions more to be discovered. The total number of invertebrate species could be five, 10, or even 30 million, compared to more than 66,000 vertebrates.

One reason for the success of invertebrates is the variety of ways they reproduce. Sponges and corals, for example, produce both eggs and sperm. Social insects such as ants and bees lay eggs that can develop without fertilization—they become the males (drones).

Insects in particular are successful because they have adapted to many different conditions. They are able to survive in extreme environments, including very hot, dry habitats. And many can fly—either to escape predators or to find new sources of food, water, and shelter.

Like vertebrates, invertebrates are classified based upon their body structure, life cycle, and evolutionary history.

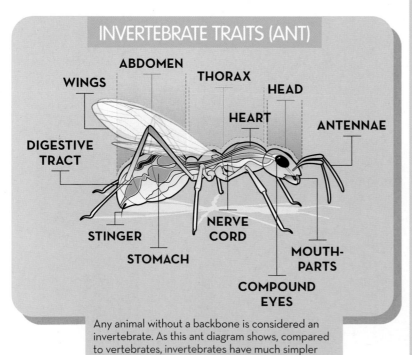

INVERTEBRATE TRAITS (ANT)

- WINGS
- ABDOMEN
- THORAX
- HEAD
- HEART
- ANTENNAE
- DIGESTIVE TRACT
- STINGER
- STOMACH
- NERVE CORD
- MOUTH-PARTS
- COMPOUND EYES

Any animal without a backbone is considered an invertebrate. As this ant diagram shows, compared to vertebrates, invertebrates have much simpler nervous, circulatory, and digestive systems.

By weight, a spider's silk is stronger than steel.

Did you know?

CLASSIFICATION OF
INVERTEBRATES

Invertebrate animals belong to one of eight large groups, listed below. These groups are each known as a phylum (FYE-lum).

1 INSECTS, ARACHNIDS, CENTIPEDES AND MILLIPEDES, CRUSTACEANS, AND HORSESHOE CRABS **(Arthropoda)**

2 SQUID, OCTOPUSES, CUTTLEFISH, SNAILS, SLUGS, AND BIVALVES **(Mollusca)**

3 JELLYFISH, CORALS, AND HYDRAS **(Cnidaria)**

4 EARTHWORMS, LEECHES, AND POLYCHAETES **(Annelida)**

5 FLUKES AND TAPEWORMS **(Platyhelminthes)**

6 ROUNDWORMS **(Nematoda)**

7 SEA STARS, SEA URCHINS, AND SEA CUCUMBERS **(Echinodermata)**

8 SPONGES **(Porifera)**

INVERTEBRATES

Wasp spiders (*Argiope bruennichi*), like the one shown here, weave orb, or circular, webs, and females have a distinctive yellow-and-black striped abdomen that resembles the markings of a wasp.

SPONGES

S ponges are the oldest animals by far—they appear in the fossil record 600 to 760 million years ago.

Most are marine animals. They look like colorful globs of plant material. Some grow like tubes; others grow as crusts over hard surfaces. They have no organs and a very simple body structure. Some sponges are "encrusting," meaning they cover the surfaces of rocks, while others are freestanding and can grow in unusual shapes and sizes.

The outer surface of a sponge is full of holes called pores. The inner surface of each pore is lined by cells that draw in water and catch food like bacteria. Porifera, the name of the sponge phylum, means "pore-bearing." Their bodies are supported by a very delicate skeleton of calcium or other minerals.

Though they do not have nerves, sponges can change their body shape by coordinating the movements of their cells. They do this to pump out water that has been filtered, along with any waste, through an exit hole. Some sponges have multiple exit holes. Others have just one.

Life spans for sponges range from a few years to thousands. Most are extremely slow-growing.

AZURE VASE SPONGE
Callyspongia plicifera

RANGE: Waters of the Caribbean Sea, Bahamas, and South Florida, U.S.A.

SIZE: 6 to 11 in (15 to 27 cm)

DIET: Bacteria and tiny marine organisms

This tubelike sponge also has folds in its body. These give it extra surface area, which creates room for more pores and more opportunities to filter food. The azure vase sponge grows as a single pink or purple tube.

STOVE-PIPE SPONGE
Aplysina archeri

RANGE: Atlantic Ocean, Caribbean Sea, coastal waters of Venezuela

SIZE: 5 ft (1.5 m)

DIET: Bacteria and tiny marine organisms

The stove-pipe sponge and many other tubelike sponges filter water for food and oxygen by taking it in through pores close to the bottom of the tube. Then they pump out the extra water through a large hole at the top.

Did you know? Sponge skeletons and fingernails are made of similar material.

BARREL SPONGE
Xestospongia testudinaria

RANGE: Tropical waters of the western Pacific

SIZE: Up to 8 in (20 cm) tall and 8 in (20 cm) wide

DIET: Bacteria and tiny marine organisms

Barrel sponges are among the largest sponges in the world. They are long-living and sometimes called the "redwoods of the deep." A related species, the giant barrel sponge, found in the Caribbean Sea and adjacent waters can grow big enough to fit a car inside.

DEAD MAN'S FINGER SPONGE
Neoesperiopsis spp.

RANGE: Tropical waters
SIZE: 19.7 in (50 cm)
DIET: Bacteria and tiny marine organisms

These sponges are freestanding, like the barrel and vase sponges, and are recognized by their fingerlike projections. They vary in color from dull brown or gray to orange.

FRESHWATER SPONGE
Spongilla lacustris

RANGE: North America, Europe, Asia

SIZE: .07 in to 3.2 ft (2 mm to 1 m)

DIET: Bacteria and tiny marine organisms

Like corals, many freshwater sponges have algae growing in their cells that give them a green color. The sponge benefits from the energy produced by the algae (by photosynthesis), and the algae have a place to live.

WORMS

There are three groups of worms: flatworms, annelids—worms with a segmented body cavity, which include earthworms and leeches—and roundworms.

Flatworms are the simplest of these worms, with no body cavity. They absorb oxygen and food directly through their skin. Their flat bodies allow more surface area for absorption. Examples are parasitic worms like flukes (trematodes) and tapeworms (cestodes), and nonparasitic worms like planarians. Life spans range from one year to unlimited in the case of planarians, which can regenerate.

Annelids have a body cavity and a complete digestive tract. Leeches are found in freshwater, marine, and terrestrial habitats, and many feed on animal blood. Many earthworms live in soil and feed on decaying plants. Life spans range from four to eight years.

Roundworms have a body cavity, digestive tract, and complex lifestyles. Many are parasites, which could explain why they may be the single most numerous animals on land and in the sea. Life spans range from one to two years.

HAMMERHEAD WORM
Bipalium simrothi

RANGE: Indonesia

SIZE: Up to 20 in (50 cm)

DIET: Earthworms and other invertebrates

This worm is a terrestrial, carnivorous flatworm. It feeds on its prey—including snails, slugs, earthworms, and insects—by pushing the inside of its mouth out to cover its prey in mucous that dissolves it. Then it ingests it.

CHRISTMAS TREE WORM
Spirobranchus giganteus

RANGE: Tropical and subtropical waters around the world

SIZE: Up to 8 in (20 cm)

DIET: Tiny marine organisms

This annelid is a type of "bristle" worm. Each segment contains a hard core of chitin for protection, a pair of footlike structures covered in bristles that help it move, and elaborate mouth parts. It is named for the two spiraling crowns of hairlike tentacles it uses to breathe and catch food. When startled, it quickly retracts into a burrow that it has made in live coral.

LEECH
Hirudo medicinalis

RANGE: Western and southern Europe

SIZE: 8 in (20 cm)

DIET: Blood

There are more than 700 species of leeches. *Hirudo medicinalis* has a sucker on one end and a tiny, three-part jaw with sharp teeth on the other. Adults feed on the blood of mammals by attaching to their host with suckers and biting through its skin. After a full meal, the leech may increase up to 11 times its body size!

C. ELEGANS
Caenorhabditis elegans

RANGE: Temperate climates

SIZE: Microscopic: .04 in (1 mm)

DIET: Bacteria and decaying vegetable matter

This tiny, transparent roundworm has been studied extensively in the lab and was the first multicellular animal to have its genome sequenced (1998). It has also been to the International Space Station and back.

COMMON EARTHWORM
Lumbricus terrestris

RANGE: Native to Europe; introduced to North America and Australia

SIZE: 8 to 10 in (20 to 25 cm)

DIET: Soil and decomposing matter such as leaves and roots

The common earthworm has been introduced to forests all over the world. Because they eat a lot of leaf litter in a short time, they are changing habitats, disrupting the lives of native animals and plants.

INVERTEBRATES

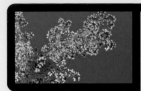

CORALS

Corals, sea anemones, and jellyfish are in the phylum Cnidaria (ni-DAIR-ee-uh). All have stinging cells, and all are much more complex than they seem.

Corals are colonies of tiny animals called polyps (POL-ips) that have permanently attached to the seafloor. Each has a saclike body. One end is attached to a calcium skeleton; the other end is open and surrounded by tentacles. Corals can't move, so they depend on currents to flush nutrients in and wastes out.

Most corals use their stinging cells to feed on plankton and small fish at night. During the day, shallow-water corals also get energy from symbiotic algae that live in their stomachs. Using sunlight and waste products from the coral, the algae carry out photosynthesis. The energy and oxygen created help the coral grow and build the calcium structures known as coral reefs. These algae also give corals their color. Coral life spans range from 20 to thousands of years.

MAT ZOANTHID
Zoanthus pulchellus

RANGE: Caribbean Sea; Bahamas; Florida, U.S.A.

SIZE: 0.5 in (1.3 cm)

DIET: Energy from photosynthesis by symbiotic algae; small fish; plankton

The corals in the zoanthid (zoe-AN-thid) group live as single polyps, long strands, or soft mats in a variety of marine habitats. The mat-like structure is made up of many individual coral polyps attached to bits of sand and rock.

BUBBLE CORAL
Plerogyra sinuosa

RANGE: Mostly found in Indian and Pacific Oceans; also Red Sea, Gulf of Aden, East China Sea, the waters off Southeast Asia and Japan

SIZE: 6 in (15 cm)

DIET: Energy from photosynthesis by symbiotic algae; small fish; plankton

Bubble corals, like all shallow-water corals, rely on their algae for energy during the day. Their polyps contract, or deflate, at night when their stinging tentacles become active. Bubble corals have extra tentacles called sweepers.

CAULIFLOWER CORAL
Pocillopora meandrina

RANGE: Indian and Pacific Oceans

SIZE: 20 in (50 cm)

DIET: Energy from photosynthesis by symbiotic algae; small fish; plankton

This coral looks like cauliflower when its polyps are extended and active. Also called brush corals, cauliflower corals may be either domed or branched. Their colors range from pink to brown.

Did you know? Some corals grow in the direction of the water current.

WHIP CORAL
Cirrhipathes (genus)

RANGE: Indian and Pacific Oceans

SIZE: 3 ft (91 cm)

DIET: Energy from photosynthesis by symbiotic algae; small fish; plankton

Whip corals look a bit like barbed wire and cannot retract their polyps. Their calcium skeleton is also dark. Depending on their algae, they may be green, yellow, brown, or gray.

STAGHORN CORAL
Acropora cervicornis

RANGE: Caribbean; Bahamas; Florida, U.S.A.

SIZE: 1 to 8 ft (0.3 to 2.4 m)

DIET: Energy from photosynthesis by symbiotic algae; small fish; plankton

Many coral species take years to grow one inch (2.5 cm). But staghorn coral can grow up to eight inches (20 cm) a year. This species is endangered because of habitat damage, pollution, collecting, and an infection called white-band disease.

ANEMONES AND JELLIES

Anemones (a-NEM-o-neez) are cnidarians with a polyp body shape like corals, but they are much bigger. They range from very small to as large as a bowling pin. They also hold on to the seafloor or coral reef using a muscular foot.

Some anemones feed only on plankton; many have symbiotic algae. The majority also capture larger animals with their stinging tentacles, including mussels, crabs, sea urchins, and even small fish.

Life spans for sea anemones range from 10 to 80 years.

Jellyfish are not fish at all! They are free-floating, upside-down polyps, a body shape known as medusa. They have three cell layers like corals and anemones. The difference is the middle layer is greatly expanded with a jellylike substance. They move by contracting and expanding their umbrellalike bell.

Some jellyfish are so small they are barely visible. The largest—the giant Nomura's jellyfish—can weigh 440 pounds (200 kg). All feed on plankton, crustaceans, fish, and other jellyfish.

Life spans for jellyfish range from a few hours to six months, though there may be a few long-living species.

GIANT GREEN ANEMONE
Anthopleura xanthogrammica

RANGE: Pacific Ocean along the west coast of North and Central America, from Alaska to Panama

SIZE: Height: 7 by 12 in (17.5 by 30 cm); crown diameter: 10 in (25 cm)

DIET: Mussels, small fish, crabs, sea urchins

Green anemones are found in cooler water—often in shallow tide pools. Their bright green color is a combination of pigmented cells and the color of the algae that live in their cells. Mussels are their preferred food.

MEDITERRANEAN JELLYFISH
Cotylorhiza tuberculata

RANGE: Mediterranean, Aegean, and Adriatic Seas

SIZE: Diameter: up to 14 in (35 cm)

DIET: Plankton

This jellyfish is also known as the fried egg jellyfish because of the way it looks from above. It is able to move on its own, rather than depending on the water current.

FISH-EATING ANEMONE
Urticina piscivora

RANGE: Alaska to California's Channel Islands, U.S.A.

SIZE: Height: 8 in (20 cm); crown diameter: 4 in (10 cm)

DIET: Shrimp, small fish, plankton

Fish-eating anemones are a cool-water species often found in kelp forests. Like many of their relatives, they capture shrimp and small fish using their tentacles and immobilize their prey with toxins ejected through microscopic barbs.

PURPLE TUBE ANEMONE
Cerianthus membranaceus

RANGE: Indo-Pacific waters

SIZE: 1 to 15 in (3 to 40 cm)

DIET: Plankton

Tube anemones are close relatives of sea anemones and live partially buried in the ocean floor. Their tentacles secrete a mucus that hardens to form a tube, which it uses like a burrow. They are nocturnal and feed on plankton and debris.

DEADLY JELLIES

Jellyfish can be found in bodies of water all around the world. They often are feared for their painful sting, though some species don't actually sting at all. But there are a select few that pack a potent punch.

The sea wasp (Chironex fleckeri), a type of box jellyfish, is the most venomous marine animal in the world. With tentacles stretching 10 feet (3 m) long, it has a powerful toxin that attacks the nervous system, heart, and skin. Each tentacle contains 20,000 stinging cells, and one jellyfish has enough venom to kill 20 grown humans!

Another dangerous box jelly is the much smaller Irukandji (Malo kingi), which measures roughly one inch (2.5 cm), including the tentacles. It can fire its stingers at its victims. The result usually is not death, but symptoms called the Irukandji syndrome: intense backache, headache, nausea, and anxiety.

INVERTEBRATES

SNAILS AND SLUGS

G astropods—snails and slugs—are the most common type of mollusks, and the second-most-common group of animals after insects! At least 60,000 species have been discovered so far.

Slugs have either no shell or a very tiny one, whereas all snails have shells, which they use for protection. Many can close off the entrance to their shell with a horny plate known as an operculum (o-PER-cyoo-lum).

All gastropods have a head with eyespots and tentacles, a digestive tract that runs the length of their body, and a muscular foot. These features give this group its name. "Gastropod" means "stomach foot" in Greek.

Snails and slugs are found worldwide and in all habitat types. Some are herbivores; others are carnivores. About two-thirds live in salt water, a few live in freshwater, and the rest are terrestrial. Many are edible, such as the abalone and conch. Life spans range from three to eight years.

PACIFIC SIDEBAND SNAIL
Monadenia fidelis

RANGE: Pacific coast of North America

SIZE: 0.9 to 1.4 in (2.2 to 3.6 cm)

DIET: Decaying material

Land snails have either two or four sensory tentacles on their heads to detect smells, and two eyespots to detect motion. The eyes are located either at the end of two of the tentacles or, as in the Pacific sideband, at the base.

YELLOW BANANA SLUG
Ariolimax californicus

RANGE: Pacific Northwest of North America

SIZE: Up to 10 in (25 cm)

DIET: Leaves, dead plant material, fungi, animal droppings

Banana slugs, one of the largest land slugs, can move fast—up to 6.5 inches (16.5 cm) per minute. Their bodies are more streamlined without a shell. To keep their skin moist, they secrete a slimy mucus.

RED SLUG
Arion rufus

RANGE: Europe; introduced in United States

SIZE: 0.6 to 7 in (1.5 to 18 cm)

DIET: Plants, decaying material, feces, carrion

The red slug is an omnivorous land slug native to Europe that has been introduced in the United States, where it has become a big problem. It eats anything, including crops like strawberries, cabbage, and clover.

NUDIBRANCH
Dendronotus frondosus

RANGE: Northeast and northwest Atlantic Ocean

SIZE: 4 in (10 cm)

DIET: Sponges, anemones, other invertebrates

Nudibranchs are a type of sea slug. They are carnivores, and most release toxic chemicals when disturbed. Their bright colors are a warning to predators to stay away.

WHITE-LIPPED SNAIL
Cepaea hortensis

RANGE: Western and central Europe

SIZE: Shell height: 0.4 to 0.6 in (1 to 1.6 cm)

DIET: Leaves, wood, bark, stems, fruit, flowers, insects

The white-lipped snail is found in woods, grasslands, and sandy shores. As in most shelled gastropods, it has a coiled shell with an opening on the right side. The shell is used for protection from predators and the environment.

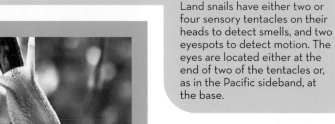

CLAMS, OYSTERS, MUSSELS, AND SCALLOPS

Clams, oysters, mussels, and scallops have two cuplike shells connected by a hinge. This is the reason for the name bivalve, which means "two shells." Like gastropods, they have a strong foot muscle. Instead of using it to move, however, they use it to close their shell.

Most bivalves are filter feeders. They have two siphons: one that pumps water in, and one that pumps water out over the gills, which trap plankton. Most bury themselves under the sea or riverbed. A few attach themselves to rocks. Some, like scallops, swim using their siphons.

Oysters and freshwater mussels often produce pearls. These begin as grains of sand that lodge in the mantle, a very thin tissue that covers the body and secretes the shell. In response, the animal covers the sand with the same material it uses to produce the inner surface of its shell. The result is a smooth, usually white, pebble-like structure.

Life spans range from two to 40 years for smaller species and longer for larger ones.

BIG MOLLUSKS

There are three types of mollusks: gastropods, bivalves, and cephalopods. All share two features: a nervous system and muscular feet, or arms. Many also have shells, usually for protection.

Mollusk shells are made of calcium carbonate, the same material as coral reefs. It is much harder than chitin, the protein found in the exoskeletons of insects and crustaceans.

Bivalves, like clams, oysters, and mussels, have two external shells joined by a hinge. Among the gastropods, land snails have a single external shell.

Only a few cephalopods have shells. The nautilus has an external shell, the cuttlefish has an internal shell called a cuttlebone, and the vampire squid has a vestigial, or remnant, internal shell called a gladius.

ELECTRIC FLAME SCALLOP
Ctenoides ales

RANGE: Indo-Pacific waters
SIZE: 1 to 3 in (2.5 to 7.6 cm)
DIET: Plankton

Also called the disco clam and the electric file clam, this clam can turn its lips—the tissue just under each half of its shell—a bright color, like a flash of light.

WAVY-RAYED LAMPMUSSEL
Lampsilis fasciola

RANGE: North American Great Lakes and Ohio-Mississippi drainage south to Tennessee River system
SIZE: Up to 3.1 in (8 cm)
DIET: Plankton

When the eggs of the wavy-rayed lampmussel hatch, they release larvae that attach to the gills of largemouth and smallmouth bass. There, they develop into juveniles, drop off, and mature to adults on the lake bottom.

NUTTALL'S COCKLE
Clinocardium nuttallii

RANGE: Native to the coastlines of California and the Pacific Northwest; found from the Bering Sea to Southern California
SIZE: Up to 5.5 in (14 cm)
DIET: Plankton

With its shell closed and viewed from the side, this clam is shaped like a heart. Most of the time, it lies buried under the sand or mud with only a part of its shell visible. Younger clams are lighter in color compared to older ones.

BAY SCALLOP
Argopecten irradians

RANGE: Atlantic Ocean
SIZE: Up to 3 in (7.5 cm)
DIET: Plankton

Populations of bay scallops have been decreasing, as development and pollution have damaged their seagrass habitat. Another reason? Sharks are being overfished. In the food web, sharks eat rays, and rays eat scallops. Fewer sharks means there are more rays to eat more scallops.

FROM THE FIELD:

Martina Panisi

OBÔ GIANT SNAIL

When people think of snails, they usually picture something more or less the size of a coin. But the yellow eggs of the Obô giant snail (*Archachatina bicarinata*) are as big as a coin—the snail itself is big enough to hold in two hands! Obô giant snails exist only in the most remote forests on the São Tomé and Príncipe Islands off the coast of West Africa. They have spiraling black shells and four tentacles. Their eyes are on the two longer tentacles up top. They use their shorter, lower tentacles to smell when searching for food.

I had been studying data and searching for information on these snails for months before I ever saw one in its native forest. I finally saw one, and we named it Filippo after my field mate Filipa, who spotted it first. The snail didn't pull back into its shell to protect itself like other species of giant snails do. Instead, it just stared at us. It wasn't scared. That's when I understood how innocent and vulnerable these creatures are, and my colleagues and I decided that we had to do something to keep this species from disappearing.

In some ways, Obô giant snails are a lot like humans. They have their favorite spots to sleep and their favorite foods, and they like to take baths. For research purposes, I kept some at home for a while. At night I could hear "scratch, scratch" sounds as they used the thousand micro teeth on their tongues to eat the fruits and vegetables I gave them. One thing I discovered was that they're not as slow as they seem. They escaped from their boxes one night, and in the morning I found them in the weirdest places—everywhere from the ceiling to the kitchen sink.

Studying species is important. Sometimes, we don't understand the value of another living being until we really observe it, learn its story, and understand its beautiful characteristics.

RANGE OF THE
ARCHACHATINA
BICARINATA
(OBÔ GIANT SNAIL)

0   700 miles

0   700 kilometers

EUROPE

AFRICA

*São Tomé and
Príncipe Islands*

ATLANTIC OCEAN

OBSERVATION TIPS

1 Don't go alone. Have a local guide and a good team of people when entering the forest.

2 Wear waterproof clothing. You'll probably have to cross several rivers, and there's a good chance it will be raining.

3 Beware of Naja snakes, venomous, black snakes found in the forests where Obô giant snails live.

4 Wash your hands before and after handling so you and the snails don't pass any diseases to each other.

Martina Panisi is a conservation biologist and environmental educator. To highlight the critical role that invertebrates play in the health of ecosystems, she helped create the "Forest Giants" project. Using the story of the Obô giant snail's decline, she and her team are teaching people why it is important to conserve native biodiversity and how everyone, from children to adults, can help.

In the past 20 years, the population of Obô giant snails has declined more than 75 percent. Habitat loss and people harvesting too many snails for food and medicine are both problems. However, some of this drop occurred after the West African giant land snail was introduced to the islands in the 1980s, spread to the native snail's habitat, and possibly passed on a disease. Today, West African giant land snails outnumber their endemic cousins and have taken over most of the area where they once lived.

INVERTEBRATES

235

OCTOPUSES
AND RELATIVES

n Greek, "cephalopod" (SEF-a-low-pod) means "head foot." The animals in this group have large heads and strong, muscular feet—lots of them. The octopus, for example, has eight. Its feet are called arms because they attach to the head, not the body. Nautilus have the most with 90.

Some cephalopods have external shells, like the nautilus, whereas others have internal ones, like squid and cuttlefish. All have a strong parrotlike beak. The only hard part of the octopus's body is its beak. This soft body allows it to squeeze through tiny holes.

Most cephalopods are predators that feed on marine animals, grabbing their prey with their arms and pushing it into their mouths. They have well-developed eyes and excellent vision. They also can change the color of their skin to match their environment.

When threatened, most of these animals secrete a milky black substance known as ink. This gives them time to hide or jet away from the predator. Life spans range from six months to five years.

GIANT PACIFIC OCTOPUS
Enteroctopus dofleini

RANGE: Pacific Ocean

SIZE: 14 to 30 ft (4.2 to 9 m)

DIET: Clams, crab, fish, squid

The giant Pacific octopus has six-foot (1.8-m)-long arms, each with hundreds of touch- and taste-sensitive suckers. Since it hunts at night, the octopus relies on its specialized vision to find a place to feed and on its arms to find prey.

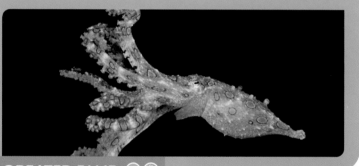

CARIBBEAN REEF SQUID
Sepioteuthis sepioidea

RANGE: Florida, U.S.A.; Caribbean, Central America, northern South America

SIZE: 8 in (20 cm)

DIET: Fish and shrimp

This squid takes water into its head and shoots it out a siphon to move quickly to catch food or escape a predator. It can even jet itself into the air.

GREATER BLUE-RINGED OCTOPUS
Hapalochlaena lunulata

RANGE: Northern Australia and tropical western Pacific Ocean

SIZE: Up to 4.7 in (12 cm)

DIET: Fish, crabs, mollusks

The saliva of this octopus contains highly toxic venom that is made from bacteria in its salivary glands. One bite paralyzes the octopus's prey.

CUTTLEFISH
Sepia officinalis

RANGE: North Atlantic Ocean, English Channel, Mediterranean Sea

SIZE: 12 to 20 in (30 to 49 cm)

DIET: Crustaceans and fish

Like octopus, cuttlefish have eyes that can see both forward and backward at the same time. In addition to eight arms, they have two long tentacles used for grabbing prey.

BIGFIN REEF SQUID
Sepioteuthis lessoniana

RANGE: Indo-Pacific waters

SIZE: 1.5 to 13 in (3.8 to 33 cm)

DIET: Crustaceans and fish

The oval squid has pigmented cells in its skin, especially around its eyes. In the light, some of these cells turn metallic red and green. Others turn the same color as the light shining on them.

ECHINODERMS

The name "echinoderm" (ee-KINE-o-derm) means "spiny skin" in Greek. The animals in this group are found only in salt water and include sea stars, brittle stars, sea urchins, sand dollars, and sea cucumbers. All have a delicate skeleton made of calcium; skin that is prickly, bumpy, or covered with spines; and tubelike feet. They are mostly herbivores that feed on algae and scavengers that eat decomposing animal and plant material. Some also eat other invertebrates.

Though they may not look like it, all echinoderms are shaped like a bicycle wheel with spokes. The mouth is in the center, and there are usually five arms, or rays. This form is easy to see in sea stars—also called starfish—except they are not fish! The rays of a sea urchin can be seen in the animal's bare skeleton, which often washes up on beaches. Sea cucumbers have tentacles around their mouth, also arranged in rays.

Life spans are up to five years for sea cucumbers, 35 for sea stars, and 100 or more for sea urchins.

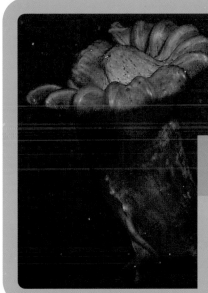

SWIMMING SEA CUCUMBER
Enypniastes eximia

RANGE: All oceans

SIZE: Up to 12 in (30 cm)

DIET: Dead organisms, bottom sediment, algae

The swimming, or pink, sea cucumber is more mobile than other sea cucumbers. It swims up the water column—as far as 3,280 feet (1,000 m) above the ocean floor—and back down. When threatened, it produces bioluminescence, and then sheds its brightly lit skin.

RED SLATE PENCIL URCHIN
Heterocentrotus mammillatus

RANGE: Indo-Pacific waters, including Hawaii

SIZE: 5 to 10 in (15 to 25 cm)

DIET: Mainly algae

The spines of the red slate pencil urchin were once used to write on slate boards—like blackboards. Like all urchins, it has tiny bones in its mouth that function like teeth to scrape up its food. It is a nocturnal feeder.

BLUE SEA STAR
Linckia laevigata

RANGE: Indo-Pacific waters

SIZE: 12 in (30 cm)

DIET: Dead organisms and algae

The blue sea star has tubular, rounded arms. Like many other sea stars, it can regrow a damaged arm. It also can detach one as a way to distract predators, such as other sea stars, shrimp, and sea anemones.

CHOCOLATE CHIP STARFISH
Protoreaster nodosus

RANGE: Indo-Pacific waters

SIZE: 12 in (30 cm)

DIET: Algae, decomposing seagrass

Also called the horned sea star, the chocolate chip starfish feeds mostly on algae. It expels its stomach to digest its food. This species is named for its resemblance to cookie dough.

BLUE SEA URCHIN
Echinothrix diadema

RANGE: Indo-Pacific waters

SIZE: Diameter of 4 to 8 in (10 to 20 cm)

DIET: Mainly algae

Sea urchins are an important source of food for sea otters, wolf eels, and triggerfish. The urchin's spines are for protection and are not venomous, though some species have short stingers in between the spines that can be toxic.

INVERTEBRATES

CRABS, SHRIMP, AND
LOBSTERS

rabs, shrimp, lobsters, barnacles, and crayfish belong to a diverse group of animals called crustaceans (cruh-STAY-shunz). A type of arthropod, crustaceans have a hard outer covering, called an exoskeleton, and segmented bodies. Unlike other arthropods, crustaceans' bodies are sometimes divided into two parts instead of three. That includes the abdomen and in some, a cephalothorax, or fused head and thorax. Most crustaceans also have branched limbs, two pairs of antennae, and jointed legs. Some have large claws. All breathe through gills.

Most crustaceans live in water, mainly in the ocean. Some, including many types of crabs, also live on land. As long as their gills stay damp, they can breathe.

Like all arthropods, crustaceans molt, or shed their exoskeleton and grow a new one. Some also have shells. Barnacles make shells to cover their bodies. The shells expand as the barnacles grow and molt inside. Hermit crabs find shells—or sometimes sea anemones or sponges—to protect the back half of their bodies. Only the front half is covered with a hard exoskeleton.

Life spans range from about a month to a speculated 100 years.

RED SWAMP CRAYFISH
Procambarus clarkii

RANGE: Native to south-central United States and northeastern Mexico

SIZE: 2.2 to 4.7 in (5.5 to 12 cm)

DIET: Insect larvae, tadpoles, snails

These dark red crayfish live in many different freshwater habitats, but they avoid places with strong currents. During drought or periods of cold, they burrow into the ground. Females also burrow when they lay eggs—up to 500 at a time. Growing hatchlings stay attached to the mother until they molt twice.

ORANGUTAN CRAB
Achaeus japonicus

RANGE: Indo-Pacific waters

SIZE: 0.8 in (2 cm)

DIET: Marine invertebrates

This fuzzy little decorator crab's body and legs are covered with long red hairs similar to those of an orangutan. It collects tiny plants and animals, shells, and other items and attaches them to its body for camouflage. But it's hard for this crab to hide. It spends most of its time on bright white bubble corals!

STRAWBERRY HERMIT CRAB
Coenobita perlatus

RANGE: Coastal shorelines of Indo-Pacific islands in the south-central Pacific Ocean

SIZE: 3.1 in (8 cm)

DIET: Dead and rotting material along the seashore

Though most of its relatives are aquatic, the strawberry hermit crab is terrestrial. It lives in coastal areas, visiting the sea at night to refill its shell with water, feeding along the way. These crabs live in groups and trade shells among one another.

SPANISH SLIPPER LOBSTER
Scyllarides aequinoctialis

RANGE: Caribbean; Bahamas; South Florida, U.S.A.; as far south as São Paulo, Brazil

SIZE: 6 to 12 in (15 to 30 cm)

DIET: Scallops, clams, mussels, oysters

This species is named for the slipper-like pair of legs it uses to open the shells of its prey. Like true lobsters, it is long-living and caught for food.

ARTHROPODS

All arthropods have segmented bodies covered with a hard outer skeleton, or exoskeleton, and several pairs of legs. Insects have three pairs of legs; millipedes have hundreds. The name of this group means "jointed foot" in Greek. Most have claws, bristles, or pads instead of feet, and many can fly.

Insects are by far the most numerous types of arthropods, but there are four others: crustaceans, which include lobsters, shrimp, and crabs; arachnids, which include spiders, ticks, and mites; centipedes and millipedes; and horseshoe crabs.

Arthropods have hard bodies made of chitin that require special conditions to fossilize well. Arthropod fossils are not as common in the fossil record as mollusk shells or echinoderms that are made of calcium carbonate, which is much harder than chitin.

COLEMAN SHRIMP
Periclimenes colemani

RANGE: West Pacific Ocean

SIZE: 0.8 in (2 cm)

DIET: Parasites, algae, plankton

Many smaller shrimp feed on parasites found on fish. They are known as cleaner shrimp. They wait inside a sea anemone or, as in the case of the Coleman shrimp, a sea urchin, and pick their meals off the fish that visit.

PEACOCK MANTIS SHRIMP
Odontodactylus scyllarus

RANGE: Indo-Pacific waters

SIZE: 1.2 to 7.1 in (3 to 18 cm)

DIET: Snails, slugs, other crustaceans, bivalves

Peacock mantis shrimp use their club-shaped feet to smash open hard prey like snails and mussels. They also have excellent color vision used in mating and for spotting predators like barracuda. Females carry their eggs under their tails.

Did you know?
A female lobster carries its eggs under its abdomen.

SMOOTH GOOSENECK BARNACLE
Lepas anatifera

RANGE: Tropical and subtropical ocean waters

SIZE: Shell size: up to 2 in (5 cm)

DIET: Plankton

Barnacles create their own shells. They also make a glue-like chemical to attach their head to a rock, dock, or even a whale; they then wave their feet in the water to catch plankton.

SPOTTED SPINY LOBSTER
Panulirus guttatus

RANGE: Caribbean Sea; Bahamas; Florida, U.S.A.

SIZE: 5 to 18 in (13 to 45 cm)

DIET: Snails, clams, crabs, sea urchins, carrion

These animals migrate in large groups along the seafloor. They communicate with each other and ward off predators by rubbing their antennae on their bodies to make different sounds.

SALLY LIGHTFOOT CRAB
Grapsus grapsus

RANGE: Pacific coast of Mexico; Central and South America, including Galápagos Islands

SIZE: 2 to 3.1 in (5 to 8 cm)

DIET: Mostly algae; parasites; also dead and decomposing animals and plants

This species is named for the way it moves: very quickly on the tips of its claws, changing directions in a flash. On the Galápagos Islands, the Sally Lightfoot crab has a symbiotic relationship with the marine iguana: It picks off the iguana's ticks for food.

SPIDERS,
SCORPIONS, TICKS, AND MITES

Spiders, scorpions, ticks, and mites are called arachnids (a-RACK-nidz), which is Greek for "spider." All have eight legs. Many of the 100,000 species in this group are venomous, but only 25 species of scorpions are dangerous to people. Spiders also have glands that produce silk, which they use for building webs to capture insects, for building egg sacs, and for climbing.

Some arachnids look as though they have more than eight legs. This is because they have two pairs of leglike structures. The first, called chelicerae (kuh-LIS-eh-ree), are used for feeding and defense. The second, called pedipalps (PEH-duh-palps), are used for capturing food, walking, and reproduction. Scorpions, for example, have a set of claws they use to grab and crush their prey.

Except for mites, the animals in this group predigest their food. They mix digestive juices with bits of food in their mouths and swallow the liquid, spitting out any hard parts.

Life spans range from seven to 25 years.

BOLD JUMPING SPIDER
Phidippus audax

RANGE: North America and parts of Central America

SIZE: 0.5 to 0.8 in (1.3 to 2 cm)

DIET: Insects

Bold jumping spiders are identified by their bright-green or blue chelicerae, or chewing mouthparts. All jumping spiders have large forward-facing eyes that give them very good depth perception for jumping to catch their insect prey.

GIANT VELVET MITE
Dinothrombium (genus)

RANGE: Southwestern United States

SIZE: 0.2 to 0.6 in (4 to 15 mm)

DIET: Young: parasitic on grasshoppers; adults: termite eggs

The giant velvet mite is much larger than other mites and their close relatives, ticks. The result is they are easy to see in the soil.

VINEGAROON
Mastigoproctus giganteus

RANGE: Southern United States, Mexico

SIZE: 2 in (5 cm) without whip

DIET: Termites, cockroaches, crickets

The vinegaroon is a type of whip scorpion. Instead of a venomous stinger, it has a long, whiplike structure that senses vibrations. Acid glands at the base of the tail spray an irritating chemical called acetic acid, or vinegar—hence its name.

BARK SCORPION
Centruroides sculpturatus

RANGE: Southwestern United States

SIZE: 3.1 in (8 cm)

DIET: Crickets, cockroaches

Bark scorpions are found anywhere there is shade and a large supply of their favored prey: insects, especially crickets and roaches. As a result, they often are found in people's homes. Their sting is painful and can be fatal.

ROCKY MOUNTAIN WOOD TICK
Dermacentor andersoni

RANGE: Rocky Mountains, U.S.A., southwestern Canada

SIZE: Up to .25 in (6 mm)

DIET: Blood of mammals

This tick requires three hosts to complete its life cycle. Larvae feed on small mammals, nymphs feed on slightly larger ones, and adults feed on deer and dogs—sometimes even people.

CENTIPEDES AND MILLIPEDES

Centipedes and millipedes are arthropods with lots of legs! Each has dozens to hundreds of body segments. Centipedes have one pair of legs for each segment except for the first and last. Millipedes have two pairs. Both types of animals have simple digestive tracts and—like many land-dwelling arthropods—breathe through tiny holes in their skin called spiracles (SPIR-uh-kulz).

Millipedes feed on decaying plants and fruits and are found all over the world in a variety of habitats. They can open or close their spiracles, depending on the amount of moisture in their environment. They lack eyes and find food using their antennae.

Centipedes prey on insects, which they kill by using their first pair of legs to inject venom. Unlike millipedes, they cannot close their spiracles and are found only in moist habitats or where they can find shelter. They also are flatter, with longer legs, which makes them very fast movers.

Life spans are up to seven years for centipedes and millipedes.

HOUSE CENTIPEDE
Scutigera coleoptrata

RANGE: Mediterranean; also introduced across Europe, Asia, North America

SIZE: 0.4 to 2.4 in (1 to 6 cm)

DIET: Worms, snails, fly larvae, bedbugs, other arthropods

There are several species of house centipedes, so named because they are very common in people's homes, where they feed on bedbugs, cockroaches, and other insects. With a rigid body and 15 pairs of long legs, they run as fast as some insects fly.

NORTH AMERICAN MILLIPEDE
Narceus americanus

RANGE: North America

SIZE: Up to 4 in (10 cm)

DIET: Decaying plants and insects

North American millipedes are usually found under logs or piles of wet leaves. They feed at night and are a favorite food of shrews as well as of frogs, lizards, beetles, and some birds.

GIANT AFRICAN MILLIPEDE
Archispirostreptus gigas

RANGE: Africa

SIZE: 13.2 in (33.5 cm)

DIET: Decaying plants

When millipedes are threatened, they curl up into a spiral so only their hard, outer covering, or exoskeleton, is exposed. They also secrete an irritating liquid from holes in their skin. The giant African millipede usually has 256 legs.

GIANT DESERT CENTIPEDE
Scolopendra heros

RANGE: Southern United States and northern Mexico

SIZE: 6.5 to 8 in (17 to 20 cm)

DIET: Small arthropods, toads, small snakes

This venomous centipede is also known as the giant redheaded centipede because some have dark blue bodies with red heads; others are all reddish brown. Its stinging front legs are long, curled, and always light tan.

Did you know?

Although "millipede" comes from the Latin words for "thousand" and "feet," no millipede has a thousand legs.

INSECTS

nsects are by far the most numerous animals on Earth. About a million have been described so far.

The main insect groups are beetles, butterflies and moths, flies, bees and wasps, and ants. Other, smaller groups—still large relative to the rest of the animal world—are grasshoppers, mantises, walking sticks, cockroaches, termites, earwigs, and wingless insects such as fleas, lice, and silverfish.

They are found in every habitat worldwide and play a range of roles in the food web, from pollinators and food to pests, parasites, and carriers of disease. The only place where there are relatively few insects is the ocean, where other arthropod groups are dominant.

Insects are identified by a three-part body (head, thorax, and abdomen), three pairs of legs, large eyes, and two antennae. Most have wings. Many have complicated life cycles, where the larval form takes years to become an adult.

Life spans (including all stages of the life cycle) range from 60 days for fruit flies to 17 years for some cicadas.

HORSE LUBBER GRASSHOPPER
Taeniopoda eques

RANGE: Southwestern United States, Mexico

SIZE: 2.5 in (6.4 cm)

DIET: Plants; sometimes carrion or other insects

The horse lubber grasshopper cannot fly and can barely jump, unlike most other grasshoppers, crickets, katydids, and locusts. For defense, it eats toxic plants so it tastes nasty to any animal that tries to eat it.

PRAYING MANTIS
Mantis religiosa

RANGE: Europe; introduced to North America

SIZE: 2 to 3 in (5 to 7.5 cm)

DIET: Caterpillars, flies, butterflies, bees, moths

Also known as the European mantis, this insect is used to control plant pests in gardens and nurseries. This ambush predator hunts by sight—it can swivel its head 180 degrees in each direction. It uses its forelegs to capture its insect prey.

GIANT DEAD LEAF MANTIS
Deroplatys desiccata

RANGE: Southeast Asia

SIZE: 3.5 in (9 cm)

DIET: Flying insects

Like all mantises, the giant dead leaf mantis uses camouflage to surprise its prey and to protect itself from predators, such as bats. If disturbed, it will fall to the ground and stay motionless, like a leaf.

GIANT PRICKLY STICK INSECT
Extatosoma tiaratum

RANGE: Australia

SIZE: 6 to 8 in (15 to 20 cm)

DIET: Plants, especially eucalyptus, raspberry, oak, rose

Stick insects are vegetarians that, like mantises, use camouflage to hide from predators. The female giant prickly stick insect is larger than the male and unable to fly, so she has sharp spines on her head as an extra means of protection.

GIANT COCKROACH
Blaberus giganteus

RANGE: Central America

SIZE: 3.5 in (9 cm)

DIET: Plants and sometimes animal material

Cockroaches communicate with one another by releasing chemicals in the air and leaving a trail of feces. The result is a swarm of these insects. They are nocturnal insects that run away from light. Most eat almost anything.

BEETLES

Almost half (up to 400,000) of all named insect species are beetles. They are found in all habitats except marine and polar ones, and they are potential prey for all kinds of animals. For protection, they have an armor-like exoskeleton and a hard outer pair of wings that protects their true flying wings. Most beetles fly. There are also aquatic species that dive, often taking an air bubble down with them.

Most beetles have additional forms of defense. These include camouflage, mimicking wasps and other stinging insects, and the ability to spray nasty-smelling chemicals from glands in their abdomen. The bombardier beetle takes this one step further: It has two chemicals in separate glands that it mixes to create a popping sound and a burst of heat.

The feeding habits of beetles range from species that are general herbivores, insectivores, or scavengers, to those that specialize in eating certain plants, pollen, fungi, or dung. Many eat aphids and other insects that are damaging to crops. There are also more than 1,000 species of beetles that parasitize, eat, or live with ants.

Life spans (including all stages of the life cycle) range from weeks to 12 years.

MULTICOLORED ASIAN LADY BEETLE
Harmonia axyridis

RANGE: Native to Asia; introduced worldwide

SIZE: 0.2 to 0.4 in (5 to 8 mm)

DIET: Insects, insect larvae and eggs, ripe fruit

Commonly called ladybugs, they are not bugs at all. This beetle and other species were introduced to control aphids.

BROWN DUNG BEETLE
Onthophagus gazella

RANGE: Native to Africa, Asia; introduced worldwide

SIZE: Up to 1.3 in (3.3 cm)

DIET: Dung; also fungi, carrion, decomposing plants

All species of dung beetles eat animal manure, or dung. Where introduced, the dung beetle is especially good at cleaning up after cows. Males and females work in pairs to bury food for later use and to feed their young.

LONGHORNED BEETLE
Clytus ruricola

RANGE: Eastern North America

SIZE: 0.4 to 0.6 in (1 to 1.5 cm)

DIET: Larvae: decaying hardwood trees; adults: pollen, nectar

Although harmless, this beetle looks—and acts—as if it could sting. Like many wasps, it is found on flowers and makes a buzzing noise when disturbed. This type of mimicking is called Batesian mimicry.

FIGEATER BEETLE
Cotinis mutabilis

RANGE: Southwestern United States, Mexico

SIZE: 1.25 in (3.2 cm)

DIET: Ripe fruit, sap

This beetle's favorite fruit is figs. Like all beetles, it has two prominent antennae, claws on its feet, and two pairs of wings. The second flying pair is protected by the first, which is hard, like the exoskeleton.

243

MANY INSECTS HAVE SHAPES AND COLORS that mimic their surroundings, but few are as curious-looking as the treehopper. Treehoppers have oddly shaped structures that sprout from their backs. These outgrowths may look like helicopter propellers, ants, wasps, thorns ... or even feces. Some species, like the nymph clown treehopper seen here, also sport bright colors that may be a sign for predators to stay away.

BUGS

People often use the words "bugs" and "insects" as catch-all terms for creepy-crawly critters. But these words aren't interchangeable. Bugs are a group of insects; not all insects are bugs. The main types of bugs are cicadas and relatives; aphids and relatives; and true bugs, which include the water bugs.

All bugs have sucking mouthparts used to pierce their food and ingest the fluid inside. Most are plant-sap eaters. The exceptions are in the true bug group. Pond skaters and assassin bugs, for example, prey on insects. Bedbugs and kissing bugs feed on blood.

True bugs are distinguished from other bugs by their wings. Their forewings are thicker and leathery where they attach to the body. The rest of the wing is soft and clear, like a membrane. At rest, the tips of the forewings cross over and are held flat across the back. If these bugs have a second set of wings, they are also soft and clear. In some animals, like bedbugs, the wings are tiny.

Life spans range from 30 days for aphids to 17 years for cicadas.

BROWN MARMORATED STINK BUGS
Halyomorpha halys

RANGE: Asia; introduced to the United States

SIZE: 0.5 to 0.7 in (1.2 to 1.7 cm)

DIET: Plants

Stinkbugs are now major agricultural pests in countries where they are not native but have been introduced. Like all true bugs, they suck fluid out of plants and leave them damaged. They release a stinky chemical as a means of defense.

RED APHID
Acyrthosiphon pisum

RANGE: Worldwide

SIZE: .16 in (4 mm)

DIET: Sap of legumes such as peas, clover, alfalfa, beans

The aphid's ability to reproduce rapidly makes it a worldwide cause of crop damage. Most aphids are produced from unfertilized eggs and are born live at a rate of about 100 a month. A newly hatched aphid already has eggs growing inside it!

MAGIC CICADA
Magicicada septendecim

RANGE: North America

SIZE: 1.5 in (3.8 cm)

DIET: Juices from the roots of plants, especially deciduous trees

Newly hatched magic cicadas burrow underground to feed on tree roots. They climb back out 17 years later to breed! They molt into adults, and the males start singing to attract a mate. Within six weeks, eggs are laid and the adults die.

Did you know? A water bug uses its middle legs for rowing and back legs for steering.

MILKWEED ASSASSIN BUG
Zelus longipes

RANGE: Southern North America; Central America; most of South America; parts of the Caribbean

SIZE: Up to 0.7 in (1.8 cm)

DIET: Soft-bodied insects

This bug hides in leaves until an insect lands on its sticky front legs. It inserts its mouthparts to paralyze, then digest the food.

POND SKATER
Gerridae (genus)

RANGE: Worldwide except polar regions

SIZE: 0.1 to 0.6 in (0.3 to 1.6 cm)

DIET: Insects

Pond skaters have thousands of tiny hairs that cover their body and repel water. They use their front legs to detect ripples in the water made by their prey—struggling insects that cannot walk on water, like spiders and bees.

FLIES

The main groups of flies are true flies, dragonflies and damselflies, mayflies, and relatives. All are found worldwide and require access to water or a moist environment for reproduction.

Examples of true flies are horseflies, gnats, midges, mosquitoes, fruit flies, and the housefly. These insects have only one set of wings. Their feeding styles and mouthparts vary, though. Some are plant-sap eaters; others suck blood or feed on carrion.

Some true flies have larvae that are parasitic, meaning they require a living host. The screwworm fly, for example, lays its eggs near open wounds. After the larvae hatch, they feed on living tissue. Other flies, like the greenbottle fly, have parasitic larvae—often called maggots—that feed on dead tissue.

Dragonflies and damselflies are predators that feed on mosquitoes and other insects. Mayflies feed on plants as larvae.

Life spans range from 21 days for houseflies to one day for adult mayflies.

COMMON HORSEFLY
Tabanus bovinus

RANGE: Worldwide

SIZE: 0.3 to 1 in (0.8 to 2.5 cm)

DIET: Flower, nectar, pollen; blood of vertebrates

Male horseflies feed on nectar and pollen, but females require a blood meal for reproduction. They usually choose a mammal, like a horse or a cow, and in the process they can transmit disease.

MAYFLY
Potamanthus luteus

RANGE: Worldwide; many in North America

SIZE: .04 to 1.2 in (0.1 to 3 cm)

DIET: Plant material, algae, debris

Young mayflies are aquatic insects for a long period of time: months to years. During this time, they feed on algae. Once they mature into adults, they mate almost immediately and die within a day.

HOUSEFLY
Musca domestica

RANGE: Worldwide

SIZE: .16 to .31 in (4 to 8 mm)

DIET: Decaying fruit and vegetables

Like all true flies, houseflies have a single pair of flight wings attached to their midsection, or thorax, and a tiny pair of nonfunctional wings, or halteres, behind those. True flies are in the order Diptera, which means "two wings" in Greek.

COMMON BLUE DAMSELFLY
Enallagma cyathigerum

RANGE: Worldwide

SIZE: 5 in (13.5 cm)

DIET: Mostly insects, but will eat anything they can digest

Damselflies are closely related to dragonflies. Both have compound eyes that give them a wide-angle view for hunting insects. Damselfly eyes are widely spaced; dragonfly eyes are so large they touch each other.

BLUE DASHER
Pachydiplax longipennis

RANGE: Most of the U.S., southern Canada, northern Mexico

SIZE: 1 to 1.7 in (2.5 to 4.3 cm)

DIET: Small flying insects

Dragonflies, like the blue dasher, catch their prey in midair. They are capable of flying up to 60 miles an hour (97 km/h) with their very distinctive, membrane-like wings. The second pair is wider than the first and both are held out to the sides.

BUTTERFLIES
AND MOTHS

Butterflies and moths are flying insects with colorful scales on their wings. Their patterned, and often brightly colored, wings are used for defense as well as breeding and territorial displays. Many have wings with spots that mimic eyespots to confuse predators. Others contain toxic chemicals from eating specific plants. Some look like toxic species, but are not. These are called mimics.

Butterflies and moths go through a similar life cycle known as metamorphosis: egg-larvae-pupa-adult. Larvae, or caterpillars, feed on leaves; adults feed on flower nectar or pollen and are important pollinators.

Butterflies and moths differ in a number of ways. Butterflies have thin antennae with clubs at the ends, are more likely to be active during the day, and rest with their wings closed. The pupa is a clear membrane and is called a chrysalis (KRIS-uh-lis). Moths have thicker, fuzzy antennae, are more active at night, and rest with their wings open. The pupa is either buried or wrapped in silk and is known as a cocoon.

Life spans for adult butterflies and moths range from a day to a year.

MONARCH BUTTERFLY
Danaus plexippus

RANGE: North and South America, Caribbean, Australia, New Zealand, western Europe, islands of the Pacific and Atlantic Oceans

SIZE: Wingspan: 3.4 to 4.9 in (8.6 to 12.4 cm)

DIET: Milkweed plant, nectar

The monarch's orange color warns predators of its nasty taste, caused by milkweed toxins. Monarchs migrate between Canada and Mexico, a journey that requires several generations.

SIX-SPOT BURNET MOTH
Zygaena filipendulae

RANGE: Europe

SIZE: 1.2 to 1.6 in (3 to 4 cm)

DIET: Adult: flower nectar; caterpillar: leaves of lotus plants and clover

The six-spot burnet moth belongs to a group of day-flying moths in which the adults as well as the caterpillars are toxic. The bright spots warn predators that the moth contains hydrogen cyanide, a very toxic chemical.

LUNA MOTH
Actias luna

RANGE: North America

SIZE: 1 in (2.5 cm); wingspan: 4 to 5 in (10 to 12.7 cm)

DIET: Caterpillar: foliage of hickory, walnut, sweetgum, other kinds of trees

Adult luna moths do not eat—they do not even have mouthparts. The adults live for only one week in order to breed. They reproduce once a year in cooler areas and up to three times a year in warmer areas.

SILKMOTH
Bombyx mori

RANGE: Asia; introduced worldwide

SIZE: 4 in (10 cm)

DIET: Mulberry tree leaves

The silkmoth was first bred in China for its silk 5,000 years ago. As its larva, called a silkworm, enters the pupa stage, it wraps itself in silk to form a cocoon. To make one pound (454 g) of silk requires 2,000 to 3,000 cocoons.

ZEBRA SWALLOWTAIL BUTTERFLY
Protographium marcellus

RANGE: Eastern United States and southeastern Canada

SIZE: 4 in (10 cm)

DIET: Pawpaw and dwarf pawpaw

Like many moth and butterfly species, the zebra swallowtail feeds on a specific group of plants. Caterpillars feed on the leaves of the pawpaw; adults feed on the tree's flower nectar. These butterflies are found only in areas where paw-paws grow.

GLASSWING BUTTERFLY
Greta oto

RANGE: Mexico to Panama

SIZE: Wingspan: 2.2 to 2.4 in (5.6 to 6 cm)

DIET: Flower nectar

Instead of using their wings to scare predators with bright colors, the glasswing butterfly uses its wings to hide. Their wings are clear, except for the borders and the veins that support them. These butterflies are also called little mirrors.

Did you know?
Blue morphos spend most of their 115-day lives as caterpillars.

BLUE MORPHO BUTTERFLY
Morpho peleides

RANGE: Tropical forests of Latin America, from Mexico to Colombia

SIZE: 8 in (20 cm)

DIET: Adult: rotting fruit, tree sap, fungi, wet mud; caterpillar: plants from the pea family

The males of the blue morpho butterfly are brightly colored; the females are brown and yellow. Males use their bright colors both for defense—to scare away birds—and to establish their territory during the breeding season.

POLYPHEMUS MOTH
Antheraea polyphemus

RANGE: North America

SIZE: 6 in (15 cm)

DIET: Adult: does not eat; caterpillar: leaves of broadleaf trees and shrubs such as sweetgum, birch, hickory, maple, rose

Male and female polyphemus moths look similar in many ways. Both have purple eyespots. But the male has thicker, fuzzier antennae, and the female has a larger body for carrying eggs. As in all moths, the cocoon is made of silk.

RED CRACKER BUTTERFLY
Hamadryas amphinome

RANGE: Tropical Americas from central Mexico and Cuba south to Argentina

SIZE: Wingspan: 3 in (7.6 cm)

DIET: Adult: rotting fruit and other nonfloral resources; caterpillar: leaves

Wing color is only one of the features used to identify butterflies. For example, red cracker butterflies are related to glasswing butterflies because both are four-footed. They have six legs like all insects, but the first pair is very short.

ORNATE MOTH
Utetheisa ornatrix

RANGE: Nova Scotia to Florida, U.S.A.; west to Minnesota, Kansas, and Texas, U.S.A.

SIZE: Wingspan: 1.2 to 1.6 in (3 to 4 cm)

DIET: Flowering plants

The larvae of ornate moths feed on plants like sweet clover that contain chemicals toxic to birds, bats, and spiders. By the time the adult emerges from the cocoon, it has high levels of these toxins in its saliva, which it spits for defense.

BEES AND WASPS

Bees and wasps are closely related to ants. All have long antennae with at least 10 segments. Females also lay eggs using a leglike structure called an ovipositor. In some species, the ovipositor is also a stinger used for paralyzing prey or for defense. All bees, wasps, and ants go through complete metamorphosis. Adult bees are usually found on flowers and feed their young either stored pollen or other insects.

Bees are pollen gatherers—and pollinators. There are more than 20,000 species. Most are solitary, meaning they live in small groups with a single breeding female and her offspring. Pollen is gathered to feed the young; sometimes it is mixed with nectar to make a paste.

Seven species of bees are called honeybees because they convert nectar to honey and store it in large amounts. European honeybees are able to do this because they are highly social, or eusocial, meaning they live in large groups called colonies that include a queen bee and thousands of offspring with specific duties. Honeybees also do a "waggle dance" to let other bees know which direction to go to search for nectar.

Most wasps are parasites of other insects. Some are eusocial like honeybees, but they hunt other insects. These include paper wasps, yellow jackets, and hornets.

Life spans range from two to five years.

ASIAN GIANT HORNET
Vespa mandarinia

RANGE: Eastern and southeastern Asia; most common in Japan

SIZE: Length up to 2.2 in (5.5 cm); wingspan up to 3 in (7.6 cm)

DIET: Insects including beetles, hornworms, and mantids

Also known as the Japanese giant hornet, this is the largest hornet species on Earth. In 2019, colonies of this species were discovered in the Pacific Northwest region of the United States and British Columbia, Canada, most likely brought to North America via shipping containers.

DISAPPEARING BEES

Beginning in 2006, beekeepers noticed that entire colonies of their bees (*Apis mellifera*, European honeybee) were mysteriously disappearing, abandoning their hives overnight. The phenomenon was so great they gave it a name: Colony Collapse Disorder. It's not just happening in managed honeybee colonies. Many species of wild bees are at risk, too. So what's going on? For starters, food is harder for bees to come by because people are cutting down the weed flowers on which bees feed. The use of chemicals called insecticides, intended to keep insects from destroying crops, are detrimental to honeybee populations as well. In addition, pollution, mites, and diseases can kill entire bee colonies.

This is a big problem because honeybees play an important role in our ecosystem. Wild bees pollinate at least 80 percent of all plants, including crops. They, along with managed bees, are needed to grow many of the foods we eat; without them we wouldn't have foods such as apples, carrots, cucumbers, and almonds.

ORCHID BEE
Eulaema bombiformis

RANGE: Brazil, Paraguay, Argentina

SIZE: .12 to 1.1 in (0.3 to 2.7 cm)

DIET: Pollen and nectar

Orchid bees are known for their long tongues, which measure up to 1.6 inches (4 cm). They pollinate hundreds of species of orchid flowers in tropical forests and use their tongues to access hard-to-reach flower nectar.

EUROPEAN HONEYBEE
Apis mellifera

RANGE: Europe, western Asia, Africa

SIZE: .39 to .79 in (1 to 2 cm)

DIET: Pollen and nectar

The European honeybee was first domesticated 6,000 years ago and is used worldwide for honey production and pollination. Workers are nonbreeding females that build the nest, gather pollen, and make honey. The males, or drones, fertilize females.

PAPER WASP
Polistes fuscatus

RANGE: Temperate areas of North America

SIZE: .59 to .83 in (1.5 to 2.1 cm)

DIET: Nectar, other insects

These wasps are named for the material they use to make their nests: a mix of plant fibers and their own saliva. In addition to nectar, this social species feeds on flies, caterpillars, and beetle larvae.

ANTS

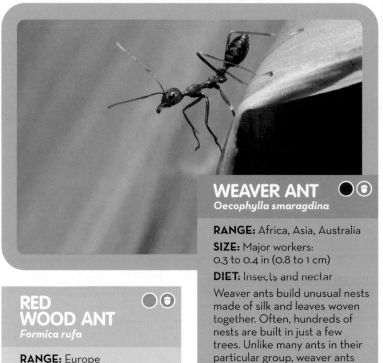

Ants look like a lot like wasps. All have stingers and many have wings during the breeding stage. But ants have bent, or elbowed, antennae and a waist, which makes their rear end look large. All ant species are either highly social—or eusocial—or they parasitize other eusocial ants.

Eusocial means that ants live in large colonies in which different types of ants have different jobs. For example, there are nonbreeding, wingless females called workers that dig tunnels and find food; soldier ants that protect the colony; and winged males and females, or queens, that breed. The males and queen ant look very different from the other ants in the colony, so the worker females are the ones used to identify the species.

Ants nest on the ground and in trees. Most are predators or scavengers that also eat nectar and fruit if available. Some, like leafcutter ants, eat fungi. Adults eat only liquid food because of their narrow necks. Larvae eat solid food and sometimes regurgitate—bring back up—liquid food for adults.

Life spans range from one to 20 years.

WEAVER ANT
Oecophylla smaragdina

RANGE: Africa, Asia, Australia
SIZE: Major workers: 0.3 to 0.4 in (0.8 to 1 cm)
DIET: Insects and nectar

Weaver ants build unusual nests made of silk and leaves woven together. Often, hundreds of nests are built in just a few trees. Unlike many ants in their particular group, weaver ants don't sting; they spray formic acid, an irritating chemical.

RED WOOD ANT
Formica rufa

RANGE: Europe
SIZE: 0.4 in (1 cm)
DIET: Insects

Red wood ants live in forests and feed on aphids and other insects, including other ants. They build large, dome-shaped nests, usually in clearings on the forest floor. Each colony may have hundreds of egg-producing females. They are threatened because of deforestation.

EASTERN CARPENTER ANT
Camponotus pennsylvanicus

RANGE: Worldwide
SIZE: Up to 0.7 in (1.8 cm)
DIET: Nectar, aphids, other soft-bodied insects

Carpenter ants nest in damp or dead wood, including wood in houses, and destroy it. Termites also destroy wood in homes, but they leave holes packed with mud. Carpenter ants leave sawdust.

LEAFCUTTER ANT
Atta sexdens

RANGE: Central and South America
SIZE: .12 to .94 in (0.3 to 2.4 cm)
DIET: Fungi

Worker leafcutter ants carry leaves from the forest back to their nest along an obvious trail. The leaves are food for fungi that they farm and eat. They build large underground nests with as many as 2,000 chambers growing the fungi.

INSIDE AN ANTHILL

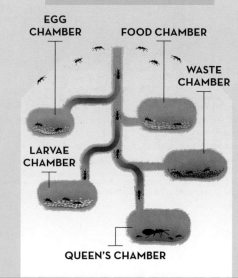

EGG CHAMBER

FOOD CHAMBER

WASTE CHAMBER

LARVAE CHAMBER

QUEEN'S CHAMBER

Worker ants haul bits of soil to the colony entrance and leave them there, eventually creating a mound, or anthill.

Marina Arbetman

PATAGONIAN BUMBLEBEE

I n 2006 I joined a wonderful group of people studying pollination in the Patagonian region of Argentina. As we trekked through the forest, it was hard to miss the native Patagonian bumblebees *(Bombus dahlbomii)*. They were everywhere, and they're HUGE! Sometimes called "flying mice," the big, fuzzy queens can grow up to 1.6 inches (4 cm) long. They are the biggest bumblebees in the world. They make a very loud buzzing noise as they fly from one flower to another. But they're not aggressive, and they won't sting you as long as you don't bother them.

Three years later I started working on a new project with the research team, and we returned to the forest where we had conducted our previous study. Although we knew the bees existed in other places, we didn't see a single Patagonian bumblebee in that forest. One possible reason we considered was climate change, which we knew to be affecting some species. But if climate change were the only reason, we would still expect to find the bees there because climate change takes time. We couldn't find them anywhere in that forest.

It appeared to us that Patagonian bumblebees had been replaced by another species, the buff-tailed bumblebee, which companies in Chile had been importing to pollinate farmers' crops. My colleagues and I wondered if the new bumblebees were carrying a parasite or some other infection and passing it on to the Patagonian bumblebees. After careful study, our hunch turned out to be right. We found the same parasite in both species.

Argentina's government has always banned the import of non-native bumblebees, but Chile has not. The bees fly right over country borders, so it's hard to stop them from spreading the parasites. We will continue with our studies, but this isn't just a scientific issue. It's an educational battle, as well. We will use what we learn to work for policy changes to stop all imports of non-native bees to the region. Hopefully, one day we can focus on helping the Patagonian bumblebee recover in the best environment possible.

NORTH
AMERICA

ATLANTIC
OCEAN

SOUTH
AMERICA

PACIFIC
OCEAN

Patagonia

RANGE OF THE
*BOMBUS
DAHLBOMII*
(PATAGONIAN
BUMBLEBEE)

0   1,000 miles

0   1,000 kilometers

ANTARCTICA

OBSERVATION TIPS

1 Go to southern South America. That's the only place this endangered species still exists.

2 Search for Magellan fuchsia or Peruvian lilies, some of the Patagonian bumblebee's favorite flowers.

3 Look, listen for a loud buzz, and be patient. Sightings of these bumblebees are now rare in most areas.

4 Don't touch! Patagonian bumblebees aren't aggressive, but they might sting you if they feel threatened.

Marina Arbetman teaches at the National University of Comahue and is a researcher at the Pollination Ecology Group of CONICET in Bariloche, Argentina. After seeing Patagonian bumblebees vanish from their native habitat in such a short period of time, she is focused on helping to restore their population in her country.

INVERTEBRATES

The Patagonian bumblebee is the only native bumblebee in the Patagonian region of Chile and Argentina. It has a large, fuzzy, ginger-colored body. Its abdomen, legs, and wings are black. Mostly found in temperate forests and mountain meadows, it builds a nest in the soil, under tree trunks, and around tree roots. It is an important pollinator that uses its long tongue to sip nectar from flowers of many different colors, shapes, and sizes. Once common across Argentina and Chile, its population has plummeted in the past 15 years. Scientists aren't sure how many of these endangered bumblebees remain.

RECORDS

D id you know that some invertebrates live more than 200 years, or that some are more toxic than any other animals in the world? Check out these record-holding rock stars of the invertebrate world to learn more.

BIGGEST →
Giant Squid
Architeuthis dux

Perhaps one of the most curious creatures of the deep, the giant squid is one interesting invertebrate. This supersize squid can grow to a massive 18 feet (5.5 m) long and weigh almost a ton (0.9 t)! Not only that, it boasts the largest eye of any animal on Earth—about 10 inches (25 cm) in diameter—roughly the size of a volleyball. Scientists don't know a lot about this mysterious monster, mostly because it lives at depths of 660 to 2,300 feet (200 to 700 m), but they do know that it can go into battle with a huge sperm whale and win.

BEST BITE →
Trap-Jaw Ant
Odontomachus bauri

The teeny-tiny trap-jaw ant might not be much to look at, but when it snaps its jaws shut—watch out. Those chompers are closing at speeds anywhere from 62 to 145 miles an hour (100 to 233 km/h)! Some scientists even estimate their jaws can snap shut about 2,300 times faster than humans can blink their eyes. Not only that, the force behind that bite is estimated to be 300 times the ant's body weight. That means that if it were the size of the average adult human, its bite would be strong enough to easily crush a refrigerator.

MOST INTELLIGENT →
Common Octopus
Octopus vulgaris

It's a close race to the head of the class, but for scientists, the selection of the smartest is kind of a toss-up between the octopus and squid, with the common octopus inching ahead just slightly. Part of an elite group of mollusks called cephalopods, octopuses and squids have big brains relative to their body sizes and can do things that scientists once thought only "intellectual" animals could do. The common octopus can complete simple mazes, solve problems, and even play—kind of like an eight-armed dog.

MOST TOXIC →
Box Jellyfish
Chironex fleckeri

If you've spent your life avoiding venomous spiders, beware! There are far more dangerous invertebrates out there. Fortunately, you're completely safe from them on land. Box jellyfish, which live off the coast of Australia, are believed to be the most toxic animals in the world. With 60 15-foot (4.6-m)-long tentacles, one jellyfish contains enough venom to kill 60 adult humans. Despite that, one animal will stare a box jellyfish in the tentacles and live to tell the tale: Sea turtles are completely immune to the venom. In fact, they eat these jellies as a snack!

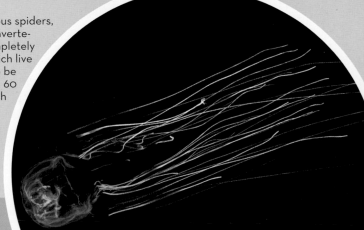

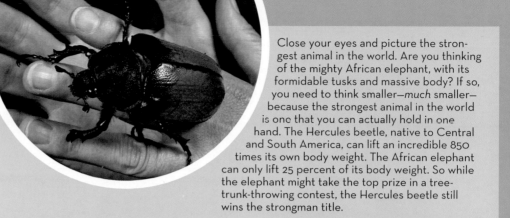

STRONGEST →
Hercules Beetle
Dynastes hercules

Close your eyes and picture the strongest animal in the world. Are you thinking of the mighty African elephant, with its formidable tusks and massive body? If so, you need to think smaller—*much* smaller—because the strongest animal in the world is one that you can actually hold in one hand. The Hercules beetle, native to Central and South America, can lift an incredible 850 times its own body weight. The African elephant can only lift 25 percent of its body weight. So while the elephant might take the top prize in a tree-trunk-throwing contest, the Hercules beetle still wins the strongman title.

FASTEST GROWING →
Giant Tubeworms
Riftia pachyptila

Deep in the darkest depths of the ocean lives the fastest-growing animal on Earth—the giant tubeworm! These cool creatures grow near hydrothermal vents one to three miles (1.6 to 4.8 km) under the ocean surface. Not only can they survive the crushing pressure and boiling temperatures, they thrive, growing up to 33 inches (84 cm) per year. Amazingly, giant tubeworms can reach a maximum of six feet (1.8 m) long, even though they have no mouth or digestive system!

BEST REGENERATION →
Planaria torva

It's no problem if this invertebrate loses its head—it will just grow another one! *Planaria torva* is an expert at growing body parts. If one of these flatworms is cut in two, both parts of the worm are able to grow whatever body part it needs and become a whole flatworm in just a couple of days. This is known as regeneration. Scientists are studying *Planaria* regeneration to learn if human cells could act in a similar way and repair or grow new tissue.

LEGGIEST →
Illacme plenipes

The *Illacme plenipes* might not have the longest legs in the animal kingdom but it certainly has the most. Millipedes, contrary to their name ("millipede" comes from the words for "thousand" and "legs" in Latin), do not have a thousand legs. But this one comes pretty close. Female *Illacme plenipes*, which are native to California, U.S.A., have an estimated 750 legs—at least 50 more than other millipede species—and males have about half that number. Which do you think would win in a race?

INVERTEBRATES

Want to know where these record-holding invertebrates live around the world? Take a look at this range map to find out.

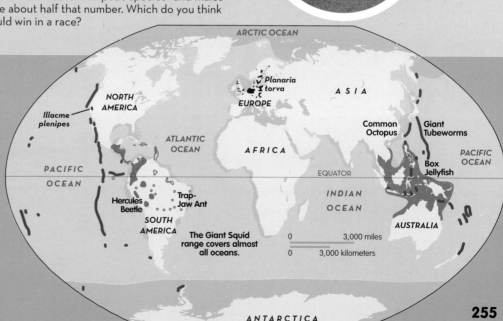

RANGES OF RECORD-SETTING INVERTEBRATES
- Giant Squid
- Trap-Jaw Ant
- Common Octopus
- Box Jellyfish
- Hercules Beetle
- Giant Tubeworms
- *Planaria torva*
- *Illacme plenipes*

The Giant Squid range covers almost all oceans.

With more than 1,000 additional animals in one easy-to-read list, this section introduces even more amazing creatures. Dig in and discover fast facts about everything from what a green sea turtle eats to where a bamboo rat lives, and so much more.

Habitat key:

- SHRUBLAND/BUSH
- GRASSLAND
- SAVANNA
- DESERT/DRY/DRY AND ROCKY
- TROPICAL FOREST/SUBTROPICAL/RAINFOREST
- TEMPERATE FOREST/WOODLAND
- CONIFEROUS FOREST/WOODLAND
- MOUNTAINS/HIGHLANDS/SLOPES/TEMPERATE AND TROPICAL
- POLAR REGIONS/ARCTIC/TUNDRA AND ANTARCTIC
- FRESHWATER/FLOWING/RIVERS/STREAMS
- FRESHWATER/STILL/WETLANDS/BOGS/SWAMPS/PONDS/LAKES
- OCEANS AND OPEN SEA
- COASTAL/INSHORE AREAS (INCLUDES MANGROVE SWAMPS)
- CORAL REEFS/SEAGRASS
- CAVES AND CAVERNS
- URBAN AREAS/CITIES/INDOOR PARKS/GARDENS
- FARMLAND/RURAL AREAS/ABANDONED STRUCTURES

MAMMALS

Status key:
- ALERT
- IN TROUBLE
- STABLE
- UNDER STUDY
- NOT LISTED
- DOMESTICATED

COMMON NAME	SCIENTIFIC NAME	SIZE	RANGE	HABITAT	DIET
MONOTREMES AND MARSUPIALS					
Western long-beaked echidna	*Zaglossus bruijni*	11 to 36.3 lb (5 to 16.5 kg)	New Guinea		insects
Tiger or spotted-tail quoll	*Dasyurus maculatus*	4 to 15.4 lb (1.8 to 7 kg)	Australia		mostly small and medium-size mammals, birds, invertebrates, reptiles
Numbat	*Myrmecobius fasciatus*	10.6 to 26.5 oz (300 to 752 g)	southern Australia		termites, ants, other invertebrates
Red kangaroo	*Macropus rufus*	up to 198 lb (90 kg)	Australia		plant-eaters: grasses and dicotyledonous flowering plants
Tammar wallaby	*Macropus eugenii*	8.8 to 20 lb (4 to 9.1 kg)	Australia and New Zealand		herbivorous: grasses
Parma wallaby	*Macropus parma*	7 to 13 lb (3.2 to 5.9 kg)	Australia and New Zealand		herbivorous: reedy grasses and herbaceous plant parts
Goodfellow's tree kangaroo	*Dendrolagus goodfellowi*	16.3 lb (7.4 kg)	Indonesia and Papua New Guinea		fruit, flowers, grasses
Long-nosed potoroo	*Potorous tridactylus*	1.5 to 4 lb (0.7 to 1.8 kg)	Australia		plants, roots, fungi, insects
Sugar glider	*Petaurus breviceps*	3.9 oz (110 g)	Australia, Indonesia, Papua New Guinea		omnivorous: pollen, nectar, insects (and their larvae), arachnids, small vertebrates
Leadbeater's possum	*Gymnobelideus leadbeateri*	3.5 to 6 oz (100 to 170 g)	Australia		small invertebrates and tree juices
Ringtail possum	*Pseudocheirus peregrinus*	1.1 to 2.2 lb (0.5 to 1 kg)	Australia		folivorous: mainly eucalyptus leaves; also flowers, buds, nectar, fruit
Gray cuscus	*Phalanger orientalis*	2.2 to 11 lb (1 to 5 kg)	Indonesia and southwest Pacific islands		leaves, fruit, other plant material
Common or coarse-haired wombat	*Vombatus ursinus*	44 to 77 lb (20 to 35 kg)	Australia		herbivorous: native grasses, roots of shrubs and trees, sedges, mat rushes, fungi
Eastern barred bandicoot	*Perameles gunnii*	23 oz (640 g)	Australia and Tasmania		mainly invertebrates such as earthworms, grubs, beetles; small vertebrates; some plants
RODENTS					
Greater cane rat	*Thryonomys swinderianus*	6.6 to 19.8 lb (3 to 9 kg)	Africa		mainly grasses and cane
Small five-toed jerboa	*Allactaga elater*	2.1 oz (58.7 g)	Asia Minor		seeds, insects, succulent parts of plants
Common or black-bellied hamster	*Cricetus cricetus*	12.7 to 15.9 oz (359 to 451 g)	Eurasia from Belgium to Siberia		seeds, grains, roots, potatoes, green plants, insect larvae
Bank vole	*Myodes glareolus*	0.6 to 0.7 oz (17 to 20 g)	Europe through Central Asia		leaves; seeds, grains, nuts; fruit
Brown lemming	*Lemmus sibiricus*	1.6 to 4.6 oz (45 to 130 g)	Siberia and North America		live plant parts
Tree shrew	*Tupaia glis*	5 oz (142 g)	Southeast Asia		insects, spiders, seeds, buds
Woodland jumping mouse	*Napaeozapus insignis*	0.6 to 1.2 oz (17 to 35 g)	northeastern North America		arthropods; worms; leaves, roots, tubers; seeds, grains, nuts; fruit; bryophytes
Armored rat	*Hoplomys gymnurus*	7.7 to 28.8 oz (220 to 820 g)	Central and South America		seeds, grains, nuts; fruit, insects
Bamboo rat	*Rhizomys sumatrensis*	1.1 to 8.8 lb (0.5 to 4 kg)	southern China, Nepal, eastern India		bamboo, plants, seeds, fruit

COMMON NAME	SCIENTIFIC NAME	SIZE	RANGE	HABITAT	DIET
Eurasian beaver	Castor fiber	28.6 to 77.1 lb (13 to 35 kg)	Europe and Asia		bark, leaves, plants
Lowland paca	Cuniculus paca	15 to 26 lb (7 to 12 kg)	east-central Mexico south to Paraguay		fruit, leaves, buds, flowers
Red-rumped agouti	Dasyprocta leporina	6.6 to 13 lb (3 to 5.9 kg)	South America		seeds and fruit
Desmarest's hutia	Capromys pilorides	2.2 to 19.8 lb (1 to 9 kg)	Cuba		leaves, fruit, bark; some vertebrates including lizards
Patagonian mara	Dolichotis patagonum	17.9 lb (8.1 kg)	Argentina		plant material: grasses and low shrubs
North African crested porcupine	Hystrix cristata	22 to 66.1 lb (10 to 30 kg)	Italy; sub-Saharan and Mediterranean coast of Africa		herbivorous: bark, roots, tubers, rhizomes, bulbs, fallen fruit, cultivated crops
North American porcupine	Erethizon dorsatum	11 to 30.8 lb (5 to 14 kg)	North America		buds, twigs, bark; roots and stems of flowering plants
Rock cavy	Kerodon rupestris	2 to 2.2 lb (0.9 to 1 kg)	northeastern Brazil		leaves, buds, flowers, bark
Damara mole rat	Cryptomys damarensis	3 to 7 oz (86 to 202 g)	southwestern and central Africa		herbivorous: mostly roots, bulbs, tubers, aloe leaves; also some invertebrates
Guinea pig	Cavia porcellus	1.5 to 2.4 lb (0.7 to 1.1 kg)	no longer exist in the wild		hay, grasses, leafy greens
Plains viscacha	Lagostomus maximus	4.4 to 17.6 lb (2 to 8 kg)	Paraguay, Argentina, Bolivia		any kind of vegetation; seeds, grasses
Northern viscacha	Lagidium peruanum	2 to 3.5 lb (0.9 to 1.6 kg)	Andes		tough grasses, lichens, mosses
Degu	Octodon degus	6 to 10.6 oz (170 to 300 g)	west-central Chile		plants, bulbs, tubers
Coypu	Myocastor coypus	11 to 22 lb (5 to 10 kg)	South America		aquatic vegetation; stems, leaves, roots, bark
Douglas's squirrel	Tamiasciurus douglasii	5 to 11 oz (141 to 312 g)	Pacific coast of North America		pine seeds; also twigs, sap, leaves, buds, acorns and other nuts, mushrooms, fruit, berries
White-tailed antelope squirrel	Ammospermophilus leucurus	3.4 to 4.1 oz (96 to 117 g)	western United States		leaves; seeds, grains, nuts; fruit; insects
Red squirrel	Tamiasciurus hudsonicus	7 to 10 oz (197 to 282 g)	North America		primarily seeds of conifer trees
Golden-mantled ground squirrel	Spermophilus lateralis	4.2 to 13.9 oz (120 to 394 g)	Canada and United States		fungi, nuts, acorns, seeds, forbs, flowers, bulbs, fruit, shrubs, leafy greens
Siberian flying squirrel	Pteromys volans	4.6 oz (130 g)	Scandinavia, Russia, Asia, China		green plants, young branches, berries, seeds, nuts, catkins, pinecones, pine needles
Hoary marmot	Marmota caligata	17.6 to 22 lb (8 to 10 kg)	North America		mostly herbivorous: sedges, fescues, mosses, lichens, willows; also flowers
Olympic marmot	Marmota olympus	6.8 to 24.2 lb (3.1 to 11 kg)	Olympic National Park in Washington State (U.S.A.)		meadow flora, including avalanche lilies, sub-alpine lupine, mountain buckwheat; grasses
Himalayan marmot	Marmota himalayana	8.8 to 20.3 lb (4 to 9.2 kg)	Asia, Europe, North America		herbivorous: flowering plants
Eastern chipmunk	Tamias striatus	2.3 to 4 oz (66 to 115 g)	eastern North America		nuts, acorns, seeds, mushrooms, fruit, corn; insects, bird eggs, mice, other small vertebrates
Chinchilla	Chinchilla lanigera	1.1 to 1.8 lb (500 to 800 g)	mountains of northern Chile		mainly grass and seeds
BATS					
Egyptian fruit bat	Rousettus aegyptiacus	2.8 to 6 oz (80 to 170 g)	Africa and Middle East		pulp and juice of very ripe fruit; also fruit from trees, such as lilac, fig, baobab, mulberry
Pacific flying fox	Pteropus tonganus	0.4 to 2.4 lb (0.2 to 1.1 kg)	American Samoa, Fiji, other Pacific islands		fruit, flowers, nectar, pollen
Long-nosed nectar bat	Leptonycteris yerbabuenae	0.8 oz (23 g)	Central and North America		nectar and pollen from night-blooming flowers; cactus fruit
Greater bulldog bat	Noctilio leporinus	2.1 to 2.8 oz (60 to 78 g)	South and Central America		fish, crustaceans, stinkbugs, crickets, scarab beetles, moths, winged ants, other insects
Spectral bat	Vampyrum spectrum	6 to 6.3 oz (170 to 180 g)	South and Central America		birds, rodents, bats
Big brown bat	Eptesicus fuscus	0.8 oz (23 g)	North, Central, and South America		insects, especially beetles
Hoary bat	Lasiurus cinereus	0.7 to 1.2 oz (20 to 35 g)	North, Central, and South America		moths, flies, beetles, small wasps and their relatives, grasshoppers, termites, dragonflies
Red bat	Lasiurus borealis	.25 to 0.5 oz (7 to 13 g)	eastern United States		insects
RABBITS AND RELATIVES					
European hare	Lepus europaeus	6.6 to 11 lb (3 to 5 kg)	Europe to Central Asia		leaves, buds, roots, fruit, berries, fungi, twigs, bark
European rabbit	Oryctolagus cuniculus	3.3 to 5.5 lb (1.5 to 2.5 kg)	every continent except Asia and Antarctica		grasses, leaves, buds, tree bark, roots
Marsh rabbit	Sylvilagus palustris	2.6 to 4.9 lb (1.2 to 2.2 kg)	southeastern United States		herbivorous: blackberries, rhizomes, bulbs, cattails, water hyacinths, other marsh plants
Antelope jackrabbit	Lepus alleni	6 to 10.4 lb (2.7 to 4.7 kg)	western coast of Mexico; southern Arizona (U.S.A.)		leaves, grasses, plants
Large-eared pika	Ochotona macrotis	4.2 oz (120 g)	Central Asia		grasses, sedges, twigs, flowers
SHREWS AND SMALL INSECTIVORES					
Large-eared tenrec	Geogale aurita	.18 to 0.3 oz (5 to 8.5 g)	Madagascar		insects, especially termites
Short-eared elephant shrew	Macroscelides proboscideus	1.4 to 1.8 oz (40 to 50 g)	Botswana, Namibia, South Africa		insects, especially termites and ants; other small invertebrates

MAMMALS

COMMON NAME	SCIENTIFIC NAME	SIZE	RANGE	HABITAT	DIET
Southern African hedgehog	*Atelerix frontalis*	5 to 20 oz (150 to 555 g)	southern Africa and Angola		mainly insects; also carrion, fungi, frogs, lizards, bird eggs and chicks, small mice
Western European hedgehog	*Erinaceus europaeus*	28 to 42 oz (0.8 to 1.2 kg)	Europe and Central Asia		worms, slugs, caterpillars, other invertebrates; frogs; berries; bird eggs and chicks
Rock hyrax	*Procavia capensis*	up to 9.5 lb (4.3 kg)	Africa and Arabian Peninsula		leaves, grasses, small plants, berries, fruit

ANTEATERS, ARMADILLOS, AND SLOTHS

COMMON NAME	SCIENTIFIC NAME	SIZE	RANGE	HABITAT	DIET
Southern three-banded armadillo	*Tolypeutes matacus*	3.1 to 3.5 lb (1.4 to 1.6 kg)	South America		ants and termites
Nine-banded armadillo	*Dasypus novemcinctus*	8 to 17 lb (3.6 to 7.7 kg)	North, Central, and South America		insects, spiders, small reptiles, amphibians, eggs
Giant armadillo	*Priodontes maximus*	41 to 71 lb (18.7 to 32 kg)	northern South America		termites, ants, some other small animals
Aardvark	*Orycteropus afer*	88.1 to 181 lb (40 to 82 kg)	Africa		insects, especially ants and termites

DOGS, WOLVES, AND RELATIVES

COMMON NAME	SCIENTIFIC NAME	SIZE	RANGE	HABITAT	DIET
African wild dog	*Lycaon pictus*	40 to 80 lb (18 to 36 kg)	Africa		small antelope such as impala and bush duiker; old, sick, or injured larger animals
Dingo dog	*Canis familiaris*	21 to 43 lb (9.5 to 19.5 kg)	western and central Australia		sheep, rabbits, rats, wallabies, birds, reptiles, human garbage
Maned wolf	*Chrysocyon brachyurus*	44 to 50.7 lb (20 to 23 kg)	Brazil		large rodents, including pacas and agoutis; birds, reptiles, frogs, insects, snails
Red wolf	*Canis rufus*	44 to 88 lb (20 to 40 kg)	southeastern United States		rodents, ungulates; other small mammals, including raccoons, white-tailed deer, muskrats
Crab-eating fox	*Cerdocyon thous*	11 to 17.6 lb (5 to 8 kg)	South America		small rodents (mice and rats), lizards, frogs, crabs, insects, fruit
Bat-eared fox	*Otocyon megalotis*	6.6 to 11.7 lb (3 to 5.3 kg)	Africa		insects, other arthropods; also small rodents, lizards, bird eggs and chicks; plants
Gray fox	*Urocyon cinereoargenteus*	4.4 to 19.8 lb (2 to 9 kg)	North, Central, and South America		omnivorous: small vertebrates, fruit, invertebrates
Arctic fox	*Vulpes lagopus*	11.5 lb (5.2 kg)	Eurasia, North America, Greenland, Iceland		ground-dwelling birds; lemmings and other small mammals; insects, berries, carrion
Kit fox	*Vulpes macrotis*	3.5 to 6 lb (1.6 to 2.7 kg)	southwestern United States; Mexico		primarily rodents and rabbits, including prairie dogs and kangaroo rats
Red fox	*Vulpes vulpes*	6.6 to 30.8 lb (3 to 14 kg)	Northern Hemisphere		rodents, rabbits, hares, birds, insects, invertebrates; fruit; berries

SKUNKS AND STINK BADGERS

COMMON NAME	SCIENTIFIC NAME	SIZE	RANGE	HABITAT	DIET
Western hog-nosed skunk	*Conepatus leuconotus*	4.4 to 9.9 lb (2 to 4.5 kg)	southern United States; Mexico		insects, grubs, snakes, small mammals, fruit
Pygmy spotted skunk	*Spilogale pygmaea*	5 to 11 oz (150 to 320 g)	Pacific coast of Mexico		insects, fruit, berries, small mammals, birds, reptiles
Sunda stink badger	*Mydaus javanensis*	3.1 to 7.9 lb (1.4 to 3.6 kg)	Sumatra, Java, Borneo		insects, worms, grubs, plants

OTTERS, WEASELS, AND RELATIVES

COMMON NAME	SCIENTIFIC NAME	SIZE	RANGE	HABITAT	DIET
Chinese ferret-badger	*Melogale moschata*	2.2 to 6.6 lb (1 to 3 kg)	China, Taiwan, Southeast Asia		small rodents, amphibians, insects, and other invertebrates; sometimes fruit
Hog badger	*Arctonyx collaris*	15.4 to 30.8 lb (7 to 14 kg)	Southeast Asia		worms, invertebrates, fruit, roots
Eurasian badger	*Meles meles*	14.5 to 36.8 lb (6.6 to 16.7 kg)	Ireland, Spain, Russia, China, Japan		earthworms, small animals, bulbs, fruit, nuts
North American river otter	*Lontra canadensis*	11 to 30.8 lb (5 to 14 kg)	Canada and United States		amphibians; fish; turtles; crayfish, crabs, and other invertebrates
Southern river otter	*Lontra provocax*	3.3 to 3.8 ft (1 to 1.2 m)	Chile and parts of Argentina		fish, crustaceans, mollusks, birds
Sea otter	*Enhydra lutris*	30.8 to 99.1 lb (14 to 45 kg)	East Asia to North America		clams, mussels, snails, abalone, and other mollusks; sea urchins
European otter	*Lutra lutra*	14.9 lb (6.7 kg)	Eurasia south of the tundra line and North Africa		fish; crustaceans; clams; small mammals, amphibians, birds; eggs; insects; worms
Spotted-necked otter	*Hydrictis maculicollis*	8.8 lb (4 kg)	central Africa		mainly fish; also frogs, crabs, mollusks, aquatic insects, larvae
Hairy-nosed otter	*Lutra sumatrana*	11 to 13 lb (5 to 8 kg)	Southeast Asia		fish and crustaceans
Marine otter	*Lontra felina*	6.6 to 11 lb (3 to 5 kg)	Pacific coast of South America		crustaceans, mollusks, other invertebrates; fish; also birds, small mammals
African clawless otter	*Aonyx capensis*	23.4 to 46.3 lb (11 to 21 kg)	Africa		crabs, mollusks, fish, reptiles, frogs, birds, small mammals
Tayra	*Eira barbara*	6.6 to 13.2 lb (3 to 6 kg)	Central and South America		omnivorous; small mammals, especially the spiny rat
Greater grison	*Galictis vittata*	3 to 8.4 lb (1.4 to 4 kg)	Central and South America		small mammals, such as chinchillas, viscachas, agoutis, mice; frogs; worms
Striped polecat or zorilla	*Ictonyx striatus*	2.2 to 3 lb (1 to 1.4 kg)	Africa		carnivorous: small rodents, frogs, lizards, snakes, birds, bird eggs, beetles
American marten	*Martes americana*	0.6 to 2.9 lb (0.3 to 1.3 kg)	North America		squirrels; small animals and insects; fruit; nuts
Black-footed ferret	*Mustela nigripes*	1.4 to 2.5 lb (0.6 to 1.1 kg)	North America		mainly prairie dogs; sometimes mice, ground squirrels, other small animals
American mink	*Neovison vison*	1.5 to 3.5 lb (0.7 to 1.6 kg)	United States		crayfish; small frogs; rabbits, mice, other small mammals; fish; ducks, other waterfowl
Long-tailed weasel	*Mustela frenata*	2.8 to 15.9 oz (80 to 450 g)	North America		small rodents

CIVETS, FOSSAS, AND RELATIVES

COMMON NAME	SCIENTIFIC NAME	SIZE	RANGE	HABITAT	DIET
African palm civet	*Nandinia binotata*	3.3 to 11 lb (1.5 to 5 kg)	sub-Saharan Africa		rodents, insects, birds, fruit bats, eggs, carrion, pineapples, fallen fruit

COMMON NAME	SCIENTIFIC NAME	SIZE	RANGE	HABITAT	DIET
Large spotted genet	*Genetta tigrina*	1.9 to 7 lb (.84 to 3.2 kg)	southern Africa		seeds, fruit, insects, rodents, snakes, skinks, geckos
Yellow mongoose	*Cynictis penicillata*	17.6 to 28.8 oz (500 to 800 g)	southern Africa		insects, grasses, seeds, birds, reptiles, amphibians

MONGOOSES

COMMON NAME	SCIENTIFIC NAME	SIZE	RANGE	HABITAT	DIET
Indian gray mongoose	*Herpestes edwardsi*	1.1 to 8.8 lb (0.5 to 4 kg)	Arabia, Nepal, India, Pakistan, Sri Lanka		mice, rats, lizards, snakes, beetles

RACCOONS, RED PANDAS, AND RELATIVES

COMMON NAME	SCIENTIFIC NAME	SIZE	RANGE	HABITAT	DIET
White-nosed coatimundi	*Nasua narica*	6.6 to 11 lb (3 to 5 kg)	Arizona (U.S.A.), Cent. Am., Colombia, Ecuador		omnivorous: prefers all types of insects; will eat fruit and small mammals
Cacomistle	*Bassariscus sumichrasti*	31.7 oz (900 g)	Central America		omnivorous; fruit, eggs, lizards, insects, tree frogs, birds, mice
Northern raccoon	*Procyon lotor*	4 to 23 lb (2 to 10 kg)	North America and northern South America		aquatic animals, small land animals, birds, nuts, seeds, turtle eggs, fruit, corn
Olingo	*Bassaricyon gabbii*	2.1 to 3.3 lb (1 to 1.5 kg)	Nicaragua to Bolivia		small vertebrates, insects, nectar, flowers, fruit

HYENAS AND AARDWOLVES

COMMON NAME	SCIENTIFIC NAME	SIZE	RANGE	HABITAT	DIET
Brown hyena	*Hyaena brunnea*	75 to 160 lb (34 to 73 kg)	Angola and southern Africa		carrion, insects, rodents, fungi, fruit

BEARS

COMMON NAME	SCIENTIFIC NAME	SIZE	RANGE	HABITAT	DIET
Spectacled bear	*Tremarctos ornatus*	132 to 441 lb (60 to 200 kg)	South America		mainly leaves, fruit, and roots; berries, cacti, shrubs, honey, sugarcane
American black bear	*Ursus americanus*	85.9 to 901 lb (39 to 409 kg)	North America		fruit, berries, nuts, roots, honey, insects, small mammals, fish, carrion

LARGE CATS

COMMON NAME	SCIENTIFIC NAME	SIZE	RANGE	HABITAT	DIET
Asiatic lion	*Panthera leo persica*	300 to 500 lb (135 to 230 kg)	Gir Forest in India		sambar and chital deer, wild boar, water buffalo, livestock
Sumatran tiger	*Panthera tigris sondaica*	295 to 340 lb (135 to 155 kg)	Indonesia		monkeys, porcupines, tapir, deer, wild pig, pheasants

SMALL AND MEDIUM CATS

COMMON NAME	SCIENTIFIC NAME	SIZE	RANGE	HABITAT	DIET
Asiatic golden cat	*Pardofelis temminckii*	26.5 to 33.1 lb (12 to 15 kg)	Asia		muntjac, small deer, birds, hares, snakes, squirrels and other rodents, reptiles, birds
Domestic cat	*Felis catus*	9 to 11.9 lb (4.1 to 5.4 kg)	every continent except Antarctica		most depend on human-supplied food; feral cats may hunt rodents, birds
Jungle cat	*Felis chaus*	8.8 to 35.3 lb (4 to 16 kg)	Middle East and Asia		rodents, frogs, birds, hares, fish, lizards, snakes, insects, livestock, fruit (in winter)
Wild cat	*Felis silvestris*	7.7 to 11 lb (3.5 to 5 kg)	Europe, Asia, Africa		small rodents and ground-dwelling birds
Geoffroy's cat	*Leopardus geoffroyi*	6.6 to 16 lb (3 to 7.4 kg)	southern half of South America		rodents, hares, lizards, insects, sometimes frogs and fish
Kodkod	*Leopardus guigna*	3.3 to 6.6 lb (1.5 to 3 kg)	Chile		primarily small rodents, reptiles, birds, large insects
African golden cat	*Caracal aurata*	7.7 to 39.7 lb (3.5 to 18 kg)	equatorial Africa		tree hyraxes, red duikers, small antelopes, monkeys, birds
Marbled cat	*Pardofelis marmorata*	5.3 to 11 lb (2.4 to 5 kg)	Himalaya, Myanmar, Southeast Asia		primarily birds and arboreal small mammals
Spanish lynx	*Lynx pardinus*	24.2 to 33 lb (11 to 15 kg)	western Europe		small mammals, primarily European rabbits
Leopard cat	*Prionailurus bengalensis*	6.6 to 15.4 lb (3 to 7 kg)	Asia		small mammals such as rodents and lizards; small birds
Cougar	*Puma concolor*	63.8 to 264 lb (29 to 120 kg)	North and South America		moose, elk, deer, caribou, squirrels, muskrats, rabbits; also birds
Jaguarundi	*Puma yagouaroundi*	9.9 to 19.8 lb (4.5 to 9 kg)	south Texas and Arizona (U.S.A.) to north Argentina		small mammals, reptiles, birds, frogs, fish
Caracal	*Caracal caracal*	17.6 to 41.8 lb (8 to 19 kg)	Africa, Central Asia, southwestern Asia		hyraxes, hares, rodents, antelopes, small monkeys; birds; reptiles

SEALS, SEA LIONS, AND FURRED SEALS

COMMON NAME	SCIENTIFIC NAME	SIZE	RANGE	HABITAT	DIET
New Zealand fur seal	*Arctocephalus forsteri*	66 to 550 lb (30 to 250 kg)	New Zealand and Australia		aquatic species, including arrow squid, octopus, barracuda, jade mackerel
New Zealand sea lion	*Phocarctos hookeri*	300 to 903 lb (136 to 410 kg)	New Zealand		small fish, crabs, octopus, mussels, penguins
South American sea lion	*Otaria flavescens*	308 to 771 lb (140 to 350 kg)	South American coastlines		fish, cephalopods, crustaceans, other invertebrates
Australian sea lion	*Neophoca cinerea*	231 to 661 lb (105 to 300 kg)	Australia		fish, including whiting, rays, small sharks; squid; cuttlefish; fairy penguins
Gray seal	*Halichoerus grypus*	330 to 485 lb (150 to 220 kg)	sub-Arctic waters of the North Atlantic Ocean		fish; some crustaceans and mollusks
Hooded seal	*Cystophora cristata*	352 to 661 lb (160 to 300 kg)	eastern coast of North America north of Maine		fish, such as redfish, herring, polar cod, flounder; also octopus and shrimp
Weddell seal	*Leptonychotes weddellii*	881 to 1,322 lb (400 to 600 kg)	Antarctica		notothenioid (Antarctic) fish, squid, crustaceans
Harbor seal	*Phoca vitulina*	176 to 375 lb (80 to 170 kg)	North Atlantic and North Pacific Oceans		crustaceans, mollusks, squid, fish
Harp seal	*Pagophilus groenlandicus*	264 to 297 lb (120 to 135 kg)	Arctic and North Atlantic Oceans		fish and crustaceans

SEA COWS

COMMON NAME	SCIENTIFIC NAME	SIZE	RANGE	HABITAT	DIET
Amazonian manatee	*Trichechus inunguis*	1,060 lb (480 kg)	Amazon Basin in South America		aquatic grasses and flowers; water lettuce
African manatee	*Trichechus senegalensis*	790 lb (360 kg)	west coast of Africa		aquatic vegetation

MAMMALS

COMMON NAME	SCIENTIFIC NAME	SIZE	RANGE	HABITAT	DIET
COWS, SHEEP, AND GOATS					
Gaur	*Bos gaurus*	1,432 to 2,203 lb (650 to 1,000 kg)	Nepal, India to Indochina, Malay Peninsula		green grasses; also coarse, dry grasses; forbs, leaves
Water buffalo	*Bubalus arnee*	551 to 2,643 lb (250 to 1,200 kg)	Bhutan, Cambodia, India, Myanmar, Nepal, and Thailand		grasses; also herbs, aquatic plants, leaves, crops, vegetation along rivers and streams
African or cape buffalo	*Syncerus caffer*	660 to 1,980 lb (300 to 900 kg)	middle of the African continent		herbivorous: grasses
European bison or wisent	*Bison bonasus*	660 to 2,200 lb (300 to 1,000 kg)	mainland Europe		primarily grazers; also browsers, eating leaves, ferns, twigs, bark, acorns
ANTELOPES AND PRONGHORNS					
Greater kudu	*Tragelaphus strepsiceros*	264 to 693 lb (120 to 315 kg)	Africa		herbivorous: leaves, herbs, fruit, vines, flowers, some new grasses
Impala	*Aepyceros melampus*	99 to 132 lb (45 to 60 kg)	Africa		grasses, leaves, flowers, fruit
Topi	*Damaliscus lunatus*	198 to 323 lb (90 to 147 kg)	Africa		almost entirely grasses
Springbok	*Antidorcas marsupialis*	72.6 to 101 lb (33 to 46 kg)	South Africa		leaves of shrubs and bushes; grasses
Blackbuck	*Antilope cervicapra*	70.4 to 94.6 lb (32 to 43 kg)	India and Nepal; introduced to U.S. and Argentina		primarily grasses; also leaf litter, flowers, fruits
Dorcas gazelle	*Gazella dorcas*	30.8 to 39.6 lb (14 to 18 kg)	northern Africa		flowers, leaves, pods of acacia trees; also fruit and leaves
Salt's dik-dik	*Madoqua saltiana*	4.4 to 13.2 lb (2 to 6 kg)	Africa		leaves of scrub and bushes; buds; plants; flowers; fruit; herbs
Sable antelope	*Hippotragus niger*	484 to 524 lb (220 to 238 kg)	Africa		foliage and herbs; grasses
Arabian oryx	*Oryx leucoryx*	220 to 462 lb (100 to 210 kg)	Middle East		grasses and shrubs
Nilgai	*Boselaphus tragocamelus*	264 to 528 lb (120 to 240 kg)	India		browsers: grasses; also fruit and sugarcane
Steenbok	*Raphicerus campestris*	15.4 to 35.2 lb (7 to 16 kg)	Africa		grasses, roots, tubers of some plants; shoots of bushland trees and shrubs
Saiga	*Saiga tatarica*	66 to 99 lb (30 to 45 kg)	Asia		grasses, low-growing shrubs
Sitatunga	*Tragelaphus spekii*	110 to 275 lb (50 to 125 kg)	Africa		grazers and browsers: especially foliage of *Alchornea cordifolia*
Bongo	*Tragelaphus eurycerus*	463 to 892 lb (210 to 405 kg)	Africa		grazers and browsers: leaves, flowers, twigs, thistles, garden produce, cereals
Defassa waterbuck	*Kobus ellipsiprymnus*	352 to 660 lb (160 to 300 kg)	Africa		variety of grasses, long and short
Yellow-backed duiker	*Cephalophus silvicultor*	99.1 to 176 lb (45 to 80 kg)	Africa		fruit, leaves, seeds, buds, bark, shoots
DEER AND ELK					
Marsh deer	*Blastocerus dichotomus*	196 to 275 lb (89 to 125 kg)	South America		herbivorous: mainly aquatic and riparian vegetation
Taruca	*Hippocamelus antisensis*	151 lb (68.6 kg)	Argentina, Chile, Peru		herbivorous: sedges and grasses
Mule deer	*Odocoileus hemionus*	94.6 to 330 lb (43 to 150 kg)	western North America		woody and herbaceous forage; acorns, legume seeds, fleshy fruits
Chital	*Axis axis*	60 to 100 lb (27 to 45 kg)	India		grasses; flowers; fruit; sedges
Tufted deer	*Elaphodus cephalophus*	37.4 to 110 lb (17 to 50 kg)	China and Myanmar		grasses, other plant material; leaves, twigs, fruit; sedges, forbs, woody growth
Indian muntjac	*Muntiacus muntjak*	30.8 to 77 lb (14 to 35 kg)	southern and southeastern Asia		omnivorous: herbs, fruit, bird eggs, small animals, sprouts, seeds, grasses
Sambar	*Rusa unicolor*	240 to 572 lb (109 to 260 kg)	southern Asia		leaves, berries, grasses, bark from young trees, fallen fruit, herbs, buds
Javan deer	*Rusa timorensis*	163 to 352 lb (74 to 160 kg)	southern Asia		primarily grasses and leaves
Chinese water deer	*Hydropotes inermis*	26.4 to 40.8 lb (12 to 18.5 kg)	China and Korea		reeds, coarse grasses, beets, other vegetation
Himalayan musk deer	*Moschus leucogaster*	24 to 40 lb (10 to 18 kg)	Himalaya		herbivorous: grasses, forbs, mosses, lichen, twigs, shoots, plant leaves
Water chevrotain	*Hyemoschus aquaticus*	15.4 to 33 lb (7 to 15 kg)	Africa		grasses, leaves, fruit; some insects, crabs, fish, worms, small mammals
Greater mouse-deer	*Tragulus napu*	11 to 17.6 lb (5 to 8 kg)	southern Asia		fallen fruit and berries, aquatic plants, leaves, buds, shrubs, grasses
GIRAFFES					
Giraffe	*Giraffa camelopardalis*	2,599 to 4,251 lb (1,180 to 1,930 kg)	sub-Saharan Africa		acacia tree foliage, buds, fruit; grasses; plants; grains; leaves; flowers; seed pods
HIPPOS AND PIGS					
Pygmy hippopotamus	*Hexaprotodon liberiensis*	352 to 605 lb (160 to 275 kg)	West Africa		leaves, swamp vegetation, fallen fruit, roots, tubers
Bushpig	*Potamochoerus larvatus*	119 to 253 lb (54 to 115 kg)	Africa		roots, rhizomes, bulbs, tubers, fruit, insect larvae; invertebrates, small vertebrates, carrion
Giant hog	*Hylochoerus meinertzhageni*	396 to 605 lb (180 to 275 kg)	Africa		grasses, plants, leaves, buds, roots, berries, fruit
Pygmy hog	*Sus salvanius*	17.6 lb (8 kg)	northwestern Assam, India		roots, tubers, other plant parts; insects, eggs, young birds, reptiles
Babirusa	*Babyrousa babyrussa*	94.6 to 220 lb (43 to 100 kg)	Indonesia		roots, berries, tubers, leaves, fallen fruit, fungi
Chacoan peccary	*Catagonus wagneri*	63.9 to 108 lb (29 to 49 kg)	Paraguay, Bolivia, southern Brazil		cacti, seeds of leguminous plants

COMMON NAME	SCIENTIFIC NAME	SIZE	RANGE	HABITAT	DIET
White-lipped peccary	*Tayassu pecari*	55.1 to 88.1 lb (25 to 40 kg)	southern Mexico; South America		fruit, leaves, roots, seeds, mushrooms, worms (Annelida), insects
CAMELS AND RELATIVES					
Guanaco	*Lama guanicoe*	286 to 341 lb (130 to 155 kg)	North America, Europe, Australia		low shrubs, lichens, mountain vegetation
Vicuña	*Vicugna vicugna*	121 to 143 lb (55 to 65 kg)	central and southern Andes		herbivorous: grasses, plants, woody shrubs
HORSES AND RELATIVES					
Przewalski's horse	*Equus ferus*	441 to 661 lb (200 to 300 kg)	original species: steppe zone of Europe and Asia		herbivorous: grasses, plants, fruit; sometimes bark, leaves, buds
Grevy's zebra	*Equus grevyi*	769 to 993 lb (349 to 451 kg)	northern Africa and southern Ethiopia		herbivorous grazers: tough grasses and forbs; leaves
Mountain zebra	*Equus zebra*	528 to 818 lb (240 to 372 kg)	southern and southwestern Africa		primarily grasses
Kulan	*Equus hemionus*	441 to 573 lb (200 to 260 kg)	southern Mongolia, Russia, China, Iran, India		herbivorous: perennial grasses, herbs, bark
TAPIRS					
Mountain or woolly tapir	*Tapirus pinchaque*	300 to 400 lb (136 to 182 kg)	northern Andes, Peru, Ecuador, Colombia		herbivorous: tough, fibrous leaves of shrubs; myrtle trees; pampas grass
BALEEN WHALES					
Bowhead whale	*Balaena mysticetus*	165,000 to 220,000 lb (75,000 to 100,000 kg)	Northern Hemisphere		planktonic crustaceans; epibenthic organisms; some benthic organisms
Blue whale	*Balaenoptera musculus*	418,502 lb (190,000 kg)	all oceans		mostly krill; other planktonic crustaceans
North Atlantic right whale	*Eubalaena glacialis*	121,145 to 209,251 lb (55,000 to 95,000 kg)	North Atlantic and North Pacific Oceans		aquatic crustaceans and zooplankton
Humpback whale	*Megaptera novaeangliae*	66,000 lb (30,000 kg)	Arctic, Atlantic, Indian, and Pacific Oceans		planktonic crustaceans and fish
Pygmy right whale	*Caperea marginata*	9,912 lb (4,500 kg)	Atlantic, Indian, and Pacific Oceans		krill
DOLPHINS, PORPOISES, AND OTHER TOOTHED WHALES					
Long-finned pilot whale	*Globicephala melas*	3,968 to 8,378 lb (1,800 to 3,800 kg)	all oceans except polar; Med. and Black Seas		squid; fish such as cod and turbot
Beluga whale	*Delphinapterus leucas*	2,976 to 3,307 lb (1,350 to 1,500 kg)	Arctic, Atlantic, and Pacific Oceans		smelt, flounder, sculpins, salmon, cod; invertebrates such as crab, octopus, squid
Narwhal	*Monodon monoceros*	1,982 to 3,524 lb (900 to 1,600 kg)	Arctic and Atlantic Oceans		squid, crabs, shrimp, fish
Sperm whale	*Physeter macrocephalus*	77,093 to 110,132 lb (35,000 to 50,000 kg)	all oceans except polar; Med. and Black Seas		large, deep-water squid; some fish, lobsters, other marine life
Cuvier's beaked whale	*Ziphius cavirostris*	6,608 lb (3,000 kg)	all oceans except polar; Med. and Black Seas		squid and deep-water fish
False killer whale	*Pseudorca crassidens*	2,018 to 4,056 lb (916 to 1,842 kg)	all oceans except polar; Med. and Black Seas		primarily fish and squid
Short-beaked common dolphin	*Delphinus delphis*	220 to 299 lb (100 to 136 kg)	all oceans except polar; Med. and Black Seas		small fish; squid and octopus
Risso's dolphin	*Grampus griseus*	661 to 1,102 lb (300 to 500 kg)	all oceans except polar; Med. and Black Seas		fish, krill, crustaceans, cephalopods; greater argonaut (paper nautilus)
Harbor porpoise	*Phocoena phocoena*	99 to 132 lb (45 to 60 kg)	all oceans except polar; Med. and Black Seas		smooth, nonspiny fish; cephalopods
Vaquita	*Phocoena sinus*	66 to 121 lb (30 to 55 kg)	Pacific Ocean		tuna and other teleost fish; squid
Atlantic white-sided dolphin	*Lagenorhynchus acutus*	396 to 550 lb (180 to 250 kg)	Atlantic Ocean		shrimp, smelt, hake, squid, herring
Irrawaddy dolphin	*Orcaella brevirostris*	251 to 293 lb (114 to 133 kg)	Indian and Pacific Oceans		fish, cephalopods, crustaceans
Amazon River dolphin	*Inia geoffrensis*	217 to 407 lb (99 to 185 kg)	South America		fish and some crustaceans
Ganges River dolphin	*Platanista gangetica*	112 to 196 lb (51 to 89 kg)	southern Asia		variety of aquatic animals; fish, crustaceans
LEMURS					
Aye-aye	*Daubentonia madagascariensis*	6 lb (3 kg)	Madagascar		insect larvae, plant shoots, fruit, eggs
Gray mouse lemur	*Microcebus murinus*	2.1 oz (60 g)	Madagascar		insects, small reptiles, plants, fruit, flowers
Fork-marked lemur	*Phaner furcifer*	10.6 to 17.6 oz (300 to 500 g)	coastal and western Madagascar		gum of temperate deciduous trees
Indri	*Indri indri*	15 to 22 lb (7 to 10 kg)	northeastern Madagascar		leaves, shoots, fruit
Diademed sifaka	*Propithecus diadema*	11 to 15 lb (5 to 7 kg)	eastern Madagascar		leaves, shoots, fruit, flowers
Woolly lemur	*Avahi laniger*	1.3 to 2.9 lb (0.6 to 1.3 kg)	northwestern and eastern Madagascar		fruit, leaves, buds
Black lemur	*Eulemur macaco*	3.3 to 6.6 lb (1.5 to 3 kg)	Madagascar and nearby islands		mainly fruit; reportedly mushrooms and millipedes; flower nectar; seed pods
Bamboo lemur	*Hapalemur griseus*	33 oz (935 g)	Madagascar		mainly bamboo; also grasses, fruit, leaves
POTTOS, LORISES, AND GALAGOS					
Northern lesser galago	*Galago senegalensis*	3.2 to 9.6 oz (90 to 270 g)	sub-Saharan Africa		insects, spiders, scorpions, young birds, lizards, seeds, fruit, nectar
Greater galago	*Otolemur crassicaudatus*	2.2 to 4.4 lb (1 to 2 kg)	East Africa		insects, reptiles, birds, bird eggs, plant material

COMMON NAME	SCIENTIFIC NAME	SIZE	RANGE	HABITAT	DIET
Slow loris	*Nycticebus coucang*	21.1 to 24.1 oz (599 to 685 g)	Southeast Asia		insects, bird eggs, small birds, fruit, shoots
Slender loris	*Loris tardigradus*	4.6 to 8.1 oz (130 to 230 g)	Sri Lanka		insects, small birds, bird eggs, lizards, leaves, shoots
Potto	*Perodicticus potto*	1.3 to 3.5 lb (0.6 to 1.6 kg)	equatorial Africa		insects, snails, fruit, leaves
MONKEYS					
Sooty mangabey	*Cercocebus atys*	11 to 31 lb (5 to 14 kg)	coastal West Africa		omnivorous: fruit, seeds, small animals
Drill	*Mandrillus leucophaeus*	25 to 55 lb (11.5 to 25 kg)	Cameroon		plant matter, fruit, leaves; insects, small invertebrate and vertebrate animals
Mona monkey	*Cercopithecus mona*	4.4 to 13.2 lb (2 to 6 kg)	southwest Africa		mostly fruit; also sprouts, young leaves, invertebrates
Blue monkey	*Cercopithecus mitis*	8.8 to 13.2 lb (4 to 6 kg)	equatorial Africa		mainly fruit and leaves; also slow-moving slugs and worms
De Brazza's monkey	*Cercopithecus neglectus*	8.8 to 15.4 lb (4 to 7 kg)	Africa, especially eastern		leaves, shoots, fruit, berries, insects, lizards
Crowned guenon	*Cercopithecus pogonias*	5.7 to 9.9 lb (2.6 to 4.5 kg)	West Africa		fruit; also insects, leaves
Patas monkey	*Erythrocebus patas*	15 to 29 lb (7 to 13 kg)	sub-Saharan Africa		fruit, seeds, roots, leaves, lizards, insects, bird eggs
Gray-cheeked mangabey	*Lophocebus albigena*	males: 24 to 55 lb (11 to 25 kg)	Central Africa		mainly fruit and seeds
Gelada baboon	*Theropithecus gelada*	28 to 46 lb (13 to 21 kg)	Ethiopia, Eritrea		herbivorous: grasses, seeds
Yellow baboon	*Papio cynocephalus*	15 to 29 lb (7 to 13 kg)	East Africa		grasses, pods, seeds, fruit, roots, leaves, buds, bark, flowers, insects, meat
Hamadryas baboon	*Papio hamadryas*	20 to 47 lb (9 to 21 kg)	northern Africa		omnivorous: birds, mammals; reptiles; eggs; leaves, roots, tubers, seeds, grains, nuts, fruit
Japanese macaque	*Macaca fuscata*	19 to 25 lb (8.4 to 11.3 kg)	Japan		mainly nuts, berries, buds, leaves, bark
Stump-tailed macaque	*Macaca arctoides*	16 to 23 lb (7 to 10.4 kg)	Southeast Asia		leaves, fruit, roots, crops
Liontail macaque	*Macaca silenus*	6 to 22 lb (3 to 10 kg)	India, Western Ghats mountains		fruit; also leaves, stems, flowers, buds, fungi; some insects, lizards, frogs, small mammals
Bonnet macaque	*Macaca radiata*	8 to 15 lb (4 to 7 kg)	India, Western Ghats mountains		leaves, fruit, nuts, seeds, insects, eggs; sometimes lizards
Western red colobus	*Procolobus badius*	15 to 27 lb (7 to 12 kg)	West Africa		primarily leaves; also shoots, fruit, flowers
Proboscis monkey	*Nasalis larvatus*	15 to 48 lb (7 to 22 kg)	Borneo		fruit, seeds, young leaves, shoots of mangrove; also some invertebrates
Mitered leaf monkey	*Presbytis melalophos*	13.2 lb (6 kg)	Malay Peninsula, Sumatra, western Borneo		leaves, seeds, fruit, flowers, roots
Douc langur	*Pygathrix nemaeus*	21 lb (9.6 kg)	Vietnam, Cambodia		mainly leaves; also unripe fruit, their seeds and flowers
Hanuman langur	*Semnopithecus entellus*	22 to 29 lb (10 to 13 kg)	South and Central Asia		leaves, fruit, flowers, insects; also bark, gum, soil
Golden snub-nosed monkey	*Rhinopithecus roxellana*	26 to 44 lb (12 to 20 kg)	southwestern China		lichens, fruit, seeds, leaves, buds, sometimes small animals
Northern night monkey	*Aotus trivirgatus*	28.2 oz (800 g)	tropical South America		fruit; leaves, insects, spiders; also some small mammals and birds
Black spider monkey	*Ateles paniscus*	18 to 20 lb (8.5 to 9 kg)	South America north of Amazon River		mainly fruit; some flowers, mature seeds, tips of roots, fungi
Humboldt's woolly monkey	*Lagothrix lagotricha*	6 to 22 lb (3 to 10 kg)	Central and South America		fruit; also leaves, seeds, some insects
Brown capuchin monkey	*Cebus apella*	2.9 to 10.6 lb (1.3 to 4.8 kg)	South America		fruit; also vegetation, seeds, pith, eggs, birds, small mammals, insects, reptiles
Geoffroy's tamarin	*Saguinus geoffroyi*	12.3 to 15.9 oz (350 to 450 g)	Central and South America		insects and fruit; also small lizards; flowers; nectar found in secondary growth
Black-mantled tamarin	*Saguinus nigricollis*	16.7 oz (475 oz)	South America		insects, leaves, fruit
Golden-headed lion tamarin	*Leontopithecus chrysomelas*	10.6 to 24.7 oz (300 to 700 g)	Brazil		insectivorous, frugivorous; also invertebrates such as spiders and snails
Common marmoset	*Callithrix jacchus*	10.6 to 12.7 oz (300 to 360 g)	Brazil		tree sap; also insects, spiders, fruit flowers, nectar
White-eared marmoset	*Callithrix aurita*	10.8 oz (306 g)	Brazil		insectivorous: ants, termites, larvae, caterpillars, insect galls, large-winged insects
Goeldi's marmoset	*Callimico goeldii*	13.9 to 30.3 oz (393 to 860 g)	northern Amazon forests of South America		plant matter, including berries; insects; small vertebrates
Bolivian titi monkey	*Callicebus donacophilus*	2.1 lb (950 g)	Bolivia, Brazil		primarily frugivorous; also leaves, seeds, insects
Black bearded saki	*Chiropotes satanas*	5.7 to 7 lb (2.6 to 3.2 kg)	northern Amazonian and Guianas, South America		seeds of fruit and nuts; also fruit, flowers, leaf stalks, insects
APES AND TARSIERS					
Western lowland gorilla	*Gorilla gorilla*	397 to 606 lb (180 to 275 kg)	West Africa		plant material, such as leaves, buds, berries, stalks, bark, ferns
Red-cheeked gibbon	*Nomascus gabriellae*	15.4 to 24.2 lb (7 to 11 kg)	southeastern Asia		leaves, flowers, shoots, insects
Hoolock gibbon	*Hoolock hoolock*	13 to 15 lb (6 to 6.8 kg)	southern Asia		fruit, leaves, shoots; sometimes spiders, insects, larvae, bird eggs
Spectral tarsier	*Tarsius tarsier*	3.6 to 4.6 oz (102 to 130 g)	Indonesia		ants, beetles, cockroaches, scorpions, lizards, bats, snakes, birds, small mammals

BIRDS

COMMON NAME	SCIENTIFIC NAME	SIZE	RANGE	HABITAT	DIET
DUCKS, GEESE, AND SWANS					
Mandarin duck	*Aix galericulata*	16 to 19.3 in (41 to 49 cm)	China, eastern Siberia, Japan		aquatic plants; rice
Mallard duck	*Anas platyrhynchos*	19.7 to 25.6 in (50 to 65 cm)	worldwide		insects, aquatic invertebrates and vegetation, seeds, grains
Northern pintail duck	*Anas acuta*	20.1 to 29.9 in (51 to 76 cm)	worldwide		grains, seeds, aquatic insects, crustaceans
American black duck	*Anas rubripes*	21.3 to 23.2 in (54 to 59 cm)	Canada to the Gulf Coast and Bermuda		seeds, roots, grains, aquatic plants, fish
Speckled teal	*Anas flavirostris*	14.6 to 16.9 in (37 to 43 cm)	eastern South America		seeds, insects, vegetation
Eurasian wigeon	*Anas penelope*	16.5 to 20.5 in (42 to 52 cm)	Europe, Asia, Africa, United States		aquatic vegetation; grasses
Northern shoveler	*Anas clypeata*	17.3 to 20.1 in (44 to 51 cm)	Europe, Asia, Africa, North America		aquatic invertebrates
Velvet scoter	*Melanitta fusca*	18.9 to 22.8 in (48 to 58 cm)	Europe, Asia, Canada, coastal United States		mollusks, crustaceans, insects
Canvasback duck	*Aythya valisineria*	18.9 to 22 in (48 to 56 cm)	Mexico, United States, western Canada		seeds, vegetation, insects
Surf scoter	*Melanitta perspicillata*	18.9 to 23.6 in (48 to 60 cm)	Canada, United States, Baja California, British Isles		freshwater invertebrates
Bufflehead	*Bucephala albeola*	12.6 to 15.7 in (32 to 40 cm)	Canada, United States, northern Mexico		seeds and aquatic invertebrates
Lesser scaup	*Aythya affinis*	15.4 to 18.1 in (39 to 46 cm)	Canada, U.S., Central America, Caribbean		aquatic vegetation and insects, seeds, crustaceans
Hawaiian goose	*Branta sandvicensis*	21 to 26 in (53 to 66 cm)	Hawaiian Islands		grasses, seeds, berries, flowers
Egyptian goose	*Alopochen aegyptiaca*	25 to 29 in (63 to 73 cm)	Africa and Europe		grains and vegetation; some insects
Greylag goose	*Anser anser*	29.9 to 35 in (76 to 89 cm)	Europe, western Russia, northern Africa		grasses, plants, aquatic animals
Tundra swan	*Cygnus columbianus*	47.2 to 57.9 in (120 to 147 cm)	Siberia, Alaska, Canada, Europe, Asia, U.S.		aquatic plants, seeds, grains
Northern screamer	*Chauna chavaria*	34 in (86 cm)	northwestern Venezuela and northern Colombia		aquatic vegetation
Southern screamer	*Chauna torquata*	32 to 37 in (81 to 95 cm)	much of South America		plants, seeds, leaves
Magpie goose	*Anseranas semipalmata*	27.6 to 35.4 in (70 to 90 cm)	Australia and New Guinea		seeds and grasses
CHICKENS, TURKEYS, AND RELATIVES					
Vulturine guineafowl	*Acryllium vulturinum*	24 to 28 in (61 to 71 cm)	central East Africa		seeds, roots, insects
Northern bobwhite quail	*Colinus virginianus*	8 to 9.7 in (20.3 to 24.7 cm)	southeastern Ontario (Can.) to Mexico		vegetation, fruit, invertebrates
Bearded-wood partridge	*Dendrortyx barbatus*	8.7 to 14.2 in (22 to 36 cm)	Mexico, mainly along the Gulf coast		fruit, nuts, vegetation
Chukar	*Alectoris chukar*	13.4 to 15 in (34 to 38 cm)	Greece to Asia; U.S.; Hawaii; New Zealand		grasses, seeds, fruit
Black francolin	*Francolinus francolinus*	13.4 to 14.3 in (34 to 36 cm)	Middle East and South Asia		vegetation and insects
Indian peafowl	*Pavo cristatus*	59 in (150 cm)	Asia, Australia, New Zealand, U.S., Bahamas		vegetation, insects, worms, frogs, snakes
Himalayan monal pheasant	*Lophophorus impejanus*	24.8 to 28.3 in (63 to 72 cm)	South Asia and China		vegetation, seeds, insects
Domestic chicken	*Gallus gallus domesticus*	14 to 34 in (35.6 to 86.4 cm)	worldwide		insects, seeds, grains, mice, small reptiles
Satyr tragopan	*Tragopan satyra*	24 to 28 in (61 to 71 cm)	central and eastern parts of Himalaya		vegetation, berries, fruit
Temminck's tragopan	*Tragopan temminckii*	25.2 in (64 cm)	China, India, Myanmar, Vietnam		vegetation, seeds, insects
Spruce grouse	*Falcipennis canadensis*	15.3 to 15.9 in (39 to 40.5 cm)	Canada and northern United States		pine and spruce needles; invertebrates
Willow ptarmigan	*Lagopus lagopus*	13.8 to 17.3 in (35 to 44 cm)	Arctic North America, Greenland, Europe, Asia		insects, willow buds, grasses, roots, flowers seeds
Greater prairie chicken	*Tympanuchus cupido*	16.9 in (43 cm)	midwestern United States		leaves, buds, fruit, insects
Plain chachalaca	*Ortalis vetula*	21.7 in (55 cm)	Central America, Mexico, southern Texas (U.S.A.)		leaves, berries, buds
Wattled curassow	*Crax globulosa*	32.3 to 35 in (82 to 89 cm)	northern half of South America		fish, insects, fruit, seeds
Blue-throated piping guan	*Pipile cumanensis*	27.2 in (69 cm)	northern half of South America		fruit and flowers
Maleo	*Macrocephalon maleo*	21.7 to 23.6 in (55 to 60 cm)	Indonesian islands of Sulawesi and Buton		fruit, seeds, insects
Hamerkop	*Scopus umbretta*	22 in (56 cm)	Africa, Saudi Arabia, Yemen		frogs, fish, insects

COMMON NAME	SCIENTIFIC NAME	SIZE	RANGE	HABITAT	DIET
NIGHTJARS, POTOOS, AND RELATIVES					
Lyre-tailed nightjar	*Uropsalis lyra*	23.6 in (60 cm)	mountains of South America		insects
Common pauraque	*Nyctidromus albicollis*	11 to 11.8 in (28 to 30 cm)	Texas (U.S.A.), Mexico, Cent. and S. America		insects
Common nighthawk	*Chordeiles minor*	8.7 to 9.4 in (22 to 24 cm)	North, Central, and South America		insects
Eastern whip-poor-will	*Antrostomus vociferus*	8.7 to 10.2 in (22 to 26 cm)	Canada to Central America		insects
Oilbird	*Steatornis caripensis*	16.1 to 19.3 in (41 to 49 cm)	Panama and northern half of South America		fruits
HUMMINGBIRDS AND SWIFTS					
Blue-throated hummingbird	*Lampornis clemenciae*	4.3 to 4.7 in (11 to 12 cm)	United States: Arizona to New Mexico; Texas		nectar
Rufous-tailed hummingbird	*Amazilia tzacatl*	4 to 4.8 in (10 to 12 cm)	central-east Mexico to Ecuador		nectar
Ruby-throated hummingbird	*Archilochus colubris*	2.8 to 3.5 in (7 to 9 cm)	North America to Costa Rica and Caribbean		nectar
Allen's hummingbird	*Selasphorus sasin*	3.5 in (9 cm)	Pacific coast of North America to Mexico		nectar
Common swift	*Apus apus*	6.3 to 6.7 in (16 to 17 cm)	Europe to North Africa; east to Siberia and China		insects
White-throated swift	*Aeronautes saxatalis*	5.9 to 7.1 in (15 to 18 cm)	western United States; Mexico; Central America		insects
Pacific swift	*Apus pacificus*	7.1 to 8.3 in (18 to 21 cm)	Southeast Asia, eastern Russia, south to Australia		insects
Chimney swift	*Chaetura pelagica*	4.7 to 5.9 in (12 to 15 cm)	North and South America		insects
PARROTS					
Salmon-crested cockatoo	*Cacatua moluccensis*	19.7 in (50 cm)	South Maluku, Indonesia		seeds, fruit, nuts, insects
Sulfur-crested cockatoo	*Cacatua galerita*	23.6 in (60 cm)	Australia, New Zealand, New Guinea		seeds, fruit, buds, insect larvae (grubs)
Cockatiel	*Nymphicus hollandicus*	12.8 in (32 cm)	throughout Australia; introduced to Tasmania		seeds
Violet-necked lory	*Eos squamata*	10.6 in (27 cm)	Maluku Islands, Indonesia		fruit (palm, fig) and nectar
Kakapo	*Strigops habroptila*	25.2 in (64 cm)	southernmost New Zealand		fruit, seeds, vegetation
Kea	*Nestor notabilis*	18.9 in (48 cm)	mountains of South Island, New Zealand		leaves, buds, berries, carrion
Fischer's lovebird	*Agapornis fischeri*	5 to 5.9 in (12.7 to 15 cm)	north-central Tanzania		seeds
Sun parakeet	*Aratinga solstitialis*	11.8 in (30 cm)	northern Brazil and Guianas into Venezuela		seeds, fruit, berries
Eclectus parrot	*Eclectus roratus*	13.8 in (35 cm)	New Guinea region		seeds, fruit, nuts, leaf buds, blossoms
Puerto Rican Amazon parrot	*Amazona vittata*	11.8 in (30 cm)	Puerto Rico		fruit, flowers, leaves, seeds
Thick-billed parrot	*Rhynchopsitta pachyrhyncha*	15 in (38 cm)	western Sierra Madre Mountains of Mexico		pine nuts
Hyacinth macaw	*Anodorhynchus hyacinthinus*	37.4 to 39.4 in (95 to 100 cm)	eastern Amazon in Brazil; east Bolivia; Paraguay		palm fruit and nuts
Scarlet macaw	*Ara macao*	31.5 to 38.4 in (80 to 96.5 cm)	southern Mexico; Central and South America		seeds, fruit, bark, leaves, flowers
Brown-throated parakeet	*Eupsittula pertinax*	9.8 in (25 cm)	northernmost South America into Panama		seeds, fruit, flowers
Budgerigar	*Melopsittacus undulatus*	5.9 to 7.9 in (15 to 20 cm)	Australia and southwest Florida		grasses and seeds of ground vegetation
Rose-ringed parakeet	*Psittacula krameri*	14.6 to 16.9 in (37 to 43 cm)	northern Uganda to North Africa, Asia		fruit, seeds, flowers, nectar, seeds
Senegal parrot	*Poicephalus senegalus*	7.9 to 9.8 in (20 to 25 cm)	western sub-Saharan Africa		fruit, seeds, buds, flowers
WOODPECKERS, TOUCANS, AND RELATIVES					
Acorn woodpecker	*Melanerpes formicivorus*	7.5 to 9.1 in (19 to 23 cm)	United States, Mexico, Central America		insects, acorns, sap, fruit
Arizona woodpecker	*Dryobates arizonae*	7.1 to 7.9 in (18 to 20 cm)	Sierra Madre Mts. in U.S.; Mexico to Arizona (U.S.A.)		insects, larvae, fruit, acorns
Black-backed woodpecker	*Picoides arcticus*	9.1 in (23 cm)	Alaska to New England region in United States		larvae and insects
Lemon-throated barbet	*Eubucco richardsoni*	5.1 to 6.3 in (13 to 16 cm)	northwestern South America		insects, seeds, fruit
Scarlet-hooded barbet	*Eubucco tucinkae*	6.7 in (17 cm)	eastern Peru, slightly into Brazil and Bolivia		insects and fruit
Keel-billed toucan	*Ramphastos sulfuratus*	17 to 22 in (42 to 55 cm)	southern Mexico to Colombia and Venezuela		fruit, seeds, small reptiles, insects, bird eggs and young
Channel-billed toucan	*Ramphastos vitellinus*	19.7 in (50 cm)	northern South America		fruit, small reptiles, frogs
Collared aracari	*Pteroglossus torquatus*	16.1 in (41 cm)	southern Mexico to Colombia and Venezuela		insects, eggs, fruit
Saffron toucanet	*Pteroglossus bailloni*	13.8 to 15.4 in (35 to 39 cm)	southern Brazil and just into Paraguay		fruit; bird eggs and young

COMMON NAME	SCIENTIFIC NAME	SIZE	RANGE	HABITAT	DIET
Whitehead's trogon	Harpactes whiteheadi	11.4 in (29 cm)	northern Borneo		insects
Guianan puffbird	Notharchus macrorhynchos	11.4 in (29 cm)	Guianas into Brazil and Venezuela		insects, especially army ants
Black-fronted nunbird	Monasa nigrifrons	9.8 in (25 cm)	Amazon River region of South America		insects, lizards, frogs
Three-toed jacamar	Jacamaralcyon tridactyla	5.5 to 13 in (14 to 34 cm)	southeastern Brazil		insects

RATITES

COMMON NAME	SCIENTIFIC NAME	SIZE	RANGE	HABITAT	DIET
Slaty-breasted tinamou	Crypturellus boucardi	10.8 in (27.5 cm)	parts of Central America just into Mexico		insects, fruit, seeds
Great spotted kiwi	Apteryx haastii	17.7 to 19.7 in (45 to 50 cm)	South Island, New Zealand		insects, snails, spiders, earthworms, crayfish, fruits

GULLS, PUFFINS, AND SANDPIPERS

COMMON NAME	SCIENTIFIC NAME	SIZE	RANGE	HABITAT	DIET
Tufted puffin	Fratercula cirrhata	14.2 to 15.7 in (36 to 40 cm)	northern Pacific Ocean		fish and invertebrates
Black guillemot	Cepphus grylle	11.8 to 12.6 in (30 to 32 cm)	North Atlantic and Arctic Oceans		fish and invertebrates
Ancient murrelet	Synthliboramphus antiquus	7.9 to 9.4 in (20 to 24 cm)	northern Pacific coasts		crustaceans and other invertebrates, larval fish
Cassin's auklet	Ptychoramphus aleuticus	9.1 in (23 cm)	Pacific coasts of North America		crustaceans and other invertebrates, larval fish
Marbled murrelet	Brachyramphus marmoratus	9.4 to 9.8 in (24 to 25 cm)	Pacific coasts of North America		fish
Eurasian thick-knee	Burhinus oedicnemus	15.7 to 17.3 in (40 to 44 cm)	Europe, Asia, northern Africa		invertebrates and small rodents, reptiles
Killdeer	Charadrius vociferus	7.9 to 11 in (20 to 28 cm)	North America; Central America to South America		insects and other invertebrates
Black-bellied plover	Pluvialis squatarola	11 to 11.4 in (28 to 29 cm)	Arctic; all tropical and subtropical coasts		insects and other invertebrates
Southern lapwing	Vanellus chilensis	12.6 to 15 in (32 to 38 cm)	most of South America		insects and other invertebrates
Snowy sheathbill	Chionis albus	13.4 to 16.1 in (34 to 41 cm)	Antarctic Peninsula and eastern Argentina		invertebrates and carrion
Burchell's courser	Cursorius rufus	9.4 in (24 cm)	Angola, Botswana, Namibia, South Africa		insects and seeds
Australian pratincole	Stiltia isabella	7.5 to 9.4 in (19 to 24 cm)	Australia to Indonesia and New Guinea		insects and spiders
Black oystercatcher	Haematopus bachmani	16.5 to 18.5 in (42 to 47 cm)	Pacific coast of North America to Baja California		mussels and limpets, other invertebrates
Northern jacana	Jacana spinosa	6.7 to 9 in (17 to 23 cm)	Mexico to Panama, including Caribbean		insects and aquatic vegetation
California gull	Larus californicus	18.5 to 21.3 in (47 to 54 cm)	parts of North America from Mexico to Canada		fish, insects, small mammals, grains
Western gull	Larus occidentalis	22 to 26 in (56 to 66 cm)	Pacific coast of North America to Baja California		marine invertebrates, fish, carrion
Elegant tern	Thalasseus elegans	15.3 to 16.5 in (39 to 42 cm)	Pacific coast of the Americas		fish
Plains wanderer	Pedionomus torquatus	5.9 to 7.5 in (15 to 19 cm)	Australia		seeds, invertebrates, leaves
Double-banded sandgrouse	Pterocles bicinctus	7.1 in (18 cm)	southern Africa		seeds
Hawaiian stilt	Himantopus himantopus	13.8 to 15.4 in (35 to 39 cm)	eastern Hawaiian Islands		small fish, seeds, insects
Australian painted-snipe	Rostratula australis	8.7 to 9.8 in (22 to 25 cm)	eastern Australia		marine invertebrates, insects, seeds
Spotted sandpiper	Actitis macularius	7.1 to 7.9 in (18 to 20 cm)	Americas, including Caribbean		marine invertebrates, small fish, insects
Sanderling	Calidris alba	7.1 to 7.9 in (18 to 20 cm)	Arctic areas; coastlines of all oceans and seas		invertebrates
Black turnstone	Arenaria melanocephala	8.7 to 9.8 in (22 to 25 cm)	North American coasts and Ecuador		aquatic invertebrates
Marbled godwit	Limosa fedoa	16.5 to 18.9 in (42 to 48 cm)	Canada; coasts of the United States and Mexico		insects and other invertebrates
Stilt sandpiper	Calidris himantopus	7.9 to 9.1 in (20 to 23 cm)	Arctic, U.S., Central and South America, Caribbean		insects
Long-billed curlew	Numenius americanus	19.7 to 25.6 in (50 to 65 cm)	Canada, United States, Mexico		insects, crustaceans, other invertebrates
Greater yellowlegs	Tringa melanoleuca	11.4 to 13 in (29 to 33 cm)	Canada, U.S., Mex., Cent. and S. Am., Caribbean		invertebrates, frogs, seeds, berries
Long-tailed jaeger	Stercorarius longicaudus	15 to 24.8 in (38 to 63 cm)	Arctic Circle, South America, South Africa		rodents, small birds, insects
Least seedsnipe	Thinocorus rumicivorus	5.9 in (15 cm)	South America		seeds and vegetation

ALBATROSSES, PELICANS, AND RELATIVES

COMMON NAME	SCIENTIFIC NAME	SIZE	RANGE	HABITAT	DIET
Oriental darter	Anhinga melanogaster	28 to 31.1 in (71 to 79 cm)	South and Southeast Asia		fish, amphibians, aquatic invertebrates
Brandt's cormorant	Phalacrocorax penicillatus	27.6 to 31.1 in (70 to 79 cm)	Pacific coast of North America		fish and squid
Pelagic cormorant	Phalacrocorax pelagicus	20.1 to 29.9 in (51 to 76 cm)	Pacific coasts of Asia and North America		fish and marine invertebrates
Red-tailed tropicbird	Phaethon rubricauda	30.7 to 31.9 in (78 to 81 cm)	tropical waters of Indian and Pacific Oceans		fish and squid

COMMON NAME	SCIENTIFIC NAME	SIZE	RANGE	HABITAT	DIET
Masked booby	Sula dactylatra	29.1 to 33.9 in (74 to 86 cm)	tropical waters worldwide		fish and squid
Red-footed booby	Sula sula	27.2 to 31.1 in (69 to 79 cm)	tropical and subtropical waters worldwide		fish and squid
Wandering albatross	Diomedea exulans	43.3 to 53.1 in (110 to 135 cm)	oceans south of the Tropic of Capricorn		fish and squid
Royal albatross	Diomedea epomophora	42.1 to 48 in (107 to 122 cm)	southern oceans worldwide		cephalopods, fish, crustaceans
Magellanic diving petrel	Pelecanoides magellani	7.5 in (19 cm)	southern South America and Falkland Islands		crustaceans, other aquatic invertebrates, small fish
Polynesian storm petrel	Nesofregetta fuliginosa	9.4 to 10.2 in (24 to 26 cm)	tropical Pacific islands		fish, cephalopods, crustaceans
Scopoli's shearwater	Calonectris diomedea	18.1 in (46 cm)	Atlantic Ocean to Gulf of Mexico; Med. Sea		squid, crustaceans, fish
Streaked shearwater	Calonectris leucomelas	18.9 in (48 cm)	western Pacific Ocean; coasts of eastern Asia		fish and squid
HERONS, FLAMINGOS, AND RELATIVES					
Yellow-crowned night-heron	Nyctanassa violacea	21.7 to 27.6 in (55 to 70 cm)	U.S., Mexico, Cent. and S. America, Caribbean		crustaceans, reptiles, small mammals
Black-crowned night-heron	Nycticorax nycticorax	22.8 to 26 in (58 to 66 cm)	North America, Africa, Europe into Asia		invertebrates, fish, rodents, lizards
Little blue heron	Egretta caerulea	22 to 29.1 in (56 to 74 cm)	North America to South America		small fish, frogs, invertebrates
Boat-billed heron	Cochlearius cochlearius	21.3 in (54 cm)	Mexico to northern half of South America		fish, crustaceans, insects
Snowy egret	Egretta thula	22 to 26 in (56 to 66 cm)	North, Central, and South America		fish, crustaceans, insects
Reddish egret	Egretta rufescens	27.6 to 31.5 in (70 to 80 cm)	Caribbean; Mexico to Cent. and S. America		small fish, frogs, crustaceans
Wood stork	Mycteria americana	33.5 to 45.3 in (85 to 115 cm)	Mexico, Caribbean, Cent. and S. America		small fish; frogs; insects, other invertebrates
African sacred ibis	Threskiornis aethiopicus	25.5 to 29.5 in (65 to 75 cm)	sub-Saharan Africa to Iraq; Europe		insects, frogs, reptiles, fish
Speckled mousebird	Colius striatus	14 in (35.6 cm)	most of sub-Saharan Africa		fruit, leaves, buds
PIGEONS AND DOVES					
White-tipped dove	Leptotila verreauxi	9.8 to 12.2 in (25 to 31 cm)	Mexico; Central and South America		seeds, fruit, invertebrates
African-collared dove	Streptopelia roseogrisea	10.2 to 10.6 in (26 to 27 cm)	Arabian Peninsula and northern Africa		seeds
Common ground dove	Columbina passerina	5.9 to 7.1 in (15 to 18 cm)	southern United States to northern South America		seeds and vegetation
Rock dove	Columbia livia	12 in (30.5 cm)	Asia; now worldwide		grains and seeds
Band-tailed pigeon	Patagioenas fasciata	13 to 15.7 in (33 to 40 cm)	British Columbia (Canada) to Argentina		seeds, fruit, flowers
Pink pigeon	Nesoenas mayeri	13 in (33 cm)	Mauritius		buds, leaves, flowers, fruit, seeds
White-crowned pigeon	Patagioenas leucocephala	13 to 13.8 in (33 to 35 cm)	Caribbean and Bahamas to South Florida		fruit and berries; sometimes insects
White-naped pigeon	Columba albinucha	13.4 in (34 cm)	Africa: Lake Albert region and Cameroon		berries and fruit
Inca dove	Columbina inca	7.1 to 9.1 in (18 to 23 cm)	southwestern U.S. and northern Central America		seeds
KINGFISHERS, HORNBILLS, AND RELATIVES					
Amazon kingfisher	Chloroceryle amazona	11.4 to 11.8 in (29 to 30 cm)	Mexico, Central America, South America		insects and amphibians
African pygmy kingfisher	Ceyx pictus	4.7 in (12 cm)	sub-Saharan Africa except southwestern tip		insects and amphibians
Sulawesi lilac kingfisher	Cittura cyanotis	11 in (28 cm)	central Indonesia		insects
Woodland kingfisher	Halcyon senegalensis	7.9 to 9.1 in (20 to 23 cm)	sub-Saharan Africa except southern tip		invertebrates, insects, fish, other birds
Blue-winged kookaburra	Dacelo leachii	11 to 17 in (28 to 42 cm)	northern Australia; southern New Guinea		snakes and invertebrates
Laughing kookaburra	Dacelo novaeguineae	17.7 in (45 cm)	eastern and southern Australia; Tasmania		fish, invertebrates, insects, reptiles
Southern yellow-billed hornbill	Tockus leucomelas	18.9 to 23.6 in (48 to 60 cm)	southern Africa		small animals, fruit, insects
Northern ground hornbill	Bucorvus abyssinicus	39.4 in (100 cm)	belt across Africa from Mauritania to Ethiopia		reptiles, mammals, insects
Indian roller	Coracias benghalensis	12.6 to 13.5 in (32 to 34 cm)	India east to northern Southeast Asia		insects and amphibians
Dollarbird	Eurystomus orientalis	9.8 to 11.4 in (25 to 29 cm)	eastern Asia to Australian coasts		insects
Rainbow bee-eater	Merops ornatus	7.4 to 10.6 in (19 to 27 cm)	Australia; eastern Indonesia to Solomon Islands		bees and wasps
Amazonian motmot	Momotus momota	15.7 in (40 cm)	northeastern Mexico to northern Argentina		insects and fruit
Green woodhoopoe	Phoeniculus purpureus	17 in (43.2 cm)	sub-Saharan Africa except Congo River Basin		insects and spiders
Jamaican tody	Todus todus	3.5 to 4.3 in (9 to 11 cm)	Jamaica		insects and fruit

COMMON NAME	SCIENTIFIC NAME	SIZE	RANGE	HABITAT	DIET
CUCKOOS AND RELATIVES					
Common cuckoo	Cuculus canorus	13 in (33 cm)	Europe, Asia, sub-Saharan Africa		insects
Striped cuckoo	Tapera naevia	11.8 in (30 cm)	southern Mexico to South America		insects
Yellow-billed cuckoo	Coccyzus americanus	10.2 to 11.8 in (26 to 30 cm)	Canada, U.S., Mexico, Caribbean, South America		insects
Smooth-billed ani	Crotophaga ani	11.8 to 14.2 in (30 to 36 cm)	Caribbean into South America		insects, lizards, fruit
Livingstone's turaco	Tauraco livingstonii	17.7 in (45 cm)	southeastern Africa from Tanzania to South Africa		fruit
White-bellied go-away bird	Corythaixoides leucogaster	13.8 to 29.5 in (35 to 75 cm)	Horn of Africa south to Tanzania		fruit, invertebrates, seeds
Gray go-away-bird	Corythaixoides concolor	18.1 to 20.1 in (46 to 51 cm)	across southern Africa except southern tip		fruit, flowers, leaves, insects
Ruspoli's turaco	Tauraco ruspolii	15.7 in (40 cm)	southern Ethiopia		fruit
EAGLES, FALCONS, HAWKS, AND OWLS					
African fish eagle	Haliaeetus vocifer	24.8 to 30.3 in (63 to 77 cm)	sub-Saharan Africa		fish and carrion
Golden eagle	Aquila chrysaetos	27.5 to 33 in (70 to 84 cm)	Europe, Asia, Africa, North America		small animals, insects, carrion
Tawny eagle	Aquila rapax	25.5 to 28.3 in (65 to 72 cm)	India and Africa		small animals, carrion, insects
Harpy eagle	Harpia harpyja	35 in (88.9 cm)	Mexico to northern South America		sloths, primates, reptiles, birds, small mammals
Common black hawk	Buteogallus anthracinus	21 in (53 cm)	U.S. to South America; Cuba; Isle of Pines		snakes, frogs, fish, crabs
Roadside hawk	Buteo magnirostris	12.2 to 16.1 in (31 to 41 cm)	Mexican coasts, Central America, South America		insects and small mammals
Swallow-tailed kite	Elanoides forficatus	19.7 to 25.2 in (50 to 64 cm)	southeastern U.S. and northern South America		insects, snakes, frogs
Secretary bird	Sagittarius serpentarius	34 in (86.4 cm)	sub-Saharan Africa		insects and small mammals
Northern goshawk	Accipiter gentilis	20.9 to 25.2 in (53 to 64 cm)	parts of North America; Europe; parts of Asia		birds, mammals, reptiles
Turkey vulture	Cathartes aura	25.2 to 31.8 in (64 to 81 cm)	throughout the Americas except Canada		carrion, rotten fruit and vegetables, insects
King vulture	Sarcoramphus papa	27.9 to 31.8 in (71 to 81 cm)	Mexico to South America		carrion
Merlin	Falco columbarius	9.4 to 11.8 in (24 to 30 cm)	parts of Northern Hemisphere		small birds
Peregrine falcon	Falco peregrinus	14.2 to 19.3 in (36 to 49 cm)	worldwide except rainforests and Arctic regions		birds, mostly pigeons and doves
Lesser kestrel	Falco naumanni	11.8 to 14.2 in (30 to 36 cm)	Europe and Asia; most of sub-Saharan Africa		insects, other invertebrates, small mammals
Common kestrel	Falco tinnunculus	11.8 to 14.1 in (30 to 36 cm)	Europe, Asia, sub-Saharan Africa		small mammals, reptiles, amphibians
Crested caracara	Caracara cheriway	19.3 to 22.8 in (49 to 58 cm)	United States–Mexico border to Panama		insects, small animals, carrion
Long-eared owl	Asio otus	13.8 to 15.7 in (35 to 40 cm)	North America and Eurasia		small mammals
Eurasian eagle-owl	Bubo bubo	22.8 in (58 cm)	Eurasia except polar regions and southern Asia		small animals and large insects
Barred owl	Strix varia	16.9 to 19.7 in (43 to 50 cm)	eastern United States and southern Canada		small animals and invertebrates
Spotted owl	Strix occidentalis	18.5 to 18.9 in (47 to 48 cm)	western North America		small mammals
Boreal owl	Aegolius funereus	8.3 to 11 in (21 to 28 cm)	Alaska and Canada; northern Eurasia		small mammals, birds, insects
Elf owl	Micrathene whitneyi	4.9 to 5.6 in (12.4 to 14.2 cm)	southwestern United States to western Mexico		insects
Tawny owl	Strix aluco	15 in (38 cm)	Europe to Asia; Himalaya to coast of China		small mammals, birds, insects
Northern hawk-owl	Surnia ulula	14.2 to 17.7 in (36 to 45 cm)	Alaska and Canada; northern Eurasia		small mammals and birds
Mottled owl	Ciccaba virgata	12.2 in (31 cm)	Mexico; Central and South America		insects, small mammals, birds, reptiles
LOONS AND GREBES					
Arctic loon	Gavia arctica	15.7 to 31.8 in (40 to 81 cm)	Arctic to Baja California; Med.; East China Sea		fish and aquatic invertebrates
Yellow-billed loon	Gavia adamsii	35 in (88.9 cm)	Arctic North Am., Europe, Asia, Gulf of Alaska		fish and other aquatic invertebrates
Pacific loon	Gavia pacifica	22.8 to 29.1 in (58 to 74 cm)	western coast of U.S., northern Canada, Alaska		fish and other aquatic invertebrates
CRANES, BUSTARDS, AND RELATIVES					
Sunbittern	Eurypyga helias	18.5 in (47 cm)	South America to Central America and Mexico		amphibians, crustaceans, insects
Masked finfoot	Heliopais personatus	22 in (56 cm)	Bangladesh to Sumatra		small fish and insects
Limpkin	Aramus guarauna	25.2 to 28.7 in (64 to 73 cm)	United States, Caribbean, Mexico to Argentina		snails and mussels

BIRDS

COMMON NAME	SCIENTIFIC NAME	SIZE	RANGE	HABITAT	DIET
Red-legged seriema	*Cariama cristata*	35.4 in (90 cm)	South America		insects, rodents, lizards, birds
Wattled crane	*Bugeranus carunculatus*	68.9 in (175 cm)	eastern Africa from Ethiopia to South Africa		vegetation, small aquatic animals and insects
Siberian crane	*Leucogeranus leucogeranus*	45.3 in (115 cm).	Russia to western Siberia; Iran; India; China		vegetation, insects, small mammals, fish
American coot	*Fulica americana*	15.5 to 16.9 in (39.4 to 42.9 cm)	southern Canada; United States		aquatic plants and insects
King rail	*Rallus elegans*	15 to 18.9 in (38 to 48 cm)	eastern United States to Mexico and Caribbean		crustaceans, small fish, insects
Subdesert mesite	*Monias benschi*	11.8 to 12.6 in (30 to 32 cm)	Madagascar		terrestrial invertebrates, seeds, fruit

ANTBIRDS AND RELATIVES

COMMON NAME	SCIENTIFIC NAME	SIZE	RANGE	HABITAT	DIET
Olivaceous woodcreeper	*Sittasomus griseicapillus*	5.2 to 7.6 in (13.1 to 19.3 cm)	South and Central America		ants, beetles, spiders and other arthropods
Rufous-fronted antthrush	*Formicarius rufifrons*	7.1 in (18 cm)	Bolivia, Brazil, Peru		insects and other arthropods
Giant antpitta	*Grallaria gigantea*	10.4 in (26.5 cm)	Colombia and Ecuador		insects and larvae
Zimmer's tapaculo	*Scytalopus zimmeri*	3 to 5.5 in (10 to 14 cm)	Argentina and Bolivia		insects and seeds
Black-chinned antbird	*Hypocnemoides melanopogon*	4.3 to 4.7 in (11 to 12 cm)	South America		insects

FLYCATCHERS AND RELATIVES

COMMON NAME	SCIENTIFIC NAME	SIZE	RANGE	HABITAT	DIET
Acadian flycatcher	*Empidonax virescens*	5.5 to 5.9 in (14 to 15 cm)	eastern United States and northern South America		insects and larvae
Olive-sided flycatcher	*Contopus cooperi*	7.1 in to 7.9 in (18 to 20 cm)	North, Central, and South America		insects
Yellow-bellied flycatcher	*Empidonax flaviventris*	5.1 to 5.9 in (13 to 15 cm)	northern United States, Canada, central Mexico		insects and arthropods
Hammond's flycatcher	*Empidonax hammondii*	4.7 to 5.5 in (12 to 14 cm)	western United States and Canada; Central America		insects
Black phoebe	*Sayornis nigricans*	6.3 in (16 cm)	southern U.S., Mexico, northern South America		insects, small fish, berries
Rose-throated becard	*Pachyramphus aglaiae*	6.3 to 7.1 in (16 to 18 cm)	Central America and coastal Mexico		insects and berries
Red-capped manakin	*Ceratopipra mentalis*	3.9 in (10 cm)	Central America and northern South America		fruit
Andean cock-of-the-rock	*Rupicola peruvianus*	12.6 in (32 cm)	Andes		fruit, small animals, insects

CROWS AND RELATIVES

COMMON NAME	SCIENTIFIC NAME	SIZE	RANGE	HABITAT	DIET
Common raven	*Corvus corax*	22.1 to 27.2 in (56 to 69 cm)	North and Central America; Europe; Africa; Asia		amphibians, reptiles, birds, small mammals, carrion
Green jay	*Cyanocorax yncas*	11.4 in (29 cm)	Texas (U.S.A.) to Honduras; South America		insects, seeds, vegetation, other arthropods
California scrub-jay	*Aphelocoma californica*	11 to 11.8 in (28 to 30 cm)	western United States and parts of Mexico		insects, fruit, nuts
Black-billed magpie	*Pica hudsonia*	17.7 to 23.6 in (45 to 60 cm)	western North America; parts of southwest U.S.		invertebrates, grains, acorns, carrion
Magnificent bird of paradise	*Cicinnurus magnificus*	6.3 to 10.2 in (16 to 26 cm)	mountains of New Guinea		fruit and insects
Blue bird of paradise	*Paradisaea rudolphi*	11.8 in (30 cm)	mountains of Papua New Guinea		fruit and some arthropods
Loggerhead shrike	*Lanius ludovicianus*	7.9 to 9.1 in (20 to 23 cm)	southern Canada; United States; Mexico		insects, amphibians, reptiles, birds
White-eyed vireo	*Vireo griseus*	4.3 to 5.1 in (11 to 13 cm)	eastern U.S., eastern Mexico, Belize, Caribbean		insects and some fruit
Hawaiian elepaio	*Chasiempis sandwichensis*	5.5 in (14 cm)	island of Hawaii		insects and spiders

SONGBIRDS

COMMON NAME	SCIENTIFIC NAME	SIZE	RANGE	HABITAT	DIET
Horned lark	*Eremophila alpestris*	6.3 to 7.9 in (16 to 20 cm)	North America; Arctic Eurasia; Europe to China		seeds and insects
Mountain chickadee	*Poecile gambeli*	4.3 to 5.5 in (11 to 14 cm)	Canada and United States		insects, spiders, seeds
Tufted titmouse	*Baeolophus bicolor*	5.5 to 6.3 in (14 to 16 cm)	eastern half of United States		insects, berries, seeds, acorns
American treecreeper	*Certhia americana*	4.7 to 5.5 in (12 to 14 cm)	United States, Canada, Mexico, Central America		insects, spiders, ants, seeds
Grass wren	*Cistothorus platensis*	3.9 to 4.7 in (10 to 12 cm)	U.S., Canada, Central and South America		insects
Wood thrush	*Hylocichla mustelina*	7.5 to 8.3 in (19 to 21 cm)	eastern N. America; Central America to Mexico		insects and insect larvae, fruit, snails, small salamanders
Western bluebird	*Sialia mexicana*	6.3 to 7.5 in (16 to 19 cm)	western North America		insects, seeds, fruit
American dipper	*Cinclus mexicanus*	5.5 to 7.9 in (14 to 20 cm)	western North America to Central America		aquatic invertebrates
Black-and-white warbler	*Mniotilta varia*	4.3 to 5.1 in (11 to 13 cm)	Canada, U.S., Caribbean, Mexico, Cent. and S. Am.		butterflies (caterpillars), insects, spiders
Sage thrasher	*Oreoscoptes montanus*	7.9 to 9.1 in (20 to 23 cm)	southwestern Canada, western U.S., Mexico		insects and berries
Common starling	*Sturnus vulgaris*	7.9 to 9.1 in (20 to 23 cm)	Eurasia, Africa, N. America, Aust., New Zealand		insects, spiders, berries

268

COMMON NAME	SCIENTIFIC NAME	SIZE	RANGE	HABITAT	DIET
Bali myna	*Leucopsar rothschildi*	9.8 in (25 cm)	Indonesia: Bali and Nusa Penida		insects, seeds, fruit, worms, small reptiles
Red-billed oxpecker	*Buphagus erythrorynchus*	7.5 to 8.7 in (19 to 22 cm)	eastern Africa		insects, mostly ectoparasites of large mammals
Brown-eared bulbul	*Hypsipetes amaurotis*	11 in (28 cm)	Japan, Korean Peninsula, coastal China		berries, flowers, insects, fruits
Golden-fronted leafbird	*Chloropsis aurifrons*	8.7 to 10.2 in (22 to 26 cm)	Himalaya to India, Sri Lanka, southern Asia		nectar, insects, fruit
Bananaquit	*Coereba flaveola*	4.1 to 4.5 in (10.5 to 11.5 cm)	South America, southern Mexico, Caribbean		nectar
Varied bunting	*Passerina versicolor*	4.3 to 5.5 in (11 to 14 cm)	most of Mexico into southwest Texas (U.S.A.)		seeds, grasses, cactus fruit
Dark-eyed junco	*Junco hyemalis*	5.5 to 6.3 in (14 to 16 cm)	North America and southern Mexico		seeds, insects, some spiders
White-throated towhee	*Melozone albicollis*	8.3 to 9.8 in (21 to 25 cm)	Mexico		insects, seeds, fruit
Chestnut-collared longspur	*Calcarius ornatus*	5.1 to 6.5 in (13 to 16.5 cm)	United States to Canada and Mexico		insects, spiders, seeds
Rusty blackbird	*Euphagus carolinus*	8.3 to 9.8 in (21 to 25 cm)	Alaska and across Canada; eastern United States		acorns, seeds, fruit, grasshoppers, aquatic insects
Altimira oriole	*Icterus gularis*	8.3 to 9.8 in (21 to 25 cm)	Gulf coast of Mexico; parts of Central America		insects and fruit
Baltimore oriole	*Icterus galbula*	6.7 to 7.5 in (17 to 19 cm)	North, Central, and South America; Caribbean		insects, spiders, nectar, fruit
Common grackle	*Quiscalus quiscula*	11 to 13.4 in (28 to 34 cm)	North America east of the Rocky Mountains		seeds, fruits, insects, other arthropods
Boat-tailed grackle	*Quiscalus major*	10.2 to 14.6 in (26 to 37 cm)	Atlantic and Gulf coasts of United States		arthropods, crustaceans, snails, frogs, turtles, lizards, grain, fruit, tubers
Bronzed cowbird	*Molothrus aeneus*	7.9 in (20 cm)	Central America, Mexico, United States		seeds and insects
American goldfinch	*Spinus tristis*	4.3 to 5.1 in (11 to 13 cm)	United States into southern Canada and Mexico		seeds
Oahu amakihi	*Chlorodrepanis flava*	4.7 to 5.1 in (12 to 13 cm)	Honolulu, Hawaii		nectar, insects and other arthropods, fruit
'I'iwi	*Drepanis coccinea*	4.7 in (12 cm)	Hawaiian Islands		nectar, insects, spiders
Common waxbill	*Estrilda astrild*	4.7 in (12 cm)	sub-Saharan Africa, Americas, Med., Oceania		seeds and insects
Pin-tailed whydah	*Vidua macroura*	5.5 in (14 cm)	sub-Saharan Africa		seeds
Red wattlebird	*Anthochaera carunculata*	13.8 in (35 cm)	southern Australia		nectar and insects
Rail babbler	*Eupetes macrocerus*	11 to 11.8 in (28 to 30 cm)	Malay Peninsula, Sumatra, Borneo		insects and spiders
Western whipbird	*Psophodes nigrogularis*	7.9 to 9.8 in (20 to 25 cm)	isolated pockets in southern Australia		insects and spiders
Satin bowerbird	*Ptilonorhynchus violaceus*	11.8 in (30 cm)	east coast of Australia		fruit, flowers, leaves, insects
Brown treecreeper	*Climacteris picumnus*	6.2 to 7 in (16 to 18 cm)	eastern Australia		insects and insect larvae
Lark sparrow	*Chondestes grammacus*	5.9 to 6.7 in (15 to 17 cm)	U.S., except eastern; Canada; most of Mexico		seeds and insects
Elegant sunbird	*Aethopyga duyvenbodei*	4.6 in (12 cm)	Sangihe, Indonesia		nectar and insects
Hermit thrush	*Catharus guttatus*	5.5 to 7.1 in (14 to 18 cm)	North and Central America		insects, small invertebrates, amphibians and reptiles, fruit, shrubs, plants
PENGUINS					
King penguin	*Aptenodytes patagonicus*	33.5 to 37.4 in (85 to 95 cm)	islands surrounding Antarctica		cephalopods, small fish, squid
Royal penguin	*Eudyptes schlegeli*	26 to 30 in (65 to 75 cm)	Macquarie Island, Australia		fish, squid, krill
Humboldt penguin	*Spheniscus humboldti*	26 to 28 in (66 to 70 cm)	coastal Peru and Chile and offshore islands		fish, squid, crustaceans
Galápagos penguin	*Spheniscus mendiculus*	20.9 in (53 cm)	Galápagos Islands		small fish
Snares penguin	*Eudyptes robustus*	19.7 to 23.6 in (50 to 60 cm)	Snares Islands, New Zealand		krill, squid, fish
Fiordland penguin	*Eudyptes pachyrhynchus*	21.7 in (55 cm)	southern New Zealand islands		krill, fish, squid

REPTILES

- ● ALERT
- ● UNDER STUDY
- ● IN TROUBLE
- ● NOT LISTED
- ● STABLE
- ● DOMESTICATED

COMMON NAME	SCIENTIFIC NAME	SIZE	RANGE	HABITAT	DIET
CROCODILES, CAIMANS, AND ALLIGATORS					
Black caiman	*Melanosuchus niger*	20 ft (6 m)	northern and central South America		mollusks; fish, other aquatic vertebrates; also terrestrial vertebrates, including capybara
Mugger crocodile	*Crocodylus palustris*	13 to 16.4 ft (4 to 5 m)	India, Pakistan, Sri Lanka		crustaceans, fish, frogs, birds, monkeys, squirrels
Cuban crocodile	*Crocodylus rhombifer*	up to 10.5 ft (3.5 m)	Cuba: Zapata and Lanier Swamps		primarily turtles, fish, small mammals
Siamese crocodile	*Crocodylus siamensis*	about 9.8 ft (3 m)	Southeast Asia		fish; also amphibians, reptiles, small mammals
African dwarf crocodile	*Osteolaemus tetraspis*	about 6.3 ft (1.9 m)	west-central Africa		fish, crustaceans, amphibians
African slender-snouted crocodile	*Crocodylus cataphractus*	up to 13 ft (4 m)	central Africa		fish, frogs, snakes, shrimp, crabs, waterbirds, mammals
Tuatara	*Sphenodon punctatus*	15.7 to 23.5 in (50 to 60 cm)	islands off the coast of New Zealand		spiders, insects, worms
Chinese alligator	*Alligator sinensis*	4.6 to 4.9 ft (1.4 to 1.5 m)	Lower Yangtze River Basin, China		snails, clams, fish, waterfowl, small mammals
TURTLES					
Pig-nose turtle	*Carettochelys insculpta*	21.7 to 27.6 in (55 to 70 cm)	New Guinea and northern Australia		fruit of pandanus and figs; also mollusks, worms, crustaceans
Red-bellied short-necked turtle	*Emydura subglobosa*	5.2 to 10 in (13.3 to 25.5 cm)	coastal Australia and New Guinea		fish, mollusks, crustaceans, phytoplankton, worms, algae, leaves, flowers, carrion
Green sea turtle	*Chelonia mydas*	3.3 to 3.9 ft (1 to 1.2 m)	tropical and subtropical oceans worldwide		mostly herbivorous: sea algae, shallow-water grasses
Hawksbill sea turtle	*Eretmochelys imbricata*	2.1 to 3.7 ft (0.6 to 1.1 m)	tropical regions of Atlantic and Pacific Oceans		sponges, sea jellies, other coelenterates; also mollusks, fish, crustaceans, algae
Olive ridley sea turtle	*Lepidochelys olivacea*	27.6 in (70 cm)	Indian and southern Atlantic Oceans		invertebrates and protochordates such as jellyfish, snails, shrimp, crabs
Kemp's ridley sea turtle	*Lepidochelys kempii*	22 to 30 in (55 to 75 cm)	Atlantic Ocean to Gulf of Mexico		floating crabs, shrimp, jellyfish, mollusks, some vegetation
Flatback sea turtle	*Natator depressus*	about 35 in (90 cm)	east Indian Ocean and southwest Pacific Ocean		seafloor life such as cuttlefish, hydroids, soft corals, crinoids, mollusks, jellyfish
Alligator snapping turtle	*Macrochelys temminckii*	1 to 1.3 ft (0.8 to 1 m)	southern and midwestern United States		fish, mollusks, carrion, and other turtles
European pond turtle	*Emys orbicularis*	4.7 to 15 in (12 to 38 cm)	Europe, Africa, Middle East, Asia		generalist carnivore: small aquatic animals; worms, insects, frogs, fish
Diamondback terrapin	*Malaclemys terrapin*	5.5 to 9 in (14 to 23 cm)	eastern United States		snails, other mollusks, fish, insects, crustaceans, carrion
Common slider	*Trachemys scripta*	4 to 11.4 in (10 to 29 cm)	southeastern U.S.; Central and South America		aquatic insects, fish, crustaceans, snails, tadpoles, mollusks; also plant matter
Painted turtle	*Chrysemys picta*	3.5 to 9.8 in (9 to 25 cm)	North America		mainly plants, small animals (fish, crustaceans, aquatic insects), some carrion
North American wood turtle	*Glyptemys insculpta*	6.3 to 9.8 in (16 to 25 cm)	eastern Canada and northeastern United States		slugs, snails, worms, insects, tadpoles, leaves, berries, other plant food
Bog turtle	*Glyptemys muhlenbergii*	3.1 to 4.5 in (8 to 11.4 cm)	eastern United States		small invertebrates such as insects, snails, worms; seeds, berries, vegetation
River cooter	*Pseudemys concinna*	9 to 12 in (23 to 30 cm)	eastern United States		mainly herbivorous: eelgrass, elodea, algae; also small fish, insects, other animal food
American red-bellied turtle	*Pseudemys rubriventris*	10.2 to 12.5 in (26 to 32 cm)	mid-Atlantic United States		mostly aquatic vegetation and algae; also crayfish, snails, fish, and tadpoles
Southeast Asian box turtle	*Cuora amboinensis*	8 in (20 cm)	Southeast Asia		vegetables, fruit, mushrooms, aquatic plants; also waxworms, fish, insects
False map turtle	*Graptemys pseudogeographica*	3.5 to 10.6 in (9 to 27 cm)	midwestern United States		mollusks, insects, fish carrion; some vegetation
Furrowed wood turtle	*Rhinoclemmys pulcherrima*	7 to 8 in (18 to 20 cm)	Central America		fruits, plant shoots, insects
Black-breasted leaf turtle	*Geoemyda spengleri*	about 4.5 in (11.5 cm)	China, Vietnam		snails, insects, leaves, fruits
Yellow mud turtle	*Kinosternon flavescens*	4 to 6 in (10.2 to 15.2 cm)	midwestern United States and northern Mexico		snails, worms, insects, tadpoles
Eastern mud turtle	*Kinosternon subrubrum*	2.8 to 4.9 in (7 to 12.5 cm)	eastern United States		mostly insects, mollusks, crustaceans, amphibians, carrion
South American river turtle	*Podocnemis expansa*	3.5 ft (1.1 m)	northern South America		aquatic vegetation
Madagascan big-headed turtle	*Erymnochelys madagascariensis*	about 20 in (50 cm)	Madagascar		plants overhanging water; also small vertebrates
South African helmeted terrapin	*Pelomedusa galeata*	upper shell: 5.9 to 7.1 in (15 to 18 cm)	southern Africa		frogs, tadpoles, mollusks, invertebrates, carrion
Big-headed turtle	*Platysternon megacephalum*	6 to 7 in (15 to 18 cm)	southeastern Asia		small marine and terrestrial animals including fish, mollusks, worms
TORTOISES					
Leopard tortoise	*Stigmochelys pardalis*	11.8 to 27.5 in (30 to 70 cm)	eastern and southern Africa		berries and other fruits when available
Radiated tortoise	*Astrochelys radiata*	up to 16 in (40 cm)	southern Madagascar		grasses, fruit, plants

COMMON NAME	SCIENTIFIC NAME	SIZE	RANGE	HABITAT	DIET
Russian tortoise	*Testudo horsfieldii*	6 to 10 in (15 to 26 cm)	Russia, Afghanistan, China		weeds, grasses, twigs, flowers, fruits
Gopher tortoise	*Gopherus polyphemus*	9 to 15.2 in (23 to 38.7 cm)	southeastern United States		grasses and leaves
Indian star tortoise	*Geochelone elegans*	5.9 to 15 in (15 to 38 cm)	southeastern Pakistan; India; Sri Lanka		grasses, leaves, fruit, flowers; also insects, carrion, dung
Aldabra giant tortoise	*Aldabrachelys gigantea*	35.5 to 55 in (90 to 140 cm)	Seychelles		grasses, leaves, woody plant stems, herbs, sedges
Red-footed tortoise	*Chelonoidis carbonaria*	up to 20.1 in (51 cm)	eastern Amazon Basin; Caribbean islands		fruit, grasses, flowers, fungi, carrion, invertebrates
South American yellow-footed tortoise	*Chelonoidis denticulata*	up to 32 in (82 cm)	Amazon Basin		leaves, vines, roots, bark, fruit, flowers; also fungi, insects, snails
African spurred tortoise	*Geochelone sulcata*	up to 32.6 in (83 cm)	Sahara and Sahel, Africa		grasses and succulent plants
Asian giant tortoise	*Manouria emys*	19.7 to 23.6 in (50 to 60 cm)	southeastern Asia		grasses, vegetables, leaves, fruit
Forest hinge-back tortoise	*Kinixys erosa*	up to 14.7 in (37.5 cm)	central and western Africa		fungi, fruit, plant matter, invertebrates, carrion
Bell's hinge-back tortoise	*Kinixys belliana*	6 to 8.6 in (15 to 22 cm)	sub-Saharan Africa		leaves, grasses, sedges, fallen fruit, sugarcane, fungi; insects, snails, millipedes
Home's hinge-back tortoise	*Kinixys homeana*	up to 8.7 in (22.3 cm)	West Africa		mostly insects; also mushrooms, seeds, frogs, and carrion
Hermann's tortoise	*Testudo hermanni*	up to 10 in (20 cm)	Mediterranean Europe		mostly vegetarian: fruit, flowers, leaves; also slugs, snails, animal remains
Common tortoise	*Testudo graeca*	about 10 in (20 cm)	eastern Europe; North Africa		weeds and grasses
Spiny softshell turtle	*Apalone spinifera*	5 to 19 in (12.7 to 48 cm)	central to eastern United States		macroinvertebrates, including aquatic insects, crayfish; also fish
Smooth softshell turtle	*Apalone mutica*	4.5 to 14 in (11.5 to 35.6 cm)	central United States		amphibians, fish, snails, mollusks, arthropods, worms
Florida softshell turtle	*Apalone ferox*	5.9 to 29 in (15 to 73.6 cm)	southeastern United States		snails, insects, crustaceans, fish, amphibians, small turtles
IGUANAS, CHAMELEONS, AND RELATIVES					
Agama lizard	*Agama agama*	7.9 to 9.8 in (20 to 25 cm)	sub-Saharan Africa		ants, grasshoppers, beetles, termites; also small mammals and reptiles, vegetation
Frilled lizard	*Chlamydosaurus kingii*	33 in (85 cm)	northern Australia and southern New Guinea		mostly small invertebrates
Chinese water dragon	*Physignathus cocincinus*	up to 35 in (90 cm)	India, China, East and Southeast Asia		plants, insects; some small fish or other vertebrates
Central bearded dragon	*Pogona vitticeps*	13 to 24 in (33 to 61 cm)	eastern and central Australia		plant matter, insects, occasional small rodents or lizards
Common flying dragon	*Draco volans*	7.6 to 8.3 in (19.3 to 21.1 cm)	Philippine islands		mostly ants and termites
Sailfin lizard	*Hydrosaurus amboinensis*	4.8 ft (1.4 m)	Indonesia and New Guinea		plants, small animals, insects
Mediterranean chameleon	*Chamaeleo chamaeleon*	8 to 15 in (20.3 to 38.1 cm)	southern Europe and northern Africa		invertebrates, young birds, reptiles; some vegetation
Flap-necked chameleon	*Chamaeleo dilepis*	up to 15 in (38 cm)	southern and eastern Africa		insects
Jackson's three-horned chameleon	*Chamaeleo jacksonii*	6 to 14 in (15 to 35 cm)	East Africa		mainly insects and spiders
Namaqua chameleon	*Chamaeleo namaquensis*	5.5 to 6.2 in (14 to 16 cm)	southern Africa		locusts, crickets, beetles, small snakes, scorpions
Lesser chameleon	*Furcifer minor*	6 to 10 in (15.2 to 25.4 cm)	Madagascar		invertebrates
Parson's chameleon	*Calumma parsonii*	18.5 to 24.4 in (47 to 62 cm)	Madagascar		large insects and small vertebrates
Horned leaf chameleon	*Brookesia superciliaris*	3 to 4.7 in (8 to 12 cm)	Madagascar		insects
Smooth helmeted iguana	*Corytophanes cristatus*	12 to 16 in (30 to 40 cm)	Central America		insects
Brown basilisk	*Basiliscus vittatus*	about 23.6 in (60 cm)	Latin America		mostly insects; also fallen berries
Leopard lizard	*Gambelia sila*	up to 14 in (35.7 cm)	California (U.S.A.)		insects, including grasshoppers, beetles, bees, ants, wasps; also plant matter, lizards
Marine iguana	*Amblyrhynchus cristatus*	24 to 30 in (60 to 75 cm)	Galápagos Islands		marine algae
Lau banded iguana	*Brachylophus fasciatus*	up to 31 in (80 cm)	Fiji and Tonga		leaves, flowers, fruit; also insects
Land iguana	*Conolophus subcristatus*	3 to 3.9 ft (0.9 to 1.2 m)	Galápagos Islands		plants, fruit of prickly pear cactus
Black spiny-tailed iguana	*Ctenosaura similis*	3.3 to 4.1 ft (1 to 1.25 m)	Mexico, Panama, Central America		small animals, such as rodents, bats, frogs, insects, small birds
Rhinoceros iguana	*Cyclura cornuta*	2 to 3.9 ft (0.6 to 1.2 m)	Hispaniola		leaves, fruits, flowers, seeds; sometimes animal matter
Grand Cayman blue iguana	*Cyclura lewisi*	16.3 to 20.3 in (41.5 to 51.6 cm)	Grand Cayman Island		mostly plant matter, including leaves and stems; also fruits, nuts, flowers
Lesser Antillean iguana	*Iguana delicatissima*	15 to 17 in (39 to 43 cm)	Caribbean		leaves, flowers, fruits
Desert iguana	*Dipsosaurus dorsalis*	up to 15 in (38 cm)	western United States and northwestern Mexico		foliage and fruit of desert plants; also invertebrates
Chuckwalla	*Sauromalus ater*	up to 16 in (40 cm)	western United States and northwestern Mexico		fruits, leaves, flowers
Fence lizard	*Sceloporus undulatus*	3.5 to 7.5 in (9 to 19 cm)	Mexico and United States		insects and other arthropods, including ants, weevils, beetles, spiders, centipedes; also snails

COMMON NAME	SCIENTIFIC NAME	SIZE	RANGE	HABITAT	DIET
Zebra-tailed lizard	Callisaurus draconoides	6 to 9.2 in (15 to 23.4 cm)	southwestern U.S. and northern Mexico		insects, plant material, sloughed skin of other lizards; also eggs, insect larvae, carrion
Brown anole	Anolis sagrei	1.2 to 2.7 in (3.5 to 6.8 cm)	southern United States; Mexico; Caribbean		insects, including moths, beetles, flies, grasshoppers; worms, snails, other invertebrates
Green anole	Anolis carolinensis	4 to 8 in (10.2 to 20.3 cm)	southeast U.S.; Hawaii; Caribbean; Japan		arthropods, including beetles, flies, spiders; also mollusks, grains, seeds
Lava lizard	Microlophus albemarlensis	6.7 to 10 in (17 to 25 cm)	Galápagos Islands		moths, flies, beetles, grasshoppers, ants, other insects; spiders, centipedes, other arthropods
Speckled worm lizard	Amphisbaena fuliginosa	12 to 18 in (30 to 45 cm)	Panama, Trinidad, northern and central South America		small vertebrates and insects
Red worm lizard	Amphisbaena alba	up to 30 in (75 cm)	Panama to central South America		earthworms, beetles, ants, termites, spiders, crickets, larvae of various insects
Mediterranean worm lizard	Blanus cinereus	4 to 8 in (10 to 20 cm)	Portugal and Spain		earthworms and small insects
Florida worm lizard	Rhineura floridana	10 to 14 in (25 to 35 cm)	southeastern United States		worms, spiders, termites
Two-legged worm lizard	Bipes biporus	6.5 to 9.5 in (17 to 24 cm)	Baja California		worms and termites
GECKOS, SKINKS, AND MONITORS					
Leopard gecko	Eublepharis macularius	8 to 10 in (20 to 25 cm)	Middle East and northwest India		scorpions, beetles, spiders, grasshoppers
Common house gecko	Hemidactylus frenatus	3 to 5.9 in (7.5 to 15 cm)	tropical and subtropical regions worldwide		insects, spiders, smaller geckos
Kuhl's flying gecko	Gekko kuhli	up to 4.2 in (10.8 cm)	Southeast Asia		mainly insects
Standing's day gecko	Phelsuma standingi	up to 12 in (30.5 cm)	Madagascar		insects
Lined day gecko	Phelsuma lineata	4 to 5.7 in (10 to 14.5 cm)	Madagascar and Mauritius		insects
Northern alligator lizard	Elgaria coerulea	about 10 in (25 cm)	western United States and southwestern Canada		insects, ticks, spiders, millipedes, snails
Southern alligator lizard	Elgaria multicarinata	2.8 to 7 in (7.3 to 17.8 cm)	western United States; Mexico		insects and other small creatures; scorpions, black widow spiders
Madrean alligator lizard	Elgaria kingii	up to 12.6 in (32 cm)	southwestern U.S. and northern Mexico		insects and spiders
Texas alligator lizard	Gerrhonotus ophiurus	up to 20 in (50.8 cm)	south Texas (U.S.A.) and eastern Mexico		arthropods, small rodents, snakes, other lizards
European glass lizard	Pseudopus apodus	up to 4.4 ft (1.3 m)	Greece, eastern Europe, western Asia		slugs, snails, other invertebrates
Armadillo lizard	Cordylus cataphractus	3 to 4.1 in (7.5 to 10.5 cm)	west coast of South Africa		mainly insects, especially termites and beetles; millipedes; scorpions; plant material
Augrabies flat lizard	Platysaurus broadleyi	6 to 8 in (15 to 20 cm)	South Africa		insects, especially flies; also small berries
Rough-scaled plated lizard	Gerrhosaurus major	about 9 in (22.9 cm)	East and Central Africa		fruit, flowers, invertebrates, small vertebrates, including smaller lizards
Yellow-throated plated lizard	Gerrhosaurus flavigularis	up to 18 in (45 cm)	sub-Saharan Africa		insects and vegetation
Common wall lizard	Podarcis muralis	up to 9 in (23 cm)	Europe		insects such as flies and beetles; also spiders, earthworms, slugs, other invertebrates
Ibiza wall lizard	Podarcis pityusensis	6 to 8.5 in (15 to 21 cm)	Balearic Islands, Spain		primarily invertebrates, especially ants and beetles; also spiders; plant matter
Blotched blue-tongue lizard	Tiliqua nigrolutea	9.8 to 11.8 in (25 to 30 cm)	Australia		variety of plants and animals, especially snails and beetles
Spotted skink	Niveoscincus ocellatus	1.3 to 3 in (3.4 to 7.4 cm)	Tasmania		invertebrates and berries
Emerald skink	Lamprolepis smaragdina	3.2 to 4.2 in (8 to 10.7 cm)	Admiralty Islands, Marshall Islands, Indonesia		insects
Great Plains skink	Plestiodon obsoletus	3.9 to 5.5 in (10 to 14 cm)	western United States and northern Mexico		insects, spiders, small lizards
Otago skink	Oligosoma otagense	10 to 12 in (25 to 30 cm)	New Zealand		insects, fleshy fruit, smaller lizards
Shingleback lizard	Tiliqua rugosa	16 to 18 in (41 to 46 cm)	Australia		omnivorous: snails and plants
Common garden skink	Lampropholis guichenoti	up to 1.6 in (4 cm)	southern Australia		primarily insects
Florida sand skink	Neoseps reynoldsi	4 to 5 in (10 to 13 cm)	Florida (U.S.A.)		arthropods, including beetle larvae, termites, spiders, larval ant lions; other invertebrates
Common tegu	Tupinambis teguixin	23.6 to 35.4 in (60 to 90 cm)	northern South America		insects and other invertebrates, birds, small mammals, other lizards, carrion
Argentine giant tegu	Salvator merianae	3 to 4 ft (0.9 to 1.2 m)	Argentina, Bolivia, Brazil, Paraguay		wide range of animals and fruit
Giant ameiva	Ameiva ameiva	4.7 to 7.1 in (12 to 18 cm)	Florida and northern South America		insects, spiders, snails, other small invertebrates, small lizards
New Mexico whiptail lizard	Cnemidophorus neomexicanus	9.3 to 14.5 in (23.5 to 37 cm)	southwestern U.S. and northern Mexico		grasses and leaves
Desert night lizard	Xantusia vigilis	1.5 to 2.8 in (4 to 7 cm)	southwestern United States; Mexico		termites, ants, beetles, flies
Water monitor lizard	Varanus salvator	3 to 4.6 ft (0.9 to 1.4 m)	Southeast Asia		small mammals, especially rats; fish; crocodiles; birds; frogs; snakes; tortoises
Borneo earless monitor	Lanthanotus borneensis	up to 20 in (50 cm)	Indonesia		earthworms, crustaceans, fish
Crocodile monitor lizard	Varanus salvadorii	6.6 to 16.4 ft (2 to 5 m)	New Guinea		mainly birds; in captivity will eat mice, rats, chickens
Mexican beaded lizard	Heloderma horridum	29.5 to 35.4 in (75 to 90 cm)	Mexico		birds, eggs, small mammals, lizards, frogs, insects

COMMON NAME	SCIENTIFIC NAME	SIZE	RANGE	HABITAT	DIET
SNAKES					
Coral cylinder snake	*Anilius scytale*	about 27 in (70 cm)	northern South America		other snakes, caecilians, amphisbaenids
Pygmy python	*Antaresia perthensis*	16.5 to 24.4 in (42 to 62 cm)	western Australia		small mammals such as bats; also amphibians
Rosy boa	*Charina trivirgata*	1.4 to 3.7 ft (0.4 to 1.1 m)	southwestern United States; Mexico		birds, reptiles, small mammals
Emerald tree boa	*Corallus caninus*	5 to 6.5 ft (1.5 to 2 m)	northern South America		birds, rodents, lizards
Rainbow boa	*Epicrates cenchria*	3.3 to 6.5 ft (1 to 2 m)	southern Central America; South America		birds, lizards, small mammals
Kenyan sand boa	*Gongylophis colubrinus*	up to 30 in (77 cm)	northeast Africa		lizards and small rodents
Yellow anaconda	*Eunectes notaeus*	7.9 to 15 ft (2.4 to 4.6 m)	parts of South America		birds, bird eggs, small mammals, turtles, lizards; also fish, fish carrion, caimans
Carpet python	*Morelia spilota*	6.5 to 13 ft (2 to 4 m)	New Guinea and Australia		lizards, birds, small mammals
Green tree python	*Morelia viridis*	6 to 7.8 ft (1.8 to 2.4 m)	Australia, Indonesia, Papua New Guinea		small reptiles, invertebrates, mammals, birds
Burmese python	*Python molurus*	16 to 23 ft (5 to 7 m)	East and Southeast Asia		primarily rodents and other mammals; also birds, amphibians, reptiles
Brongersma's short-tailed python	*Python brongersmai*	5 to 8 ft (1.5 to 2.5 m)	Singapore, Malay Peninsula		rodents
Reticulated python	*Python reticulatus*	20 to 33 ft (6 to 10 m)	Indonesia		birds and mammals
Round Island boa	*Casarea dussumieri*	3.3 to 5 ft (1 to 1.5 m)	Mauritius		lizards
Mexican burrowing python	*Loxocemus bicolor*	up to 5.2 ft (1.6 m)	Central America		rodents and lizards
Caicos Islands dwarf boa	*Tropidophis greenwayi*	about 15 in (38 cm)	Caicos Island		lizards, frogs; sometimes invertebrates
Large shield-tailed snake	*Pseudotyphlops philippinus*	18 to 20 in (45 to 50 cm)	Sri Lanka		earthworms
Sunbeam snake	*Xenopeltis unicolor*	3.3 to 4.3 ft (1 to 1.3 m)	Southeast Asia		frogs, lizards, snakes, small mammals
Western threadsnake	*Leptotyphlops humilis*	7 to 16 in (18 to 41 cm)	southwestern United States; Mexico		small invertebrates, especially ant broods, termites
Brahminy blind snake	*Ramphotyphlops braminus*	6 to 7 in (15 to 18 cm)	Middle East and North Africa		ants, termites and their eggs and larvae
Arafura file snake	*Acrochordus arafurae*	5 to 8.2 ft (1.5 to 2.5 m)	eastern Indonesia, New Guinea, North Australia		almost exclusively fish
Common kingsnake	*Lampropeltis getula*	.26 to 5 ft (.08 to 1.5 m)	eastern and midwestern United States		snakes, lizards, mice, birds
Eastern rat snake	*Pantherophis alleghaniensis*	3.5 to 6 ft (1.1 to 1.8 m)	southern and midwestern United States		mainly mice and rats; also chipmunks, moles, other small rodents
Common garter snake	*Thamnophis sirtalis*	1.5 to 4.5 ft (0.5 to 1.4 m)	United States		worms, amphibians, slugs, snails, insects, leeches, crayfish, small fish, other snakes
Green vine snake	*Oxybelis fulgidus*	5 to 6.5 ft (1.5 to 2 m)	Central and South America		birds and lizards
Dark green whipsnake	*Hierophis viridiflavus*	up to 6.2 ft (1.9 m)	western Europe		lizards, frogs, mammals, birds, other snakes
Eastern racer	*Coluber constrictor*	3 to 6.2 ft (0.9 to 1.9 m)	southern Canada; United States		mainly insects, spiders, small frogs, small reptiles, young rodents, shrews
Red corn snake	*Pantherophis guttata*	2 to 6 ft (0.6 to 1.8 m)	United States		young feed on lizards and tree frogs; adults eat larger prey such as mice, rats, birds, bats
Common slug snake	*Pareas monticola*	12 to 30 in (30 to 76 cm)	India, southwest China, Vietnam		slugs and snails
Common bronzeback snake	*Ophidiocephalus taeniatus*	about 11 in (27 cm)	Australia		invertebrates: termites, cockroach nymphs, spiders, beetle and moth larvae
Ringneck snake	*Diadophis punctatus*	10 to 18.1 in (25.5 to 46 cm)	Canada, Mexico, United States		small salamanders, lizards, frogs; earthworms, juvenile snakes of other species
Northern water snake	*Nerodia sipedon*	2 to 4.6 ft (0.6 to 1.4 m)	southeastern Canada and eastern United States		fish, crayfish, other snakes, turtles, birds, small mammals, large insects, leeches
Mangrove snake	*Boiga dendrophila*	up to 6.6 ft (2 m)	Southeast Asia		lizards, frogs, birds, small mammals
Boomslang	*Dispholidus typus*	3.9 to 6.6 ft (1.2 to 2 m)	sub-Saharan Africa		lizards, especially chameleons; birds
Green whip snake	*Hierophis viridiflavus*	up to 5 ft (1.5 m)	western Europe		mainly lizards; also rodents and other small mammals
Aesculapian rat snake	*Elaphe longissima*	up to 6.6 ft (2 m)	Europe		rodents, shrews, moles, birds, bird eggs
False water cobra	*Hydrodynastes gigas*	6 to 10 ft (1.8 to 3 m)	South America		fish and amphibians; also small animals
Western hognose snake	*Heterodon nasicus*	14.2 to 36.6 in (36 to 93 cm)	western United States and southern Canada		toads
Natal black snake	*Macrelaps microlepidotus*	3 to 3.9 ft (0.9 to 1.2 m)	South Africa		frogs, especially rain frogs; lizards; rodents, especially rats and mice; other snakes
Wart snake	*Acrochordus granulatus*	13.1 to 65.6 ft (4 to 20 m)	coasts of Southeast Asia, Indonesia, northern Aust.		small fish, snails, small crustaceans
Schokari sand racer	*Psammophis schokari*	about 4.3 ft (1.3 m)	Southeast Asia, Middle East, North Africa		lizards, small birds, rodents, other snakes
Northern death adder	*Acanthophis praelongus*	up to 28 ft (70 m)	Australia, New Guinea, and nearby islands		small mammals, lizards, birds
King cobra	*Ophiophagus hannah*	up to 18 ft (5.5 m)	Southeast Asia		cold-blooded animals, especially other snakes

COMMON NAME	SCIENTIFIC NAME	SIZE	RANGE	HABITAT	DIET
Coastal taipan	Oxyuranus scutellatus	up to 11 ft (3.3 m)	southern Papua New Guinea; Indonesia; Aust.		rats, lizards, bandicoots and other small mammals
Red spitting cobra	Naja pallida	up to 5 ft (1.5 m)	North Africa		amphibians; also rodents, birds
Eastern coral snake	Micrurus fulvius	20 to 30 in (51 to 76 cm)	southern United States		small lizards; snakes
Black mamba	Dendroaspis polylepis	7.3 to 8.9 ft (2.2 to 2.7 m)	Africa		mostly small mammals, such as squirrels, dassies, and other rodents, hyraxes
Crocker's sea snake	Laticauda crockeri	27 to 34 in (70 to 88 cm)	Solomon Islands		fish
Blue-lipped sea krait	Laticauda laticaudata	up to 3.5 ft (1.1 m)	Indian Ocean and Southeast Asia		eels
Banded sea krait	Laticauda colubrina	2.5 to 11.8 ft (0.7 to 3.5 m)	Indian Ocean and Southeast Asia		eels
Western brown snake	Pseudonaja nuchalis	up to 5.9 ft (1.8 m)	Australia		mice, other small mammals, reptiles
King brown snake	Pseudechis australis	up to 8.2 ft (2.5 m)	Australia, Indonesia, New Guinea		reptiles, especially lizards, snakes, other king browns; also birds, mammals, frogs
Yellow-bellied sea snake	Pelamis platurus	up to 3.7 ft (1.1 m)	Indian and Pacific Oceans; South China Sea		carnivorous: fish
Olive-brown sea snake	Aipysurus laevis	up to 6.6 ft (2 m)	Australia, Southeast Asia, areas in Oceania		fish; also fish eggs, shrimp, crabs, mollusks
Turtle-headed sea snake	Emydocephalus annulatus	up to 3 ft (0.9 m)	Australia, Southeast Asia, areas in Oceania		fish eggs
North-western Mangrove sea snake	Ephalophis greyae	up to 26 in (66 cm)	northwestern coast of Australia		fish
Eastern diamondback rattlesnake	Crotalus adamanteus	3.3 to 7.9 ft (1 to 2.4 m)	southern United States		primarily small mammals, from mice to rabbits; also birds
Sidewinder rattlesnake	Crotalus cerastes	18 to 24 in (45 to 61.5 cm)	southwestern United States; Mexico		lizards, burrowing rodents such as kangaroo rats and pocket mice, birds
Western diamond-back rattlesnake	Crotalus atrox	up to 5 ft (1.5 m)	southwestern United States; Mexico		small mammals, birds, lizards
Prairie rattlesnake	Crotalus viridis	0.8 to 5.4 ft (.25 to 1.7 m)	Canada, United States, Mexico		small mammals, ground-nesting birds, amphibians, reptiles, including other snakes
Eastern copperhead	Agkistrodon contortrix	about 30 in (76.2 cm)	Mexico and United States		rodents, frogs, lizards, small snakes, amphibians, insects, especially cicadas
South American bushmaster	Lachesis muta	6.6 to 11.8 ft (2 to 3.6 m)	Trinidad and northern South America		small rodents and other mammals

AMPHIBIANS

- ● ALERT
- ● IN TROUBLE
- ● STABLE
- ● UNDER STUDY
- ● NOT LISTED
- ● DOMESTICATED

COMMON NAME	SCIENTIFIC NAME	SIZE	RANGE	HABITAT	DIET
SALAMANDERS					
Northwestern salamander	Ambystoma gracile	5.5 to 8.7 in (14 to 22 cm)	western North America		soft-bodied invertebrates, including annelids, mollusks, amphipods, isopods, copepods
Spotted salamander	Ambystoma maculatum	5.9 to 9.8 in (15 to 25 cm)	eastern to midwestern United States		insects, crustaceans, tadpoles
Blue-spotted salamander	Ambystoma laterale	3.9 to 5.5 in (10 to 14 cm)	northeastern U.S. and southeastern Canada		invertebrates, including worms, insects, centipedes, snails, slugs, spiders
Reticulated flatwoods salamander	Ambystoma bishopi	3.5 to 5.1 in (9 to 13 cm)	southeastern United States		earthworms, insects, other invertebrates
Flatwoods salamander	Ambystoma cingulatum	3.5 to 5.3 (9 to 13.5 cm)	southeastern United States		earthworms, insects, other invertebrates
Mole salamander	Ambystoma talpoideum	3.2 to 4.7 in (8 to 12 cm)	southeastern United States		aquatic insects, tadpoles, earthworms, arthropods, other invertebrates
Jefferson's salamander	Ambystoma jeffersonianum	4.2 to 8.2 in (10.7 to 21 cm)	northeastern U.S. and southeastern Canada		insects and other invertebrates
Marbled salamander	Ambystoma opacum	3.5 to 4.2 in (9 to 10.7 cm)	eastern United States		small worms, insects, slugs, snails
Three-toed amphiuma	Amphiuma tridactylum	18 to 43 in (46 to 110 cm)	southern United States		crayfish, insects, worms, snails, small fish, small reptiles, other amphibians
Two-toed amphiuma	Amphiuma means	14.4 to 29.9 in (36.8 to 76 cm)	southeastern United States		salamanders, small frogs, crayfish, range of smaller invertebrates
One-toed amphiuma	Amphiuma pholeter	up to 12.9 in (33 cm)	southern United States		various invertebrates, such as worms, crustaceans, snails
Japanese giant salamander	Andrias japonicus	up to 4.9 ft (1.5 m)	Japan		fish, worms, crustaceans
Chinese giant salamander	Andrias davidianus	up to 3.3 ft (1 m)	China		aquatic invertebrates such as crayfish and crabs; fish, frogs
Pacific giant salamander	Dicamptodon tenebrosus	up to 13.5 in (34 cm)	northwestern United States		invertebrates, including insect larvae and adults; mollusks; crayfish and other crustaceans

COMMON NAME	SCIENTIFIC NAME	SIZE	RANGE	HABITAT	DIET
Idaho giant salamander	*Dicamptodon aterrimus*	6.7 to 9.8 in (17 to 25 cm)	western United States	(icons)	adults eat terrestrial invertebrates, small snakes, shrews, mice, other salamanders
California giant salamander	*Dicamptodon ensatus*	about 11.8 in (30 cm)	California (U.S.A.)	(icons)	land snails and slugs; insects, including beetles, caddisfly larvae, moths, flies
Cope's giant salamander	*Dicamptodon copei*	up to 8.1 in (20.5 cm)	northwestern United States	(icons)	invertebrates
Japanese clawed salamander	*Onychodactylus japonicus*	4.2 to 7.2 in (10.6 to 18.4 cm)	Japan	(icons)	primarily insects and their larvae; also other invertebrates, such as spiders, millipedes, snails
Fischer's long-tailed clawed salamander	*Onychodactylus fischeri*	about 6.7 in (17 cm)	China, Korea, and the Russian Far East	(icons)	terrestrial insects and millipedes
Siberian salamander	*Salamandrella keyserlingii*	4.7 to 6.2 in (12 to 16 cm)	Russia and China	(icons)	insects, small snails, earthworms; occasionally small fish
Western Chinese mountain salamander	*Batrachuperus pinchonii*	5 to 6 in (13 to 15 cm)	China	(icons)	aquatic and terrestrial invertebrates, especially insects
Alpine stream salamander	*Batrachuperus tibetanus*	6.7 to 8.3 in (17 to 21.1 cm)	China	(icons)	small crustaceans; aquatic and terrestrial insects
Longdong stream salamander	*Batrachuperus londongensis*	6.1 to 10.4 in (15.5 to 26.5 cm)	China	(icons)	aquatic and terrestrial invertebrates, especially insects
Taichu salamander	*Hynobius sonani*	3.9 to 4.7 in (10 to 12 cm)	Taiwan	(icons)	invertebrates
Tokyo salamander	*Hynobius tokyoensis*	3.1 to 5.1 in (8 to 13 cm)	around Tokyo, Japan	(icons)	invertebrates
Oki salamander	*Hynobius okiensis*	4.7 to 5.2 in (12.1 to 13.3 cm)	Japan	(icons)	invertebrates
Taiwan salamander	*Hynobius formosanus*	about 3.9 in (10 cm)	Taiwan	(icons)	sow bugs, earthworms, other terrestrial invertebrates
Red-backed salamander	*Plethodon cinereus*	2.2 to 5 in (5.7 to 12.7 cm)	northeastern U.S. and southeastern Canada	(icons)	small terrestrial arthropods; sometimes snails, slugs, small earthworms
Red-cheeked salamander	*Plethodon jordani*	3.25 to 7.5 in (8.5 to 18.5 cm)	Appalachian Mountains	(icons)	millipedes, beetles, insect larvae
Four-toed salamander	*Hemidactylium scutatum*	2 to 4 in (5 to 10.2 cm)	eastern United States	(icons)	insects (beetles, flies, ants, bristletails) and their larvae, spiders, mites, snails, worms
Slimy salamander	*Plethodon glutinosus*	4.5 to 8 in (11.5 to 20 cm)	eastern to midwestern United States	(icons)	ants, beetles, sowbugs, earthworms
Salvin's mushroom tongue salamander	*Bolitoglossa salvinii*	3.9 to 4.7 in (10 to 12 cm)	El Salvador and Guatemala	(icons)	small invertebrates, such as insects
Blind cave salamander	*Proteus anguinus*	7.8 to 11.8 in (20 to 30 cm)	Bosnia, Croatia, Italy, Slovenia, France	(icons)	small invertebrates, other arthropods; wide variety of insect larvae
Mudpuppy	*Necturus maculosus*	7.8 to 12.9 in (20 to 33 cm)	midwestern United States	(icons)	aquatic organisms, including crayfish, insect larvae, small fish, fish eggs, snails, amphibians
Neuse River waterdog	*Necturus lewisi*	6 to 9.1 in (15.2 to 23 cm)	eastern United States	(icons)	crayfish, other crustaceans, insect larvae and nymphs, mollusks, plant remains, worms
Gulf Coast waterdog	*Necturus beyeri*	6.2 to 8.6 in (16 to 22 cm)	Gulf Coast of United States	(icons)	crayfish, isopods, amphipods, mayflies, dragonflies, sphaeriid clams
Dwarf waterdog	*Necturus punctatus*	0.4 to 0.6 in (1.2 to 1.6 cm)	southeastern United States	(icons)	mollusks, worms, crustaceans, spiders, centipedes, insects, other salamanders
Olympic torrent salamander	*Rhyacotriton olympicus*	up to 3.9 in (10 cm)	northeastern United States	(icons)	aquatic and semiaquatic invertebrates, including larval and adult beetles, flies, snails
Gold-striped salamander	*Chioglossa lusitanica*	up to 6.5 in (16.4 cm)	Portugal and Spain	(icons)	invertebrates: spiders, flies, beetles
NEWTS					
Sword-tailed newt	*Cynops ensicauda*	4 to 7 in (10.3 to 17.9 cm)	Japan	(icons)	aquatic and terrestrial invertebrates, including snails, slugs, tadpoles, newt eggs
California newt	*Taricha torosa*	5 to 8 in (12.5 to 20 cm)	California (U.S.A.)	(icons)	invertebrates: earthworms, snails, slugs, sowbugs
Great crested newt	*Triturus cristatus*	4 to 5.5 in (10 to 14 cm)	Europe	(icons)	aquatic invertebrates; some large prey, such as smooth newts, dragonflies
Spot-tailed warty newt	*Paramesotriton caudopunctatus*	4.8 to 6.1 in (12.2 to 15.4 cm)	China	(icons)	insect larvae, arthropods, snails, frog eggs, earthworms
Kurdistan newt	*Neurergus microspilotus*	5.5 to 5.9 in (14 to 15 cm)	Iran	(icons)	invertebrates
Cyan newt	*Hypselotriton cyanurus*	2.8 to 3.9 in (7.3 to 10 cm)	China	(icons)	invertebrates
SIRENS					
Greater siren	*Siren lacertina*	20 to 35 in (50 to 90 cm)	southeastern United States	(icons)	snails, insect larvae, small fish
Dwarf siren	*Pseudobranchus striatus*	4 to 9 in (10 to 22 cm)	southeastern United States	(icons)	aquatic invertebrates
CAECILIANS					
Mexican caecilian	*Dermophis mexicanus*	4 to 23.5 in (10 to 60 cm)	Central America	(icons)	invertebrates, including earthworms, termites, immature grasshoppers and crickets; lizards
Marbled caecilian	*Epicrionops marmoratus*	11.8 in (30 cm)	Ecuador	(icons)	earthworms and soil arthropods
Banded caecilian	*Scolecomorphus vittatus*	5.5 to 14.8 in (14.1 to 37.6 cm)	Tanzania	(icons)	large, surface-active earthworms; soil arthropods
Cayenne caecilian	*Typhlonectes compressicauda*	12 to 23.5 in (30 to 60 cm)	northern South America	(icons)	invertebrates
TOADS					
Harlequin frog	*Atelopus varius*	1 to 2.4 in (2.5 to 6 cm)	Costa Rica and Panama	(icons)	arthropods, including flies, wasps, ants, caterpillars, spiders
Cane toad	*Rhinella marina*	6 to 9.4 in (15 to 24 cm)	Central and South America	(icons)	insects, especially ants, termites, beetles; other invertebrates; frogs, lizards, mice

COMMON NAME	SCIENTIFIC NAME	SIZE	RANGE	HABITAT	DIET
Natterjack toad	*Epidalea calamita*	1.9 to 2.7 in (5 to 7 cm)	Europe		moths, woodlice, other insects
Woodhouse's toad	*Anaxyrus woodhousii*	up to 5 in (12.7 cm)	western United States and northern Mexico		small terrestrial arthropods
Canadian toad	*Anaxyrus hemiophrys*	1.5 to 3.3 in (3.7 to 8.3 cm)	northern United States; Canada		worms, beetles, ants
Puerto Rican crested toad	*Peltophryne lemur*	2.5 to 4.7 in (6.4 to 12 cm)	Puerto Rico and British Virgin Islands		worms, insect larvae, insects, other invertebrates
Cuchumatan golden toad	*Incilius aurarius*	2.1 to 3.2 in (5.4 to 7.9 cm)	Guatemala and Mexico		small invertebrates
Western toad	*Anaxyrus boreas*	2 to 5 in (5.1 to 2.7 cm)	western Canada; Mexico; United States		variety of invertebrates, including worms, spiders, moths, beetles, ants
Great Plains toad	*Anaxyrus cognatus*	1.8 to 3.1 in (4.5 to 9 cm)	western Canada; United States; Mexico		insectivorous: moths, flies, cutworms, beetles
Yosemite toad	*Anaxyrus canorus*	1.8 to 2.9 in (4.5 to 7.5 cm)	California (U.S.A.)		primarily insectivorous, including bees, ants, mosquitoes, spiders, centipedes, beetles
Wyoming toad	*Anaxyrus baxteri*	up to 2.7 in (6.8 cm)	Wyoming (U.S.A.)		ants, beetles, other arthropods
Malayan dwarf toad	*Ingerophrynus divergens*	1.1 to 2.1 in (2.8 to 5.5 cm)	Brunei, Indonesia, Malaysia		arthropods, especially ants and termites
Arroyo toad	*Anaxyrus californicus*	1.8 to 3.4 in (4.6 to 8.6 cm)	western United States; Mexico		variety of invertebrates, mostly ants
Himalayan toad	*Duttaphrynus himalayanus*	5.1 to 5.2 in (13 to 13.2 cm)	China, India, Nepal, Pakistan		grasshoppers, moths, ants, other invertebrates
Flat-backed toad	*Sclerophrys maculata*	1.4 to 2.3 in (3.8 to 6 cm)	sub-Saharan Africa		insects, especially ants, beetles
FROGS					
Green and black poison dart frog	*Dendrobates auratus*	1 to 2.2 in (2.5 to 5.7 cm)	Colombia, Nicaragua, Panama, Costa Rica, U.S.		small invertebrates, especially ants
Harlequin poison dart frog	*Oophaga histrionica*	1 to 1.5 in (2.5 to 3.8 cm)	Colombia		small invertebrates, including ants, termites, small beetles, other small arthropods
Dyeing poison frog	*Dendrobates tinctorius*	1.5 to 2.3 in (4 to 6 cm)	Brazil, French Guiana, Guyana, Suriname		ants, termites, other small insects, small spiders
Yellow-headed poison frog	*Dendrobates leucomelas*	1.2 to 2 in (3.1 to 5 cm)	Brazil, Colombia, Guyana, Venezuela		ants, termites, tiny beetles, crickets, other small insects, spiders
Striped poison dart frog	*Phyllobates lugubris*	0.8 to 0.9 in (2 to 2.3 cm)	Costa Rica, Nicaragua, Panama		ants, mites, beetles
Black-legged poison dart frog	*Phyllobates bicolor*	1.2 to 1.6 in (3.2 to 4.2 cm)	Colombia		ants, mites, beetles
Oriental fire-bellied toad	*Bombina orientalis*	1.4 to 3.2 in (3.5 to 8 cm)	China, Korea, Russia		terrestrial invertebrates: worms, mollusks, insects
Midwife toad	*Alytes obstetricans*	about 2.2 in (5.5 cm)	Europe		invertebrates
Painted frog	*Discoglossus pictus*	1.2 to 1.6 in (3.2 to 4.1 cm)	Algeria, Italy, Malta, Tunisia, France, Spain		invertebrates
Shovel-nosed frog	*Hemisus marmoratus*	0.8 to 1.9 in (2.2 to 4.9 cm)	Africa		ants and termites
Spotted snout-burrower	*Hemisus guttatus*	2 to 3 in (5 to 8 cm)	South Africa		termites and earthworms
Mountain chorus frog	*Pseudacris brachyphona*	1 to 1.3 in (2.6 to 3.4 cm)	eastern United States		insects, including beetles, bugs, ants; spiders
Cuban tree frog	*Osteopilus septentrionalis*	1 to 4.7 in (2.5 to 12 cm)	Cuba and the Caribbean islands		cockroaches and moths
Gray tree frog	*Dryophytes versicolor*	1.1 to 2 in (2.8 to 5 cm)	Canada and United States		insects and their larvae
Green tree frog	*Dryophytes cinereus*	1.3 to 2.5 in (3.2 to 6.4 cm)	United States		flies, mosquitoes, other small insects
Hourglass tree frog	*Dendropsophus ebraccatus*	1.1 to 1.4 in (2.8 to 3.7 cm)	Mexico, Central America, Colombia, Ecuador		probably small arthropods
Barking tree frog	*Dryophytes gratiosus*	2 to 2.8 in (5.1 to 7 cm)	eastern United States		arboreal insects; crickets
Yucatán shovel-headed tree frog	*Triprion petasatus*	1.8 to 2.9 in (4.8 to 7.5 cm)	Belize, Guatemala, Honduras, Mexico		variety of small arthropods and small frogs
Pine Barrens tree frog	*Hyla andersonii*	1.1 to 1.8 in (3 to 4.7 cm)	United States		small invertebrates, including flies, crickets, small slugs, snails, beetles, butterflies, moths
Chinese tree frog	*Hyla chinensis*	0.9 to 1.2 in (2.5 to 3.3 cm)	China and Taiwan		variety of arthropods
Japanese tree frog	*Dryophytes japonicus*	up to 1.7 in (4.5 cm)	China, Japan, Korea, Mongolia, Russia		variety of arthropods
Mountain tree frog	*Dryophytes eximius*	0.7 to 2.2 in (1.9 to 5.6 cm)	Mexico		insects, shrubs, dense grasses
Squirrel tree frog	*Dryophytes squirellus*	0.9 to 1.4 in (2.3 to 3.7 cm)	United States and Bahamas		insects and other small prey
Lemur leaf frog	*Agalychnis lemur*	up to 1.9 in (5 cm)	Colombia, Costa Rica, Panama		probably a variety of arthropods
Sardinian tree frog	*Hyla sarda*	1.5 in (3.8 cm)	France and Italy		probably a variety of arthropods
Lemon yellow tree frog	*Hyla savignyi*	1.1 to 1.8 in (3 to 4.7 cm)	western Asia and Arabian Peninsula		probably a variety of arthropods
Pacific tree frog	*Pseudacris regilla*	1 to 1.9 in (2.5 to 4.8 cm)	western Canada; United States; Mexico		probably a variety of arthropods
Mountain chorus frog	*Pseudacris brachyphona*	1 to 1.3 in (2.6 to 3.4 cm)	Appalachian Mountains		mostly insects, especially beetles, ants; also spiders, earthworms

COMMON NAME	SCIENTIFIC NAME	SIZE	RANGE	HABITAT	DIET
Brimley's chorus frog	*Pseudacris brimleyi*	up to 1.4 in (3.5 cm)	East Coast of United States		probably a variety of arthropods
Spotted chorus frog	*Pseudacris clarkii*	1.2 in (3 cm)	southern United States; Mexico		probably a variety of arthropods
Strecker's chorus frog	*Pseudacris streckeri*	up to 1.9 in (4.8 cm)	southern United States		probably a variety of arthropods
Green and golden bell frog	*Litoria aurea*	up to 4.3 in (10.8 cm)	Australia and New Zealand		insects and other frogs
Booroolong frog	*Litoria booroolongensis*	1.7 in (4.5 cm)	Australia		probably a variety of arthropods
Yellow-spotted tree frog	*Litoria castanea*	up to 3.1 in (8 cm)	Australia		probably a variety of arthropods
Dainty green tree frog	*Litoria gracilenta*	1.7 in (4.5 cm)	Australia		probably a variety of arthropods
Leaf green tree frog	*Litoria phyllochroa*	1.5 in (4 cm)	Australia		probably a variety of arthropods
Marsupial frog	*Assa darlingtoni*	up to 0.8 in (2 cm)	Australia		arthropods
Horned marsupial frog	*Gastrotheca cornuta*	up to 3 in (7.7 cm)	Colombia, Costa Rica, Ecuador, Panama		probably a variety of arthropods
Cinnamon-bellied reed frog	*Hyperolius cinnamomeoventris*	up to 1.1 in (2.8 cm)	Africa		probably mostly insects
Delicate spiny reed frog	*Afrixalus delicatus*	up to 1 in (2.5 cm)	Africa		probably mostly insects
Knysna spiny reed frog	*Afrixalus knysnae*	1 in (2.5 cm)	South Africa		probably mostly insects
Brown tree frog	*Litoria ewingii*	1.1 to 1.5 in (3 to 5 cm)	Australia and New Zealand		probably mostly insects
Hamilton's frog	*Leiopelma hamiltoni*	up to 1.9 in (4.9 cm)	New Zealand		probably mostly insects
Helmeted water toad	*Caudiverbera caudiverbera*	up to 12.8 in (32 cm)	Chile and Argentina		aquatic insect larvae, fish, frogs, small birds, mammals
Chaco horned frog	*Chacophrys pierottii*	2.1 in (5.5 cm)	central South America		probably small arthropods
Monte Iberia dwarf frog	*Eleutherodactylus iberia*	0.4 in (1 cm)	Cuba		probably small arthropods
Mexican white-lipped frog	*Leptodactylus fragilis*	about 1.9 in (5 cm)	Central and South America		mostly arthropods
Mountain chicken frog	*Leptodactylus fallax*	up to 8.2 in (21 cm)	Dominica and Montserrat		probably small arthropods
Labyrinth frog	*Leptodactylus labyrinthicus*	up to 7.1 in (18 cm)	central South America		probably small arthropods
Moustached frog	*Leptodactylus mystacinus*	up to 2.6 in (6.7 cm)	South America		probably small arthropods
Emerald forest frog	*Hylorina sylvatica*	up to 2.6 in (6.6 cm)	Argentina and Chile		small arthropods
Lake Titicaca frog	*Telmatobius culeus*	up to 5.3 in (13.7 cm)	Bolivia and Peru		amphipods, snails, aquatic insects, tadpoles, fish
Asian spadefoot frog	*Megophrys montana*	4.4 in (11.1 cm)	Indonesia		relatively large prey, including cockroaches, scorpions, snails
Long-nosed horned frog	*Megophrys nasuta*	up to 5 in (12.7 cm)	Southeast Asia		arachnids, nestling rodents, lizards, other frogs
Eastern narrow-mouthed toad	*Gastrophryne carolinensis*	up to 1.5 in (3.8 cm)	southeastern coast of United States		small invertebrates, especially ants, beetles, termites
Ornate narrow-mouthed frog	*Microhyla ornata*	up to 1 in (2.5 cm)	southern Asia		small invertebrates
Malaysian painted frog	*Kaloula pulchra*	up to 3 in (7.5 cm)	southern Asia		ants and other small insects
Turtle frog	*Myobatrachus gouldii*	1.7 in (4.5 cm)	Australia		termites
Eastern banjo frog	*Limnodynastes dumerilii*	2 to 3.2 in (5.2 to 8.3 cm)	Australia		probably arthropods
Crucifix frog	*Notaden bennettii*	2.1 in (5.5 cm)	Australia		probably arthropods
Orange-bellied frog	*Geocrinia vitellina*	1 in (2.5 cm)	Australia		probably small arthropods
White-bellied frog	*Geocrinia alba*	1 in (2.5 cm)	Australia		probably small arthropods
Northern Corroboree frog	*Pseudophryne pengilleyi*	1 to 1.2 in (2.5 to 3 cm)	Australia		adults consume mainly ants
Southern Corroboree frog	*Pseudophryne corroboree*	1 to 1.2 in (2.5 to 3 cm)	Australia		mainly small invertebrates such as ants
Desert froglet	*Crinia deserticola*	0.7 in (1.8 cm)	Australia		probably small arthropods
Sunset frog	*Spicospina flammocaerulea*	1.3 in (3.5 cm)	Australia		probably small arthropods
Marbled frog	*Limnodynastes convexiusculus*	2.1 in (5.5 cm)	Australia, Indonesia, Papua New Guinea		probably arthropods
Western bullfrog	*Limnodynastes dorsalis*	2.7 in (7 cm)	Australia		probably arthropods
Giant bullfrog	*Limnodynastes interioris*	3.5 in (9 cm)	Australia		probably arthropods
Spotted grass frog	*Limnodynastes tasmaniensis*	1.7 in (4.5 cm)	Australia		probably arthropods

COMMON NAME	SCIENTIFIC NAME	SIZE	RANGE	HABITAT	DIET
Red rain frog	Scaphiophryne gottlebei	up to 1.5 in (4 cm)	Madagascar	(icons)	insects
Large toadlet	Pseudophryne major	up to 1.5 in (4 cm)	Australia	(icons)	probably small arthropods
Eastern spadefoot toad	Scaphiopus holbrookii	1.75 to 3 in (4.5 to 7.8 cm)	eastern United States	(icons)	worms and various arthropods
Northern spadefoot toad	Notaden melanoscaphus	up to 1.9 in (4.9 cm)	Australia	(icons)	small arthropods
Common spadefoot toad	Neobatrachus sudelli	1.6 In (4 cm)	Australia	(icons)	probably arthropods
Parsley frog	Pelodytes punctatus	1.6 in (4 cm)	France, Italy, Portugal, Spain	(icons)	small invertebrates, including crickets and flies
Surinam toad	Pipa pipa	up to 0.7 in (1.7 cm)	northern South America	(icons)	worms, insects, crustaceans, small fish
Pickerel frog	Lithobates palustris	1.7 to 3 in (4.3 to 7.8 cm)	western Canada; United States	(icons)	small insects and other invertebrates
Green frog	Lithobates clamitans	3 to 4.9 in (7.5 to 12.5 cm)	eastern North America	(icons)	insects and other invertebrates, including slugs, spiders, flies, snails, crayfish, moths
Goliath frog	Conraua goliath	6.7 to 12.6 in (17 to 32 cm)	Africa	(icons)	insects, crustaceans, fish, mollusks, small mammals, amphibians
Northern red-legged frog	Rana aurora	2 to 5.3 in (5 to 13.3 cm)	Canada and United States	(icons)	probably invertebrates
Common frog	Rana temporaria	2.4 to 3.7 in (6 to 9.5 cm)	Europe	(icons)	insects and their larvae, snails, worms, wood lice, spiders
Sahara frog	Pelophylax saharicus	up to 4.1 in (10.5 cm)	northern Africa	(icons)	probably mainly invertebrates
Amami tip-nosed frog	Odorrana amamiensis	up to 4 in (10.1 cm)	Japan	(icons)	probably mainly invertebrates
Columbia spotted frog	Rana luteiventris	4 in (10 cm)	western Canada and western United States	(icons)	probably mainly invertebrates
Crawfish frog	Rana areolata	up to 4.6 in (11.8 cm)	central United States	(icons)	insects, small crayfish, reptiles, amphibians
Northern leopard frog	Lithobates pipiens	2 to 4.4 in (5 to 11.1 cm)	Central and North America	(icons)	terrestrial invertebrates: spiders, insects and their larvae, earthworms, slugs, snails
Wood frog	Lithobates sylvatica	1.3 to 3 in (3.5 to 7.6 cm)	Canada and United States	(icons)	insects and other small invertebrates: spiders, beetles, bugs, slugs, snails
Mountain yellow-legged frog	Rana muscosa	1.5 to 3.5 in (4 to 8.9 cm)	western United States	(icons)	aquatic and terrestrial invertebrates: beetles, ants, bees, wasps, flies, dragonflies
Florida bog frog	Lithobates okaloosae	up to 1.8 in (4.8 cm)	northern Florida (U.S.A.)	(icons)	probably mostly small invertebrates
African bullfrog	Pyxicephalus adspersus	up to 9.6 in (24.5 cm)	Africa	(icons)	vertebrates: mammals, birds, snakes, lizards, frogs
Larut torrent frog	Amolops larutensis	up to 2.1 in (5.4 cm)	southern Asia	(icons)	terrestrial and aquatic animals, especially insects
Assam sucker frog	Amolops formosus	up to 3.3 in (8.5 cm)	Asia	(icons)	unconfirmed
Crowned or Victoria forest frog	Astylosternus diadematus	up to 2.7 in (7 cm)	Africa	(icons)	small forest-floor arthropods
Kinugasa flying frog	Zhangixalus arboreus	up to 3.2 in (8.2 cm)	Japan	(icons)	insects
Reinwardt's flying frog	Rhacophorus reinwardtii	up to 3.1 in (7.9 cm)	southern Asia	(icons)	canopy insects
Wallace's flying frog	Rhacophorus nigropalmatus	up to 4 in (10 cm)	southern Asia	(icons)	mainly insects
Golden mantella	Mantella aurantiaca	0.7 to 1 in (2 to 2.6 cm)	Madagascar	(icons)	insectivorous, especially termites, fruit flies, ants
Darwin's frog	Rhinoderma darwinii	up to 1.2 in (3.1 cm)	Argentina and Chile	(icons)	mainly insects and other small invertebrates
Mexican burrowing toad	Rhinophrynus dorsalis	1.9 to 2.7 in (5 to 7 cm)	Central America	(icons)	termites
Gardiner's Seychelles frog	Sechellophryne gardineri	up to 0.4 in (1.1 cm)	Seychelles	(icons)	small invertebrates
Hairy frog	Trichobatrachus robustus	about 4.3 in (11 cm)	Africa	(icons)	insects and other arthropods
Tanzanian screeching frog	Arthroleptis tanneri	up to 2.2 in (5.5 cm)	United Republic of Tanzania	(icons)	forest-floor arthropods, including small spiders
Coastal tailed frog	Ascaphus truei	1 to 2 in (2.5 to 5 cm)	western Canada; United States	(icons)	terrestrial and aquatic insects; other invertebrates
Rocky Mountain tailed frog	Ascaphus montanus	1.2 to 2 in (3 to 5 cm)	Canada and United States	(icons)	terrestrial and aquatic insects
Pumpkin toadlet	Brachycephalus ephippium	0.5 to 0.7 in (1.25 to 2 cm)	Brazil	(icons)	small arthropods, especially springtails; also insect larvae, mites

FISH

Legend:
- ● ALERT
- ● IN TROUBLE
- ● STABLE
- ● UNDER STUDY
- ● NOT LISTED
- ● DOMESTICATED

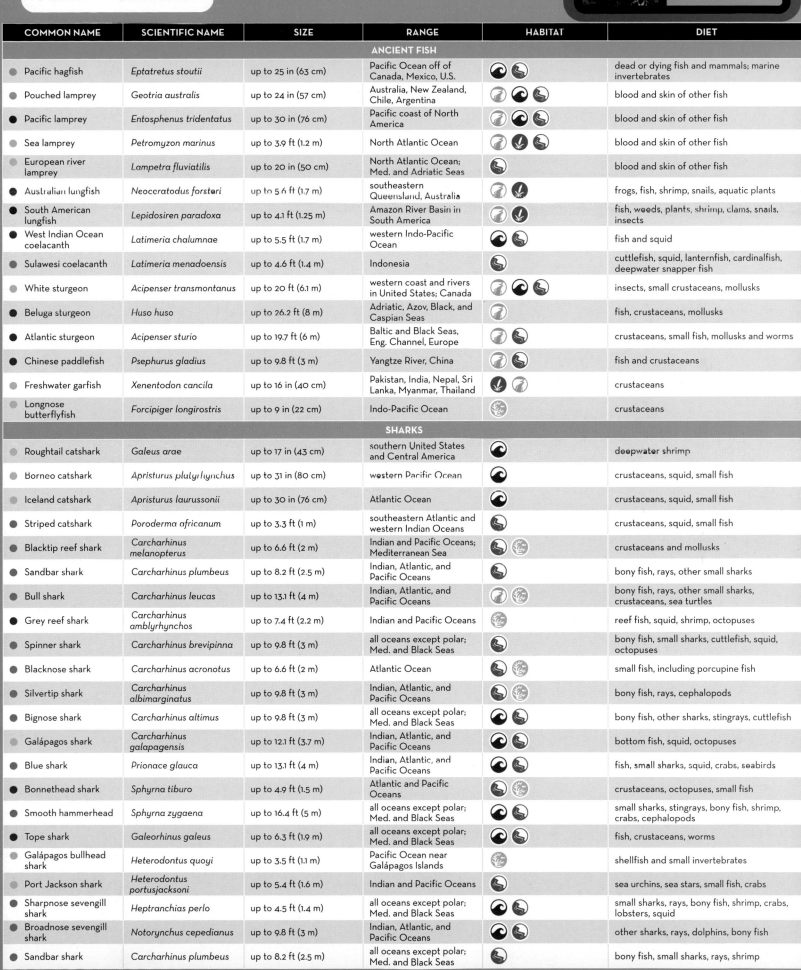

COMMON NAME	SCIENTIFIC NAME	SIZE	RANGE	HABITAT	DIET
ANCIENT FISH					
Pacific hagfish	*Eptatretus stoutii*	up to 25 in (63 cm)	Pacific Ocean off of Canada, Mexico, U.S.		dead or dying fish and mammals; marine invertebrates
Pouched lamprey	*Geotria australis*	up to 24 in (57 cm)	Australia, New Zealand, Chile, Argentina		blood and skin of other fish
Pacific lamprey	*Entosphenus tridentatus*	up to 30 in (76 cm)	Pacific coast of North America		blood and skin of other fish
Sea lamprey	*Petromyzon marinus*	up to 3.9 ft (1.2 m)	North Atlantic Ocean		blood and skin of other fish
European river lamprey	*Lampetra fluviatilis*	up to 20 in (50 cm)	North Atlantic Ocean; Med. and Adriatic Seas		blood and skin of other fish
Australian lungfish	*Neoceratodus forsteri*	up to 5.6 ft (1.7 m)	southeastern Queensland, Australia		frogs, fish, shrimp, snails, aquatic plants
South American lungfish	*Lepidosiren paradoxa*	up to 4.1 ft (1.25 m)	Amazon River Basin in South America		fish, weeds, plants, shrimp, clams, snails, insects
West Indian Ocean coelacanth	*Latimeria chalumnae*	up to 5.5 ft (1.7 m)	western Indo-Pacific Ocean		fish and squid
Sulawesi coelacanth	*Latimeria menadoensis*	up to 4.6 ft (1.4 m)	Indonesia		cuttlefish, squid, lanternfish, cardinalfish, deepwater snapper fish
White sturgeon	*Acipenser transmontanus*	up to 20 ft (6.1 m)	western coast and rivers in United States; Canada		insects, small crustaceans, mollusks
Beluga sturgeon	*Huso huso*	up to 26.2 ft (8 m)	Adriatic, Azov, Black, and Caspian Seas		fish, crustaceans, mollusks
Atlantic sturgeon	*Acipenser sturio*	up to 19.7 ft (6 m)	Baltic and Black Seas, Eng. Channel, Europe		crustaceans, small fish, mollusks and worms
Chinese paddlefish	*Psephurus gladius*	up to 9.8 ft (3 m)	Yangtze River, China		fish and crustaceans
Freshwater garfish	*Xenentodon cancila*	up to 16 in (40 cm)	Pakistan, India, Nepal, Sri Lanka, Myanmar, Thailand		crustaceans
Longnose butterflyfish	*Forcipiger longirostris*	up to 9 in (22 cm)	Indo-Pacific Ocean		crustaceans
SHARKS					
Roughtail catshark	*Galeus arae*	up to 17 in (43 cm)	southern United States and Central America		deepwater shrimp
Borneo catshark	*Apristurus platyrhynchus*	up to 31 in (80 cm)	western Pacific Ocean		crustaceans, squid, small fish
Iceland catshark	*Apristurus laurussonii*	up to 30 in (76 cm)	Atlantic Ocean		crustaceans, squid, small fish
Striped catshark	*Poroderma africanum*	up to 3.3 ft (1 m)	southeastern Atlantic and western Indian Oceans		crustaceans, squid, small fish
Blacktip reef shark	*Carcharhinus melanopterus*	up to 6.6 ft (2 m)	Indian and Pacific Oceans; Mediterranean Sea		crustaceans and mollusks
Sandbar shark	*Carcharhinus plumbeus*	up to 8.2 ft (2.5 m)	Indian, Atlantic, and Pacific Oceans		bony fish, rays, other small sharks
Bull shark	*Carcharhinus leucas*	up to 13.1 ft (4 m)	Indian, Atlantic, and Pacific Oceans		bony fish, rays, other small sharks, crustaceans, sea turtles
Grey reef shark	*Carcharhinus amblyrhynchos*	up to 7.4 ft (2.2 m)	Indian and Pacific Oceans		reef fish, squid, shrimp, octopuses
Spinner shark	*Carcharhinus brevipinna*	up to 9.8 ft (3 m)	all oceans except polar; Med. and Black Seas		bony fish, small sharks, cuttlefish, squid, octopuses
Blacknose shark	*Carcharhinus acronotus*	up to 6.6 ft (2 m)	Atlantic Ocean		small fish, including porcupine fish
Silvertip shark	*Carcharhinus albimarginatus*	up to 9.8 ft (3 m)	Indian, Atlantic, and Pacific Oceans		bony fish, rays, cephalopods
Bignose shark	*Carcharhinus altimus*	up to 9.8 ft (3 m)	all oceans except polar; Med. and Black Seas		bony fish, other sharks, stingrays, cuttlefish
Galápagos shark	*Carcharhinus galapagensis*	up to 12.1 ft (3.7 m)	Indian, Atlantic, and Pacific Oceans		bottom fish, squid, octopuses
Blue shark	*Prionace glauca*	up to 13.1 ft (4 m)	Indian, Atlantic, and Pacific Oceans		fish, small sharks, squid, crabs, seabirds
Bonnethead shark	*Sphyrna tiburo*	up to 4.9 ft (1.5 m)	Atlantic and Pacific Oceans		crustaceans, octopuses, small fish
Smooth hammerhead	*Sphyrna zygaena*	up to 16.4 ft (5 m)	all oceans except polar; Med. and Black Seas		small sharks, stingrays, bony fish, shrimp, crabs, cephalopods
Tope shark	*Galeorhinus galeus*	up to 6.3 ft (1.9 m)	all oceans except polar; Med. and Black Seas		fish, crustaceans, worms
Galápagos bullhead shark	*Heterodontus quoyi*	up to 3.5 ft (1.1 m)	Pacific Ocean near Galápagos Islands		shellfish and small invertebrates
Port Jackson shark	*Heterodontus portusjacksoni*	up to 5.4 ft (1.6 m)	Indian and Pacific Oceans		sea urchins, sea stars, small fish, crabs
Sharpnose sevengill shark	*Heptranchias perlo*	up to 4.5 ft (1.4 m)	all oceans except polar; Med. and Black Seas		small sharks, rays, bony fish, shrimp, crabs, lobsters, squid
Broadnose sevengill shark	*Notorynchus cepedianus*	up to 9.8 ft (3 m)	Indian, Atlantic, and Pacific Oceans		other sharks, rays, dolphins, bony fish
Sandbar shark	*Carcharhinus plumbeus*	up to 8.2 ft (2.5 m)	all oceans except polar; Med. and Black Seas		bony fish, small sharks, rays, shrimp

FISH

COMMON NAME	SCIENTIFIC NAME	SIZE	RANGE	HABITAT	DIET
Crocodile shark	Pseudocarcharias kamoharai	up to 3.6 ft (1.1 m)	Indian, Atlantic, and Pacific Oceans		bony fish, squid, shrimp
Shortfin mako shark	Isurus oxyrinchus	up to 14.6 ft (4.4 m)	all oceans except polar; Med. and Black Seas		bony fish, other sharks, cephalopods
Thresher shark	Alopias vulpinus	up to 18.8 ft (5.7 m)	all oceans except polar; Med. and Black Seas		bony fish, squid, octopuses, crustaceans
Porbeagle shark	Lamna nasus	up to 11.5 ft (3.5 m)	all oceans; Mediterranean and Black Seas		small fish, other sharks, squid
Arabian carpetshark	Chiloscyllium arabicum	up to 31 in (80 cm)	western Indian Ocean		squid, crustaceans, eels
Zebra shark	Stegostoma fasciatum	up to 11.6 ft (3.5 m)	Indian and Pacific Oceans		crustaceans and sea snakes
Whitespotted bambooshark	Chiloscyllium plagiosum	up to 37 in (95 cm)	Indian and Pacific Oceans		bony fish and crustaceans
Common sawshark	Pristiophorus cirratus	up to 4.5 ft (1.4 m)	eastern Indian and south-western Pacific Oceans		small fish and crustaceans
Longnose velvet dogfish	Centroscymnus crepidater	up to 4.3 ft (1.3 m)	Atlantic, Indian, and Pacific Oceans		fish and cephalopods
Angular roughshark	Oxynotus centrina	up to 4.9 ft (1.5 m)	Atlantic Ocean; Mediterranean and Black Seas		worms
Spined pygmy shark	Squaliolus laticaudus	up to 8.7 in (22 cm)	Atlantic, Indian, and Pacific Oceans		squid and lanternfish
Bramble shark	Echinorhinus brucus	up to 6.6 ft (2 m)	Atlantic, Indian, and Pacific Oceans		smaller sharks, bony fish, crabs
Prickly shark	Echinorhinus cookei	up to 13.1 ft (4 m)	Indian and Pacific Oceans		small sharks, fish, squid
Atlantic angel shark	Squatina dumeril	up to 4.9 ft (1.5 m)	Atlantic Ocean		fish and crustaceans
Pacific angel shark	Squatina californica	up to 5 ft (1.5 m)	Pacific Ocean		fish and squid
Blackfin ghostshark	Hydrolagus lemures	up to 35 in (88 cm)	Indian and Pacific Oceans		small fish

SKATES AND RAYS

COMMON NAME	SCIENTIFIC NAME	SIZE	RANGE	HABITAT	DIET
Long-tailed butterfly ray	Gymnura poecilura	up to 8.2 ft (2.5 m)	Indian and Pacific Oceans		fish, mollusks, crustaceans
Japanese butterfly ray	Gymnura japonica	up to 3.3 ft (1 m)	Pacific Ocean		fish
Spiny butterfly ray	Gymnura altavela	up to 13.1 ft (4 m)	Atlantic Ocean; Mediterranean and Black Seas		fish, crustaceans, mollusks, plankton
Australian butterfly ray	Gymnura australis	up to 37 in (94 cm)	Indian and Pacific Oceans		fish
Smooth butterfly ray	Gymnura micrura	up to 4.5 ft (1.4 m)	Atlantic Ocean		fish and shrimp
Atlantic devil ray	Mobula hypostoma	up to 3.9 ft (1.2 m)	coasts of the western Atlantic Ocean		small fish and crustaceans
Deepwater stingray	Plesiobatis daviesi	up to 8.9 ft (2.7 m)	Atlantic Ocean		fish, crabs, lobsters, eels, shrimp
Largetooth sawfish	Pristis pristis	up to 23 ft (7 m)	Indian and Pacific Oceans		sea stars, clams, sea anemones, small fish
Blue-spotted fantail ray	Taeniura lymma	up to 14 in (35 cm)	Indian and Pacific Oceans		mollusks, shrimp, crabs
Ocellate river stingray	Potamotrygon motoro	up to 20 in (50 cm)	South America		mollusks, crustaceans, fish
Porcupine river stingray	Potamotrygon histrix	up to 16 in (40 cm)	Argentina, Brazil, Paraguay		invertebrates
Melbourne skate	Spiniraja whitleyi	up to 6.6 ft (2 m)	coasts of southern Australia; Tasmania		crustaceans
Sydney skate	Dipturus australis	up to 22 in (55 cm)	Indian and Pacific Oceans		crustaceans
Thornback skate	Raja clavata	up to 4.6 ft (1.4 m)	southwest Pacific Ocean		crustaceans
California skate	Raja inornata	up to 30 in (76 cm)	Atlantic Ocean; Mediterranean and Black Seas		worms and crustaceans
Longnose skate	Raja rhina	up to 5.9 ft (1.8 m)	Pacific Ocean		worms and crustaceans
African ray	Raja africana	up to 31 in (80 cm)	eastern Atlantic and south-western Mediterranean		crustaceans and bony fish
Spotted skate	Raja montagui	up to 33 in (84 cm)	Atlantic Ocean; Mediterranean and Black Seas		crustaceans
Speckled skate	Raja polystigma	up to 24 in (60 cm)	Mediterranean and Black Seas		crustaceans and bony fish
Big skate	Raja binoculata	up to 8 ft (2.4 m)	northeastern and eastern-central Pacific Ocean		crustaceans and bony fish
Starry skate	Raja asterias	up to 28 in (70 cm)	Mediterranean and Black Seas		crustaceans
Blonde ray	Raja brachyura	up to 4.1 ft (1.2 m)	Atlantic Ocean; Mediterranean and Black Seas		crustaceans
Atlantic guitarfish	Rhinobatos lentiginosus	up to 30 in (76 cm)	Atlantic Ocean		mollusks and crustaceans
Marbled electric ray	Torpedo marmorata	up to 3.3 ft (1 m)	Atlantic Ocean; Mediterranean and Black Seas		small fish
Undulate skate	Raja undulata	up to 3.3 ft (1 m)	Atlantic Ocean; Mediterranean and Black Seas		crustaceans and worms

COMMON NAME	SCIENTIFIC NAME	SIZE	RANGE	HABITAT	DIET
EELS					
● Abyssal cutthroat eel	*Meadia abyssalis*	up to 29 in (73 cm)	Indo-Pacific Ocean		small fish and crustaceans
● Gray cutthroat eel	*Synaphobranchus affinis*	up to 5.2 ft (1.6 m)	Atlantic, Indian, and Pacific Oceans		invertebrates and fish
● Brown garden eel	*Heteroconger longissimus*	up to 20 in (51 cm)	eastern Atlantic Ocean		plankton
● Taiwanese moray eel	*Gymnothorax taiwanensis*	up to 21 in (52 cm)	northwest Pacific: Taiwan		crustaceans and fish
● Little conger eel	*Gnathophis habenatus*	up to 17 in (43 cm)	Indo-Pacific Ocean		crustaceans and fish
● Swollen-headed conger eel	*Bassanago bulbiceps*	up to 27 in (69 cm)	southwest Pacific Ocean		crustaceans and fish
● White ribbon eel	*Pseudechidna brummeri*	up to 3.4 ft (1 m)	Indo-Pacific Ocean		crustaceans and fish
● Death-banded snake-eel	*Ophichthus frontalis*	up to 34 in (86 cm)	Pacific Ocean		crustaceans and fish
● European eel	*Anguilla anguilla*	up to 4.4 ft (1.3 m)	Europe		invertebrates
● Java spaghetti eel	*Moringua javanica*	up to 3.9 ft (1.2 m)	Indo-Pacific Ocean		fish and crustaceans
● Rusty spaghetti eel	*Moringua ferruginea*	up to 4.6 ft (1.4 m)	Indo-Pacific Ocean		fish and crustaceans
● Slender snipe eel	*Nemichthys scolopaceus*	up to 4.3 ft (1.3 m)	all oceans except polar		crustaceans
● Avocet snipe eel	*Avocettina infans*	up to 31 in (80 cm)	all oceans except polar		crustaceans
● Gulper eel	*Saccopharynx ampullaceus*	up to 5.2 ft (1.6 m)	eastern Atlantic Ocean		fish
● Clown knifefish	*Chitala chitala*	up to 4 ft (1.2 m)	South Asia		aquatic insects, mollusks, fish
● Glass knifefish	*Eigenmannia virescens*	up to 17 in (44 cm)	South America		insects
● Lesser spiny eel	*Macrognathus aculeatus*	up to 15 in (38 cm)	Asia		small fish
● Malabar spiny eel	*Macrognathus guentheri*	up to 12 in (30 cm)	India		small fish
● Asian swamp eel	*Monopterus albus*	up to 3.3 ft (1 m)	South Asia and United States		fish and crustaceans
● Marbled swamp eel	*Synbranchus marmoratus*	up to 4.9 ft (1.5 m)	Central and South America		fish and invertebrates
COD AND RELATIVES					
● Pacific cod	*Gadus macrocephalus*	up to 3.9 ft (1.2 m)	North Pacific Ocean		fish, octopuses, crustaceans
● Offshore silver hake	*Merluccius albidus*	up to 28 in (70 cm)	western-central Atlantic Ocean		fish, crustaceans, squid
DEEP-SEA FISH					
● Kroyer's deep-sea angler fish	*Ceratias holboelli*	30 in (77 cm)	all oceans except polar		fish and crustaceans
● Soft leafvent angler	*Haplophryne mollis*	5.9 in (15 cm)	tropical and subtropical parts of all oceans		fish and crustaceans
● Short dragonfish	*Eurypegasus draconis*	up to 3.9 ft (1.2 m)	Australia, Oceania, parts of Asia and Africa		insects, worms, crustaceans
TROUT AND SALMON					
● Pink salmon	*Oncorhynchus gorbuscha*	up to 30 in (76 cm)	Pacific and Arctic Oceans		insects
● Masu salmon	*Oncorhynchus masou masou*	up to 31 in (79 cm)	northwestern Pacific Ocean		insects, fish, crustaceans
● Coho salmon	*Oncorhynchus kisutch*	up to 3.5 ft (1.1 m)	North Pacific Ocean		fish, jellyfish, squid
● Chinook salmon	*Oncorhynchus tshawytscha*	up to 4.9 ft (1.5 m)	Arctic and northwest to northeast Pacific Oceans		insects and crustaceans
● Chum salmon	*Oncorhynchus keta*	up to 3.3 ft (1 m)	North Pacific Ocean and Bering Sea		crustaceans, fish, squid
● Brown trout	*Salmo trutta trutta*	up to 4.6 ft (1.4 m)	Europe and Asia		insects, mollusks, crustaceans, and small fish
● Bull trout	*Salvelinus confluentus*	up to 3.4 ft (1 m)	Canada and United States		invertebrates and small fish
● Golden trout	*Oncorhynchus aguabonita*	up to 28 in (71 cm)	North America		insects and small crustaceans
● Apache trout	*Oncorhynchus apache*	up to 23 in (58 cm)	United States		insects
CATFISH, PIRANHAS, AND RELATIVES					
● Black tetra	*Gymnocorymbus ternetzi*	up to 3.1 in (8 cm)	South America		worms, crustaceans, plants
● Glowlight tetra	*Hemigrammus erythrozonus*	up to 1.2 in (3 cm)	South America: Essequibo River		worms, crustaceans, plants
● African moon tetra	*Bathyaethiops caudomaculatus*	up to 3.1 in (8 cm)	Africa		worms, crustaceans, plants
● Copper tetra	*Hasemania melanura*	up to 1.6 in (4 cm)	South America: Iguaçu River Basin		worms, crustaceans, plants
● Johnny darter	*Etheostoma nigrum*	up to 2.8 in (7 cm)	North America		insects and larvae

COMMON NAME	SCIENTIFIC NAME	SIZE	RANGE	HABITAT	DIET
Gulf darter	*Etheostoma swaini*	up to 3.1 in (8 cm)	North America		insects and larvae
Least darter	*Etheostoma microperca*	up to 1.6 in (4 cm)	North America		larvae and microcrustaceans
Spotted hatchetfish	*Gasteropelecus maculatus*	up to 2 in (5 cm)	Central and South America		crustaceans, larvae, insects
Marbled hatchetfish	*Carnegiella strigata*	up to 1.6 in (4 cm)	South America		crustaceans and insects
Torrent sucker	*Thoburnia rhothoeca*	up to 7.1 in (18 cm)	North America		plants and larvae
Desert sucker	*Catostomus clarkii*	up to 13 in (33 cm)	North America		diatoms, detritus, invertebrates
Longnose sucker	*Catostomus catostomus*	up to 25 in (64 cm)	North America		invertebrates
Mottled loach	*Paracanthocobitis botia*	up to 5.9 in (15 cm)	South Asia		invertebrates
Jonklaas's loach	*Lepidocephalichthys jonklaasi*	up to 2.4 in (6 cm)	Sri Lanka		invertebrates
Almorha loach	*Botia almorhae*	up to 5.9 in (15 cm)	India		invertebrates
Crucian carp	*Carassius carassius*	up to 25 in (64 cm)	Europe		plankton, plants, invertebrates
Bighead carp	*Hypophthalmichthys nobilis*	up to 4.8 ft (1.5 m)	China		zooplankton and algae
Hoven's carp	*Leptobarbus hoevenii*	up to 3.3 ft (1 m)	Asia		plankton, plants, invertebrates
Sailfin molly	*Poecilia latipinna*	up to 5.9 in (15 cm)	North America		algae and plant material
Blackstripe topminnow	*Fundulus notatus*	up to 3.1 in (8 cm)	Canada and midwestern United States		insects and larvae
Golden topminnow	*Fundulus chrysotus*	up to 3.5 in (9 cm)	North American Coastal Plain		insects and larvae
Mummichog	*Fundulus heteroclitus*	up to 5.9 in (15 cm)	western Atlantic Ocean		phytoplankton, crustaceans, larvae
Salt Creek pupfish	*Cyprinodon salinus*	up to 3.1 in (8 cm)	California (U.S.A.)		algae and small snails
Grass carp	*Ctenopharyngodon idella*	up to 4.9 ft (1.5 m)	Asia		aquatic plants and insects
Green swordtail	*Xiphophorus hellerii*	up to 6.3 in (16 cm)	Mexico and Central America		insects, crustaceans, worms
Guppy	*Poecilia reticulata*	up to 2.4 in (6 cm)	South America		zooplankton and insects
Foureyes	*Anableps microlepis*	up to 13 in (32 cm)	Central and South America		insects
Slender walking catfish	*Clarias nieuhofii*	up to 20 in (50 cm)	Southeast Asia		insects and crustaceans
Philippine catfish	*Clarias batrachus*	up to 18.5 in (47 cm)	Southeast Asia		insects, fish, crustaceans
Striped eel catfish	*Plotosus lineatus*	up to 13 in (32 cm)	Indo-Pacific Ocean		crustaceans, mollusks, fish
African glass catfish	*Pareutropius debauwi*	up to 5 in (13 cm)	Central Africa		crustaceans, mollusks, worms, fish, insects
Giant river catfish	*Sperata seenghala*	up to 4.9 ft (1.5 m)	Bangladesh, India, Nepal		fish
African catfish	*Clarias gariepinus*	up to 5.6 ft (1.7 m)	Africa		insects, crustaceans, other invertebrates
PERCH AND RELATIVES					
Nile tilapia	*Oreochromis niloticus*	up to 24 in (60 cm)	Africa		phytoplankton and algae
Guinean tilapia	*Coptodon discolor*	up to 9.1 in (23 cm)	West Africa		vegetation and invertebrates
Black drum	*Pogonias cromis*	up to 5.6 ft (1.7 m)	western Atlantic Ocean		crustaceans and fish
Freshwater drum	*Aplodinotus grunniens*	up to 37.4 in (95 cm)	North and Central America		aquatic insects and fish
Striped snakehead	*Channa striata*	up to 3.3 ft (1 m)	South Asia		snakes, frogs, insects, crustaceans
Barca snakehead	*Channa barca*	up to 3.4 ft (1.1 m)	Australia		fish
Orange roughy	*Hoplostethus atlanticus*	up to 30 in (75 cm)	Australia		fish, shrimp, squid
Silver roughy	*Hoplostethus mediterraneus*	up to 17 in (42 cm)	Atlantic, Indian, and Pacific Oceans		fish, shrimp, squid
Gulf flashlightfish	*Phthanophaneron harveyi*	up to 3.1 in (8 cm)	eastern Pacific Ocean		crustaceans
Splitfin flashlight fish	*Anomalops katoptron*	up to 14 in (35 cm)	Pacific Ocean		zooplankton
White bass	*Morone chrysops*	up to 17.7 in (45 cm)	Canada and United States		aquatic invertebrates and fish
Yellow bass	*Morone mississippiensis*	up to 18.1 in (46 cm)	North America		fish
Bluespot mullet	*Moolgarda seheli*	up to 24 in (60 cm)	Indo-Pacific Ocean		algae and diatoms
Starry flounder	*Platichthys stellatus*	up to 36 in (91 cm)	North Pacific Ocean		crustaceans, worms, small fish

COMMON NAME	SCIENTIFIC NAME	SIZE	RANGE	HABITAT	DIET
European flounder	*Platichthys flesus*	up to 24 in (60 cm)	Atlantic; Arctic; Mediterranean and Black Seas		small fish and invertebrates
European plaice	*Pleuronectes platessa*	up to 3.3 ft (1 m)	Europe		mollusks
Atlantic halibut	*Hippoglossus hippoglossus*	up to 15.4 ft (4.7 m)	Atlantic Ocean		fish
Greenland halibut	*Reinhardtius hippoglossoides*	up to 4.3 ft (1.3 m)	circumglobal, Northern Hemisphere		crustaceans and fish
Dover sole	*Solea solea*	up to 28 in (70 cm)	eastern Atlantic Ocean		worms, fish, crustaceans
Spotted rainbowfish	*Glossolepis maculosus*	up to 2 in (5 cm)	Papua New Guinea		shrimp and worms
Red rainbowfish	*Glossolepis incisus*	up to 4.7 in (12 cm)	Indonesia		insects and crustaceans
Atlantic silverside	*Menidia menidia*	up to 5.9 in (15 cm)	western Atlantic Ocean		shrimp, squid, worms
Panama silverside	*Atherinella panamensis*	up to 4.3 in (11 cm)	Pacific Ocean		zooplankton and larvae
Common halfbeak	*Hyporhamphus unifasciatus*	up to 12 in (30 cm)	western Atlantic Ocean and Caribbean		algae and small animals
Ballyhoo halfbeak	*Hemiramphus brasiliensis*	up to 22 in (55 cm)	Atlantic Ocean and Caribbean		seagrasses and small animals
Jumping halfbeak	*Hemiramphus archipelagicus*	up to 13 in (34 cm)	Indo-Pacific Ocean		algae and small animals
Keeltail needlefish	*Platybelone argalus*	up to 20 in (50 cm)	Atlantic, Indian, and Pacific Oceans		small fish
Timucu	*Strongylura timucu*	up to 24 in (61 cm)	western Atlantic Ocean		small fish
Ninespine stickleback	*Pungitius pungitius*	up to 3.5 in (9 cm)	Europe and Asia		insects and larvae
Redmouth whalefish	*Rondeletia loricata*	up to 4.3 in (11 cm)	worldwide in tropical to temperate seas		crustaceans
TUNA, MARLIN, SWORDFISH, AND RELATIVES					
Albacore	*Thunnus alalunga*	up to 4.6 ft (1.4 m)	all oceans except polar; Med. and Black Seas		crustaceans, fish, squid
Atlantic bluefin tuna	*Thunnus thynnus*	up to 15 ft (4.6 m)	Atlantic Ocean; Mediterranean and Black Seas		crustaceans, fish, squid
Guachanche barracuda	*Sphyraena guachancho*	up to 6.6 ft (2 m)	Australia		fish and squid
Atlantic blue marlin	*Makaira nigricans*	up to 16.4 ft (5 m)	Atlantic; Pacific; Mediterranean and Black Seas		fish
Indo-Pacific blue marlin	*Makaira mazara*	up to 16.4 ft (5 m)	Indo-Pacific Ocean		squid, fish, crustaceans
Indo-Pacific sailfish	*Istiophorus platypterus*	up to 11.4 ft (3.5 m)	all oceans except polar; Med. and Black Seas		fish and crustaceans
SCORPIONFISH AND SCULPINS					
Orange filefish	*Aluterus schoepfii*	up to 23.6 in (60 cm)	western Atlantic Ocean		algae and seagrass
Titan triggerfish	*Balistoides viridescens*	up to 30 in (75 cm)	Indo-Pacific Ocean		crustaceans and mollusks
Ocean sunfish	*Mola mola*	up to 10.9 ft (3.3 m)	warm and temperate zones of all oceans		fish, jellyfish, zooplankton
Northern puffers	*Sphoeroides maculatus*	up to 14.2 in (36 cm)	western Atlantic Ocean		shellfish
White-spotted puffer	*Arothron hispidus*	up to 20 in (50 cm)	Indo-Pacific Ocean		crustaceans, mollusks, worms
Leatherjackets	*Oligoplites saurus*	up to 13.8 in (35 cm)	western Atlantic Ocean		fish and crustaceans
Honeycomb cowfish	*Acanthostracion polygonius*	up to 20 in (50 cm)	western Atlantic Ocean		sponges and crustaceans
Scrawled cowfish	*Acanthostracion quadricornis*	up to 22 in (55 cm)	Atlantic Ocean		sponges and crustaceans
Buffalo trunkfish	*Lactophrys trigonus*	up to 22 in (55 cm)	western Atlantic Ocean		crustaceans, mollusks, worms
Frillfin turkeyfish	*Pterois mombasae*	up to 12 in (31 cm)	Indo-Pacific Ocean		fish and crustaceans
Blue rockfish	*Sebastes mystinus*	up to 24 in (61 cm)	eastern Pacific Ocean		krill, other marine invertebrates, fish
Fringelip flathead	*Sunagocia otaitensis*	up to 12 in (30 cm)	Indo-Pacific Ocean		fish and crustaceans
Dusky flathead	*Platycephalus fuscus*	up to 3.9 ft (1.2 m)	western Pacific Ocean		fish and crustaceans
European bullhead	*Cottus gobio*	up to 7.1 in (18 cm)	Europe		crustaceans and insects
Alpine bullhead	*Cottus poecilopus*	up to 5.9 in (15 cm)	Europe		algae, crustaceans, insects
Estuarine stonefish	*Synanceia horrida*	up to 24 in (60 cm)	Indo-Pacific Ocean		crustaceans and small fish
Dwarf scorpionfish	*Synanceia nana*	up to 5.5 in (14 cm)	western Indian Ocean		crustaceans
REEF FISH AND SEAHORSES					
Belly pipefish	*Hippichthys heptagonus*	up to 5.9 in (15 cm)	Indian and Pacific Oceans		fish

COMMON NAME	SCIENTIFIC NAME	SIZE	RANGE	HABITAT	DIET
Freshwater pipefish	*Pseudophallus mindii*	up to 6.3 in (16 cm)	Central and South America		fish
Spotted seahorse	*Hippocampus kuda*	up to 12 in (30 cm)	Indian and Pacific Oceans		zooplankton
Short-snouted seahorse	*Hippocampus hippocampus*	up to 5.9 in (15 cm)	Atlantic Ocean; Mediterranean and Black Seas		zooplankton
Blue-and-yellow wrasse	*Anampses lennardi*	up to 11 in (28 cm)	Indian Ocean		invertebrates
Bluestreak cleaner wrasse	*Labroides dimidiatus*	up to 5.5 in (14 cm)	Indo-Pacific Ocean		crustaceans
Nassau grouper	*Epinephelus striatus*	up to 4 ft (1.2 m)	Atlantic Ocean		crustaceans and fish
White grouper	*Epinephelus aeneus*	up to 3.9 ft (1.2 m)	Atlantic Ocean		crustaceans and fish
Banded archerfish	*Toxotes jaculatrix*	up to 12 in (30 cm)	Asia and Oceania		insects and vegetation
Spotted archerfish	*Toxotes chatareus*	up to 16 in (40 cm)	Asia and Oceania		insects and vegetation
Bluehead combtooth blenny	*Ecsenius lividanalis*	up to 2 in (5 cm)	western Pacific Ocean		algae and plant material
Lined rockskipper	*Blenniella bilitonensis*	up to 6.3 in (16 cm)	western Pacific Ocean		algae
Goldring bristletooth	*Ctenochaetus strigosus*	up to 5.9 in (15 cm)	Australia		detritus
Giant gourami	*Osphronemus goramy*	up to 28 in (70 cm)	Asia		plants, fish, frogs
Snakeskin gourami	*Trichopodus pectoralis*	up to 10 in (25 cm)	Asia		aquatic vegetation
Common dragonet	*Callionymus lyra*	up to 12 in (30 cm)	eastern Atlantic Ocean		invertebrates, crustaceans, worms
Blotchfin dragonet	*Callionymus filamentosus*	up to 7.9 in (20 cm)	Indo-West Pacific Ocean		invertebrates, crustaceans, worms
Puntang goby	*Exyrias puntang*	up to 6.3 in (16 cm)	western Pacific Ocean		crustaceans
Dartfish	*Myxodagnus belone*	up to 3.1 in (8 cm)	western-central Atlantic Ocean		crustaceans
Vermiculated spinefoot	*Siganus vermiculatus*	up to 18 in (45 cm)	Indo-West Pacific Ocean		algae and plant material
Foxface rabbitfish	*Siganus vulpinus*	up to 10 in (25 cm)	western Pacific Ocean		algae and plant material
John's snapper	*Lutjanus johnii*	up to 38 in (97 cm)	Indo-West Pacific Ocean		fish and invertebrates
Blacktail snapper	*Lutjanus fulvus*	up to 16 in (40 cm)	Indo-Pacific Ocean		fish and shrimp
Kelpfish	*Chironemus marmoratus*	up to 16 in (40 cm)	southwest Pacific Ocean		invertebrates and fish
Giant kelpfish	*Heterostichus rostratus*	up to 24 in (61 cm)	eastern Pacific Ocean		crustaceans and fish
Mediterranean parrotfish	*Sparisoma cretense*	up to 20 in (50 cm)	Atlantic Ocean; Mediterranean and Black Seas		invertebrates and algae
Rivulated parrotfish	*Scarus rivulatus*	up to 16 in (40 cm)	western Pacific Ocean		algae
Orange clownfish	*Amphiprion percula*	up to 4.3 in (11 cm)	western Pacific Ocean		zooplankton
Clown anemonefish	*Amphiprion ocellaris*	up to 4.3 in (11 cm)	Indo-Pacific Ocean		zooplankton and algae

INVERTEBRATES

- ● ALERT
- ● IN TROUBLE
- ● STABLE
- ● UNDER STUDY
- ● NOT LISTED
- ● DOMESTICATED

COMMON NAME	SCIENTIFIC NAME	SIZE	RANGE	HABITAT	DIET
SPONGES					
Brown bowl sponge	*Cribrochalina vasculum*	8 to 18 in (20 to 45 cm)	Caribbean, Bahamas, South Florida (U.S.A.)		bacteria and tiny marine organisms
Touch-me-not sponge	*Neofibularia nolitangere*	1 to 4 ft (0.3 to 1.2 m)	Caribbean, Bahamas, Florida, northeast Brazil		bacteria and tiny marine organisms
Yellow tube sponge	*Aplysina fistularis*	2 to 4 ft (0.6 to 1.2 m)	Caribbean, Bahamas, Florida, northeast Brazil		bacteria and tiny marine organisms
Black-ball sponge	*Ircinia strobilina*	11.8 to 23.6 in (30 to 60 cm)	Caribbean, Bahamas, Florida, north and eastern Brazil		bacteria and tiny marine organisms
Stinker sponge	*Ircinia felix*	6 to 12 in (15 to 30 cm)	Caribbean, Bahamas, Florida, Guyana		bacteria and tiny marine organisms
Dark volcano sponge	*Svenzea zeai*	11.8 to 35.4 in (30 to 90 cm)	Caribbean and Florida		bacteria and tiny marine organisms

COMMON NAME	SCIENTIFIC NAME	SIZE	RANGE	HABITAT	DIET
Pink lumpy sponge	Monanchora unguifera	4 to 16 in (10 to 40 cm)	southwestern Caribbean		bacteria and tiny marine organisms
Orange elephant ear sponge	Agelas clathrodes	2 to 6 ft (0.6 to 1.8 m)	Caribbean, Bahamas, Florida		bacteria and tiny marine organisms
Row pore rope sponge	Aplysina cauliformis	4 to 8 ft (1.2 to 2.5 m)	Caribbean, Bahamas, Brazil		bacteria and tiny marine organisms
Red encrusting sponge	Monanchora arbuscula	4 to 10 in (10 to 25 cm)	Caribbean, Bahamas, Florida		bacteria and tiny marine organisms
Red boring sponge	Cliona delitrix	6 to 12 in (15 to 30 cm)	Caribbean and Bahamas		bacteria and tiny marine organisms
Yellow calcareous sponge	Arturia canariensis	2 to 4 in (5 to 10 cm)	Caribbean, Bahamas, Florida		bacteria and tiny marine organisms
Orange icing encrusting sponge	Mycale laevis	4 to 18 in (10 to 45 cm)	Caribbean, Bahamas, Florida		bacteria and tiny marine organisms
Golf ball sponge	Cinachyrella australiensis	up to 3 in (8 cm)	Indo-West Pacific Ocean		bacteria and tiny marine organisms
Fan sponge	Phyllospongia lamellosa	up to 3 ft (1 m)	Indo-West Pacific Ocean		bacteria and tiny marine organisms
Bath sponge	Spongia officinalis	diameter: 13.8 in (35 cm)	Mediterranean Sea		bacteria and tiny marine organisms
WORMS					
Racing stripe flatworm	Pseudoceros bifurcus	up to 2.4 in (6 cm)	western Pacific Ocean		tiny marine organisms
Leopard flatworm	Pseudobiceros pardalis	1 to 2 in (2.5 to 5 cm)	Caribbean, Bahamas, Florida		tiny marine organisms
Bearded fireworm	Hermodice carunculata	4 to 6 in (10 to 15 cm)	Caribbean, Bahamas, Florida		corals, anemones, small crustaceans
Star horseshoe worm	Pomatostegus stellatus	.75 to 1.5 in (1.8 to 3.8 cm)	Caribbean, Bahamas, Florida		tiny marine organisms
Indian feather-duster worm	Sabellastarte spectabilis	up to 4 in (10 cm)	Indo-Pacific Ocean and Hawaii		tiny marine particles
Pork tapeworm	Taenia solium	6.6 to 23 ft (2 to 7 m)	worldwide	(in hosts)	food from human host
Sheep liver fluke	Fasciola hepatica	1 in (2.5 cm)	Europe, Mexico, Central America	(in hosts)	sheep blood and liver
Dugesia flatworm	Dugesia sagitta	0.4 in (1 cm)	Corfu in Greece		tiny marine organisms
Freshwater planarian	Schmidtea mediterranea	up to 0.8 in (2 cm)	Europe		protozoans, tiny snails, worms
Green earthworm	Allolobophora chlorotica	1.2 to 2.4 in (3 to 8 cm)	Europe, Asia, North Africa; introduced worldwide		soil feeders
Black worm	Lumbriculus variegatus	3.9 in (10 cm)	Europe and North America		microorganisms and organic material
Sludge worm	Tubifex tubifex	7.9 in (20 cm)	worldwide		bacteria and sediments
Grindal worm	Enchytraeus buchholzi	0.5 to 1.5 in (1.2 to 3.8 cm)	many areas worldwide		anything organic
Kinabalu giant red leech	Mimobdella buettikoferi	27.5 in (70 cm)	Borneo		worms, such as the Kinabalu giant earthworm
Japanese mountain leech	Haemadipsa zeylanica	up to 2.4 in (6 cm)	Japan		blood
CORALS					
Branching fire coral	Millepora alcicornis	1 to 18 in (2.5 to 45 cm)	Caribbean, Bahamas, Florida		plankton and other microorganisms
Venus sea fan	Gorgonia flabellum	2 to 3.5 ft (0.6 to 1 m)	Caribbean and Bahamas		plankton and other microorganisms
Corky sea finger	Briareum asbestinum	5.9 to 23.6 in (15 to 60 cm)	Caribbean, Bahamas, Florida		algae and small particles
Colorful sea rod	Diodogorgia nodulifera	4 to 12 in (10 to 30 cm)	Caribbean, Bahamas, Florida		algae and small particles
Feather black coral	Antipathes pennacea	1 to 5 ft (0.3 to 1.5 m)	Caribbean and Bahamas		algae and small particles
Ten-ray star coral	Madracis decactis	1 to 6 in (2.5 to 15 cm)	Caribbean and Bahamas		algae and small particles
Grooved brain coral	Diploria labyrinthiformis	1 to 4 ft (0.3 to 1.2 m)	Caribbean, Bahamas, Florida		algae and small particles
Knobby brain coral	Diploria clivosa	6 in to 4 ft (15 to 120 cm)	Caribbean, Bahamas, Florida		algae and small particles
Thin leaf lettuce coral	Agaricia tenuifolia	4 to 12 ft (1 to 3.5 m)	northwest Caribbean		algae and small particles
Smooth flower coral	Eusmilia fastigiataa	polyps: .75 to 1.25 in (2 to 3 cm)	Caribbean, Bahamas, Florida		algae and small particles
Common razor coral	Fungia scutaria	4 to 7 in (10 to 18 cm)	Indo-Pacific Ocean, Hawaii, Red Sea		algae and small particles
Common mushroom coral	Fungia fungites	11.8 in (30 cm)	Indo-Pacific Ocean, Australia, Red Sea		algae and small particles
Elkhorn coral	Acropora palmata	29.5 in (75 cm)	southern Florida to northern Venezuela		algae and small particles
Fire coral	Millepora alcicornis	29.5 in (75 cm)	Caribbean Sea		algae and small particles
ANEMONES AND JELLIES					
Sun anemone	Stichodactyla helianthus	disc: 4 to 6 in (10 to 15 cm)	Caribbean and Bahamas		fish, shrimp, isopods, amphipods, plankton

INVERTEBRATES

COMMON NAME	SCIENTIFIC NAME	SIZE	RANGE	HABITAT	DIET
Warty sea anemone	Bunodosoma cavernata	1 to 3 in (2.5 to 7.6 cm)	Caribbean, Bahamas, Florida, Gulf of Mexico		fish, shrimp, isopods, amphipods, plankton
Elegant anemone	Actinoporus elegans	7 to 9 in (18 to 23 cm)	Caribbean		fish, shrimp, isopods, amphipods, plankton
Leathery sea anemone	Heteractis crispa	up to 20 in (50 cm)	Indo-Pacific, Australia, Polynesia, Red Sea		fish, shrimp, isopods, amphipods, plankton
Hermit crab anemone	Calliactis polypus	up to 3 in (7.6 cm)	Indo-Pacific Ocean, Hawaii, Red Sea		fish, shrimp, isopods, amphipods, plankton
Orange ball corallimorph	Pseudocorynactis caribbeorum	1 to 2 in (2.5 to 5 cm)	Caribbean and Bahamas		fish, shrimp, isopods, amphipods, plankton
Christmas tree hydroid	Pennaria disticha	3 to 5 in (7.6 to 13 cm)	Caribbean, Bahamas, Florida, Hawaii		plankton
Upside-down jelly	Cassiopea frondosa	5 to 10 in (12 to 26 cm)	Caribbean, Bahamas, Florida		zooplankton, algae, aquatic crustaceans and other marine invertebrates
Sea thimble jellyfish	Linuche unguiculata	0.5 to .75 in (1.25 to 2 cm)	circumtropical		aquatic crustaceans and other marine invertebrates, zooplankton, algae
Sponge zoanthid	Parazoanthus parasiticus	.25 in (7 mm)	Caribbean, Bahamas, Florida, Bermuda		algae, aquatic crustaceans and other marine invertebrates, zooplankton
Red-spot comb jelly	Eurhamphaea vexilligera	1 to 2 in (2.5 to 5 cm)	Pacific, Caribbean, Gulf of Mexico, Fla., Bermuda		zooplankton: mollusk and fish larvae, copepods, amphipods, krill
Stinging bush hydroid	Macrorhynchia robusta	4 to 8 in (10 to 20 cm)	Caribbean, Bahamas, Florida		zooplankton: mollusk and fish larvae, copepods, amphipods, krill
Spotted jelly	Mastigias pupua	24 in (61 cm)	Pacific and Indian Oceans; China Sea		zooplankton
Lion's mane jellyfish	Cyanea capillata	11 to 70 in (30 to 180 cm)	Arctic, North Atlantic, and North Pacific Oceans		mainly fish
Box jellyfish, or sea wasp	Chironex fleckeri	10 ft (3 m)	Australia, New Guinea to Philippines, Asia		fish and aquatic crustaceans
SNAILS AND SLUGS					
Black slug	Arion ater	1 to 6 in (2.5 to 15 cm)	England; Pacific Northwest (U.S.A.)		fungi, plants, worms, insects, decaying vegetation, feces
Lewis's moon snail	Euspira lewisii	up to 5 in (13 cm)	Pacific coast, Vancouver Island (Canada) to Mexico		clams, mussels, mollusks
Painted elysia	Thuridilla picta	0.5 to 1 in (1 to 2.5 cm)	Caribbean, Bahamas, Florida		algae
Spotted sea hare	Aplysia dactylomela	3 to 8 in (7.6 to 20 cm)	circumtropical		algae
Lettuce sea slug	Elysia crispata	2 to 4 in (5 to 10 cm)	Caribbean, Bahamas, Florida		algae
Purple-spotted sea goddess	Hypselodoris marci	0.5 to 1 in (1.2 to 2.5 cm)	Bay Islands (Honduras), Belize, Venezuela		algae
Fried-egg nudibranch	Phyllidia varicosa	2 to 3 in (5 to 8 cm)	Indo-Pacific Ocean, Hawaii, Red Sea		sponges
Tiger cowry	Cypraea tigris	3 to 5 in (7 to 12 cm)	Indo-Pacific Ocean, Hawaii, Red Sea		soft corals, sponges, anemones
Queen conch	Strombus gigas	6 to 9 in (15 to 23 cm)	Caribbean, Bahamas, South Florida		algae and detritus
West Indian top snail	Cittarium pica	2 to 4 in (5 to 10 cm)	Caribbean, Bahamas, Florida		algae; sometimes detritus
Edible snail	Helix pomatia	1.5 to 2 in (3.8 to 5 cm)	central and eastern Europe		leaves, fruit, flowers, sap or other plant fluids
CLAMS, OYSTERS, MUSSELS, AND SCALLOPS					
Antillean fileclam	Lima pellucida	.75 to 1 in (1.8 to 2.5 cm)	Caribbean, Bahamas, Florida		plant and animal plankton
Atlantic thorny oyster	Spondylus americanus	3 to 5 in (8 to 13 cm)	Caribbean, Bahamas, Florida		plant and animal plankton
Frond oyster	Dendostrea frons	1.5 to 2.5 in (4 to 6 cm)	Caribbean, Bahamas, Florida		plant and animal plankton
Giant clam	Tridacna gigas	up to 4.3 ft (1.3 m)	Indo-Pacific Ocean and Great Barrier Reef		plant and animal plankton
Smooth giant clam	Tridacna derasa	up to 24 in (60 cm)	Indo-West Pacific Ocean and Australia		plankton
Fluted giant clam	Tridacna squamosa	up to 16 in (40 cm)	Indo-Pacific Ocean		plankton
Fuzzy West Indian chiton	Acanthopleura granulata	up to 4 in (10 cm)	Caribbean, Bahamas, Florida		plant plankton
California mussel	Mytilus californicus	up to 10 in (25 cm)	eastern Pacific Ocean		plankton and other microorganisms
Freshwater pearl mussel	Margaritifera margaritifera	4.5 in (11.5 cm)	Norway to Spain and Great Britain		plankton and other microorganisms
Zebra mussel	Dreissena polymorpha	up to 0.8 in (2 cm)	Great Lakes and many North American rivers		bacteria, blue-green algae, small green algae, protozoans
Deep sea scallop	Placopecten magellanicus	5.9 in (15 cm)	northwest Atlantic and western-central Pacific		plant plankton
OCTOPUSES AND RELATIVES					
Common octopus	Octopus vulgaris	11.8 to 35.4 in (30 to 90 cm)	widely distributed; Mediterranean and Black Seas; Atlantic, Indian, and Pacific Oceans		gastropods and bivalves
Caribbean reef octopus	Octopus briareus	up to 3.3 ft (1 m)	Caribbean, Bahamas, Florida, Central America, northern South America		crabs, marine worms, fish and shrimp
Chambered nautilus	Nautilus pompilius	8 to 10 in (20 to 25 cm)	Indo-Pacific Ocean		carrion (dead animals); also crabs and fish
Broadclub cuttlefish	Sepia latimanus	6 to 20 in (15 to 50 cm)	Indo-Pacific Ocean and Great Barrier Reef		crustaceans and fish

COMMON NAME	SCIENTIFIC NAME	SIZE	RANGE	HABITAT	DIET
European squid	*Loligo vulgaris*	5.9 to 9.8 in (15 to 25 cm)	Europe and Mediterranean Sea		small fish and crustaceans
Greater blue-ringed octopus	*Hapalochlaena lunulata*	2 to 2.8 in (5 to 7 cm)	Indo-Pacific and Indian Oceans		fish, crabs, mollusks, other small marine animals
ECHINODERMS					
Chocolate chip sea cucumber	*Isostichopus badionotus*	10 to 16 in (25 to 40 cm)	warm parts of Atlantic Ocean		detritus or sediments
Pin-cushion sea star	*Culcita novaeguineae*	up to 16 in (40 cm)	Indo-Pacific Ocean, Hawaii, Polynesia		detritus; small invertebrates, including stony corals
Guilding's sea star	*Ophidiaster guildingi*	2 to 4 in (5 to 10 cm)	Caribbean Sea and Florida Keys		detritus; small invertebrates, including stony corals
Crown-of-thorns	*Acanthaster planci*	up to 32 in (80 cm)	Indo-Pacific, Hawaii, Red Sea, Polynesia, eastern Pacific		cnidarians and other marine invertebrates; algae
Beautiful feather star	*Cenometra bella*	arms up to 6 in (15 cm)	western Pacific Ocean		detritus; small invertebrates, including stony corals
Suenson's brittle star	*Ophiothrix suensonii*	2 to 3 in (5 to 8 cm)	Caribbean, Bahamas, Florida, Bermuda		detritus; small invertebrates, including stony corals
Pebble collector urchin	*Pseudoboletia indiana*	4 to 5 in (10 to 13 cm)	Indo-West Pacific Ocean		small nutritive matter in the sand
Red heart urchin	*Meoma ventricosa*	4 to 6 in (10 to 15 cm)	Caribbean, Bahamas, Florida		small nutritive matter in the sand
Donkey dung sea cucumber	*Holothuria mexicana*	up to 20 in (50 cm)	Caribbean, Bahamas, Florida Keys		algae, tiny aquatic organisms, detritus
Difficult sea cucumber	*Holothuria difficilis*	up to 5 in (13 cm)	Indo-Pacific Ocean and Hawaii		algae, tiny aquatic organisms, detritus
Giant sea cucumber	*Thelenota anax*	1.6 to 3.3 ft (0.5 to 1 m)	Indo-Pacific Ocean		algae, tiny aquatic organisms, detritus
Leopard sea cucumber	*Bohadschia argus*	10 to 20 in (25 to 50 cm)	Indo-Pacific Ocean		plankton and decaying organic matter
CRABS, SHRIMP, AND LOBSTERS					
American lobster	*Homarus americanus*	3.6 ft (1.1 m)	Atlantic coast of North America		fish, carrion, mollusks, crustaceans, algae, macroalgae
West Indian furrow lobster	*Justitia longimanus*	5 to 8 in (12 to 20 cm)	Caribbean, Florida, Bermuda, Indo-Pacific, Hawaii		fish, carrion, mollusks, crustaceans, algae, macroalgae
Red reef lobster	*Enoplometopus occidentalis*	up to 5 in (12 cm)	Indo-Pacific Ocean and Hawaii		algae, small fish, small invertebrates
Red snapping shrimp	*Alpheus* spp.	1 to 2 in (2.5 to 5 cm)	Caribbean, Bahamas, Florida		algae, small fish, small invertebrates
Magnificent anemone shrimp	*Ancylomenes magnificus*	up to 1 in (2.5 cm)	western Pacific Ocean		detritus and small invertebrates
Glass anemone shrimp	*Periclimenes brevicarpalis*	0.8 to 1.5 in (2 to 4 cm)	Indo-Pacific Ocean, Australia, Red Sea		detritus and small invertebrates
Spotted cleaner shrimp	*Periclimenes yucatanicus*	.75 to 1 in (1.8 to 2.5 cm)	Caribbean, Bahamas, South Florida		detritus and small invertebrates
Banded coral shrimp	*Stenopus hispidus*	2.4 in (6.2 cm)	Indo-Pacific Ocean		marine worms, aquatic crustaceans, other marine invertebrates, zooplankton
Hawaiian swimming crab	*Charybdis hawaiensis*	up to 3 in (7.6 cm)	central Pacific Ocean, Polynesia, Hawaii		fish, mollusks, marine worms, aquatic crustaceans, other marine invertebrates, leaves
Blue-eyed rock crab	*Percnon affine*	up to 3 in (7.6 cm)	Pacific Ocean and Hawaii		fish, mollusks, marine worms, aquatic crustaceans, other marine invertebrates, leaves
Atlantic blue crab	*Callinectes sapidus*	4.7 to 6.7 in (12 to 17 cm)	Atlantic Ocean, Asia, Europe		fish, mollusks, marine worms, aquatic crustaceans, other marine invertebrates, leaves
Japanese spider crab	*Macrocheira kaempferi*	9.8 ft (3 m)	Japan and Taiwan		fish, carrion, aquatic crustaceans, other marine invertebrates, algae
Poll's stellate barnacle	*Chthamalus stellatus*	.55 in (1.4 cm)	Atlantic, British Isles, western Indian Ocean, Mediterranean		plankton and detritus
Acorn barnacle	*Semibalanus balanoides*	up to 0.5 in (1.3 cm)	Pacific and Atlantic coasts		plankton, other microorganisms, detritus
Tasmanian giant freshwater crayfish	*Astacopsis gouldi*	15.8 in (40 cm)	Australia and Tasmania		decaying wood and small fish
SPIDERS, SCORPIONS, TICKS, AND MITES					
Fishing spider	*Dolomedes triton*	0.4 to 1 in (0.9 to 2.6 cm)	United States: Texas to the Atlantic coast		insect larvae, tadpoles, small fish
Sydney funnel-web spider	*Atrax robustus*	1 to 1.3 in (2.5 to 3.5 cm)	Sydney, Australia		beetles, cockroaches, insect larvae, land snails, millipedes; also frogs, other small vertebrates
Large Carolina wolf spider	*Hogna carolinensis*	0.7 to 1.3 in (1.8 to 3.5 cm)	United States		grasshoppers, crickets, other similar agricultural pests
Yellow garden spider	*Argiope aurantia*	.25 to 1.4 in (0.5 to 2.8 cm)	southern Canada to Costa Rica		insects, such as aphids, flies, grasshoppers, hymenopterans
Pinktoe tarantula	*Avicularia avicularia*	4.5 in (11 cm)	northern South America		crickets, cockroaches, flying insects
American dog tick	*Dermacentor variabilis*	.25 in (6.4 mm)	North America		blood from host
Brazilian wandering spider	*Phoneutria fera*	4 to 5 in (10 to 12.7 cm)	Central and South America		insects, small lizards, pinkie mice
Asian forest scorpion	*Heterometrus longimanus*	3.5 to 5 in (8.9 to 12.7 cm)	Southeast Asia		insects and other arthropods
Brown recluse spider	*Loxosceles reclusa*	0.5 in (1.3 cm)	midwestern United States		insects
Feather-legged orb weaver	*Uloborus glomosus*	.08 to 1.2 in (2 to 30 mm)	eastern North America		insects
Goliath bird-eating tarantula	*Theraphosa blondi*	up to 12 in (30 cm)	South America		insects and other invertebrates; also a wide variety of vertebrates

COMMON NAME	SCIENTIFIC NAME	SIZE	RANGE	HABITAT	DIET
Hobo spider	Tegenaria agrestis	.25 to .75 in (0.6 to 1.8 cm)	Europe and North America	(icons)	insects
Honeybee mite	Acarapis woodi	.007 in (.18 mm)	inside the bee's body	(icon)	live off host
Northern black widow spider	Latrodectus variolus	.25 to 0.5 in (0.6 to 1.3 cm)	northern Florida to southeastern Canada	(icons)	insects
Deathstalker scorpion	Leiurus quinquestriatus	3 to 4 in (8 to 11 cm)	North Africa and the Middle East	(icons)	insects and other invertebrates
CENTIPEDES AND MILLIPEDES					
Australian house centipede	Allothereua maculata	0.8 to 1 in (2 to 2.5 cm)	southern Australia	(icons)	insects and other arthropods
Mediterranean banded centipede	Scolopendra cingulata	4 to 6 in (10 to 15 cm)	southern Europe and Mediterranean	(icons)	insects and other small animals
Stone centipede	Lithobius forficatus	0.7 to 1.3 in (1.8 to 3 cm)	Europe	(icons)	insects, spiders, and other small invertebrates, including centipedes
Amazonian giant centipede	Scolopendra gigantea	12 in (30 cm)	northern South America	(icon)	small invertebrates, such as crickets, worms, snails, roaches; also lizards, toads, mice
European pill millipede	Glomeris marginata	0.2 to 0.7 in (0.7 to 2 cm)	Britain	(icons)	organic matter
Bristly millipede	Polyxenus fasciculatus	.08 in (2 mm)	Britain	(icons)	leaves and dead plant matter
Flat-backed millipede	Polydesmus angustus	.55 to 1 in (1.4 to 2.5 cm)	northwest Europe and parts of North America	(icons)	roots, dead leaves, other bits of decayed plant matter; also strawberries, other fruit
Yellow-spotted millipede	Harpaphe haydeniana	1.6 to 2 in (4 to 5 cm)	Pacific coast of North America	(icons)	humus and leaf litter
Black millipede	Tachypodoiulus niger	.59 to 1.5 (1.5 to 3.9 cm)	Europe	(icons)	encrusting algae, detritus; sometimes raspberries, other fruit
INSECTS					
Tree lobster	Dryococelus australis	5.9 in (15 cm)	Lord Howe Island in Australia	(icon)	various plants
Southern two-striped walking stick	Anisomorpha buprestoides	1.6 to 2.6 in (4.1 to 6.7 cm)	southern North America	(icon)	various plants
Pacific dampwood termite	Zootermopsis angusticollis	.04 in (1 mm)	Pacific coast of North America	(icon)	damp wood
South Asian tar baby termite	Globitermes sulphureus	.06 in (1.5 mm)	central and southern Vietnam	(icon)	wood
Common earwig	Forficula auricularia	0.5 in (1.3 cm)	worldwide, except Antarctica	(icon)	insects, detritus, fruit, plant matter
Silverfish	Lepisma saccharina	0.3 to .75 in (0.8 to 2 cm)	worldwide	(icon)	glue, wallpaper paste, bookbindings, paper, photographs, starch in clothing, cotton, linen
True katydid	Pterophylla camellifolia	1.75 to 2 in (4.5 to 5.5 cm)	east U.S. west to Texas and northeast to Ontario (Can.)	(icons)	leaves of oaks and most other deciduous trees and shrubs
Desert locust	Schistocerca gregaria	2.4 to 3.5 in (6 to 9 cm)	Africa, Middle East, Asia	(icons)	various plants
Migratory locust	Locusta migratoria	1.4 to 2 in (3.5 to 5.5 cm)	Africa, Asia, Australia and New Zealand, Europe	(icons)	various plants
Australian plague locust	Chortoicetes terminifera	0.8 to 1.8 in (2 to 4.5 cm)	Australia	(icons)	crops and other plants
Differential grasshopper	Melanoplus differentialis	1.1 to 2 in (2.8 to 5 cm)	Central America and central North America	(icons)	corn, cotton, deciduous fruit crops
Eastern lubber grasshopper	Romalea guttata	3 in (7.6 cm)	southeastern United States	(icons)	various plants
BEETLES					
Mountain pine beetle	Dendroctonus ponderosae	0.2 to 0.3 in (5 to 7.5 mm)	North America from Mexico to British Columbia	(icon)	various plants
American burying beetle	Nicrophorus americanus	1.2 to 1.4 in (3 to 3.5 cm)	U.S.: Oklahoma and Block Island, Rhode Island	(icons)	carcasses of dead animals
Bombardier beetle	Brachinus crepitans	.25 to 0.3 in (6.5 to 9.5 mm)	central and southern Europe; North Africa	(icons)	flowers, leaves, other insects
Colorado potato beetle	Leptinotarsa decemlineata	.38 in (1 cm)	North America east of the Rocky Mountains	(icon)	potatoes and related plants
Seven-spotted ladybug	Coccinella septempunctata	height: .28 to .31 in (7 to 8 mm)	western Europe; North America	(icons)	insects
Rhinoceros beetle	Dynastinae	5.9 in (15 cm)	Africa and Mediterranean	(icons)	rotten wood, plant sap, fruit, nectar
Long-horned beetle	Anoplophora glabripennis	0.8 to 1.4 in (2 to 3.5 cm)	China, Korea, United States	(icons)	wood, bark, stems; sap or other plant fluids
Cowboy beetle	Chondropyga dorsalis	0.7 to 0.9 in (2 to 2.5 cm)	southeastern Australia	(icons)	nectar-bearing shrubs and trees
Red flour beetle	Tribolium castaneum	.09 to .17 in (2.3 to 4.4 mm)	worldwide	(icon)	grain products, such as flour, cereals, pasta, biscuits, beans, nuts
Cowpea beetle	Callosobruchus chinensis	.03 to 0.8 in (0.1 to 2.2 cm)	cosmopolitan areas and tropics of the world	(icon)	beans or grains
European elm bark beetle	Scolytinae multistriatus	.19 in (5 mm)	worldwide	(icons)	tree bark
Mealworm beetle	Tenebrio molitor	0.5 to 0.7 in (1.3 to 1.8 cm)	temperate regions worldwide	(icon)	organic material
Lightning bug	Photuris pennsylvanica	.75 in (2 cm)	North America	(icons)	insects and other invertebrates

COMMON NAME	SCIENTIFIC NAME	SIZE	RANGE	HABITAT	DIET
BUGS					
Bedbug	Cimex lectularius	0.2 to .37 in (5 to 9.5 mm)	all continents except Antarctica		primarily parasitic on humans
Kissing bug	Triatoma infestans	0.2 to 1.4 in (0.5 to 3.5 cm)	South America		animal and human blood
Masked hunter assassin bug	Reduvius personatus	0.6 to 0.8 in (1.7 to 2.2 cm)	North America		small arthropods, such as woodlice, lacewings, earwigs, bedbugs
Southern green stinkbug	Nezara viridula	0.5 to 0.6 in (1.4 to 1.7 cm)	Europe, Asia, Africa, the Americas		wide variety of crop plants
Jewel bug	Chrysocoris stolli	0.2 to 0.8 in (0.5 to 2 cm)	worldwide		various plants
Hawthorn shield bug	Acanthosoma haemorrhoidale	.67 in (1.7 cm)	Europe		fruit of the hawthorn tree
Beet leafhopper	Circulifer tenellus	0.6 in (1.5 cm)	North, Central, and South America; Europe		various plants
Glassy-winged sharpshooter	Homalodisca vitripennis	0.5 in (1.2 cm)	southeastern United States		various plants
Linne's cicada	Tibicen linnei	1 to 2 in (2.5 to 5 cm)	North America		various plants
Dogday cicada	Tibicen canicularis	1 to 1.2 in (2.7 to 3.3 cm)	North America		pines and allied conifers
Common water strider	Aquarius	0.1 to 0.6 in (0.3 to 1.6 cm)	North America		small living or dead insects on the surface of water
Water measurer	Hydrometra stagnorum	0.5 in (1.3 cm)	Europe		mosquito larvae and water fleas
Giant water bug	Belostomatidae family	0.5 to 3 in (1.3 to 7.5 cm)	worldwide		aquatic arthropods, snails, small fish, amphibians
Water scorpion	Nepa apiculata	0.7 to .78 in (1.8 to 2 cm)	North America		aquatic invertebrates
FLIES					
Botfly	Cuterebra lepivora	0.5 in (1.3 cm)	West Coast of the United States		parasitic on rabbits
Gnat	Anisopodidae	.16 to .31 in (4 to 8 mm)	worldwide		various plants
Midge	Chironomidae	.04 to .39 in (0.1 to 1 cm)	worldwide		small invertebrates
Housefly	Muscidae	.16 to .28 in (4 to 7 mm)	worldwide		various types of plant and animal discharges
Common green bottle fly	Lucilia sericata	.23 to .35 in (6 to 9 mm)	worldwide		various types of plant and animal discharges
Screwworm fly	Cochliomyia macellaria	0.3 to 0.4 in (0.8 to 1 cm)	North, Central, and South America		flesh of living organisms
Emperor dragonfly	Anax imperator	3.1 in (7.8 cm)	Europe and Africa		insects and small fish
Green darner	Anax junius	up to 3.2 in (8 cm)	North America		flying insects, including butterflies and other dragonflies
Common hawker	Aeshna juncea	2.9 in (7.4 cm)	Eurasia and North America		small invertebrates
Southern yellowjack	Notogomphus praetorius	4.9 in (12.5 cm)	southern Africa		small invertebrates
Two-striped skimmer	Orthetrum caffrum	1.6 in (4 cm)	Africa		small invertebrates
Common bluetail damselfly	Ischnura heterosticta	1.3 in (3.4 cm)	Australia		small invertebrates
Mosquito	Anopheles stephensi	0.6 in (1.6 cm)	worldwide		animal and human blood
Southern house mosquito	Culex quinquefasciatus	0.6 in (1.6 cm)	India		animal and human blood
Giant forest damselfly	Megaloprepus caerulatus	7.5 in (19 cm)	Central and South America		orb-weaver spiders
Basking malachite damselfly	Chlorolestes apricans	1.7 to 1.8 in (4.3 to 4.5 cm)	South Africa		insects
BUTTERFLIES AND MOTHS					
White-barred emperor butterfly	Charaxes brutus	2.3 to 2.9 in (6 to 7.5 cm)	South Africa		fermenting fruit and tree sap
Common buckeye butterfly	Junonia coenia	1.6 to 2.4 in (4 to 6 cm)	North America		leaves and nectar
Common castor butterfly	Ariadne merione	1.1 to 1.3 in (3 to 3.5 cm)	southeastern Asia		castor bean plant
Karner blue butterfly	Lycaeides melissa samuelis	0.4 to 0.6 in (1.2 to 1.6 cm)	northwestern United States; Canada		leaves and nectar
Gulf fritillary	Agraulis vanillae	2 to 2.5 in (5.1 to 6.4 cm)	southern United States; Central America		maypops and other passion-vine species
Numata longwing butterfly	Heliconius numata	2 in (5 cm)	South America		red or orange flowers; larvae and eggs found on low-growing vines of passifloras
Australian painted lady butterfly	Vanessa kershawi	1.6 to 1.8 in (4.3 to 4.7 cm)	Australia		flower nectar
Small white butterfly	Pieris rapae	1.7 to 2.1 in (4.5 to 5.5 cm)	Europe, Asia, northern Africa, North America		leaves and nectar
Spicebush swallowtail	Papilio troilus	3.1 to 4.5 in (8 to 11.5 cm)	North America		nectar, especially honeysuckle, clover, thistle flowers
Mallow skipper	Carcharodus alceae	1 to 1.3 in (2.6 to 3.4 cm)	Europe, northern Africa, Central Asia		nectar from herbaceous plants

COMMON NAME	SCIENTIFIC NAME	SIZE	RANGE	HABITAT	DIET
Atlas moth	*Attacus atlas*	9.8 to 11.8 in (25 to 30 cm)	Southeast Asia and Malay Islands		adults do not eat
Bogong moth	*Agrotis infusa*	1.7 in (4.5 cm)	southern Australia		plant-eaters, including beets, barley, flax, alfalfa, wheat
Peppered moth	*Biston betularia*	1.5 to 2.4 in (3.7 to 6.2 cm)	most of the British Isles		deciduous trees and shrubs
Gypsy moth	*Lymantria dispar*	1.4 in (3.8 cm)	Europe, Asia, North America		various trees, especially red oaks, cherries, willows, hickories, pines
Corn earworm	*Helicoverpa zea*	1.2 to 1.7 in (3.2 to 4.5 cm)	North Am., except northern Canada and Alaska		crops and nectar
BEES AND WASPS					
Eastern carpenter bee	*Xylocopa virginica*	0.7 to 0.9 in (1.9 to 2.3 cm)	eastern and east-central U.S.; southern Canada		nectar from flowers
Southern yellow jacket	*Vespula squamosa*	0.5 to .75 in (1.2 to 1.9 cm)	eastern U.S. through Mexico to Honduras		nectar and other fluids
Bald-faced hornet	*Dolichovespula maculata*	.75 in (2 cm)	North America and southern Canada		nectar, tree sap, fruit pulp
Cuckoo bee	*Bombus vestalis*	0.6 to 0.9 in (1.5 to 2.4 cm)	Europe, Africa, Asia		flowers
Spider-hunting wasp	*Heterodotonyx bicolor*	0.4 in (1 cm)	Central and South America; East Asia		spiders
Saxon wasp	*Dolichovespula saxonica*	0.4 to 0.6 in (1.1 to 1.7 cm)	Europe: mainly Britain and Scotland		nectar and pollen
Alfalfa leafcutter bee	*Megachile rotundata*	2.4 to 7.5 in (6 to 19 cm)	Asia, Europe, North America, Africa		nectar and pollen
Orchard mason bee	*Osmia lignaria*	0.4 to 1.7 in (1.1 to 1.4 cm)	Canada; New England states in United States		flowers of trees, especially cherry, pear, apple; also quince, laburnum, blueberry
Eastern cicada killer wasp	*Sphecius speciosus*	1 to 2 in (3 to 5 cm)	east of the Rocky Mountains and south to Mexico		nectar from flowers
Organ-pipe mud dauber	*Trypoxylon politum*	1 in (2.5 cm)	United States: Maine to Florida, Kansas, Texas		spiders
Black-and-yellow mud dauber	*Sceliphron caementarium*	0.9 to 1.1 in (2.4 to 2.8 cm)	North America		nectar
Stingless honeybee	*Meliponula ferruginea*	0.8 in (2.1 mm)	Australia, Africa, Southeast Asia, Americas		nectar and honey
ANTS					
Common fire ant	*Myrmica rubra*	.08 to .23 in (2 to 6 mm)	Europe; now in Asia and North America		small animals
Argentine ant	*Linepithema humile*	.11 in (3 mm)	Americas, South Africa, Japan, Australia, Europe		plants, dead animals, rotting fruit
Pavement ant	*Tetramorium caespitum*	.13 in (3.3 mm)	eastern and southern United States; Europe		plant and animal fluids, carrion, arthropods, seeds, grains, nuts, fruit, flowers, nectar, pollen
Northern wood ant	*Formica aquilonia*	0.2 to .47 in (0.5 to 1.2 cm)	Europe		honeydew, other invertebrates, some vertebrates
Meat ant	*Iridomyrmex purpureus*	0.4 in (1 cm)	Australia		carrion, tree sap, honeydew
Inchman bull ant	*Myrmecia forficata*	0.6 to 1 in (1.5 to 2.5 cm)	Australia		invertebrates and other small animals
Jack jumper ant	*Myrmecia pilosula*	0.4 to .47 in (1 to 1.2 cm)	Australia		carrion
Fungus-growing ant	*Mycocepurus smithii*	.12 in (3 mm)	Central and South America		fungi
Bullet ant	*Paraponera clavata*	0.7 to 1.2 in (1.8 to 3 cm)	Nicaragua to Paraguay		nectar and small arthropods
Mexican leafcutter ant	*Atta mexicana*	1.2 in (3 cm)	Central and South America; southern U.S.		vegetation, such as leaves, flowers, grasses
Ghost ant	*Tapinoma melanocephalum*	0.6 in (1.5 mm)	tropical areas worldwide		sweets (fruits), grease, living or dead insects
Red harvester ant	*Pogonomyrmex barbatus*	.25 to 0.5 in (0.6 to 1.3 cm)	parts of United States into Mexico		mostly seeds; also dead insects

TREEHOPPER

GLOSSARY

Adaptation *noun* a change in the body or behavior of a species, often over many generations, making it better able to survive

Amphibian *noun* ectothermic animal with a backbone that has moist skin and no scales

Aquatic *adjective* living all or most of the time in water

Arthropod *noun* animal whose body and legs are divided into segments. The bodies of arthropods have a hard covering called an exoskeleton.

Bioluminescence *noun* light emitted by living organisms through chemical reactions in their bodes or through symbiotic bacteria capable of bioluminescence

Boreal forest *noun* a belt of coniferous, or cone-bearing, trees that stretches across northern Asia, Europe, and North America. The region experiences long, snowy winters and short, cool summers.

Breed *verb* to reproduce by giving birth to live young or laying eggs

Burrow *noun* hole or tunnel in the ground dug by an animal; *verb* to dig a hole or tunnel in the ground

Camouflage *noun* an organism's ability to disguise its appearance, often by using its coloring or body shape to blend in with its surroundings

Canopy *noun* the highest level of a forest, formed by the tops of the tallest trees

Carnivore *noun* organism that eats meat

Circumpolar *adjective* located near or inhabiting one of Earth's polar regions

Classification *noun* grouping based on physical and genetic characteristics

Climate *noun* average weather conditions of an area over an extended period of time

Colony *noun* a group of the same kind of organism living or growing together

Crustacean *noun* organism that lives mostly in water and has a hard shell and a body divided into segments

Desert *noun* an area of land that receives less than 10 inches (25 cm) of precipitation a year

DNA *noun* (deoxyribonucleic acid) chemical code that contains information about an organism's body

Domestication *noun* the process of taming and breeding an animal for human use. Domestic animals include pets, such as cats; work animals, such as oxen; and sport animals, such as horses.

Dorsal fin *noun* fin on the back of an aquatic animal that helps the animal keep its balance as it moves

Echolocation *noun* a sensory system in some animals in which sounds are emitted and their echoes interpreted to determine the direction and distance of objects. Bats and dolphins use echolocation to navigate and find food.

Ecosystem *noun* community and interactions of living and nonliving things in an area

Embryo *noun* unborn offspring produced after a male and female mate

Endangered *adjective* relating to an animal or plant that is found in such small numbers that it is at risk of becoming extinct, or no longer existing

Ectotherm *noun* an animal that does not keep its internal body temperature above that of the environment, so it moves into or out of the heat as needed; commonly called "cold-blooded"

Endotherm *noun* an animal that keeps its internal body temperature typically above that of the environment, usually within a narrow range; commonly called "warm-blooded"

Extinct *adjective* no longer existing

Fermentation *noun* the breaking down of larger chemical compounds by natural or artificial processes

Food chain *noun* series of organisms dependent on one another for food. In a food chain, one organism is a source of food for another organism, which in turn is a source of food for another.

Freshwater *adjective* containing water with little or no salt

Gastropod *noun* mollusk that has a head with eyes and feelers. A gastropod has a muscular foot under its body that it uses to move.

Genus *noun* a grouping of organisms that have many shared characteristics but cannot produce offspring together. Tigers and lions belong to the same genus, *Panthera*.

GLOSSARY

ARCTIC WOLVES

BLACK-SIDED HAWKFISH

Gills *noun* organs present in the bodies of some water-dwelling animals that help the organisms breathe. Gills absorb, or take in, oxygen from the water and send it to an organism's bloodstream.

Grassland *noun* a large, flat area of land that is covered with grasses and has few trees

Habitat *noun* a place in nature where an organism lives throughout the year or for shorter periods of time

Hatchling *noun* a very young animal that has recently hatched from its egg

Herbivore *noun* organism that eats mainly plants

Hibernation *noun* the process of reducing activity almost to sleeping to conserve food and energy, usually in winter

Incubate *verb* to keep eggs or very young organisms warm so they can hatch or grow

Indo-Pacific *noun* a region consisting of the tropical waters of the Indian Ocean, the western and central Pacific Ocean, and the seas connecting the two in the general area of Indonesia

Insectivore *noun* organism that eats mostly insects

Invertebrate *noun* an organism without a backbone. Invertebrates can include, but are not limited to, insects, arachnids, crustaceans, and mollusks.

Krill *noun* a small marine crustacean, similar to shrimp

Larva *noun* an animal in the early stage of development that looks different than how it will look in the adult stage

Lateral line *noun* a sensory organ found on the side of fish that detects movement and pressure changes in water

Life cycle *noun* process of changes undertaken by an organism or group of organisms over the course of their existence. Birth, growth, and death usually characterize the life cycle of animals.

Mammal *noun* endothermic animal with hair that gives birth to live offspring and produces milk to feed its young

Marine *adjective* living in or near the sea

Marsupial *noun* mammal that gives birth to young that are not fully developed. A marsupial usually carries its young—which can move independently—in a pouch for protection.

Metabolism *noun* chemical reactions that take place in cells and allow organisms to grow and function

Metamorphosis *noun* complete change in form and structure from one part of the life cycle to the next, such as caterpillar to pupa, and pupa to butterfly

Migration *noun* process in which a community of organisms leaves a habitat for part of the year or part of their lives, and moves to other habitats that are more hospitable

Mimicry *noun* an organism's ability to mimic, or copy, another organism's appearance or behavior

Mollusk *noun* animal with a soft body that usually lives inside a hard shell. Most mollusks live in water.

Molt *verb* to shed an outer covering, such as feathers or skin, so that it can be replaced by a new one

Nocturnal *adjective* active at night

Omnivore *noun* organism that eats a variety of organisms, including plants, animals, and fungi

Osteoderm *noun* lump of bone in the skin of reptiles that provides protection from predators

Oviparous *adjective* reproducing by laying eggs

Photophore *noun* light-emitting organ present in some bioluminescent organisms

Placenta *noun* an organ present in the body of a pregnant mammal that nourishes and maintains the embryo as it develops

Plankton *noun* microscopic plant or animal organisms that float in salt water or freshwater

Pollution *noun* introduction of harmful materials into the environment

Population *noun* a group of the same kind of organism living in the same environment

Predator *noun* animal that hunts other animals for food

Prehensile *adjective* able to seize, grasp, or hold by wrapping around an object

Prey *noun* animal that is hunted and eaten by other animals

Primate *noun* a type of mammal that is intelligent and has forward-facing eyes. Most primates have opposable thumbs.

Proboscis *noun* long, tube-shaped part of an animal's body used for feeding

Rainforest *noun* a dense forest in which at least 160 inches (406 cm) of rain falls each year

Reproduce *verb* to create offspring, by sexual or asexual means

Reptile *noun* ectothermic animal that breathes air, has a backbone, and usually has scales

Ruminant *noun* hoofed mammal with a four-chambered stomach

Scavenger *noun* organism that eats dead or rotting flesh

Species *noun* a group of similar organisms that can reproduce with one another

RED COTTON BUG

Temperate *adjective* characterized by a warm summer and a cool winter. Most temperate regions are located between the tropics and the polar regions.

RED-EYED TREE FROG

Terrestrial *adjective* living all or most of the time on land

Tundra *noun* a cold, treeless area of the Arctic region with permafrost, a layer of soil that remains frozen throughout the year

Venom *noun* a poisonous fluid in the bodies of some organisms that is injected via a bite or a sting for hunting and protection

Vertebrate *noun* an organism with a backbone. Vertebrates can include mammals, fish, reptiles, amphibians, and birds.

FIND OUT MORE

Want to learn more? Ask an adult to help you check out these resources.

WEBSITES

Defenders of Wildlife
defenders.org/junior-defenders

National Geographic Kids
natgeokids.com

National Geographic
nationalgeographic.com

University of Michigan's
Animal Diversity Web
animaldiversity.org

BOOKS

1,000 Facts About Insects
National Geographic Kids, 2018

Nerdlet: Animals
National Geographic Kids, 2020

The Ultimate Book of Sharks
National Geographic Kids, 2018

Weird But True! Animals
National Geographic Kids, 2018

National Geographic Kids
Animal Showdown series

National Geographic Kids
Face to Face series

National Geographic Kids
Readers series

National Geographic Kids
Ultimate Explorer Field
Guide series

PLACES TO VISIT

United States
Alaska SeaLife Center
alaskasealife.org

Columbus Zoo and Aquarium
columbuszoo.org

Georgia Aquarium
georgiaaquarium.org

National Aquarium
aqua.org

San Diego Zoo
sandiegozoo.org

Smithsonian's National Zoo
nationalzoo.si.edu

Canada
Toronto Zoo
torontozoo.com

Australia
Australia Zoo
australiazoo.com.au

England
Zoological Society of London
zsl.org

Singapore
Singapore Zoo
zoo.com.sg

South Africa
National Zoological Garden of
South Africa
pretoriazoo.org

TV AND MOVIES

Growing Up Wild
Disney Nature, 2016

The Hidden Kingdoms of China
National Geographic, 2020

Meet the Chimps
National Geographic, 2020

Oceans
Disney Nature, 2010

Planet of the Birds
National Geographic, 2018

Weird But True!
National Geographic

INDEX

Illustrations are indicated by **boldface.**
If illustrations are included within a page span, the entire span is **boldface.**

KAMCHATKA BROWN BEAR

INDEX

OCHRE SEA STAR

ANNA'S HUMMINGBIRD

MOUNTAIN GORILLA

INDEX

SPOTTED SALAMANDER

FENNEC FOX

INDEX

ACKNOWLEDGMENTS

Thanks go to my friends, family, and colleagues for their advice and support; to project editor Angela Modany and everyone at National Geographic who put this beautiful book together; and to the many individuals all over the world who love animals and are working tirelessly to study, celebrate, and protect them. —Dr. Lucy Spellman

The publisher would like to thank National Geographic Explorer-in-Residence Sylvia Earle; National Geographic Explorers-at-Large Beverly and Dereck Joubert; and National Geographic Explorers Vinicius Alberici, Ashish Bashyal, Otgontuya Batsuuri, Moumita Chakraborty, Brian Skerry, Pablo García Borboroglu, Lisa Dabek, Helder Espírito-Santo, Marina Arbetman, Gladys Kalema-Zikusoka, Arthur Muneza, Martina Panisi, Somphouthone Phimmachak, Zoltan Takacs, and Washington Wachira for generously contributing their stories for this book.

The publisher would like to extend its gratitude to the following for their expert review of the book's subject matter: MAMMALS: Dr. Lauren E. Y. Norman, Visiting Assistant Professor, Department of Anthropology, University of Kansas; BIRDS: Jonathan Alderfer, co-author National Geographic Field Guide to the Birds of North America, 7th edition; REPTILES AND AMPHIBIANS: Dr. Thomas Pauley, Professor Emeritus, Biology Department, Marshall University, and Rebekah Perry Franks, Wildlife Education Director, Heritage Farm Museum and Village, Huntington, West Virginia; FISH: Dr. Adela Roa-Varón, NOAA Fisheries, National Systematics Laboratory, Smithsonian Institution, National Museum of Natural History; INVERTEBRATES: Dr. Anna J. Phillips, Research Zoologist and Curator of Parasitic Worms, Department of Invertebrate Zoology, National Museum of Natural History, Smithsonian Institution. And a special thank-you to photographer Matt Propert for traveling to find and photograph hundreds of animals featured in this book.

Photo Credits

Project, ZSL EDGE of Existence Programme; 64 (RT), Sourav Mondal, Project Associate of Red Panda Project, ZSL EDGE of Existence Programme; 65 (LO LE), Sourav Mondal, Project Associate of Red Panda Project, ZSL EDGE of Existence Programme; 65 (LO RT), Sourav Mondal, Project Associate of Red Panda Project, ZSL EDGE of Existence Programme; 65 (UP), Anand Varma; 66 (civet snout), Tim Allen/NGYS; 66 (UP RT), Tim Allen/NGYS; 66 (CTR LE), Erin Blackford/NGYS; 66 (LO LE), Tim Timmins/NGYS; 66 (LO RT), Matt Propert/NGP; 67 (mongoose snout), Matt Propert/NGIC; 67 (UP), Jeff Mauritzen/NGP; 67 (CTR LE), Matt Propert/NGP; 67 (CTR RT), Suzi Eszterhas/MP; 67 (LO LE), Ashleigh Thompson/NGYS; 67 (LO RT), Matt Propert/NGP; 68 (tiger fur), Photodisc; 68 (leopard fur), Photodisc; 68 (UP), Jeff Mauritzen/NGP; 68 (CTR), Beverly Joubert/NGIC; 68 (LO LE), Iacob Emanuel Popescu/NGYS; 68 (LO RT), Matt Propert/NGP; 69 (UP), Carissa Fricano/NGYS; 69 (CTR), Theo Willems/NGYS; 69 (LO LE), Mohammed Alnaser/NGYS; 69 (LO RT), Stephanie Ayscue/NGYS; 70 (serval fur), Photodisc; 70 (ocelot fur), Photodisc; 70 (UP), Matt Propert/NGP; 70 (LO LE), Alanna Schmidt/NGYS; 70 (LO RT), Matt Propert/NGP; 71 (UP LE), Roberto De Micheli/NGYS; 71 (UP RT), Digital Vision; 71 (CTR), Amar Parikh/NGYS; 71 (LO LE), Jeff Mauritzen/NGP; 71 (LO RT), Matt Propert/NGP; 72-73, Beverly Joubert/NGIC; 72 (LO LE), Beverly Joubert/NGIC; 72 (LO CTR), Beverly Joubert/NGIC; 72 (LO RT), Beverly Joubert/NGIC; 72 (LO LE), Beverly Joubert/NGIC; 73 (LO CTR), Beverly Joubert/NGIC; 73 (LO RT), Beverly Joubert/NGIC; 73 (UP), Mark Thiessen/NGIC; 74 (two bison), Steve Siegrist/NGYS; 74 (wildebeest herd), Hannah Canepa/NGYS; 74 (UP), Don Gurewitz/NGYS; 74 (LO), Kadek Susanto/NGYS; 75 (UP LE), Matt Propert/NGIC; 75 (UP RT), Elizabeth Blaser/NGYS; 75 (CTR LE), Jonathan Pearson/NGYS; 75 (CTR RT), Linda Conrad/NGYS; 75 (LO LE), Matt Propert/NGP; 75 (LO RT), Andy Shell/Adobe Stock; 76 (camels in desert), Erdenebayar Erdenesuren/NGYS; 76 (UP), Matt Propert/NGP; 76 (CTR LE), Liran Samuni/NGYS; 76 (LO LE), Josh Smiles/NGYS; 76 (LO RT), William Jurgelski/NGYS; 77 (zebra snout), Matt Propert/NGP; 77 (UP), Linda Kenny/NGYS; 77 (CTR LE), Matt Propert/NGIC; 77 (CTR RT), Neloy Bandyopadhyay/NGYS; 77 (LO), Philip Shaw/NGYS; 78 (rhino snout), Ray Houghton/NGYS; 78 (UP), Johannes Gerhardus Swanepoel/Dreamstime; 78 (CTR LE), Luke Casey/NGYS; 78 (LO LE), Matt Propert/NGP; 78 (LO RT), Jeff Mauritzen/NGP; 79 (UP), NGYS; 79 (CTR LE), Asep Dana Setiawan/NGYS; 79 (CTR RT), Ellen Leonhardt/NGYS; 79 (LO), Joel Sartore/NGIC; 80 (savanna), Pokzin Teo/NGYS; 80 (saiga), Vitalii Zubritskyi/Dreamstime; 80 (UP), Jim Laybourn/NGYS; 80 (CTR), Jeff Mauritzen/NGP; 80 (LO LE), Jeff Mauritzen/NGP; 80 (LO RT), Matt Propert/NGP; 81 (leaping deer), James Cumming/NGYS; 81 (UP), Dorothea Arnold/NGYS; 81 (CTR), Alicia White/NGYS; 81 (LO LE), Len Hones/NGYS; 81 (LO RT), Jim Laybourn/NGYS; 82 (giraffe snout), Oscar Medina/NGYS; 82 (UP), Wolf Avni/NGYS; 82 (CTR), Daniel Rumptz/NGYS; 82 (LO LE), Matt Propert/NGP; 82 (LO RT), Jeff Mauritzen/NGP; 83 (swimming pig), Bill Lampl/NGYS; 83 (UP), Blake Ezra Cole/NGYS; 83 (CTR LE), Matt Propert/NGP; 83 (CTR RT), Matt Propert/NGP; 83 (LO LE), Jeff Mauritzen/NGP; 83 (LO RT), Kris Gironella/NGYS; 84-85, Arthur Muneza; 84 (LO LE), Gallo Images ROOTS Collection/Getty Images; 84 (LO CTR), Arthur Muneza; 84 (LO RT), Kathy Leiden, Leiden Conservation Foundation; 85 (LO LE), Charlotte Bleijenberg/iStockphoto/Getty Images; 85 (LO RT), Arthur Muneza; 85 (UP), Annabel Staff; 86 (leaping orca), Tory Kallman/NGYS; 86 (UP), Schalke fotografie/Melissa Schalke/SS; 86 (LO LE), Alex Vogel/NGYS; 86 (LO RT), Tom Middleton/SS; 87 (gray whale breaching), Mike Paterson/NGYS; 87 (UP), Brian J. Skerry/NGIC; 87 (CTR LE), Melissa Marie Sousa/NGYS; 87 (CTR RT), Paul Nicklen/NGIC; 87 (LO), Flip Nicklin/MP; 88 (lemur and pup), Jill Livingstone Mitchell/NGYS; 88 (UP), Matt Propert/NGP; 88 (CTR LE), Robyn Gianni/NGYS; 88 (CTR RT), Matt Propert/NGP; 88 (LO LE), Matt Propert/NGP; 88 (LO RT), Nick Garbutt/NPL/MP; 89 (slow loris in tree), Anup SHah/NPL/MP; 89 (UP RT), Volmar K. Wentzel/NGIC; 89 (UP LE), Bruce Davidson/NPL/MP; 89 (LO LE), Goklas Situmorang/NGYS; 89 (LO RT), Mitsuaki Iwago/MP; 90 (sitting colobus), Matt Propert/NGP; 90 (UP), James Pelton/NGYS; 90 (CTR), Lori Epstein/NGIC; 90 (LO LE), Steve Patterson/NGYS; 90 (LO RT), Mitch Walters/NGYS; 91 (UP), Josh Brown/NGYS; 91 (CTR LE), Matt Propert/NGP; 91 (CTR RT), Matt Propert/NGP; 91 (LO LE), Larissa Reinhardus/NGYS; 91 (LO RT), Francisco Disilvestro/NGYS; 92 (orangutan baby), Oreon Strusinski/NGYS; 92 (UP), Samantha Oman/NGYS; 92 (CTR RT), Cedat Sylvain/NGYS; 92 (LO LE), Cheng Shun Ling/NGYS; 92 (LO RT), Samantha Oman/NGYS; 93 (UP), Erik Sellgren/NGYS; 93 (CTR LE), ZSSD/MP; 93 (CTR RT), Connie Lemperle/NGYS; 93 (LO LE), Lisa-Noël Hawkins/NGYS; 93 (LO RT), Manuel Rangi/NGYS; 94-95, Frans Lanting/NGIC; 94 (LO LE), Frans Lanting/NGIC; 94 (LO CTR), Jo-Anne McArthur/Conservation Through Public Health; 94 (LO LE), Shannon Hibberd/NGIC; 95 (LO LE), David Pluth/NGIC; 95 (LO RT), David Pluth/NGIC; 95 (UP), Jo-Anne McArthur/Conservation Through Public Health; 96 (leopard fur), Photodisc; 96 (UP), Denis Scott/Corbis; 96 (CTR RT), Talvi/SS; 96 (CTR LE), Merlin Tuttle/Science Source; 96 (LO), Chris Johns/NGIC; 97 (UP), Erik Gauger/iStockphoto/Getty Images; 97 (CTR RT), Eric Isselée/iStockphoto/Getty Images; 97 (CTR), Stephen Babka/NGYS; 97 (LO), Paul Banton/iStockphoto/Getty Images; **BIRDS:** 98-99, duangnapa_b/SS; 99 (peacock feathers), Photodisc; 99 (brown feathers), Photodisc; 99 (toucan), mountainpix/SS; 100 (A), Digital Vision; 100 (B), TTphoto/SS; 100 (C), BogdanBoev/SS; 100 (D), Lana Canada/iStockphoto; 100 (E), Johan Swanepoel/SS; 100 (F), Grant Sullivan/NGYS; 100 (G), Yangchen Lin/NGYS; 100 (H), Chuck Wagner/SS; 100-101 (I), Sebastian Knight/SS; 101 (A), Jeff Mauritzen/NGP; 101 (B), erllre74/SS; 101 (C), N. Frey Photography/SS; 101 (D), pix2go/SS; 101 (E), Cheryl E. Davis/SS; 101 (F), mountainpix/SS; 102 (peacock feathers), PhotoDisc; 102 (toucan), SS; 102 (duckling), Nagy Melinda/SS; 102 (brown feathers), PhotoDisc; 102-103, Wendy Rentz/NGYS; 102 (A), Ursula/SS; 102 (B), Armando Mejia/NGYS; 102 (C), Matt Propert/NGP; 104 (flying owl), Darren Merrett/NGYS; 104 (UP), Eduardo Matuod/NGYS; 104 (CTR), Galal Elmissary/NGYS; 104 (LO LE), Matt Propert/NGIC; 104 (LO RT), Jeff Foott/NPL; 105 (UP LE), Matthew Armanini/NGYS; 105 (UP RT), Stuart May/NGYS; 105 (CTR LE), Scott Nolen/NGYS; 105 (CTR RT), Leon van der Velden/NGYS; 105 (LO LE), Chris Hill/SS; 105 (LO RT), Marek Kocan/NGYS; 106-107, Joel Sartore/NGIC; 106 (LO LE), Washington Wachira; 106 (LO CTR), Washington Wachira; 106 LO (RT), Washington Wachira; 107 (LO LE), Washington Wachira; 107 (LO RT), Washington Wachira; 107 (UP), Maureen Wambui; 108 (flock of geese), Ryan Struck/NGYS; 108 (UP), Matt Propert/NGP; 108 (CTR), Lindsey Stevens/NGYS; 108 (LO), Real Deal Photo/SS; 109 (UP LE), Phoo Chan/NGYS; 109 (UP RT), Frank Angileri/NGYS; 109 (UP CTR LE), Joanne Levesque/NGYS; 109 (CTR LE), Julie Maher/NGYS; 109 (CTR RT), Matt Propert/NGP; 109 (LO LE), Michael Pachis/NGYS; 109 (LO RT), Nduche Onyeaso/NGYS; 110 (avocet swimming), Steve Ellwood/NGYS; 110 (UP), Jamie Link/NGYS; 110 (CTR), David Hemmings/NGYS; 110 (LO LE), Kate Ali/NGYS; 110 (LO RT), Eric Inglebrecht/NGYS; 111 (UP LE), Jeff Waldorff/NGYS; 111 (UP RT), Boris Belchev/NGYS; 111 (CTR LE), Matt Propert/NGIC; 111 (CTR RT), Sadatali Khan/NGYS; 111 (LO LE), Guy L Brun/NGYS; 111 (LO RT), Heather Porter/NGYS; 112 (pelican bill), Tramont_ana/SS; 112 (UP), Rohit Jain/NGYS; 112 (CTR LE), Tina Greenawalt/NGYS; 112 (CTR RT), Jeff Mauritzen/NGP; 112 (LO LE), Rich Lindie/SS; 112 (LO RT), Christine Kapler/NGYS; 113 (UP LE), Joanne Lembeck/NGYS; 113 (UP RT), Adobe Stock; 113 (CTR LE), Martin Lindsay/Alamy Stock Photo; 113 (CTR RT), Dennis Stewart/NGYS; 113 (LO LE), Robert Gates/NGYS; 113 (LO RT), Bjorn Anders Nymoen/NGYS; 114 (stork eye), Matt Propert/NGP; 114 (hamerkop eye), Matt Propert/NGP; 114 (UP), Gregory Johnston/SS; 114 (CTR), Rosanne Tackaberry/Alamy Stock Photo; 114 (LO LE), visceralimage/SS; 114 (LO CTR), Matt Propert/NGP; 114 (LO RT), Matt Propert/NGP; 115 (UP LE), Matt Propert/NGP; 115 (UP CTR), Matt Propert/NGP; 115 (UP RT), Matt Propert/NGP; 115 (CTR LE), Matt Propert/NGP; 115 (CTR RT), Matt Propert/NGP; 115 (LO), Matt Propert/NGP; 116 (crested grebe), Robert McLean/NGYS; 116 (UP), Joshua White/NGYS; 116 (CTR LE), Nancy Bauer/SS; 116 (CTR RT), Simon Vale/NGYS; 116 (LO), Robert McLean/NGYS; 117 (bustard), Matt Propert/NGIC; 117 (UP), Donna McAleer/NGYS; 117 (CTR), Jeff Mauritzen/NGP; 117 (LO LE), Jeff Mauritzen/NGP; 117 (LO RT), Matt Propert/NGP; 118-119, Joel Sartore/NGIC; 118 (LO LE), Philippe Clement/NPL; 118 (LO CTR), Nyambayar Batbayar; 118 (LO RT), Joel Sartore/NGIC; 119 (LO LE), Joel Sartore/NGIC; 119 (LO RT), Jim Brandenburg/MP; 119 (UP), Taylor Mickal; 120 (curassow snout), Matt Propert/NGP; 120 (UP), Harsha Dassenaieke/NGYS; 120 (CTR), James Stugart/NGYS; 120 (LO), Matt Propert/NGP; 121 (UP LE), Ray Wilson/Alamy Stock Photo; 121 (UP RT), Randy Brogen/NGYS; 121 (CTR), Sally Roerick/NGYS; 121 (LO LE), vagabond54/SS; 121 (LO RT), Matt Propert/NGP; 122 (fruit dove), Matt Propert/NGP; 122 (UP), Richard & Susan Day/Danita Delimont/Adobe Stock; 122 (CTR LE), Matt Propert/NGP; 122 (CTR RT), Robert McLean/NGYS; 122 (LO LE), Matt Propert/NGP; 122 (LO RT), Irawan Subingar/NGYS; 123 (hornbill snout), Matt Propert/NGP; 123 (UP), Rionw Wibowo/NGYS; 123 (CTR LE), Marie Rauh/NGYS; 123 (CTR RT), Sharon Haeger/NGYS; 123 (LO LE), Axel Hilger/NGYS; 123 (LO RT), Alberto Martin del Campo/NGYS; 124 (roadrunner), Matt Propert/NGP; 124 (UP), Matt Propert/NGP; 124 (CTR LE), Matt Propert/NGP; 124 (CTR RT), Pieter Bart van Dorp/NGYS; 124 (LO LE), Matt Propert/NGP; 124 (LO RT), Matt Propert/NGP; 125 (nightjar), Soong Ng/NGYS; 125 (UP), Julian Londono/NGYS; 125 (CTR), Matt Propert/NGP; 125 (LO LE), Whaldener Endo/NGYS; 125 (LO RT), Tim Laman/NGIC; 126 (hummingbird), Jarbas Neto/NGYS; 126 (UP), Hidetoshi Takahashi/NGYS; 126 (CTR), Phil Seu/NGYS; 126 (LO LE), FLPA/Alamy Stock Photo; 126 (LO RT), All Canada Photos/Alamy Stock Photo; 127 (parrot), Dr. Nirmal kumar Sahewalla/NGYS; 127 (UP), Armando Mejia/NGYS; 127 (CTR), Matt Propert/NGP; 127 (LO LE), Anabela George/NGYS; 127 (LO RT), Gerry Ellis/MP; 128-129, Michel Poinsignon/NPL; 130 (woodpecker), Kevin Tam/NGYS; 130 (UP), Scanrail1/SS; 130 (CTR LE), Mark Lewer/NGYS; 130 (CTR RT), Reinier Munguia/NGYS; 130 (LO LE), Matt Propert/NGP; 131 (rhea), Matt Propert/NGP; 131 (UP), Heshan de Mel/NGYS; 131 (CTR LE), Matt Propert/NGP; 131 (CTR), Matt Propert/NGP; 131 (CTR RT), Frans Lanting/NGIC; 131 (LO), Jeff Mauritzen/NGP; 132 (antbird), Whaldener Endo/NGYS; 132 (UP), Fabio Schunck; 132 (CTR LE), Wil Meinderts/MP; 132 (CTR RT), Murray Cooper/MP; 132 (LO LE), James Lowen/FLPA/MP; 132 (LO RT), Murray Cooper/MP; 133 (flycatcher and young), Matt Cashore/NGYS; 133 (UP), Cissy Beasley/NGYS; 133 (CTR LE), Cissy Beasley/NGYS; 133 (CTR RT), Mark Lewer/NGYS; 133 (LO LE), Cissy Beasley/NGYS; 133 (LO RT), Myron Tay/NGYS; 134 (drongo), Mitch Walters/NGYS; 134 (UP), William Leaman/Alamy Stock Photo; 134 (CTR), Angel Di Bilio/NGYS; 134 (LO LE), Glenn Bartley/All Canada Photos/Getty Images; 134 (LO RT), Matt Propert/NGP; 135 (UP LE), Mitch Walters/NGYS; 135 (UP RT), Matt Propert/NGP; 135 (CTR LE), Raymond Barlow/NGYS; 135 (CTR RT), Jeremy Weiss/NGYS; 135 (LO LE), Liz Andersen/NGYS; 135 (LO RT), Debapratim Saha/NGYS; 136 (green magpie), Debapratim Saha/NGYS; 136 (UP), Gary Thompson/NGYS; 136 (CTR LE), All Canada Photos/Alamy Stock Photo; 136 (CTR RT), Steven Smith/NGYS; 136 (LO LE), Stubblefield Photography/SS; 136 (LO RT), Matt Propert/NGP; 137 (UP LE), Charles Sinsua/NGYS; 137 (UP RT), Esau Sanchez/NGYS; 137 (CTR LE), Alexander Viduetsky/NGYS; 137 (CTR), Yvonne Metcalfe/NGYS; 137 (CTR RT), Steve Byland/SS; 137 (LO), Steven Russell Smith Photos/SS; 138 (olive-backed sunbird), Mun Wei Phoon/NGYS; 138 (UP), Edward Mattis/NGYS; 138 (CTR), Steve Byland/SS; 138 (LO LE), Matt Propert/NGP; 138 (LO RT), Rowland Willis/NGYS; 139 (UP LE), Wolf Avni/NGYS; 139 (UP RT), Richard Cronberg/NGYS; 139 (CTR LE), Steven Smith/NGYS; 139 (CTR), Matt Propert/NGIC; 139 (CTR RT), Matt Propert/NGP; 139 (LO LE), Soong Ng/NGYS; 139 (LO RT), Stuart Clarke/NGYS; 140 (penguins diving), Anne Lucky/NGYS; 140 (UP), David Schultz/NGYS; 140 (CTR), Tomas Kotouc/NGYS; 140 (LO), David Bluestein/NGYS; 141 (UP LE), Bryce Groves/NGYS; 141 (UP RT), Digital Vision; 141 (UP CTR LE), Jessica Caton/NGYS; 141 (CTR LE), Matt Propert/NGP; 141 (CTR RT), Tom Dowden/NGYS; 141 (LO LE), Keith Szafranski/iStockphoto; 141 (LO RT), Matt Propert/NGP; 142-143, Jonathan Irish/NGIC; 142 (LO LE), Jonathan Irish/NGIC; 142 (LO CTR), Jonathan Irish/NGIC; 142 (LO RT), Ira Meyer/NGIC; 143 (LO LE), Pablo García Borboroglu; 143 (LO RT), Pablo García Borboroglu; 143 (UP), Mark Thiessen/NGP; 144 (flycatcher), Matt Cashore/NGYS; 144 (A), Svetlana Povarova Ree/NGYS; 144 (B), Raymond Barlow/NGYS; 144 (C), Jeff Mauritzen/NGP; 144 (D), Vivien Leung/NGYS; 145 (A), Matt Propert/NGP; 145 (B), Pete Oxford/MP; 145 (C), Dennis Hall/NGYS; 145 (D), Gi Singh/NGYS; **REPTILES:** 146-147, William Mahnken/Dreamstime; 147 (thorny devil), Gerry Ellis/Digital Vision; 147 (chameleon eye), Gerry Ellis/Digital Vision; 147 (snake tongue), Gerry Ellis/Digital Vision; 148 (A), SecondShot/SS; 148 (B), Ashley Whitworth/SS; 148 (C), Matt Propert/NGP; 148 (D), Shraddha Rathi/NGYS; 148 (E), Brian Scantlebury/SS; 148 (F), Cathy Keifer/SS; 148 (G), Mark Williams/NGYS; 148-149 (H), Matt Propert/NGP; 148-149 (I), iliuta goean/SS; 149 (A), Gerry Ellis/Digital Vision; 149 (B), Audrey Snider-Bell/SS; 149 (C), Dwi Yulianto/SS; 149 (D), Byron Yu/NGYS; 149 (E), Michael Bina/Dreamstime; 150 (chameleon), Gerry Ellis/Digital Vision; 150 (snake tongue), Gerry Ellis/Digital Vision; 150-151, Suhaas Premkumar/NGYS; 151 (A), Matt Propert/NGIC; 151 (B), Sree V Remella/NGYS; 151 (C), Jitindar Chadha/NGYS; 151 (D), Frans Lanting/NGIC; 152 (dwarf crocodile snout), Matt Propert/NGIC; 152 (UP), Lori Epstein/NGIC; 152 (CTR), Steve Byland/SS; 152 (LO), Joel Sartore/NGIC; 153 (UP LE), Matt Propert/NGIC; 153 (UP RT), David Doubilet/NGIC; 153 (CTR LE), Brandon Sideleau/NGYS; 153 (CTR RT), Matt Propert/NGIC; 153 (LO), Matt Propert/NGIC; 154-155, Ashish Bashyal; 154 (LO LE), Ashish Bashyal; 154 (LO CTR), Ashish Bashyal; 154 (LO RT), Ashish Bashyal; 155 (LO LE), Ashish Bashyal; 155 (LO RT), Ashish Bashyal; 155 (UP), Ashish Bashyal; 156 (turtles on log), Jitindar Chadha/NGYS; 156 (river turtle), Matt Propert/NGP; 156 (UP), Matt Propert/NGP; 156 (LO LE), Matt Propert/NGP; 156 (LO RT), Joel Sartore/NGIC; 157 (UP LE), Terry Goss/NGYS; 157 (UP RT), Joel Sartore/National Geographic Photo Ark/NGIC; 157 (CTR LE), Jeff Mauritzen/NGP; 157 (CTR RT), Glenn Upton/NGYS; 157 (LO LE), Joel Sartore/NGIC; 157 (LO RT), Elise Hinger/NGYS; 158 (pink agama), Mikael Meisen Dietmann/NGYS; 158 (UP), Matt Propert/NGP; 158 (CTR), Trevor Keyler/NGYS; 158 (LO), Matt Propert/NGIC; 159 (UP LE), Eng Chye Toh/NGYS; 159 (UP RT), Wessam Atif/NGYS; 159 (CTR RT), Gerry Ellis/Digital Vision; 159 (CTR LE), Matt Propert/NGP; 159 (LO LE), Tui De Roy/NPL; 159 (LO RT), Anri_Louise Oosthuizen/NGYS; 160-161, Alejandro Arteaga; 162 (gecko head), Matt Propert/NGP; 162 (UP), Matt Propert/NGP; 162 (CTR), Cassandre Riou/NGYS; 162 (LO LE), Robert McLean/NGYS; 162 (LO RT),

LAPPET-FACED VULTURES

Since 1888, the National Geographic Society has funded more than 14,000 research, conservation, education, and storytelling projects around the world. National Geographic Partners distributes a portion of the funds it receives from your purchase to National Geographic Society to support programs including the conservation of animals and their habitats. To learn more, visit natgeo.com/info.

For more information, visit nationalgeographic.com, call 1-877-873-6846, or write to the following address:

National Geographic Partners, LLC
1145 17th Street N.W.
Washington, DC 20036-4688 U.S.A.

For librarians and teachers: nationalgeographic.com/books/librarians-and-educators

More for kids from National Geographic: natgeokids.com

National Geographic Kids magazine inspires children to explore their world with fun yet educational articles on animals, science, nature, and more. Using fresh storytelling and amazing photography, *Nat Geo Kids* shows kids ages 6 to 14 the fascinating truth about the world—and why they should care.
kids.nationalgeographic.com/subscribe

For rights or permissions inquiries, please contact National Geographic Books Subsidiary Rights:
bookrights@natgeo.com

Designed by Amanda Larsen

National Geographic supports K–12 educators with ELA Common Core Resources. Visit natgeoed.org/commoncore for more information.

Hardcover ISBN: 978-1-4263-7230-8
Reinforced library binding ISBN: 978-1-4263-7231-5

The publisher would like to thank everyone who worked to make this edition come together: Angela Modany, associate editor; Ariane Szu-Tu, editor; Amanda Larsen, art director; Lori Epstein, photo director; Jen Agresta, project editor; Libby Romero, contributing writer; Michelle Harris, fact-checker; Mike McNey, map production; Alix Inchausti, production editor; and Anne LeongSon and Gus Tello, design production assistants.

Printed in Hong Kong
21/PPHK/1